THE SAINT-SIMONIAN RELIGION
IN GERMANY

LE PÈRE ENFANTIN

THE
SAINT-SIMONIAN RELIGION
IN GERMANY

A Study of the Young German Movement

BY

E. M. BUTLER

NEW YORK

Howard Fertig

1968

First published in 1926

HOWARD FERTIG, INC. EDITION 1968
Published by permission of the Cambridge University Press

Library of Congress Catalog Card Number: 68-9590

PRINTED IN THE UNITED STATES OF AMERICA
BY NOBLE OFFSET PRINTERS, INC.

TO
G. H. AND D. N.
SOMETIME
FELLOW-MEMBERS
OF THE
S. W. H.

PREFACE

The year 1925 was duly celebrated as the centenary of the death of the philosopher Saint-Simon, and indeed the world is in his debt, not only because he originated many interesting ideas, but also because he was the father of a movement instinct with comedy—the Saint-Simonian religion. This comedy took on a sombre hue when transplanted into Germanic soil; the Young German Movement ended disastrously for its adherents, and was sternly suppressed.

The study of the dual development of Saint-Simon's ideas in France and Germany is an interesting one; and I should like to express my warmest thanks to Professor J. G. Robertson of the University of London, who drew my attention to the possibilities latent in this subject. His great learning, placed with the utmost generosity at my disposal, his consistent kindness and encouragement, have been of invaluable help to me. I am further deeply indebted to him for the sacrifice of a great deal of his time to reading the manuscript of the present book and to correcting the proofs.

I am also under a great obligation to Newnham College for generously providing me with the means and the leisure to undertake this study, and to the authorities of the Cambridge University Press for the skilled attention they have bestowed upon the proofs. The kind and active interest of Mr Edward Bullough, whose wide knowledge of European literature embraces this subject, has assisted me very greatly; and Miss Geraldine Hedges has helped me throughout with stimulating suggestions and criticisms.

E. M. BUTLER

Newnham College,
Cambridge.
July 1926.

CONTENTS

Introduction . . . . page 1

PART ONE
SAINT-SIMON AND SAINT-SIMONISM

Chap. I. Saint-Simon 4

II. The Saint-Simonians 11

   (a) The early beginnings 11

   (b) The schisms 14

   (c) The apotheosis of Enfantin . . . 24

   (d) The trial and disbandment . . . 28

   (e) 'L'Année de la Mère' 32

   (f) The Suez Canal 35

III. Saint-Simonism 37

   (a) *Doctrine de Saint-Simon. Exposition. Première Année* 37

   (b) *Doctrine de Saint-Simon. Exposition. Deuxième Année* 42

   (c) *Enseignements d'Enfantin* . . . 46

PART TWO
SAINT-SIMONISM IN GERMANY

Chap. IV. The attitude of Germany 60

   (a) The press and the Saint-Simonians . . 60

   (b) Public opinion on Saint-Simonism . . 64

   (c) Enlightened opinion 66

   (d) The Young German women . . . 78

   (e) The disaster 84

PART THREE
HEINE AND SAINT-SIMONISM

Chap. V. Heine and the Saint-Simonians . . . 88

   (a) A conspiracy of silence 88

   (b) 1831–1833 94

   (c) Heine and Enfantin 103

   (d) The middle years 111

   (e) Home truths 117

CONTENTS

Chap. VI. Coming events . . . . . . page 129
    (*a*) 'Enfant perdu' 129
    (*b*) Saint-Simonian thoughts . . . 131
    (*c*) Conflict 135

VII. The Saint-Simonian period 138
    (*a*) The conflict resolved 138
    (*b*) Order out of chaos 142
    (*c*) *Die Romantische Schule* 144
    (*d*) *Zur Geschichte der Religion und Philosophie in Deutschland* . . . 147
    (*e*) Heine's interpretation of the doctrine . 152

VIII. Disillusion 157
    (*a*) 1836–1848 157
    (*b*) The conversion 163
    (*c*) Extent of the Saint-Simonian influence 168

PART FOUR
LAUBE AND SAINT-SIMONISM

Chap. IX. Laube's interest in Saint-Simonism . . 172
    (*a*) His knowledge and sources . . . 172
    (*b*) An interrupted journey 174
    (*c*) Uncompleted schemes 180
    (*d*) An enforced silence 186
    (*e*) The loss of interest 189
    (*f*) Inhibitions 193

X. Laube and Börne 196

XI. A Saint-Simonian society 203
    (*a*) The plot 203
    (*b*) The constant, the inconstant and the 'calm' 207
    (*c*) The 'social revolution' 215
    (*d*) Other Saint-Simonian ideas . . . 219

XII. The influence of Heine 223
    (*a*) The *Reisenovellen* 223
    (*b*) *Die Zeitung für die elegante Welt* . . 233

CONTENTS

Chap. XIII. Shades of the prison-house . . . page 241

    (*a*) Fear 241

    (*b*) The loose ends 246

    (*c*) *Die Krieger* 248

    (*d*) *Die Bürger* 251

    (*e*) The debt owed to Enfantin . . . 255

PART FIVE

GUTZKOW AND SAINT-SIMONISM

Chap. XIV. Gutzkow's criticisms of Saint-Simonism . 258

    (*a*) Karl Gutzkow 258

    (*b*) The conscious attitude 261

XV. The half-conscious interest 274

    (*a*) Under Menzel's banner 274

    (*b*) *Briefe eines Narren an eine Närrin* . . 276

XVI. The interest waxes 281

    (*a*) *Maha Guru* 281

    (*b*) The mantle of Enfantin 283

XVII. Saint-Simonism prevails 288

    (*a*) Temper 288

    (*b*) *Lucinde* 292

    (*c*) The Preface 295

XVIII. The interest wanes 300

    (*a*) *Wally, die Zweiflerin* 300

    (*b*) An 'innocent crime' 303

XIX. The interest denied 309

    (*a*) Confessions and denials 309

    (*b*) Recantations 313

    (*c*) The 'evil eye' 317

PART SIX

MUNDT AND SAINT-SIMONISM

Chap. XX. Unpromising beginnings 320

    (*a*) Theodor Mundt 320

    (*b*) Early stories 322

    (*c*) Early critical efforts 327

CONTENTS

Chap. XXI. The influence of two women . . page 331

    (a) Charlotte Stieglitz 331

    (b) Rahel Varnhagen von Ense . . . 342

    (c) *Moderne Lebenswirren* 344

XXII. Discovery of Saint-Simonism . . . 348

    (a) The discovery 348

    (b) *Madonna* 352

XXIII. The summit of his career 361

    (a) *Literarischer Zodiacus* 361

    (b) *Charlotte Stieglitz, ein Denkmal* . . 366

    (c) The catastrophic year 369

XXIV. Seven thin years 377

    (a) Deterioration 377

    (b) Marking time 380

    (c) The 'social couple' 385

XXV. A dreary ending 389

    (a) Vain repetitions 389

    (b) A fool's paradise 393

PART SEVEN

WIENBARG AND SAINT-SIMONISM

Chap. XXVI. The Saint-Simonian influence . . . 398

    (a) Ludolf Wienbarg 398

    (b) The apostle of Heine 403

    (c) The forerunner of Nietzsche . . . 412

    (d) The partner of Gutzkow . . . 419

    (e) The myth of Wienbarg 425

Conclusion 431

Index 437

PLATES

Le Père Enfantin . . . . . *Frontispiece*

Heinrich Heine . . . . . . facing page 140

Heinrich Laube . . . . . . „ „ 256

Charlotte Stieglitz . . . . . . „ „ 332

THE SAINT-SIMONIAN RELIGION
IN GERMANY

INTRODUCTION

THE word influence is not a satisfactory one, for it states only one of the terms in a problem where two at least must be known if the answer is to be found. No man is the sum total of the influences which have gone to form him. The messages of heredity are whispered in his ear; the limits of his environment press around him; the ceaseless surge of others' thoughts encroach upon his own; and yet his personal identity survives, for every man is a self-made man. The voices from the past will be heeded or disregarded; the physical conditions of existence will be accepted or overcome; those friends will be chosen who minister to his mental and spiritual needs, those ideas accepted which form the best medium for his growth; for thus and thus each one unconsciously selects. The stronger the personality the greater the skill in this game of choosing and rejecting; but it is played by the whole human race with varying success. It is no easy pastime, this struggle for the survival of personal identity, but a position maintained with great effort in the teeth of ever-renewed attacks; yet it is never finally abandoned whilst life and sanity endure.

So that the verb to influence is a misused word, generally conjugated in the passive voice; whereas the positive consent and, more than that, the personal choice are the vital facts underlying the misleading statements that Chaucer was influenced by Boccaccio, or Klopstock by *Paradise Lost*. If Chaucer had gone to Dante for his philosophy, or Klopstock for a model to *Don Quixote*, it would then be legitimate to use the verb in the negative sense; but rare indeed are such cases of alien thoughts working in the minds of men. In the same way religious, philosophical, political and social ideas, spreading from mind to mind and from one land to another, depend upon a state of receptivity before they can get under way. The prairie fire, sweeping over the plain, leaping gulleys and fording streams, does not progress so fast because each blade of grass catches fire from the next, but because the plain, burned dry by the summer sun, offers itself as a sacrifice and is ready to be consumed, or in the colder North because the sap is mounting in bracken, heather and gorse, the inflammable sap of the spring. Whilst the wind behind the conflagration urges it along, a spirit blowing whence it will; and this incalculable element is the unknown factor here, deluding pursuit and defying analysis. Some of its qualities may be discovered, many of its manifestations may be noted, but whence it comes and why, which of us shall say?

The following study of the spread of Saint-Simonian ideas in Germany, and notably among that school of writers called the Young Germans, may provide documentary evidence for a future age more apt to deal with the larger issue. I have been content to take these young men one by one and to find out what made them embrace the gospel carried to them over the Rhine; and it would appear in each case that it was their own inner promptings and deep-seated desires; so that if Enfantin had not invented Saint-Simonism, three at least and perhaps four of these writers would have invented something very similar in its stead. But behind the personal equation was the spirit abroad at that time, manifest all over the world. It was a wind that was going from West to East; it alighted in France and paused for a while over Germany before pursuing its way. It is beyond my powers to reveal it, but the incalculable element was there.

PART I

SAINT-SIMON AND SAINT-SIMONISM

CHAPTER I

SAINT-SIMON

The story of Saint-Simon and Saint-Simonism has often been told in the past[1], but it is beginning to be forgotten to-day. Many of Saint-Simon's prophecies have been fulfilled, much that his disciples worked for has been accomplished, but their names and their deeds are slipping into oblivion; so that to speak of the spread of Saint-Simonian ideas in Germany without a brief outline of the rise of Saint-Simonism in France is to give a passage out of its context, a proceeding more puzzling than enlightening where the context is not generally known. It is for this reason that I am repeating a story well worth telling for its own sake; fantastic, preposterous and romantic; absurd and yet appealing; barely credible, yet based on solid facts; no traveller's tale of some remote unheard-of island, but witnessed by sober citizens in Paris a hundred years ago.

The prologue was spoken by Claude-Henri de Rouvroy, Comte de Saint-Simon, a descendant of the duke, a curious, restless, turbulent character, who ran a most varied and eventful career, now fighting with the rebels in the American war of independence and dreaming of the Panama Canal; then leading the dissolute existence of a nobleman of the *ancien régime*; a patron of men of science and a financial speculator on the grand scale; then again sunk in extreme poverty and reduced to writing begging letters and to living on the bounty of a sometime valet. He knew a moment of despair during which he attempted his life, but the feeling that he was born to accomplish great things upheld him, and he died confident that he had achieved something towards the progress of humanity. He had a great feeling for the future, as M. Faguet observes[2]; and indeed, although Saint-Simon changed his views often and rather startlingly; although he attacked the problem he wished to solve from one angle after another and left it unsolved in the end; although his social doctrines were often ambiguously expressed; although

[1] Cf. A. J. Booth, *Saint-Simon and Saint-Simonism*, London, 1871; S. Charléty, *Histoire du Saint-Simonisme*, Paris, 1896.

[2] E. Faguet, *Politiques et moralistes du XIXe siècle*, Paris, 1903, IIe série, p. 42.

his religious views were sometimes fantastic; nevertheless throughout his writings there is a feeling that laws are changing and customs melting. Saint-Simon was learning and discovering all his life; enouncing one point of view, only to rush on to another and possibly a contradictory one; yet in this chaotic welter of opinions, deductions and ideas are to be found the germs of modern socialism, of the positive philosophy, of some principles of Fourierism and of the Saint-Simonian religion.

The spur which goaded Saint-Simon onward and would not let him rest was the realisation, vivid enough to be a revelation, that the eighteenth century with its destructive criticism had brought about an almost unparalleled state of social dissolution, and that society must be built up again with all possible speed. The time for destruction was passed, the era of reconstruction was overdue. Saint-Simon set himself a creative rather than a critical task and his disciples followed this lead. His views on the philosophy of history, on the reorganisation of society and on the part to be played by religion became the corner-stones of the Saint-Simonian system; and if the building as a whole turned out differently from anything Saint-Simon had conceived, it cannot be denied that the confused and wordy architect with his unfinished plans was responsible for the fact that there was such a building at all.

Saint-Simon's conception of history was mainly based on Condorcet's views, nevertheless he made them peculiarly his own and deduced some remarkable theories from them, which do not directly concern us here. But whilst studying the history of mankind he evolved the theory of organic and critical epochs, which became one of the favourite tenets of the Saint-Simonians, and which Bazard expounded much more clearly than the originator. Broadly speaking the organic epochs are those in which the religion of the times offers an adequate explanation of all the known facts of life; all men are therefore united by a common belief which is reflected in their institutions, and they all march together towards a common goal. In the critical epochs on the other hand knowledge has outstripped religion, which is no longer able to answer satisfactorily the questions and criticisms of thinkers and men of science. Scepticism, disorder and destruction are the result; the unbelievers grow daily among the educated; the institutions no longer reflect the prevailing beliefs and convictions; no common purpose seems assigned to humanity and egoism rears its hydra-head. Saint-Simon distinguished two organic periods in history: pre-Socratic Greece, and the period of Christian feudalism which lasted from the sixth to the sixteenth century. Socrates ushered in the critical epoch in the first case, Luther in the second; we are now, he concluded, at the end of this second critical period and a new and wonderful organic period is at hand, based on a religion which will be the expression of the knowledge of the present age.

It is no easy task to summarise the many and varied schemes which Saint-Simon proposed for the reconstruction of society in order to make it worthy of the coming epoch. He changed and remodelled these plans again and again, giving the spiritual and the temporal power now to one class and now to another, so that with each fresh pamphlet or book we are faced with a different solution of the problem. On the whole he remained faithful to the scientists, the priests of the new society; and although he treated the artists somewhat more cavalierly, still they re-emerged triumphantly at the end in the same capacity. His aristocracy was throughout an aristocracy of intellect. But his views on the temporal power underwent a complete change. Until 1818 he placed the temporal power in the hands of the proprietors; but with the publication of *L'Industrie* the industrial class was proclaimed the governing class and the proprietors were sent to herd with robbers. Thus Saint-Simon prepared the way for the glorification of industry which was to play so important a part in the Saint-Simonian doctrine. The problem of property was not solved by Saint-Simon; he regarded it as the basis of society, and was always scheming how it could be made to play a productive part in a reorganised world. The Saint-Simonians were ready with a theory which dealt with this difficulty.

Saint-Simon differed from other social reformers of his age in invoking the aid of religion that his dreams might come true. He realised that a spiritual revelation alone could inspire in the minds of men an enthusiasm strong and pure enough to result in the vast reforms which he dreamt of for the progress of humanity; and he set himself first to prophesy and later to manufacture the new religion which was to redeem the world, an expression of the accumulated knowledge of mankind. He began fantastically enough in the *Lettres d'un habitant de Genève* by basing the coming revelation on the law of gravitation, the great unifying principle of the universe. This religion was to have its priests and its temples and Newton was to be its prophet. Although Saint-Simon soon abandoned this absurd but delightful scheme, it is important here, for it contained his solitary feminist utterance, put into the mouth of the All-Highest himself. 'Les femmes seront admises à souscrire,' the divine voice announced, referring to the subscription to be opened at Newton's tomb; the contributors were to have the right to nominate the scientists and artists, the members of the Council of Newton which was to govern the world; the inclusion of women among the voters was therefore no negligible favour. But when the voice continued 'ELLES POURRONT ÊTRE NOMMÉES,'[1] Olinde Rodrigues in his edition of Saint-Simon's works not unnaturally jumped into excited capital letters preserved in the later edition. This sentence is startling enough, but it is the only contribution of the master to the woman-question. Hubbard says that it was written with a view to pleasing Madame de Staël, to whom Saint-Simon shortly afterwards made a proposal of marriage couched in remarkable terms[2]; but she declined the offer to become the mother of his son and he dropped the subject of the enfranchisement of women with singular completeness. The seed was sown however, and Madame de Staël may have much to answer for.

In the *Introduction aux travaux scientifiques* Saint-Simon distinguished three great religious cycles in the history of humanity, fetichism, polytheism and monotheism (Judaism and Christianity). The present critical epoch which had destroyed monotheism was preparing the way for a new religion which would penetrate this period with its spirit. This religion he rather hesitatingly christened by the name of physicism, and recommended that the uneducated should be allowed to cling to monotheism for the present. Then he became dissatisfied with physicism, and indeed it is even less satisfying than the law of gravitation, and since he could not at the moment think of

---

[1] *Œuvres de Saint-Simon et d'Enfantin*, Paris, 1865–1878, xv, p. 50.
[2] N. G. A. Hubbard, *Saint-Simon, sa vie et ses travaux*, Paris, 1857, p. 40.

anything to put in its place, he let the matter rest. He was to return to it however. In his historical and sociological studies he had become much interested in the influence of Christianity and its supremacy during the Middle Ages. Although Christianity in its present form seemed to him superseded and inadequate, he admired it unreservedly during its period of greatness and gave it generous and unstinted praise. This attitude was adopted by the Saint-Simonians; they prided themselves on their just appreciation of the great good Christianity had done in the past; they were however adamant in banishing it from the future. Saint-Simon did not go so far as this when towards the end of his life he wrote the *Nouveau Christianisme*.

He had attempted to commit suicide in 1823, for he was in the most pitiable circumstances, almost completely without money and thus unable to provide for the publication of his books. Since he saw himself powerless to spread those ideas which were to redeem the world from anarchy and misery, he felt that life was a worthless gift, and in a frame of mind that was not without nobility he set himself to destroy it. But fate willed otherwise; the attempt failed, and Saint-Simon lived two years longer. In the year of his death he wrote his famous pamphlet and thus completed his destiny and founded a new religion.

The *Nouveau Christianisme* begins in dialogue form to which Saint-Simon was much addicted:

Le Conservateur. Croyez-vous en Dieu?
Le Novateur. Oui, je crois en Dieu.
Le C. Croyez-vous que la religion chrétienne ait une origine divine?
Le N. Oui, je le crois...Dieu a dit: *Les hommes doivent se conduire en frères à l'égard les uns des autres*; ce principe sublime renferme tout ce qu'il y a de divin dans la religion chrétienne[1].

From this divine principle, the essence of the Christian religion, the future code of morals will be deduced; the principle itself translated into modern language, or rather adapted to modern needs, runs thus: '*La religion doit diriger la société vers le grand but de l'amélioration la plus rapide possible du sort de la classe la plus pauvre.*'[2] The Catholic and Protestant religious forms were then submitted to a searching criticism which proved con-

[1] *Œuvres de Saint-Simon et d'Enfantin*, XXIII, pp. 107–108.
[2] *Ibid.* XXIII, p. 117; cf. also p. 177.

clusively to Saint-Simon that they were by no means directing
humanity towards the aim he had defined. This then is one side
of his doctrine; the gospel of Christ reduced to the pronouncement 'Thou shalt love thy neighbour as thyself,' applied in the
broadest possible way and adapted to modern society. There is
nothing essentially new in this; it is a definite expression of
the dreams and aspirations of every true philanthropist.

But there was another tendency in the *Nouveau Christianisme*
which had been foreshadowed in other writings of Saint-Simon
and which is of fundamental importance:

L'imagination des poètes a placé l'âge d'or au berceau de l'espèce
humaine, parmi l'ignorance et la grossièreté des premiers temps;
c'était bien plutôt l'âge de fer qu'il fallait y reléguer. L'âge d'or du
genre humain n'est point derrière nous, il est au-devant, il est dans
la perfection de l'ordre social; nos pères ne l'ont point vu, nos enfants
y arriveront un jour, c'est à nous de leur frayer en la route[1].

This is the conclusion of the *Réorganisation de la société euro-
péenne*, it was summarised later: 'L'âge d'or, qu'une aveugle
tradition a placé jusqu'ici dans le passé, est devant nous,'[2] and
became one of the war-cries of the Saint-Simonian school. It is
the natural conclusion of the eighteenth-century doctrine of
progress which Saint-Simon had adopted at the outset of his
career. Applied to religion, it meant, as Bazard was to show
with greater clearness, that the doctrine of the fall of man and
all that it entailed was superseded by the doctrine of progress
with its logical conclusion of an earthly paradise in the future[3].
Since man has not fallen from his high estate but on the contrary
has progressed in the most laudable way since his creation, since
he has no dark sin to expiate before he can attain to grace and
heaven, then away with castigations and the mortification of
the flesh[4]. Here, in germ, is the conception of the Christian
anathema against the flesh which Bazard was to develop with
such fervent eloquence at a later date; and the next extract
shows clearly that Saint-Simon was preparing to re-establish
sensualism in its own rights:

[1] *Œuvres de Saint-Simon et d'Enfantin*, xv, pp. 247–248.
[2] This was the motto of the *Producteur*, founded after Saint-Simon's
death.
[3] *Œuvres de Saint-Simon et d'Enfantin*, xxxix, pp. 82–83.
[4] *Ibid.* xxiii, pp. 153–154.

Ce n'est plus sur des idées abstraites que vous devez fixer l'attention des fidèles; c'est en employant convenablement les idées sensuelles, c'est en les combinant de manière à procurer à l'espèce humaine le plus haut degré de félicité qu'elle puisse atteindre pendant sa vie terrestre, que vous parviendrez à constituer le Christianisme, religion générale, universelle et unique[1].

'Convenablement' is a saving clause certainly, although one of the utmost vagueness; but by announcing a religion whose highest aim was the moral and physical happiness of humanity, an aim which was to be attained by rendering the earth as habitable, as agreeable and as productive as possible, Saint-Simon had gone a long way towards sanctioning the 'rehabilitation of the flesh,' the rallying-cry of the Saint-Simonian school. He had set out to do nothing more startling than bring Christianity up to date, but he introduced a new principle into his religion which was to have far-reaching results. It needed only the more logical minds of Bazard and Enfantin to perceive that a religion which denied the fall of man, bracketed moral and physical well-being together and aimed rather at earthly than at spiritual bliss, could not be called Christianity at all, even though its fundamental tenet was brotherly love.

It is more than possible that the Saint-Simonians, even before the defection of Bazard and Rodrigues, went further in the matter of the sanctification of the senses than Saint-Simon would have been prepared to go; nevertheless this doctrine is implicit in the *Nouveau Christianisme*. Saint-Simon was never one to push his ideas to the last conclusion. Had he lived he might have dropped the idea of reinstating the senses as he had dropped the law of gravitation, the enfranchisement of women, the temporal power of proprietors, positive philosophy and physicism. There is nothing to show that he had arrived at his final position. He was still learning when he died. But he died at the psychological moment, bequeathing to his followers—and herein lies his greatest claim to originality—the idea that a new spiritual power was necessary to reorganise the world.

After much wandering he had put into a port from which his disciples were to set sail for a fair-seeming land. But like those tropical islands we read of in Conrad's tales, there was ugliness and cruelty beneath the luxuriant beauty of their paradise on earth.

[1] *Œuvres de Saint-Simon et d'Enfantin*, XXIII, p. 148.

CHAPTER II

THE SAINT-SIMONIANS

(a) THE EARLY BEGINNINGS

The *Nouveau Christianisme* was written at a time of great spiritual depression in France. The intellectual scepticism of the eighteenth century persisted but it had lost its liberating power. The fierce joy of those who had slain the giants of oppression and superstition could not warm the hearts of their sons. Childe Roland to the dark tower came and the frowning, sinister menace crumbled into ruins. Never again could a knight blow his dauntless challenge among those ancient hills. The brave may go on fighting when the battle is lost; only a fool or a bully has a blow to spare when the battle is won. And so it was that from the ruins of great institutions and a shattered creed there shot up the strange and fantastic flower which we have agreed to christen romance. It was not the blue flower of the German poets, for it had its roots in a different soil; more challenging but perhaps less beautiful, it symbolised nevertheless the same desire to escape from a dreary and desolate world.

Born in this age of weariness and reaction, the youth of that day trod many curious paths in search of spiritual and emotional adventure. The 'mal du siècle' attacked some sensitive and not too valiant spirits; others, like Alfred de Vigny, withdrew behind a reserved and disdainful pessimism; others again, like Lamartine, flung themselves wailing into the arms of the church, and brought a new element of romantic sadness into an ancient faith. The hero of the hour, part Napoleon, part Byron, strode, gloomy and gallant, across the stage of poetry, drama and fiction, voicing blasphemies or offering up impassioned prayers; and the swelling rhetoric of titanic defiance or the appealing harmonies of religious exaltation were alike attuned to the subjective note. Adventurers all, the French youth of 1830 were ever on the alert for new spiritual and emotional experiences; and it is well to remember in reading the almost unbelievable history of this strange religion that the spirit of de Vigny, George Sand, de

Musset and Lamartine was abroad in Paris at the time: denying, seeking, blaspheming, finding, but always in some definite personal relation to God. And Enfantin himself, with his superhuman claims, is only another incarnation of the 'héros fatal' whose great prototype had died a few years earlier tragically and miserably on the island of Saint Helena.

It is small wonder then, since it was the outcome of the very spirit which acclaimed it, that the Saint-Simonian religion had so remarkable a success; the guiding principle indeed, 'l'amélioration la plus rapide possible de la classe la plus nombreuse et la plus pauvre,' contained an almost irresistible appeal to all that is generous in human nature. Saint-Simon himself did not doubt that his gospel would bear fruit; the last hours of his life were spent expounding it to his disciples, and he died prophesying that it would prevail: 'L'avenir est à nous.'

Five years after Saint-Simon's death, the new school was already founded; the new doctrine was already being taught. Olinde Rodrigues, 'la tradition vivante' as he was called because he was the only one who had known the master personally, was a wealthy Jew, who had helped Saint-Simon with money and then financed and founded the school, bringing to it many important converts, amongst them his cousins Isaac and Emile Pereire, his friend Gustave d'Eichthal, another Jew, Charles Duveyrier and his own brother Eugène who, according to G. Weill, was the moving spirit in transforming the doctrine from a philosophy to a religion. He translated Lessing's *Erziehung des Menschengeschlechts*, and in his letters to Burns and Rességuier he formulated the new trinity. When he died he had done a great deal towards commenting and clarifying the *Nouveau Christianisme*.

Enfantin had successively abandoned a military and a commercial career, and had been studying economic and financial problems since 1823. He had met Saint-Simon once in 1825, and now at the age of thirty-three his real life lay before him; it is not his service during the siege of Paris, or his career as a traveller in wines, or his clerkship in a bank in St Petersburg which can interest us here; we leave him to the future and pass on to Bazard who had been a conspirator and a carbonaro. He

brought with him something of the rigid discipline of those who
conspire for freedom in the dark, and although he was clear and
convincing, and sincerely convinced himself of the doctrine he
taught, he seems to have had little share in the general riotous
affection which was so soon to be abroad amongst them all.

The July Revolution gave the Saint-Simonians their first
opportunity for a public manifesto; in a circular of July 27 they
exhorted their members to hold aloof from a fratricidal war,
and on July 30 they posted a proclamation in the streets demanding the abolition of all privileges of birth and the universal
classification by merit alone. Meanwhile Bazard had paid a
visit to his old carbonaro comrade Lafayette imploring him to
accept the dictatorship of the people and to inaugurate a Saint-
Simonian rule, but Lafayette had other views, and the *Jugement
de la doctrine de Saint-Simon sur les derniers évènements*, published in August 1830, was destined to have no direct influence
on contemporary politics. But the movement was growing
apace. Not only were the working men being organised in the
arrondissements somewhat after the system of Fourier's *phalan-
stères*, but missions were also sent to various parts of France,
to England and to Belgium. The South of France had been
organised since February 1830 by Rességuier, a friend and correspondent of Enfantin, and there were departmental churches
at Toulouse, Montpellier, Metz, Dijon and Lyons.

These are the dry bones of what appeared to be, until November
1831, a flourishing state of affairs. The young and active church
was gaining new members both at home and abroad, the *Globe*
daily trumpeted forth its principles and penetrated into other
countries, whilst crowds of possible and actual converts attended
the sermons in the *salle* Taitbout. Moreover the spirit of the
members of the family was one of generous enthusiasm and
ardour, of whole-hearted singleness of purpose, of the faith
which will remove mountains. Yet all was not well within, and
two disquieting symptoms were already manifest. In the first
place the two high priests were at war on a question of fundamental importance; in the second place Enfantin, by the exercise
of what appears to have been an unusual personal charm, was
already sowing the seeds of exaltation and hysteria which led

the sect into excesses and absurdities. These in their turn made
of a most respectable religion, whose basis was the broadest
possible philanthropy, and whose doctrine was founded on
science and political economy, the laughing-stock of Paris and
one of the *causes célèbres* of the world.

'Know thyself' and 'Nothing too much'; it is possible that
his good genius sometimes whispered these words in his ear,
but they fell unheeded; and in the glare of a limelight all the
more dazzling because it took the form of a halo, in the
blare of the trumpets which heralded his mystical utterances,
Enfantin marched triumphantly towards a retribution none the
less sure for being delayed, none the less tragic perhaps for taking
the character of successive anti-climaxes and a comfortable and
prosperous latter end.

(b) THE SCHISMS

The programme of reforms which the Saint-Simonians advocated included the enfranchisement of women; and here, although they might claim to be following the spirit of Saint-
Simon's teaching, it would need some good will to twist his one
utterance about women into anything like a foreshadowing of
their own views. During a discussion with Buchez in 1828 on
the nature of God Enfantin had come to the conclusion that God
was androgynous, and that his material manifestation was under
a male and a female form. Since God was both man and woman
the equality of the sexes followed inevitably. The enfranchisement of woman was to be complete: in the family, in the city,
in the temple she was to be the equal of man. No social function
could be performed without her, since the social individual was
henceforth to be the 'couple,' man and woman[1]. It was not
the complete enfranchisement of women which gave Bazard
pause. The whole sect were firm and solid on this point, and
they put the theory into practice as far as they could by admitting women into the hierarchy; they even pushed it to its
last conclusion by proclaiming that the high priest himself was
incomplete without a high priestess. Nor was this a mere statement in the air accompanied by a secret wish that the 'mère

[1] The Saint-Simonians owed this idea to Fourier.

suprême' might never materialise. Public appeals were made
in the *Globe*, expensive entertainments were organised, George
Sand was approached, and if Julie Fanfernot, a daughter of
the people, was rejected, the reasons were probably solid enough.
Bazard and Rodrigues as well as Enfantin had the 'mère
suprême' on their programme and publicly announced the fact.
Here therefore they were at one.

They were agreed as well on the principle of the 'rehabilitation of the flesh' which the master had adumbrated in the
Nouveau Christianisme. Something of emotional fervour they
added; Fourier's appeal that the passions should be allowed free
play may not have been without effect; the doctrine was developed by Enfantin along lines which might have startled
Saint-Simon, but he had certainly sanctioned the doctrine itself.
Whence then did the disagreement spring?

Fundamentally it lay in the logical nature of Enfantin's mind.
He meant what he said when he announced that senses and
spirit were both equally divine, and thereupon he applied this
doctrine to the question of marriage. Bazard had accepted the
principle but he could not swallow its logical conclusion. His
position towards the question of marriage and divorce is best
seen in the manifesto of October 1, 1830, which he and Enfantin
addressed to the President of the Chamber of Deputies:

Le christianisme a tiré les femmes de la servitude, mais il les a condamnées pourtant à la subalternité, et partout, dans l'Europe chrétienne, nous les voyons encore frappées d'interdiction *religieuse,
politique et civile*.

Les saint-simoniens viennent annoncer leur affranchissement définitif, leur complète émancipation, mais sans prétendre pour cela
abolir la sainte loi du mariage proclamée par le christianisme; ils
viennent au contraire pour *accomplir cette loi*, pour lui donner une
nouvelle sanction, pour ajouter à la puissance et à l'*inviolabilité* de
l'union qu'elle consacre[1].

Thus far they went together, but Bazard would not go a step
farther, and even at the moment of signing this manifesto,
Enfantin was dreaming of radical changes in the marriage laws;
whilst probably even before this the two chiefs were at variance,

[1] *Œuvres de Saint-Simon et d'Enfantin*, IV, p. 123.

although they kept their disagreement from the rest of the family, hoping against hope that some solution might be found.

Meanwhile Enfantin was developing the theory of the constant and the inconstant, leading to the desirability of successive unions for the latter, and on this rock the bark of their mutual agreement foundered at last. Bazard was fundamentally opposed to divorce; he might have been brought to admit its desirability in exceptional cases, but this regularisation of inconstancy stuck in his gorge.

The year 1831 was the year of the crisis with Bazard and it is necessary to follow the development of the woman-question in some detail during this period.

Claire Bazard, the first 'mother,' and wife of the high priest, was an ardent convert, an enthusiastic worker, and presumably quite as much interested in the emancipation of her sex as the men who were advocating it. But prejudices die hard, and when Jules Lechevalier, one of the youngest members of the 'collège,' proposed marriage to an actress, the first Saint-Simonian woman was horrified and dismayed[1]. This incident might well have given Enfantin pause, for if all the constant women were to show this instinctive repugnance to their inconstant sisters, the new era of love and peace would wear a rather strained expression.

Nor was this all; with a tactless sincerity that is not without its charm, Claire insisted on pouring her complaints of herself and the women in the hierarchy into Enfantin's unwilling ears. She would not allow him to live in a fool's paradise and to imagine that the women were as advanced as the men; she shook him roughly out of golden day-dreams to communicate the following discouraging report:

Je n'ai rien fait encore, mon père; je n'ai réalisé aucune de vos espérances, mon père; celles dont vous m'aviez dit de développer l'amour, d'éclairer l'esprit, de diriger les efforts, elles sont encore ce qu'elles étaient lorsque vous les avez remises entre mes mains....La hiérarchie pour nous est un vain mot, elle ne porte aucun fruit; nos réunions se passent dans le tumulte et le désordre; c'est un chaos dans lequel il serait impossible de reconnaître les inférieures de la supérieure, car la mère ne sait imposer le respect aux enfants, les

[1] *Œuvres de Saint-Simon et d'Enfantin*, III, p. 72 note.

enfants ne savent point se soumettre à la mère...l'obéissance et le respect, nous ne les éprouvons que pour le maître, et le maître, pour nous, c'est l'homme[1].

Enfantin however refused to be discouraged because the women were difficult to manage and *mère* Bazard was not at the height of the task. That would be changed at the advent of the 'mère suprême.' And the 'femme messie' would not tarry long; already visions were being vouchsafed to the elect:

Mon père! mon père! je le sens, le jour de ton hymen est proche, et déjà, près de toi, j'ai vu le trône de ma MÈRE[2].

And so back to the golden day-dreams with a heart warmed by the love and adoration expressed in this letter and typical of the feelings which he called forth in them all.

On October 13, 1831, Olinde Rodrigues read a *Note* on marriage and divorce to his colleagues. He obviously imagined that he and Enfantin were at one on the question, since he supported him during the ensuing struggle with Bazard, for it was not till some months later that he in his turn renounced Enfantin and all his works. Yet that the latter was already prepared to go much further is known from a letter to his mother written as early as August 1831, in which he stated those opinions which were to alienate Rodrigues and indeed all who understood them aright and were not dazzled by the strange glamour with which Enfantin was able to surround them.

Je crois donc fermement [Rodrigues stated in this *Note*] qu'un individu ne peut être à la *fois* l'époux que d'une seule femme, et qu'il ne peut donc l'être de plusieurs que *successivement*....Nul ne sera en état normal pour être marié, qui désirerait ou accepterait le mariage, en voyant devant lui le divorce[3].

Marriage, he continued, can only be contracted between equals in the hierarchy, and divorce between the high priest and the high priestess would mean abdication. The woman who is to seat herself on the pontifical throne will determine the limits beyond which immorality begins in successive marriages, she will reveal the 'code de la pudeur.'

This *Note* precipitated the quarrel between Bazard and

[1] *Œuvres de Saint-Simon et d'Enfantin*, III, pp. 115–117.
[2] *Ibid.* III, p. 80, letter from a disciple dated January 1, 1831.
[3] *Ibid.* IV, pp. 128 and 127.

Enfantin, and it was now an open secret in the family that a rupture was imminent. The eternal and endless arguments between the two chiefs, which had been hitherto held where none might witness them, now came to be discussed *in camera* among the elect. Louis Blanc gives a curious and distressing account of the abnormal excitement which characterised these gatherings[1]. Enfantin sometimes insisted that each member present should confess his sins; young men would faint away under the stress of their emotions, and the arguments would proceed whilst they were being carried out. On one occasion Caseaux fell into a trance and began to prophesy; on another Rodrigues insisted on a testimony from each present that the Holy Ghost dwelt within him, Rodrigues. Reynaud answered with unbelieving words, and Rodrigues fell down in a fit. The doctor was summoned, but the patient did not recover until Reynaud withdrew from the sceptical position he had adopted. The author of the *Notice historique*, commenting on this scene, adds that when Dr Fuster arrived he found everyone in a high state of fever and nervous excitement: 'Il n'y avait guère qu'Enfantin qui eût gardé tout son calme.'[2]

This painful and violent struggle was not only between opposing principles, it was also the clash of two very different temperaments; the lion and the unicorn were fighting for the crown; there is only one end to such a duel. For a moment Bazard showed symptoms of coming to heel by recognising Enfantin as supreme head of the Saint-Simonian religion and by accepting a secondary position as 'chef de dogme' beside Rodrigues, 'chef de culte'; which shows that Bazard too could be swayed by Enfantin's mysterious power; but it was a victory of short duration. On November 11, 1831, he retired completely and the Saint-Simonian gatherings knew him no more. Some virtue had gone out of him during the strife, the emotional and intellectual exhaustion produced a stroke, from which he recovered at the time, but he had only nine months to live. His wife accompanied him, giving another proof of her 'immobilité,' and there were altogether nineteen secessions on this occasion,

---

[1] L. Blanc, *Histoire de dix ans, 1830–1840*, Paris, 1844, III, pp. 128 ff.
[2] *Œuvres de Saint-Simon et d'Enfantin*, IV, p. 138.

among the renegades being Pierre Leroux, Carnot, Lechevalier, Charton, Dugied, Caseaux; and also Henri and Cécile Fournel who, however, returned later to the church.

A meeting of the family was held on November 19 at which stormy and angry speeches were made by those who threw in their lot with Bazard, and some heart-broken confessions of doubt and scepticism were heard. Reynaud announced that he would stay with Enfantin in order to protest against him. Enfantin's divine calm was not shattered; he welcomed the protestant and heard unmoved the attack made by Reynaud on the fundamental danger of his views:

La théorie que le père Enfantin professe, sur la femme, n'est qu'un détail de l'ensemble de sa théorie sur l'humanité. Je crois que cette théorie abolit toute la liberté humaine.... Votre théorie enlève à l'homme sa dignité et sa conscience[1].

It was the voice of sanity, but it was crying in a sparsely populated country.

On November 21 a second meeting was held. The empty chair by Enfantin's side was henceforward to remain as a symbol of the appeal to woman, but until the high priestess had declared herself, women must no longer remain in the hierarchy, since it was a man-made institution. Also until the 'mère suprême' should have drawn up the laws of morality no Saint-Simonian must allow himself to sin against such laws as then existed. He would be no true member of the church who failed to obey this order. Those who came to this meeting to protest were persuaded after some wrangling to retire; the young men who were left, and it was mostly the young who remained with Enfantin, were wildly enthusiastic. The charge of immorality which Bazard had brought against his colleague, and which had caused a terrible sensation, was finally removed by Rodrigues; he saluted in Enfantin: 'L'homme le plus MORAL de mon temps, le vrai SUCCESSEUR de SAINT-SIMON, le CHEF SUPRÊME de la RELIGION SAINT-SIMONIENNE.'[2]

This declaration was solemnly repeated on November 27 which is the culminating scene in the story of the schism. It was an

[1] Œuvres de Saint-Simon et d'Enfantin, IV, pp. 179 and 182.
[2] Ibid. IV, p. 201.

open meeting held in the rue Taitbout and was reported in the
Globe next day. Béranger was among the spectators. The purpose of the meeting was to organise the religious association of
the working men. Olinde Rodrigues undertook to found a Saint-
Simonian company; Barrault in an impassioned speech called
upon the artists to institute the new religious rites. But Reynaud,
the protestant, interrupted the harmony of the proceedings:

...l'argent ne peut avoir encore de puissance MORALE, puisque
vous, père ENFANTIN, d'après les termes posés par vous, vous dé-
truisez la MORALE ancienne, sans avoir la MORALE nouvelle. Vous
n'avez pas de MORALE particulièrement en ce qui concerne les rapports de l'homme et de la femme[1].

A frantic discussion ensued between Reynaud, Rodrigues,
Laurent, Talabot and Baud, which lasted an hour and a half
and over which Enfantin presided, calm, unmoved and with an
inspired air. Suddenly Baud arose and testified to his faith
in the supreme father:

'Non, Dieu n'a pas permis qu'un homme pût se placer en présence
des hommes avec cette face calme et sereine, avec cette grandeur et
cette beauté, pour qu'il s'en servît afin de les séduire et de les
perdre....'
Lorsque Baud a eu dit, notre PÈRE ENFANTIN s'est levé, et
bientôt tous ses fils étaient dans ses bras. Reynaud lui-même, après
un instant d'hésitation, s'est jeté à son cou avec transport....
'Ce que je viens de voir et d'entendre [said Félix R..., a stranger]
me fait croire à des choses que je prenais pour des fictions. Il me
semble avoir assisté au discours sur la montagne.'[2]

Enfantin's personality had gained a signal victory.

Henceforward for a space his ascendancy over his disciples
was complete, and he felt himself emboldened to proceed with
the development of his doctrine. He delivered his famous *Enseignements* sometimes in the rue Taranne, sometimes in the rue
Monsigny from November 28, 1831, to February 18, 1832,
attempting the by no means easy task of justifying his views
on morality to those members of the hierarchy who had not
followed Bazard, and, making every effort as he did, so to keep
Rodrigues by his side. More than once he regretted the absence
of the 'tradition vivante' from these assemblies, but Rodrigues

[1] *Œuvres de Saint-Simon et d'Enfantin*, IV, p. 233.
[2] *Ibid.* IV, pp. 238–240.

remained obstinately aloof, and Enfantin's voice might not reach him, charm he never so wisely. The *Enseignements* were largely in the nature of prophecies on the pronouncements of the 'mère suprême'; this temptation was irresistible, since he was now firmly established as an oracle, nay, as the Messiah himself, although still awaiting completion. Meanwhile he was straining every nerve to compel the high priestess to reveal herself, but all in vain. Peradventure she was on a journey, peradventure she was asleep; certain it is that she remained deaf to his pleadings, and that clouds were gathering on all sides.

On January 22, 1832, the government made a descent on the rue Taitbout where Barrault was about to preach; the sermon was stopped, the meeting was dissolved, and the government seals were affixed to the door. Desmoutiers, 'procureur du roi,' and Zangiacomi, 'juge d'instruction,' then proceeded to the rue Monsigny, already besieged by the police, here they seized all the papers they could find and retired. The trial began next day with the cross-questioning of Enfantin and Rodrigues and was to last six months. The bearing of the Saint-Simonians was quiet and collected during this proceeding. Always the advocates of peaceable methods, they persuaded the crowds to disperse quietly, and all were most favourably impressed by the serene and dignified bearing of Enfantin; indeed some converts were made among the soldiers on this occasion. The interference of the government was not wholly disadvantageous to the Saint-Simonians. The press, which had hitherto ridiculed them mercilessly, especially the *Figaro*, now adopted a more generous attitude.

A more telling blow awaited the new church however. Enfantin's remarkable views on the relations between men and women, which he was preaching in the *Enseignements*, were not long in reaching Rodrigues' ears, and he found in them the following new ideas, an ironic supplement to his *Note*: (a) Marriage may take place between those who are not equals in the hierarchy. (b) The child shall not know his father; the mother alone can be called upon to pronounce on this subject. (c) The high priest and the high priestess may use sensual as well as spiritual means to lead their flock upwards.

It was enough; Rodrigues, whatever he may have meant by the 'rehabilitation of the flesh,' did not mean this; his reaction to these views was refreshingly prompt and vigorous:

J'ai affirmé que dans la famille Saint-Simonienne tout enfant devait pouvoir connaître son père. Enfantin a exprimé le vœu que la femme seule fût appelée à s'expliquer sur cette grave question. Il a donc admis des cas de promiscuité religieuse, tandis que j'ai seulement admis *la sanction du divorce et la sanctification des secondes noces*[1]....

Rodrigues signed this protest 'Chef de la religion Saint-Simonienne' and shortly afterwards brought out a selection of Saint-Simon's works with a manifesto-preface. Bazard too came out of a long silence at this inopportune moment and published protests in the *Globe*:

...vous, vous êtes (involontairement, je veux le croire encore) la constatation du désordre dans la voie du MAL. *Voilà ce que vous êtes*[2].

'Dieu se retire de l'homme isolé' was the soft answer made to Bazard in the *Globe*, nevertheless things were not going very well with Enfantin. Rodrigues left in an evil hour for the church; he had undertaken to float a Saint-Simonian loan, and his secession came during the third issue. The Saint-Simonians were nearing a financial crisis. Worse than this, in spite of proclamations made by Enfantin in the *Globe* and to the provincial churches, that until the coming of the 'femme messie' the existing code of morals was to be rigorously observed, sinister rumours were afloat anent his private morality. It was high time to convince a censorious world of the purity of his motives. The propaganda must cease since there were no funds to maintain it, and a lofty impression must be produced. On April 20, 1832, the *Globe* expired with a final display of fireworks: 'DIEU m'a donné mission d'*appeler* le PROLÉTAIRE et la FEMME à une destinée nouvelle,' so ran Enfantin's undaunted announcement, and this mission was now to be accomplished in an extremely awe-inspiring manner. Enfantin was going to leave the world and retire into monastic seclusion taking forty of his disciples with him. They would live in strict celibacy

---

[1] *Globe*, February 19, 1832.
[2] *Ibid*. February 20, 1832.

until the new code of morals should be revealed to them by the 'mère suprême.' It was a master-stroke of diplomacy. The expenses of propaganda were eliminated and the evil bird of calumny was slain outright; for this sensational retreat outweighed all the sermons that they had ever preached.

Enfantin's mother had died on the same day as the final appearance of the *Globe*, and her funeral, which took place two days later, served as a curtain-raiser to the retreat. A procession was carefully arranged and several hundred disciples and friends followed Enfantin with bared heads to the cemetery. They then all accompanied the forty apostles to Ménilmontant, where Enfantin gave them a short address ending with a remarkable invitation. He summoned to his arms all those who had lost a woman they had loved or by whom they had been loved within the last twelve months. The invitation was rapturously accepted, the friends then dispersed and the apostles were left alone.

Their life in the seclusion of Ménilmontant would seem to have differed little in practice from the usual monastic routine. They lived in celibacy and employed no servants, thus accomplishing the 'change of skin' which was one of their catch-words. 'La hiérarchie a la peau trop blanche' Enfantin had said, and he set his disciples digging, brick-laying, scrubbing, polishing floors, washing plates and cooking. They rose at five, and work, which included lectures, was over by five in the afternoon. The apostles were not allowed to leave Ménilmontant, so that, although Paris might come to them, they might not go to Paris. It was a curious turn of events; behold the apostles of this religion which preached roses and raptures, the beauty of the senses and the divinity of passion, they have been swept into a monastic retreat, and are separated by a provisional vow of celibacy from their wives and from their lovers. Nor were these apostles the simple fishermen who left all and followed Christ. They were for the most part extremely intellectual men: scientists, lawyers, doctors, engineers, men with an excellent education behind them, and many with successful careers in the future, long-headed, clear-sighted Frenchmen. 'Que diable allaient-ils faire dans cette galère?' The only answer to this question lies in the personality of Enfantin. It is one of the greatest victories of this elusive quality that, in the name of a religion which promised just the reverse, he should have imposed upon forty young men, many of them married, this temporary confinement to barracks. He could have done anything with them then; the religion he preached and the charm he embodied had gone to their heads. They were prostrate before him and his will was theirs; over the life at Ménilmontant there brooded for a space the mysterious power of the priest.

(c) THE APOTHEOSIS OF ENFANTIN

Enfantin was very far from being indifferent to his worshippers. He called himself 'un de ces êtres aimants qui entraînent' and saw in his great power to love the secret of his success. And yet one cannot help feeling that other causes were at work as well, and that he possessed that strange attraction which the unbalanced sometimes wield over their more normal brethren. He certainly stirred his followers up to a pitch of frantic excitement, so that they, and not their leader, appeared to be trembling on the verge of insanity; but things are not always what they seem.

Physically and outwardly Enfantin seems to have been the type of man most readily connected with the phrase *mens sana in corpore sano*, for he was tall and handsome, with a tendency to corpulence and with a healthy love of good food. Moreover, contemporary writers are unanimous in their praise of his beauty and of his charm of expression. 'Son sourire délivre de la détresse et rend joyeux,' said Cavel, commenting on his portrait[1]; and Rose, his cousin's cook, contributed the endearing words, 'C'est bien sa bouche bonasse et ses yeux si doux.'[2]

And not only was his expression beautiful, it was also extremely serene and calm, the outward sign of a serenity of mind which rarely forsook him, and of which his biographers give innumerable examples. He was extremely proud of this attribute round which he built a miniature mythology, since the dominant characteristic of the priest was this very 'calme' which he possessed in so marked a degree and which came to symbolise

[1] *Globe*, March 27, 1832.
[2] *Œuvres de Saint-Simon et d'Enfantin*, VII, p. 12.

the harmony between two such diametrically opposed qualities
as constancy and unfaithfulness. In *La lettre sur le calme*
which was quoted and re-quoted, read and re-read, he deigned
to give the reasons for his divine calm, and magnificent and
wonderful those reasons were; yet he was by no means devoid
of judgment, and he gave proof of a certain shrewdness even
whilst he was advocating those fantastical doctrines which seem
so entirely lacking in common sense[1]; for his insistence on the
importance of respecting public morality until the new code
should be revealed is another proof that he was no vague,
unpractical dreamer, and indeed his later life showed that
he had great practical ability as well as vision in industrial
matters; whilst, most saving clause of all, on one occasion at
least, he was known to throw cold water on an ecstatic disciple.
For when Gustave d'Eichthal, the most fervent and perhaps the
most unbalanced of an adoring and ill-balanced crew, rushed
into his room one morning at half-past six to announce a vision
he had had in the night, the substance of which was the refrain:
'JÉSUS VIT EN ENFANTIN...TU ES LA FUTURE MOITIÉ du
COUPLE RÉVÉLATEUR...l'*Homme-Dieu*,' Enfantin answered:
'En l'absence de la femme je ne puis me nommer; à plus forte
raison, tu ne le peux pas'; then seeing that there was nothing
for it but to rise, if he wished to put an end to the stream of
ecstatic testimonies, he announced finally as he drew on his
stockings: 'HOMO SUM.'[2] It goes without saying that this
episode has been quoted by Enfantin's admirers in support of
his sanity of outlook. It certainly proves that the early morning
is a propitious hour for the promptings of common sense.

Yet in spite of this evidence for the defence it would seem
that Enfantin cannot have been completely sane during the
period we are considering; nor is this meant merely in the sense
in which all inspiration sins against the humdrum sanity of the
Philistine. He appears rather as a victim of an all-too-common
delusion which is typified at one end of the scale by the man
who takes himself too seriously and at the other by those

---

[1] Cf. *Œuvres de Saint-Simon et d'Enfantin*, III, p. 130, letter to Duguet
who was proselytising in Belgium, dated April 21, 1831.

[2] Cf. *ibid*. VI, pp. 185–196, 214.

Emperors of China and Napoleons who are to be met with in the saddest of societies.

His power of attraction had begun in his school-days; and in his early manhood he had walked a conquering way:

...trouvant partout...des cœurs aimants qui allaient au-devant du mien; j'ai vu beaucoup de monde, hommes, femmes, enfants, vieillards, et il m'a semblé plus tard que je pouvais consacrer à autre chose qu'à vendre des bouteilles cet heureux don qui faisait que tous s'attachaient, se *liaient*, se *reliaient* à moi....Le jour où je me fis cette question fut pour moi celui d'une nouvelle vie...je voulus connaître, et j'appris tout ce qu'avaient fait les hommes qui avaient le plus contribué au bonheur de l'humanité, à sa marche progressive....

(He instances Moses, Christ, Mohammed, Luther, Calvin, Robespierre, Napoleon, Augustine, Gregory.)

...enfin je fis société avec les lumières du monde, avec les grands hommes, c'est de là que date ma *folie*, comme disent plusieurs, c'est de là que date ma FOI...ma VIE[1].

It is in this letter that Enfantin ranks himself with 'ces êtres aimants qui entraînent'; it shows clearly enough how he became convinced of his high mission, and that with much that was lovable and admirable in his character, much that was lofty and noble in his aspirations, there went something too much like vaingloriousness, the solemnity at once touching and absurd of one who in all good faith rates himself too high.

This attitude of mind, if it is merely adumbrated in the letter to Morin, appears with startling clearness when Enfantin addresses those who are already under his spell; and it would be easy to multiply examples of letters, proclamations and speeches couched in the language of megalomania[2], but there is another and less amusing side of the question to be considered, and that is the effect which Enfantin's conception of himself and of his divine mission had on his disciples.

And of the whole strange story, this part seems the strangest and the most unreal; more unbelievable even than the fantastic search for the mystic mother which has the quality of a romantic

---

[1] *Œuvres de Saint-Simon et d'Enfantin*, III, pp. 155–157, letter to Morin, dated June 21, 1831.

[2] Cf. *ibid.* II, pp. 168–169; III, p. 109; IV, pp. 191–192.

day-dream, whereas the apotheosis of Enfantin belongs rather
to the realm of nightmare. For he was no god, as they all came
to see in time, nor was he even a great leader of men, as the
fiasco of the damming of the Nile was to prove. He was a man
not without visions, and not without ideals, but with a strange
lack of moral good taste, a strange childishness and absurd pretensions; yet for a time so confident of his high mission, and
possessed of so real a power of attraction, that he led his followers a dance that was wild indeed. I have instanced as a
proof of this power the fact that some forty apostles followed
him into seclusion at Ménilmontant; I should add that they
adopted a costume of which the wearer's name was a conspicuous feature and grew long beards. But even this *tour de
force* pales before the testimony of the state of mind of these
men as it is set forth in the sixteenth volume of the *Œuvres
complètes*, the second volume of the *Enseignements d'Enfantin*.

It seems, after this lapse of time, as if it were hardly
fair to drag these confessions again into the light of day; but
one or two quotations are necessary to complete the picture of
the abnormal excitement which surged round the figure of the
supreme priest. During the course of his *Enseignements* Enfantin often insisted that one after another of the members of
the family should make a public confession of faith; and these
professions degenerated into declarations of love and into real
confessions which often make most distressing reading. We
hear of unhappy homes, of religious doubts and despair, of
thoughts of suicide, and of dissolute lives; precious material for
those engaged in studying the 'mal du siècle.' The speakers all
testify to the solution which the Saint-Simonian religion brought
to their various problems, and all, or nearly all, speak of the
great suffering which the late crisis had caused them and which
had obviously left them in a highly strung and painfully sensitive
condition. There is a note of desperate sincerity in these outpourings which is impossible to miss; and many of the disciples,
d'Eichthal in particular, seem to be trembling on the verge of
a nervous breakdown. The confessions are interspersed with
declarations of love, with pardons begged and given, with em-
bracings and tears. It is a grotesque travesty of what may be

witnessed in a Catholic school on the eve of the first communion. The most striking point about these effusions however is the language which the disciples addressed to Enfantin and the feelings they express towards him. A few examples, chosen almost at random, will illustrate sufficiently the effect he had on them:

Béranger....je vous aime, et d'un amour *aveugle*![1]

Lambert (Philosopher, École Polytechnique). Depuis lors, PÈRE, j'ai eu la révélation de ce que VOUS êtes...et aujourd'hui je me sens capable de vous dire un mot que je n'aurais jamais dit à un homme avant d'entrer dans la doctrine; c'est que *je vous aime de tout mon cœur*[2].

Michel Chevalier. VOUS êtes l'homme au monde, je ne dirai pas que j'aime le plus maintenant, la chose est toute simple, mais il n'y a pas encore eu d'homme au monde pour lequel j'aie senti et pensé ce que j'ai senti et pensé sur VOUS[3].

Such was the nature of the incense offered to Enfantin in response to the claims he put forward; it remains to be seen if this adoration will stand the test to which the life at Ménil-montant was to subject it.

(d) THE TRIAL AND DISBANDMENT

The Saint-Simonian ceremonies which took place at Ménil-montant, and of which there were not unnaturally a considerable number, since they alone varied the monotony of the monastic routine, were elaborate and solemn in the extreme. The 'prise d'habits,' the 'ouverture des travaux du temple,' the funeral rites of Talabot who died of the cholera, all these occasions were duly celebrated by ritual song and dance; and had it not been for the cruel promptitude of Madame Bazard, Enfantin and his apostles would have graced the interment of her husband clad in the symbolical costume which they had adopted in their retreat:

Le pantalon était blanc, le gilet rouge et la tunique d'un bleu violet. Le blanc est la couleur de l'amour, le rouge celle du travail, le bleu violet celle de la foi; le costume signifiait donc que le saint-simonisme s'appuyait sur l'amour, fortifiait son cœur par le travail et était enveloppé par la foi; la coiffure et l'écharpe étaient laissées à l'initia-

---

[1] *Œuvres de Saint-Simon et d'Enfantin*, XVII, p. 126.
[2] *Ibid*. XVI, p. 64.   [3] *Ibid*. XVI, pp. 59–60.

tive individuelle; mais comme ici-bas et plus tard chacun garde la responsabilité de sa vie, le nom de tout saint-simonien devait être inscrit en grosses lettres sur sa poitrine.... Sur la poitrine d'Enfantin on lisait: Le Père; sur celle de Duveyrier: Charles, Poète de Dieu[1].

The waistcoat was made to button at the back, a symbol of fraternity and association, an ever-present reminder of the dependence of man upon his brother; the disciples also wore long beards.

The government meanwhile had been subjecting the Saint-Simonians to continual cross-examinations, since the descent on the *salle* Taitbout. The case against them was now complete, and Enfantin, Michel Chevalier, Duveyrier and Olinde Rodrigues were summoned before the court of assizes on the charge of violation of article 291 of the penal code, forbidding unauthorised reunions of more than twenty people; and on a second charge levelled against Enfantin, Duveyrier and Chevalier of outrage on public morality. This was based on an article entitled 'De la femme,' written by Duveyrier and published on February 2, 1832, in the *Globe* which was edited by Chevalier; and on an extract from the fifth *Enseignement* dealing with the relations between men and women which had appeared in the same paper.

At half-past nine on the morning of July 27, 1832, all the apostles, with Enfantin at their head, left Ménilmontant and proceeded towards the court of assizes. They were in full costume and created a sensation on their way. It was a most curious trial. Enfantin named Aglaé Sainte-Hilaire and Cécile Fournel as his counsels. This was out of order since women could not plead in court, but he refused any others and the witnesses for the defence were then called; but they were not heard because they would not take the oath without Enfantin's permission, and the judge ruled that this invalidated their oath:

...mais vous ne savez pas [Lambert exclaimed during this argument] ce qu'est cet homme. Cet homme, c'est la manifestation la plus élevée de DIEU dans l'humanité. Ce qui revient à dire que nous reconnaissons un pouvoir humain, dont les actes ont une inspiration et une sanction religieuse[2].

The judge however stood firm, and the trial proceeded without

[1] Maxime du Camp, *Souvenirs littéraires*, Paris, 1882–1883, II, p. 124.
[2] *Œuvres de Saint-Simon et d'Enfantin*, VII, p. 224.

the evidence of the witnesses for the defence. Duveyrier then rose to defend himself, and in a speech which unhappily was not reported, he turned the tables with dramatic suddenness by a terrible indictment of the immorality of his judges. He was not called 'poète de Dieu' for nothing; many years later the magistrate owned that he himself had been greatly moved by Duveyrier's flaming eloquence.

Enfantin's defence came the next day, and it is more than probable that he enjoyed himself immensely. He began by staring the judge, the jury and the audience out of countenance, speaking with maddening slowness whilst his gaze wandered from one embarrassed face to another. The irritated president could hardly contain his impatience whilst Enfantin explained that he was teaching them the powerful influence of form, flesh and senses. In the end the proceedings were interrupted until he should show more respect to the court, and when they were resumed, Enfantin preached a sermon instead of defending himself and informed an angry judge and an incensed jury of the mission he had been sent into the world to fulfil:

De cette femme MESSIE, je sens que je suis le PRÉCURSEUR; pour elle je suis ce que SAINT JEAN fut pour JÉSUS; LÀ EST TOUTE MA VIE, LÀ EST LE LIEN DE TOUS MES Actes, et ils sont logique-ment enchaînés, car ils découlent tous de ma foi dans les femmes[1].

At last the trial wore to an end, for even the speeches of Enfantin could not last for ever. Rodrigues and Barrault escaped with a nominal fine of fifty francs each; Enfantin, Duveyrier and Chevalier were condemned to one year's imprisonment and to a fine of a hundred francs. The dissolution of the society was ordered, and a hundred copies of this order were to be posted in Paris.

The law had pronounced the doom of the society, but un-necessarily, for the principle of disintegration was at work, and the law itself could not have stopped it. From the beginning of September the defections began; the apostles had not enough to do; they were leading a life not only unnatural in any case, but also entirely against the principles they proclaimed. They were, further, at too close quarters; they had lost their first en-

---

[1] *Œuvres de Saint-Simon et d'Enfantin*, VIII, p. 54 note.

thusiasm and developed in its stead an intense nervous irritability. Enfantin had misjudged the strength of his influence. It was stronger than the natural instincts of the apostles for a time, but for a time only. He could no longer hold them, so he bowed to the inevitable, and allowed one after another to slip away; to dine out, to stay out, to abandon the costume. Gradually the hierarchy melted away. 'On attendrait pour la reconstituer l'arrivée de la femme.' The experiment had proved a failure.

Léon Cogniet has painted a portrait of Enfantin in the famous costume standing before the double throne and pointing to the empty seat. It is in this attitude of waiting, whilst patience becomes impatience, that one sees him during the next few months. No harder trial could have been imagined for one of Enfantin's spirit than this interminable watching and hoping for someone who did not appear, whilst the work he was longing to do remained undone, and the enthusiasm of his disciples became cooler day by day. He made a final effort however. Instead of attempting to stem the tide of defections, he turned his mind to the best means of using the defaulters to advantage.

It was a gallant effort to adapt himself to circumstances but on the whole it failed. The church was only held together now by the hope, still persisting in some hearts, that the 'free woman' would accomplish what Enfantin had failed to accomplish. He had said too often that he was as nothing without her; they now began to believe him. Duveyrier and d'Eichthal who had been his most ecstatic disciples were gone like arrows from a bow to search for the mystic mother; they shaved their beards, donned ordinary clothes, embraced their families, wept a little over the separation from the 'supreme father,' but recovered sufficiently to pen the following gleeful lines to Hoart:

Désormais donc nous sommes INDÉPENDANTS DU PÈRE; nous allons au-devant de l'inspiration des FEMMES et de la MÈRE[1].

The capital letters tell their own story; Enfantin was no longer their chief concern. By November 14, 1832, most of them were gone, and the high priest fell into so gloomy a mood

[1] *Œuvres de Saint-Simon et d'Enfantin*, VIII, p. 164, dated November 9, 1832.

that Michel Chevalier, one of the faithful few, sent a message to
Rodrigues to come and bring him consolation. But Rodrigues
held warily aloof, and Enfantin struggled as best he might out
of the black depression which had mastered him, not without
cause.

On December 15, 1832, Enfantin and Chevalier entered Sainte-
Pélagie together to work off their condemnation. Duveyrier
never sat for his term of captivity, and I have not discovered
how he managed to escape it. The remaining apostles were sent
away from Ménilmontant, and all were released from Enfantin's
authority:

Libres! oui, vous êtes libres, vous n'êtes plus mes *enfants*, vous
êtes émancipés, vous êtes hommes, vous êtes mes amis....[1]

Despise him as a charlatan, or mock at him as mad, it is yet
impossible to deny that he had the rare gift of facing adversity
with head up and a courageous smile.

(e) 'L'ANNÉE DE LA MÈRE'

The year 1833 was rapturously welcomed by the disciples as
'l'année de la mère,' for the fever inoculated by Enfantin now
ran high in the veins of his disciples, and Barrault in particular
presented the spectacle of a man demented with excitement.
The women themselves, who had hitherto remained on the
whole unmoved, began to testify; Cécile Fournel founded a
paper called *Le Livre des actes*, and Flora Tristran and Susanne
Voilquin threw themselves into the search for the mystic mother
with more ardour than discretion. Enfantin attempted to direct
all this feverish energy from his prison, but it must have been
a sore trial to be left at the post whilst his more fortunate companions raced on without him.

On April 8, 1833, Enfantin and Chevalier were once more
tried before the court of assizes; this time however the trial
ended in an acquitment. Michel had abandoned the costume
and shaved his beard; indeed his defection was imminent; he
had withdrawn to another part of the prison, and saw as little
as possible of the master who, alas, was now thoroughly on his
nerves. Enfantin appeared in high boots and a velvet cloak

[1] *Œuvres de Saint-Simon et d'Enfantin*, VIII, p. 207.

trimmed with ermine; in this impressive apparel he stood before
his judges and spoke to them in *vers libres*:

> Car si JÉSUS a été envoyé
> Pour ENSEIGNER au monde
> La SAGESSE du PÈRE,
> Moi, je suis envoyé par mon DIEU
> PÈRE et MÈRE de TOUS et de TOUTES,
> Pour faire désirer au monde
> Sa tendresse de MÈRE[1].

Meanwhile Barrault and the 'compagnons de la femme' had set
sail for Constantinople, having been authorised by Enfantin to
seek for the 'free woman' in the East. For some time now
Enfantin had been dreaming dreams of a mysterious affinity
between himself and the Orient, and Barrault had been seeing
visions. Two young girls had declared during a hypnotic trance
that the 'femme messie' would be found in the city on the
Bosphorus. It was enough for Barrault:

> Plus d'appel à la Femme! La Femme a entendu! Plus d'attente
> de la Femme! Je veux, et mon cœur s'en gonfle d'orgueil et de joie,
> je veux, dès qu'elle paraîtra et jettera un regard autour d'elle, qu'elle
> trouve à ses côtés, docile sous sa main, mais fière, calme et imposante
> à ses ennemis, ma tête de lion[2].

Behold them therefore disembarking in full costume, saluting
all women, rich and poor, high and low, according to Enfantin's
instructions; and experiencing at the sight of the veiled ladies
more than the usual glamour, since it was extremely likely that
the 'free woman' was at that moment hidden in a harem. The
Grand Turk prevented possible complications at this point by
transporting them to Smyrna. Barrault wandered as far as
Odessa, but returned holding firm to the belief that the mystic
mother would appear in the month of May of that year, that
she would reveal herself in Constantinople, and that she would
prove to be of Jewish origin. In the meantime the fame of Lady
Hester Stanhope had reached the 'compagnons de la femme,'
and they hastened to visit her, a tremulous hope in their hearts,
for had she not also seen visions of a woman messiah? But this
strange prophetess refused to play the part that was all ready

---

[1] *Œuvres de Saint-Simon et d'Enfantin*, VIII, pp. 229–230.
[2] S. Charléty, *Histoire du Saint-Simonisme*, Paris, 1896, p. 269.

for her. The great lady gave them money, but would not further their schemes. Rigaud finally started the heresy that the 'mère suprême' would appear in India; Barrault treated this prophecy as a blasphemy; in sorrow and in anger the 'compagnons de la femme' dispersed.

On August 1, 1833, Enfantin and Chevalier were released from prison. Michel will appear no more in these pages; he was to visit America, and on his return to become one of the leading economists of the age. Enfantin, we are not surprised to learn, set his face towards the East. But he was no longer the same man. The meditations in prison had borne an unexpected fruit. Mysticism and symbolism were still the outward characteristics of his utterances, but the utterances themselves were of a profoundly practical nature. In the solitude of Sainte-Pélagie he had originated a truly great idea, an idea which pushed the 'free woman' completely into the background; indeed he had done with her for good:

> Tu as annoncé ma face d'appel à la FEMME; c'est bien....Aujourd'hui je sens que c'est ma face POLITIQUE que je dois d'abord montrer à l'Orient....
> C'est à nous de faire,
> Entre l'antique Egypte et la vieille Judée,
> Une des deux nouvelles routes d'Europe
> Vers l'Inde et la Chine,
> Plus tard nous percerons aussi l'autre
> A Panama...
> Suez
> Est le centre de notre vie de travail,
> Là nous ferons l'acte
> Que le monde attend
> Pour confesser que nous sommes
> Mâles....[1]

It is impossible to lose an illusion more completely and more robustly than Enfantin when he lost faith in the 'mère suprême,'[2] a monster whom he had created and who for a moment threatened to overpower her master. But Enfantin was no Frankenstein, and the 'mère suprême' no revengeful demon to hunt

---

[1] *Œuvres de Saint-Simon et d'Enfantin*, IX, pp. 55–57, dated August 8, 1833; Saint-Simon had advocated the piercing of the isthmus of Panama as early as 1779.

[2] Cf. *ibid*. IX, pp. 58–65.

him to his death; the life he had given her proved an illusion, she had never lived at all.

With the rejection of the mystic mother, and by this time all but the most fanatical were only too willing to consign her to limbo, the Saint-Simonians left their fruitless star-gazing and came back to solid earth. 'Ce qui doit frapper *uniquement* aujourd'hui, c'est LA PERCÉE DE SUEZ.'[1]

(f) THE SUEZ CANAL

Enfantin was cruelly treated in the matter of the Suez Canal. It was the *grand œuvre* of his life, yet it is not generally associated with his name, nor is it widely enough known that it was he who gave the first impetus towards its final completion. He was unsuccessful in interesting Mehemet Ali in the scheme in the years 1833–1834, for Mehemet Ali was more anxious just then to proceed to the damming of the Nile. The Saint-Simonians were disappointed, discouraged and angry, especially Fournel, but Enfantin, who was remarkably adaptable, and who was thirsting for action, determined to seize this opportunity and to engineer the dam himself. It was not the success he hoped for; the enterprise began well but progressed slowly, the Saint-Simonians were wretchedly paid and more or less ignored; many fell victims to the plague, and in the end they drifted apart, although Enfantin did not return to France till January 1837.

There followed the phase of the 'apostolat royal.' Enfantin for a brief but happy period saw himself as an apostle preaching to kings and great men: Louis-Philippe, Heine, Lamartine and the Duke of Orleans. This ended with the offer of a 'sous-préfecture' from the duke; if his sin were excess, the punishment was admirably adapted to the crime, and retribution was taking a peculiarly trying form. He found his level at last from a worldly point of view in the Paris-Lyon-Méditerranée which he created from three smaller companies, and of which he became general secretary in 1852.

But he never abandoned the project of the Suez Canal, and in 1846 he founded the 'Société d'études pour le canal de Suez.' France was represented by Enfantin and Arlès-Dufour; Austria

---

[1] *Œuvres de Saint-Simon et d'Enfantin*, IX, p. 98.

and Germany by Negrelli and Sellier; and England by Starbuck and Stephenson; the consulting engineers were Jules, Léon and Paulin Talabot, and the meetings were held in Enfantin's house on the first Monday in the month. Later Lesseps joined the society and his share in the work is known to the world at large. He obtained a firman granting him the concession of the canal, and when the pasha made out a list of the founders of this great undertaking, no Saint-Simonian name appeared. It was a bitter blow, but Enfantin bore it very well; there is a dignity, a simplicity and a real grandeur in his words on this occasion, which contrast favourably with his messianic utterances of earlier days[1]; and he was later to vanquish the very natural bitterness which he felt towards Lesseps:

Il importe peu que le vieux Prosper Enfantin ait subi une déception, il importe peu que ses enfants aient été trompés dans leur espoir; mais il importe que le canal de Suez soit percé, et il le sera; c'est pourquoi je remercie Lesseps et je le bénis[2].

It is altogether a pleasant picture which Maxime du Camp gives us of Enfantin in the latter years of his life; he had gathered round him something in the nature of a family once more; a family which met together on Sundays and listened to Enfantin, who would talk by the hour of the old days, and at last interrupt the eager questioner with a wistful smile: 'Tais-toi, ma vieille folie va me reprendre.' He never quite lost the old conviction of his divine mission, but he had learnt to keep it to himself:

Un soir, chez lui, on causait de différents hommes remarquables et, entre autres, de Sully et de Turgot, qui furent les deux ministres économiques de la France; il prit la parole et dit: 'Il n'y a de grands hommes que ceux qui ont fondé des religions, Zoroastre, Moïse, Jésus, Mahomet, Luther'; il s'arrêta comme si un nom qu'il n'osait prononcer eût flotté sur ses lèvres; personne ne souffla mot; nous avions tous compris et complété sa pensée[3].

[1] Cf. Maxime du Camp, *op. cit.* ii, p. 141.
[2] *Ibid.* ii, p. 142.   [3] *Ibid.* ii, pp. 136–137.

CHAPTER III

SAINT-SIMONISM

(a) DOCTRINE DE SAINT-SIMON. EXPOSITION. PREMIÈRE ANNÉE

On December 12, 1828, began the public exposition of Saint-Simon's doctrine delivered by Bazard which lasted until 1830, and which was published under the title: *Doctrine de Saint-Simon. Première année*. 1828–1829; *Deuxième année*. 1830.

The first *séance* had the challenging title: 'De la nécessité d'une doctrine sociale nouvelle,' and was a review of the state of society. Bazard drew a gloomy picture of the anarchy which had resulted from the liberty promised by the Revolution. Individualism and egoism were everywhere rampant; antagonism ruled the hour; antagonism between man and man, between church and state, between capital and labour. The fine arts were in a state of languor and decay; the elegy and satire flourished alone, for art reflects the feelings of her age. But the destructive period, amidst whose ruins society fought for life, was passed; an age of hope and peace was at hand, and love for the universal family of mankind must hasten the dawn of this new era.

In the following lectures Bazard expounded the doctrine of progress and of the organic and critical epochs. He distinguished two warring principles in the history of the race, the principle of individualism or antagonism and the principle of unity or association. The goal of humanity is universal association, and history has shown an uninterrupted progress in this direction, from individualism in its most uncompromising stage to the founding first of families, then of cities, then of nations and finally of federations or churches. This progress has continued side by side with continual strife; strife between families, cities, nations and creeds; internal strife in the family between age and youth, between man and woman. The larger the association however the less violent the dissension between each group. Nevertheless, although the progress towards association has

been immense, the main characteristic of history in the past
has been universal antagonism:

...l'empire de la force physique et l'exploitation de l'homme par
l'homme sont la cause et l'effet de l'état d'antagonisme. L'antagonisme, ayant pour cause l'emploi de la force physique, et pour
résultat l'exploitation de l'homme par l'homme, voilà le fait le plus
saillant de tout le passé[1]....

The history of the exploiting of man by his brother was then
reviewed from the earliest times. 'Le sauvage égorge son
ennemi, et souvent même en fait sa pâture'; thus Bazard began
with that apparent thoroughness which marked the school and
which made of its systems something so neat, rounded and
plausible, that it seems churlish to regard them with suspicion.
The stage of slavery which superseded cannibalism shows a
great moral and economic progress, although in this constitution
of society the material, intellectual and moral life of man is in
bondage. Serfdom marks another advance; the serf is not the
direct property of the lord; he is attached to the land, and his
moral life is his own. Later he is freed from the glebe and
granted the right of locomotion; and so we come by degrees to
the present state, the subservience of labour:

En résumé, à mesure que le cercle d'association est devenu plus
large, l'exploitation de l'homme par l'homme a diminué, l'antagonisme est devenu moins violent, et toutes les facultés humaines se
sont développées de plus en plus dans la direction pacifique[2].

In spite of the progress that has been made since the days of
slavery, and although the Christian dogma recognises no dis-
abilities of birth, a position which is theoretically sanctioned by
the political constitutions of the day, yet advantages and dis-
advantages are still inherited, and economists have pointed to
hereditary poverty. The workers are still exploited materially,
intellectually and morally, although not so intensely as the
slaves; the law, daughter of the right by conquest, gives the
monopoly of riches to a small class of men, who can thus dispose
as they wish of the instruments of labour, and who are not
themselves compelled to work.

The chief cause of this crying injustice, this continued anta-

[1] *Œuvres de Saint-Simon et d'Enfantin*, XLI, p. 190.
[2] *Ibid.* XLI, p. 201.

gonism, whose effect is the bondage of the workers, is the
constitution of property, the transmission of riches by inheritance. This law of property must therefore be abolished
gradually and peacefully. It is idle to protest that it is a
fundamental basis of society and cannot be altered, since history
has shown successive modifications in the law of inheritance;
at one time property was transmitted arbitrarily, then to the
first-born in the family, and finally divided equally amongst its
members:

Actuellement, avons-nous dit, un nouvel ordre tend à s'établir; il
consiste à transporter à l'État, devenu ASSOCIATION DES TRA-
VAILLEURS, le droit d'héritage, aujourd'hui renfermé dans la
famille domestique. Les privilèges de la *naissance*, qui ont déjà
reçu, sous tant de rapports, de si vives atteintes, doivent complète-
ment disparaître. Le seul droit à la richesse, c'est-à-dire à la dis-
position des instruments de travail, sera la *capacité* de les mettre
en œuvre.[1]

To the question, a question which is an answer in itself, Who
is to undertake this classification by merit? we hear the following
answer with no great reassurance:

...toute la question consiste donc à savoir qui aura l'autorité, qui
classera les hommes suivant leurs capacités, qui appréciera et rétri-
buera leurs œuvres; et nous répondons, quel que soit le cercle d'association que l'on ait en vue: *celui qui aime le plus* la destinée sociale[2].

'Who will that be?' say the bells of Stepney.
'I do not know,' says the great bell of Bow.

We shall meet this mythological personage later when we come
to consider the 'living law'; for the moment we will return with
Bazard to the realm of practical reforms.

This right to the instruments of labour, the capacity to use
them, is the fundamental law of the future of society; and the
germ of the institution which will be invested with the functions
of regulating the choice of enterprises, the destination of the
workers and the distribution of the instruments of labour, is
already to be found, and only needs organisation. Banks exist
already as intermediaries between capital and labour, and
exercise the function of distribution, although very imperfectly.

[1] *Œuvres de Saint-Simon et d'Enfantin*, XLI, p. 243.
[2] *Ibid.* XLI, p. 276, footnote.

The organisation of the industry of banks is the next step on the road of progress, the peaceful revolution of industry and the practical application of the new commandment: 'Toutes les institutions sociales doivent avoir pour but l'amélioration morale, physique et intellectuelle de la classe la plus nombreuse et la plus pauvre.'

The two great means by which the transformation of property may be effected peaceably, education and legislation, were then considered. There will be two kinds of education, moral or general and professional or special. The first has for its object to harmonise the prevailing ideas and sentiments with the goal of society; that is to say, it must make the pupil love and desire what it is his duty to do. Sermons and the confessional have been the means of moral education in the past; they will be modified in the future, but their importance will remain. Society will be composed of the artistic, the learned and the industrial classes; there will therefore be three kinds of professional or special education; one will develop the sympathies, the source of the fine arts; the second will develop the reasoning powers, the instrument of science; and the third will develop material activity and thus fit the pupil for an industrial life. The general education will provide the necessary first education in all these branches, after which specialisation will begin.

Legislation, whose aim is the maintenance of morality and its teaching under a particular form, must henceforward have a positive as well as a negative value. The legislators will distribute praise and remuneration for moral acts as well as blame and punishment for immorality. The jury drawn by lot will disappear; each man will be judged by his own class, artists, scientists or industrialists, but his superiors in this class will be his judges.

These are, very briefly, the chief positions the Saint-Simonian school adopted towards the social questions of the day and the reforms they necessitated. The first part of the *Exposition* is at once a masterly summing up of the doctrine of Saint-Simon, and a brilliant development of the views he expressed. It is original in the sense in which Saint-Simon's spoken and written word was alive. His theories were no dead letter to his disciples but big with consequences which they were clear-sighted enough to perceive. The *Exposition* is no academic commentary on the text, it is faithful only to the spirit of the teaching of Saint-Simon; and since no man may completely understand nor adequately interpret another, it is possible that even here they were rather the children of Saint-Simon than his followers. From confused hints, from brilliant *aperçus*, from chimerical dreams and from prophetic visions they had made an organic whole, which they presented to the world as something within the sphere of practical politics, and which it only needed good-will to establish. Nor were they without a theory as to how that good-will was to be created.

'Souvenez-vous que pour faire quelque chose de grand, il faut être passionné,' Saint-Simon had said to Rodrigues on his death-bed, and in the *Nouveau Christianisme* he had pointed to the only means by which humanity can be made to desire passionately the welfare of mankind. That means is religion, and, when the name of the religion is love, it would seem that there are no mountains which it cannot remove. So they made a new religion called love that it should remove their mountains. Here lies their strength, but here also lies their weakness. From history they had deduced the imminent appearance of a new religion, since the last critical epoch was already in its second stage; from history too they had deduced the inevitable form which this religion would take; nothing remained but to act on the *Nouveau Christianisme* and proclaim it. Theoretically they were in the right, but they overlooked the fact that they were making a servant of that which owns no master and of the unseizable an exact science. They mistook deduction for revelation and intellectual conviction for inspiration. Those who so mistook were 'passionnés' enough to accomplish great things, but the new religion never convinced humanity as a whole; and its most convinced adherents came to regard it later in its true light: an interesting philosophy of life, and a suggestive criticism of Christianity.

(b) DOCTRINE DE SAINT-SIMON. EXPOSITION.
DEUXIÈME ANNÉE

L'HUMANITÉ A UN AVENIR RELIGIEUX;—*la religion de l'avenir sera plus grande, plus puissante qu'aucune des religions du passé; son dogme sera la synthèse de toutes les conceptions, de toutes les manières d'être de l'homme;*—L'INSTITUTION SOCIALE, POLITIQUE, CONSIDÉRÉE DANS SON ENSEMBLE, SERA UNE INSTITUTION RELIGIEUSE[1].

With these brave words Bazard opened the second year of the *Exposition*. In order to prepare the ground for the new religion he then proceeded to an historical survey of Christianity and the development of religious ideas in general. He set himself to prove that fetichism, polytheism and Judaism, in spite of the great distance which separates them, and however important the progress which humanity made in passing from one to the other, have one characteristic in common; they all viewed the existence of man principally from its material side. Their gods manifested themselves physically, they received material sacrifices and tributes, and the religious law was little more than the regulation of physical activities. The material aspect of life inspired their religious conceptions and their social institutions.

With the coming of Christianity all this was changed. The beauty of the spiritual world was revealed to man, and became the dominant object of his love, his meditations and his activity. Material existence was not merely ignored and subordinated in fact, as had been the case with spiritual life in pre-Christian times; the Christian knows this part of his nature and repudiates it consciously. Accepting from earlier religions the conception of the two opposing principles of good and evil, Christianity came to see the principle of evil personified in the flesh, and the principle of good personified in the spirit; it excluded from its sanctification one of the manifestations of human existence, and thundered out through all its teachings an anathema against the flesh. This marks a great progress in the history of mankind, since the things of the spirit had been unduly subordinated; excessive materialism had been the result, the empire of force upheld by wars, the most violent expression

[1] *Œuvres de Saint-Simon et d'Enfantin*, XLII, pp. 172–173.

of antagonism. Christianity, that is to say Catholicism, thus played an essential part in the progress of humanity[1]; but there remains an important progress to be made. The Christian dogma of the fall of man, of original sin, of election and damnation, of heaven and hell, was but a further development of the primitive dualism, good and evil. Here certainly Christianity shows an advance on all preceding theologies, since it no longer regards evil as co-eternal with good. God alone, the principle of good, said the fathers of the church, had existed from all eternity, and Satan was a fallen angel. Yet they saw evil co-existing with good in the world, and a last dread division on the Day of Judgment. Christianity is then profoundly marked by this ancient dualism, that is to say with the principle of antagonism; and the characterisation of evil is the result of this error:

LA CHAIR, C'EST LE PÉCHÉ, a dit Saint-Paul; toute la doctrine de l'Église, sur le mal et sa source, se trouve en quelque sorte renfermée dans ce peu de mots[2].

The religious history of mankind as expounded by Bazard is altogether too simple. The contrast between pagan sensualism and Christian spiritualism is like an etching in black and white of a herbaceous border riotous with colour; the shapes are correct but the essential quality has vanished. The mysterious instincts, the elemental beliefs, which go to form the incalculable force called religion have no place in his system, and the merging and melting of faiths are distorted by these clear-cut outlines. To rob the pagan religions of the spiritual element which gave them birth is an even more fundamental error than to interpret the Christian dogma as a purely spiritual code. But the Saint-Simonians saw history in the grand manner of sweeping generalisations which has now fallen into disrepute. Flesh triumphant under paganism, spirit dominant under Christianity; it is not so much that they were wrong, as that they made it all too simple, too logical, and too obvious. And when Bazard goes on to declaim that the antithesis will be harmonised, the dissonance resolved in the Saint-Simonian age, it is almost like listening to an election cry:

[1] Cf. Œuvres de Saint-Simon et d'Enfantin, XLII, pp. 267–268.
[2] Ibid. XLII, p. 273.

L'aspect le PLUS FRAPPANT, le PLUS NEUF, sinon le plus important, du progrès *général* que l'humanité est AUJOURD'HUI appelée à faire, consiste, messieurs, dans la RÉHABILITATION DE LA MATIÈRE, réhabilitation qui ne pourra avoir lieu qu'autant qu'une conception religieuse nouvelle aura fait rentrer *dans l'ordre providentiel et en* DIEU *même cet élément, ou plutôt cet aspect de l'existence universelle que le christianisme a frappé de sa* RÉPROBATION[1].

It remains now to translate this dogma of a universal God into terms of social order. The new society will be a hierarchy founded on love[2]; and the chiefs of the new society are therefore to be the priests, that is to say those men in whom love is dominant, a love which embraces both the finite and the infinite. These priests will teach mankind the religion of the future, the religion of love. The scientists will be the theologians, for science is the knowledge of the universe, and the universe is God. The aim of industry is the exploiting of the globe; man in altering the globe, in changing gradually the conditions of his existence, participates in the successive manifestations of God, and continues the work of creation; industry therefore is the worship of God:

La RELIGION ou la MORALE, la THÉOLOGIE ou la *science*, le CULTE ou l'*industrie*, tels sont les trois grands aspects de l'activité sociale de l'avenir. Les PRÊTRES, les *savants*, les *industriels*, voilà la SOCIÉTÉ[3].

Science and industry are equal in the eyes of the priest. Each will have a hierarchy of its own, with a priest of science or a priest of industry respectively at its head; but these hierarchies will depend on the high priest; he constitutes and sanctions them, he unites man to man and also man to God, harmonising the social order with the universal order, the human hierarchy with the divine.

The rehabilitation of industry followed logically on the 'rehabilitation of the flesh.' The Saint-Simonians had already proposed to enfranchise industry by the abolition of the laws of inheritance, substituting for these the law of capacity. They now proceeded to establish industry in the proud position to

---

[1] *Œuvres de Saint-Simon et d'Enfantin*, XLII, p. 282.
[2] Cf. *ibid.* XLII, p. 329.   [3] *Ibid.* XLII, p. 337.

which it is entitled. They saw that the very essence of industry is service, and that therefore, looked at from the widest point of view, it is an act of worship. They were right in claiming that this position was entirely new, nor was there anything chimerical in their various industrial schemes.

Yet that there was a chimerical side to their doctrine it is impossible to deny; it becomes apparent when we consider the functions of the high priest in the hierarchy. Since there is to be a hierarchy with a high priest at its head; since he is to be invested with complete moral and political power; since everything in the last resort depends on him, and liberty, as we understand it, is to be non-existent, it is of some importance to know who he is to be and how he is to be chosen. He is to be chosen (by what machinery is not made clear, probably by revelation) in virtue of his capacity to love man and God. This is reasonable enough, since his stupendous task consists in harmonising science and industry, spirit and flesh, every conceivable irreconcilable; since, what is more, he must unite the finite to the infinite, man to God, it is not too much to ask that he shall be all-loving. But where is he to be found? We turn the last pages of the *Exposition* in some impatience, but the answer does not occur. We are told that, when the hierarchical order is established, it will be maintained by education and legislation. We are told that, as in all previous organic epochs, there will be a 'living law,' and that this law will bear the name of the man who proclaims it and who will personify it; and lest we fear that justice has gone to join liberty in the attic where back-numbers are kept, we are told in soothing tones:

Le jugement est toujours équitable, car le juge est à la fois celui qui AIME et qui *connaît* le mieux l'ordre qu'il a pour but de maintenir, et l'individu qu'il juge[1].

Finally we are silenced with the following declaration:

L'AMOUR, sous son double aspect, *concentrique* et *excentrique*, l'amour de *soi* et l'amour des *autres*, voilà, messieurs, la base de la hiérarchie, la raison de l'AUTORITÉ et de l'OBÉISSANCE que nous désirons et que nous ANNONÇONS[2].

[1] *Œuvres de Saint-Simon et d'Enfantin*, XLII, p. 429.
[2] *Ibid.* XLII, p. 431.

It is not in taking love as the basis of their religion that the Saint-Simonians can fairly be taxed with being chimerical; nor is it more than idealistic to assert that love will prove in the future a greater motive power than it has been in the past. Human nature can be changed, although infinitely slowly; and to educate man towards a greater love for his fellows is perhaps the noblest aim which a reformer can propose. But to found a hierarchy whose chief will be invested with powers as despotic as ever Tsar or Sultan knew, and to endow him off-hand with love so infinite as to pre-suppose him superhuman, this is chimerical indeed. Yet while Bazard spoke and Barrault preached, while Michel wrote and Enfantin mused, this mythical being had already been found. For was there not one amongst them whose great power of loving was already rewarded by the love of his disciples; and who by means of this power had established on a small scale a religious hierarchy which would serve as a model for the universal hierarchy of the future? Enfantin in fact seemed so exactly fitted to create the part of 'prêtre suprême' that the unworthy thought obtrudes itself: was not the part of 'prêtre suprême' created to fit Enfantin? And with this question on our lips we turn from the *Exposition de la doctrine de Saint-Simon* to the *Enseignements d'Enfantin*.

(c) *ENSEIGNEMENTS D'ENFANTIN*

In these lectures Enfantin developed that part of the doctrine which was peculiarly his own, showing step by step as he did so, that it was the logical outcome of the positions sanctioned by Bazard in the *Exposition*. His views are in sober truth the logical outcome of the doctrine of the 'rehabilitation of the flesh,' and he was therefore justified in calling Bazard a heretic. They are so pitilessly logical because he had no moral taste, but it is only fair to him to remember that the theories he advocated so boldly, and for which he was prepared to suffer, and did suffer imprisonment, were not invented to legitimise a disreputable practice. Considering what he wished to make his disciples accept, it is not surprising that he felt it necessary to speak with authority, and that, throwing aside false modesty, he should appear before them as the 'living law.'[1] He then proceeded to prepare for the new and active phase which lay before them: the organisation of industry, the appeal to women and the constitution of the rites of worship. He called upon the artists to aid him here, for the new church was also to be a new theatre: 'C'est par l'*acteur* régénéré que le chrétien sera sauvé.'[2] This applies to all artists, and to speak of artists is nearly the same thing as to speak of the priest; as Bazard in his lectures had proclaimed: 'C'est par l'artiste que le prêtre se manifeste; l'*artiste*, en un mot, est le *verbe* du PRÊTRE.'[3]

And if, in the body politic, industry must be enfranchised and reinstated, a great moral and social reform remains to be accomplished by the emancipation of women. Woman is no longer a slave, but she is treated as a minor; she is still exploited by man as labour is exploited by capital, for she is regarded as his inferior in the institution of marriage. This institution must be altered, and the complete equality of man and woman must be proclaimed; it was time to consider the question of divorce.

Enfantin distinguished two kinds of nature in men and women, the 'mobile' and the 'immobile.' The 'immobile' are steadfast, unchanging, constant, the Othellos, as he liked to call them. The 'mobile,' the Don Juans, are lighter, ardent, exalted, inconstant, in need of continual change in their personal relations. Since all our instincts, whether spiritual or sensual, are equally divine, the Othellos and Don Juans are equally respectable members of society, and the institution of marriage must recognise both. The constant will contract lasting unions, since this is their nature; the inconstant on the other hand must be granted facilities for divorce, that they may satisfy their desire for change. Both kinds of marriage will be holy in the eyes of the priests, the lasting and the successive; what is to happen when the constant marry the inconstant we are left to guess; but all such questions will be decided by the priestly couple, man and woman:

Le couple sacerdotal lie ou délie l'homme et la femme, c'est lui qui consacre leur UNION ou leur DIVORCE; car l'amour de chacun

---

[1] *Œuvres de Saint-Simon et d'Enfantin*, xɪv, pp. 103–104.
[2] *Ibid.* xɪv, p. 123.   [3] *Ibid.* xLɪɪ, p. 355.

lui est révélé, puisqu'il doit rétribuer chacun selon son amour. Tous
lui ont *confié, avoué, confessé* leur âme; tous viennent déposer en lui
le mystère de leurs pensées et de leurs actes, les douleurs ou les joies
de leur esprit et de leur chair, car le sacerdoce est HOMME ET
FEMME[1].

The supreme couple will certainly have their hands full, but they
have other duties as well. They must seek to develop the
physical and the intellectual side of each individual entrusted
to their care, not by captation, nor by seduction, but by affection and attraction[2]; Enfantin came near to poetry at times in
his efforts to show the love of beauty which lies at the root of
this conception[3]; criticism is disarmed for a moment, and if the
practical mind begins to wonder what limits are to be placed
to the influence of the priest and the priestess on the faithful,
reassurance is at hand:

> Moi HOMME, moi, SEUL, je n'en pose aucune; la femme parlera.
> La *liberté* pleine et entière que je lui offre avec toute la franchise de
> mon cœur d'homme, je veux qu'elle soit *libre* encore de me la refuser
> ou de ne l'accepter qu'en partie[4].

Enfantin sought refuge in this pronouncement again and
again. The priestly couple were to educate the faithful both
physically and spiritually; to do this satisfactorily, they must
use sensual as well as spiritual means; the question of the limits
to be placed on the use of such means flashes through the mind:
'La femme parlera.' The priest unites and harmonises in himself
the two natures, constant and inconstant, he is 'calm.' This
gave rise during the *Huitième Enseignement* to a strong protest
from Guéroult:

> ...s'il y a dans le monde ces *deux natures, constant* et *inconstant*, et
> que le PRÊTRE les unisse en lui, il devra être *constant* avec les uns
> et *inconstant* avec les autres, afin de les RELIER entre eux. Alors je
> dis que le PRÊTRE devra avoir simultanément une affection *profonde*
> et des affections *successives*, par conséquent des FAMILLES *succes-*
> *sives*....Mais il a deux FAMILLES, deux FAMILLES du sang, la
> FAMILLE de la *constance* et les FAMILLES de l'*inconstance*; il a aussi
> celle de la *fonction*, il a donc trois espèces de familles[5].

---

[1] *Œuvres de Saint-Simon et d'Enfantin*, XIV, p. 157.
[2] *Ibid.* XIV, pp. 162–163.   [3] *Ibid.* XIV, p. 163.
[4] *Ibid.* XIV, p. 164.   [5] *Ibid.* XVI, p. 24.

Either the murder is out at last, or Guéroult is cruelly maligning Enfantin, and we look for a hot denial. It does not come:

Dire quelle sera la conduite du COUPLE-PRÊTRE avec les *fidèles*, je te le repète encore une fois, cela m'est impossible, je ne le sais pas[1].

'La femme parlera.' It is perhaps not surprising, in view of the questions which she would have to decide, that no woman came forward to decide them. The part which she was to play does not bear steady contemplation. Nor is the society of the future, as Enfantin dreamed of it now, a much more pleasant object for meditation: it is impossible to characterise adequately this promiscuity under the mystical sanction of a religion at once sensual and spiritual, and offering special facilities to the supreme couple. It is with a sense of relief that we turn back to Olinde Rodrigues' *Note sur le divorce*:

A l'époux et à l'épouse appartient exclusivement ce saint état, l'*intimité* du cœur, de l'esprit et des sens, sphère mystérieuse, impénétrable, où deux *spontanéités*, se confondent, où la *vie* peut produire la *vie*[2].

And back a little further to the letter to the President of the Chamber of Deputies signed by Bazard and Enfantin:

Ils [the Saint-Simonians] demandent, comme les chrétiens, qu'un seul homme soit uni à une seule femme, mais ils enseignent que l'épouse doit devenir l'égale de l'époux; et que, selon la grâce particulière que Dieu a dévolue à son sexe, elle doit lui être associée dans l'exercice de la triple fonction du temple, de l'état et de la famille: de manière à ce que l'*individu social* qui, jusqu'à ce jour, a été l'*homme* seulement, soit désormais l'*homme* et la *femme*[3].

And back at last to the early days of the school when Enfantin declared marriage to be the basis of society, and that the priest and priestess would sanctify it, although remaining celibate themselves, eternally separated by a cloud of incense[4]. Even this absurd picture seems beautiful after studying the functions and attributes of the supreme couple in the *Enseignements d'Enfantin*.

[1] *Œuvres de Saint-Simon et d'Enfantin*, XVI, p. 25.
[2] *Ibid.* IV, p. 133.   [3] *Ibid.* IV, p. 123.
[4] *Ibid.* XXVI, pp. 6–18, letter from Enfantin to Duveyrier, August 1829.

Enfantin styled himself Saint-Simon the second; but the
school owed an almost equal debt to Fourier[1]. Nevertheless
Saint-Simon was their source of inspiration. 'À lui le souffle
initiateur, la grande direction.'[2] And in so far as Saint-Simonism
has prevailed, it has done so, if we except the growth of feminism,
along the lines laid down by Saint-Simon and not in the direction
given to it by Fourier. For looking back at the school from the
twentieth century, it becomes clear that many of the dreams of
the Saint-Simonians are now a reality, or at least a force to be
reckoned with. By their attacks on property and capital they
laid the foundation of the French socialist school, and their
significance in economic progress can hardly be exaggerated.
They advocated the establishment of the great houses of credit;
they were largely instrumental in the construction of the first
railways in France; they were the direct instigators of the
piercing of the Suez Canal. All these works live to-day and
have helped to modify the civilisation of the twentieth century.
But it is not this aspect of the Saint-Simonian doctrine which
forms the subject of the present investigation. The influence of
Saint-Simonism on the Young German movement was almost
entirely confined to the theory of the 'rehabilitation of the flesh'
with its corollary the relation between men and women. It remains to be seen how they interpreted these views, and the
literary expression they gave to them.

[1] Notably, their feminism, and also the germs of the doctrine of the
'emancipation of the flesh.'

[2] P. Janet, *Saint-Simon et le Saint-Simonisme*, Paris, 1878, p. 71.

PART II
SAINT-SIMONISM IN GERMANY

SAINT-SIMONISM IN THE GERMAN PRESS

German Papers and Journals printing articles and notices on Saint-Simonism, 1830–1835	Date of first article or notice	Remarks
Abendzeitung, Dresden, ed. Theodor Hell	March 19, 1832	Only this article
Allgemeine Zeitung, Augsburg	October 7, 1830	Frequent notices and articles from Paris correspondents (about 70)
Allgemeine Kirchenzeitung, Darmstadt, ed. Zimmermann; 1833, Bretschneider	October 23, 1830	Very frequent notices and articles; often reprints (about 116)
Allgemeine Literaturzeitung, Jena, Halle, Leipzig	March 21, 1831 (Léo)	Reviews of Carové, Bretschneider, Matter, Hahn; bibliography in 1836
Allgemeines Repertorium für die theologische und kirchliche Statistik, Berlin, ed. Rheinwald	August 16, 1833	Three articles
Annalen der gesammten theologischen Literatur und der christlichen Kirche überhaupt, Coburg and Leipzig	1831	Two articles, one by Prätorius
Ausland, Stuttgart, Tübingen, Augsburg	October 20, 1830	Frequent articles and translations, Paris correspondent (about 40)
Berlinische Nachrichten von Staats- und gelehrten Sachen (Spenersche Zeitung)		A good many references
Bibliothek der neuesten Weltkunde, Aarau, ed. Malter	1831	Two articles
Blätter für literarische Unterhaltung, Leipzig, ed. Brockhaus	November 15, 1830	Many articles (Raumer). Reviews of Bretschneider, Carové, Schiebler, Veit
Breslauer Zeitung, ed. Karl Schall		Gives some space to Saint-Simonism
Canonischer Wächter, Halle, ed. Müller	March 22, 1831 (Not procurable)	A good many notices
Eremit, Altenburg, ed. Gleich	March 23, 1831	A.K.Z. gives 3 references in 1831
Evangelische Kirchenzeitung, Berlin, ed. Hengstenberg		Several other notices

Journal	Date	Notes
Freie Kirche, Zwickau		
Freimüthiger, Berlin		
Gesellschafter, Berlin, ed. Gubitz	(Not procurable)	A.K.Z. gives 1 reference in 1831
Jahrbücher für wissenschaftliche Kritik, Berlin		A good many notices
		Several articles
Jenaische Allgemeine Literaturzeitung, Jena and Leipzig	December 1830 (Carové)	Weisse on Veit, 1834
Leipziger Tageblatt	August 1832	
Literarische und kritische Blätter der Börsenhalle, Hamburg ed. Wurm	February 19, 1832	Reviews on Bretschneider, Carové, Hahn, Veit
Literaturblatt zum Morgenblatt, Stuttgart and Tübingen, ed. Menzel	August 1, 1832	Gives some space to Saint-Simonism
Magazin für die Literatur des Auslands, Berlin, ed. Lehmann	February 29, 1832	A good many notices; reviews of Carové, Veit
Mitternachtzeitung, Brunswick, ed. Köchy		Only this article
Morgenblatt für gebildete Stände, Stuttgart and Tübingen	October 20, 1830	Veit and other articles
Neue Monatsschrift für Deutschland, historisch-politischen Inhalts, Berlin, ed. Buchholtz	1826 on Saint-Simon 1831 on Saint-Simonism	Some notices Frequent articles from Paris correspondent (about 25) Long articles and translations
Prometheus, Für Licht und Recht, Aarau, ed. Zschokke	1832	One article only
Sachsenzeitung	(Not procurable)	
Stuttgarter Zeitung		A.K.Z. gives 2 references in 1831
Theologisches Literaturblatt, zur Allgemeinen Kirchenzeitung, Darmstadt	October 19, 1831	Gives some space to Saint-Simonism Reviews of Carové, Bretschneider, Schiebler, Anon.
Zeitung für die elegante Welt, Leipzig, ed. Müller; 1833, ed. Laube	January 12, 1832	Gives very little space to the movement

SAINT-SIMONISM IN THE GERMAN PRESS (Contd.)

Date	Books, pamphlets and signed articles on Saint-Simonism, 1830–1835	Journals in which the articles appeared	French sources	German sources
1830	F. W. Carové, Criticism of Doctrine de Saint-Simon. Exposition. Première Année	Jahrbücher für wissenschaftliche Kritik, Berlin, December 1830. Nos. 115 and 116	Doctrine de Saint-Simon. Exposition. Première Année, Paris, 1830	Gives none
1831	F. W. Carové, Der Saint-Simonismus und die neuere französische Philosophie, Leipzig, 1831		Nouveau Christianisme, Paris, 1825 Doctrine de Saint-Simon. Exposition. Première Année Globe: quotes largely Mentions: Producteur } Probably Organisateur } not seen	Gives none
	Hengstenberg, Ueber die Secte der St. Simonianer in Frankreich	Evangelische Kirchenzeitung, Berlin, March 23, 1831	Nouveau Christianisme Doctrine de Saint-Simon. Exposition. Deuxième Année Appel aux Artistes Organisateur } 'Eine lange Reihe von Globe } Nummern'	Carové in Jahrbücher für wissenschaftliche Kritik
	H. Léo, Criticism of Nouveau Christianisme	Allgemeine Literaturzeitung, Halle, Jena, Leipzig, Ergänzungsblätter, March 21, 1831	Nouveau Christianisme Doctrine de Saint-Simon. Exposition. Première Année Organisateur: 'Mehrere Blätter' All sent by a Saint-Simonian friend, whose name he does not give	Blätter für literarische Unterhaltung, Leipzig, 1830, No. 319 = November 15. 'Mehrfache anderweitige ...gekommene Notizen'

Dr Matter, *Ueber die Saint-Simonisten*	*Theologische Studien und Kritiken*, Hamburg, 1822, vol. I. Dated August 1831	*Nouveau Christianisme, Doctrine de Saint-Simon. Exposition. Première Année. Deuxième Année*, Paris, 1830 *Tableau synoptique*, Paris, 1830 *Lettres sur la Religion et la Politique*, Paris, 1831 *Appel aux Artistes*, Paris, 1830 *Enseignement Central*, Paris, 1831 *Communion de la famille Saint-Simonienne*, Paris, 1831 *Prédications et conférences*: 'mündlich.' He had been to Paris	Gives none
F. A. Nelker, *St Simon's neue Glaubenslehre, oder der St Simonismus und die Philosophie des 19ten Jahrhunderts in Frankreich. Aus dem Französischen*, Augsburg, 1831 K. W. Schieber, *Der Saint-Simonismus, oder die Lehre Saint-Simon's und seiner Anhänger*, Leipzig, 1831	[Cannot trace. Reference in *Allgemeine Literatur-Zeitung, Ergänzungsblätter*, October 1836, No. 99]	*Doctrine de Saint-Simon. Exposition.* Probably *Première Année* only *Lettres sur la Religion et la Politique De la Religion Saint-Simonienne*, Paris, 1831[1] *Organisateur Globe*	Gives none

SAINT-SIMONISM IN THE GERMAN PRESS (Contd.)

Date	Books, pamphlets and signed articles on Saint-Simonism, 1830–1835	Journals in which the articles appeared	French sources	German sources
1831	Dr Warnkönig, *Die Lehre der Anhänger von Saint-Simon*	*Kritische Zeitschrift für Rechtswissenschaft und Gesetzgebung des Auslands,* Heidelberg, 1832, vol. IV, dated March 1831	*Doctrine de Saint-Simon. Exposition. Première Année* *Aux Elèves de l'Ecole Polytechnique,* Paris, 1830 *Extrait de l'Organisateur du 19 Mai,* Paris, 1831 *Globe,* October 26, 1830 *Revue Encyclopédique,* November 1830	Gives none
1832	Anonymous, *Was ist der St Simonismus? ... Nach den neuesten Quellen bearbeitet,* Quedlinburg and Leipzig, 1832		Gives none Mentions: *Producteur, Organisateur, Globe* Quotes from: *Nouveau Christianisme*	*Wendt (Enseignement Central)* Uses without acknowledgment: Hahn, and Veit in the *Magazin für die Literatur des Auslands,* Berlin, 1832
	Anonymous, *Die Saint-Simonistische Religion. Fünf Reden an die Zöglinge der polytechnischen Schule, nebst einem Vorbericht über das Leben und Charakter St Simon's. Aus dem Französischen,* Göttingen, 1832	[Cannot trace. Reference in *Allgemeine Literaturzeitung, Ergänzungsblätter,* October 1836, No. 99]	*Aux Elèves de l'Ecole Polytechnique*	
	K. G. Bretschneider, *Der Simonismus und das Christenthum,* Leipzig, 1832		*Tableau synoptique* *Lettres sur la Religion et la Politique* Extracts from *Globe* communicated to him by Wangenheim	Carové Léo *Allgemeine Kirchenzeitung,* Darmstadt, December 5, 1830, and Nos. 24 and 25, 1831 = February 8 and 10

Work	Periodical	Works referred to	Reviews, etc. cited
			Ausland, No. 4, 1831 = January 4 *Blätter für literarische Unterhaltung*, Feb. 16, 1831 (probably a mistake for Feb. 18) *Neue Monatsschrift für Deutschland*, Berlin, vols. XXI, XXII, XXXIV (1826, 1827, 1831)
A. Hahn, *Ueber die Lage des Christenthums in unserer Zeit...nebst einer Beilage: Der St Simonismus als religiös-politisches System...*, Leipzig, 1832		*Tableau synoptique* *Enseignement Central* (Wendt's translation). 'Die, welche Schiebler und Carové in ihren erschienenen bekannten Schriften benutzt haben'	Bretschneider Carové Matter Raumer Schiebler Wendt *Allgemeine Kirchenzeitung* *Evangelische Kirchenzeitung*, 'und andere Zeitschriften'
M. C. Kapff, *Der Saint-Simonismus in Frankreich*	*Tübinger Zeitschrift für Theologie*, 1832	*Nouveau Christianisme* *Doctrine de Saint-Simon. Exposition. Première Année* *Tableau synoptique* *Lettres sur la Religion et la Politique* *Producteur* *Organisateur* *Globe*	Bretschneider Carové Matter Raumer in *Blätter für literarische Unterhaltung*, January 1, 1832 *Allgemeine Zeitung*, Augsburg, No. 87, 1832 = March 6
E. Prätorius, *Ueber die Doctrine de Saint-Simon*	*Annalen der gesammten theologischen Literatur und der christlichen Kirche überhaupt*, Coburg and Leipzig, 1832	*Doctrine de Saint-Simon. Exposition. Première Année*, 2nd ed. Paris, 1830 *Globe*, June 10, 1831	Gives none

SAINT-SIMONISM IN THE GERMAN PRESS (Contd.)

Date	Books, pamphlets and signed articles on Saint-Simonism, 1830–1835	Journals in which the articles appeared	French sources	German sources
1832	F. V. Raumer, Geschichtliche Entwickelung der Begriffe von Recht, Staat und Politik, 1832, 2nd ed.	Chapter on Saint-Simonism appeared also in the Blätter für literarische Unterhaltung, January 1–3, 1832	Doctrine de Saint-Simon. Exposition. Première Année. (Does not mention as a source, but laments absence of Deuxième Année.) Enseignement Central Globe	Gives none
	A. Schlör, Der Saint-Simonismus	Neue theologische Zeitschrift, ed. Petz, 1832	[Cannot trace. Reference in Jenaische Allgemeine Literaturzeitung, Ergänzungsblätter, 1834, No. 65]	
	K. E. Schmid, Graf Heinrich von Saint-Simon und seine Jünger	Minerva, Jena, March 1832	Gives none	Bretschneider Carové
	C. Schiller, St Simonismus und Christianismus	Allgemeine Kirchenzeitung, Darmstadt, April 26, 1832	Gives none	Gives none
	M. Veit, Der Saint-Simonismus	Magazin für die Literatur des Auslands, February 29, March 2, April 2, 4, 6, July 11, 13, 1832	Doctrine de Saint-Simon. Exposition. Première Année Producteur Organisateur	Gives none
	A. Wendt, Die Saint-Simonische Religion, dargestellt von Jules Lechevalier. Aus dem Französischen	Zeitschrift für die historische Theologie, Leipzig, 1832	Enseignement Central Globe	Illgen, editor, mentions Bretschneider, Carové, Matter, Schiebler
	K. W. Wiedenfeld, Kritik des Saint-Simonismus, ein Beitrag zur richtigen Würdigung dieser Sekte in		Gives none	Gives none

1833	*ihren gefährlichen Folgen für Kirche und Staat*, Barmen and Schwelm, 1832 Sebastus, *Ueber den St Simonismus und sein Verhältniss zur katholischen Kirche*	*Der Katholik*, Mayence, 1833	*Doctrine de Saint-Simon. Exposition. Première Année* only? *Enseignement Central* (Wendt's translation) Knew some disciples, but does not say which	Bretschneider Carové Hahn Matter Schiebler
1834	M. Veit, *Saint Simon und der Saintsimonismus*, Leipzig, 1834. Appeared at the end of 1833		*Vie de Saint-Simon écrite par lui-même*, Paris, 1832 *Doctrine de Saint-Simon. Exposition. Première Année*, 3rd ed. 1831 *Œuvres de Saint-Simon*, Paris, 1832 Saint-Simon, *Système Industriel*, Paris, 1821 *Religion Saint-Simonienne*[1] *Revue Encyclopédique*, January 1832 *Globe*	Anonymous Bretschneider Carové Léo Raumer Schiebler *Ausland*, 1832 *Jenaische Allgemeine Literaturzeitung*, 1832, August, Nos. 145 and 146 *Neue Monatsschrift für Deutschland*
	C. H. Weisse, Review of Veit's book	*Jahrbücher für wissenschaftliche Kritik*, June 1834	*Livre des Actes*, etc. Gives none	Veit

[1] *Religion Saint-Simonienne. A collection of four volumes, including Nouveau Christianisme, Doctrine de Saint-Simon. Exposition. Première Année*, 2nd ed. Paris, 1830, *Lettres sur la Religion et la Politique*, numerous articles, pamphlets, 'Appels,' 'notices', and the like. On their first publication all these various essays were headed *Religion Saint-Simonienne*. Wherever possible, I have given only the real title of whatever publication is involved. Schiebler gives no guide to what he had read, but Veit had read all the various productions.

I refer to these various books, pamphlets and articles by the author's name in the following chapter; and have used the following abbreviations:—*A.Z.* = *Allgemeine Zeitung*. *A.B.* = *Ausserordentliche Beilage zur Allgemeinen Zeitung*. *A.K.Z.* = *Allgemeine Kirchenzeitung*.

CHAPTER IV

THE ATTITUDE OF GERMANY

(a) THE PRESS AND THE SAINT-SIMONIANS

The general impression that remains from a study of the contemporary newspapers is that Germany was remarkably well informed on the subject of the Saint-Simonians; some of her informants knew them personally, whilst many others attended their meetings, read their papers, kept an interested eye on their adventures, and generally possessed first-hand information, which was eagerly accepted and punctually published in the various daily organs. The newspaper-reading German public could no more be in ignorance of Saint-Simonism than of the cholera; it was perpetually being reminded of both epidemics; so that if demand creates supply in journalism, there can be no doubt that there was much demand for such news.

The attitude of the *Allgemeine Zeitung* towards the Saint-Simonians is of peculiar importance, since it was already in those days a paper of world-wide renown with many distinguished contributors; and the anonymous author of an article entitled 'Ueber den Saint-Simonismus. Aus dem Briefe eines Deutschen vom Rhein, Februar 1832'[1] arouses a lively curiosity, for the Saint-Simonians mention it as having been attributed to Heine[2]. The author, who subsequently published three more articles on the same subject[3], and was fiercely attacked in this paper[4], treated the Saint-Simonians seriously and sympathetically, and his personal relations with the members of this sect seem to have been friendly ones; nevertheless these articles are certainly not by Heine, for the style lacks his characteristic qualities completely. Moreover, the author wrote them on his return from a visit to Paris, during which he attended no Saint-Simonian

[1] *A.Z. A.B.* March 6, 1832.
[2] *Œuvres de Saint-Simon et d'Enfantin*, VI, p. 108, footnote.
[3] *A.Z. A.B.* April 17 and 18, May 21, 1832.
[4] *A.Z. A.B.* April 26, 27 and 28, 1832.

meetings; 'doch waren während meines Aufenthalts in Paris ihre Säle geschlossen.' Proelss asserts that Varnhagen von Ense wrote an anonymous article in defence of the Saint-Simonians and that it was published in the *Allgemeine Zeitung*[1]. I have been able to trace no further articles of this kind; they may therefore have been the property of Varnhagen; but the fact that they are dated from the Rhine makes such an assumption rather doubtful, as he was then living in Berlin.

The three correspondents to the *Allgemeine Zeitung* who were chiefly responsible for Saint-Simonian news signed their articles *, *†, and *** respectively. The first of these three contributors confined himself to reporting various rumours and well-known facts, judging the Saint-Simonians harshly, and giving no account of meetings and the like. I am so far without a clue to his identity. The second, *†, in view of the mistakes he sometimes made[2] and the absence of any sign of inside knowledge, may be assumed to have had no personal acquaintance among the Saint-Simonians, although he attended their meetings and was present on the second day of the trial. He allowed that their economic doctrines were important and interesting[3], but he regarded them on the whole with bitterness and dislike. This correspondent was undoubtedly J. H. Schnitzler, who later published his articles to the *Allgemeine Zeitung* in book-form[4].

The third, ***, I believe to be Donndorf, a fairly intimate friend of Heine's:

Es geht übrigens nichts bedeutendes vor, und die kleinen Lumpereyen weiss Donndorff doch immer eine Stunde früher als ich, da er sie mir erst bey Tisch erzählt[5].

This correspondent paid no attention to the Saint-Simonians until after the arrival of Heine in Paris, but from then onwards his notices and articles show traces of inside information, and

[1] J. Proelss, *Das junge Deutschland*, Stuttgart, 1892, p. 177.

[2] He speaks of 'Bezar-Lenfantin' (May 17, 1831) and is quite at sea about the schism between Bazard and Enfantin (December 8, 1831).

[3] *A.Z.* December 8, 1831.

[4] J. H. Schnitzler, *Briefe aus Paris über Frankreich im ersten Jahre seiner Juliusrevolution*, Stuttgart and Tübingen, 1832; cf. Chapter XXVI, 'Die Saint-Simonisten,' and *A.Z.* A.B. November 17, 1830; signed *†.

[5] F. Hirth, *Heinrich Heines Briefwechsel*, Munich and Berlin, 1914–1920, II, p. 12, dated January 20, 1832.

are written in general with a benevolent neutrality, which sometimes overbalances into sympathy, sometimes into mockery. In
all this I am inclined to see Heine's influence. He certainly
inspired the sympathetic article signed *** and dated January 23,
1832, on the intervention of the government[1]; for Heine wrote
to Cotta that he had been present on this occasion and had made
all haste to Donndorf, who was writing an account for the
Allgemeine Zeitung[2].

Donndorf, either directly or through the good offices of Heine,
was in a position to approach the Saint-Simonians personally.
He attended their *soirées*, was present at Mme Enfantin's funeral
and came to the trial; he watched them at the opera; he had
some speech with Chevalier during the latter's imprisonment,
and was able to report that he had abandoned the costume[3].
Most significant of all, he wrote those articles, in which the inner
scandals of the sect were revealed for the public benefit. Something in the lighter touch and the more enlightened interest;
something in the more sympathetic amusement, in the very
perversity which made him give away secrets too good to be
kept to himself, suggests the presence of a more vital personality
beside Donndorf's. If Heine were gagged by a subtle sense of
decency on the subject of the Saint-Simonians, he had perhaps
the satisfaction of talking openly to a fellow-countryman and a
fellow-journalist, thus half suggesting, half inspiring articles to
a paper in which he himself observed a profound silence on the
subject of his friends.

On the whole the impartiality and fairness for which this
paper was noted are reflected in the articles and notices on Saint-
Simonism; different opinions, clashing convictions, retorts and
counter-retorts are to be found almost side by side. Nevertheless
the judgment is on the whole unfavourable, and the underlying
fear felt by some of the writers is often apparent. The same
impression is given by the *Ausland*, although the first-hand
knowledge of the doctrine displayed by this paper makes it

[1] *A.Z.* January 29, 1832.
[2] Hirth, II, p. 13, dated January 25, 1832.
[3] *A.Z.* June 17, 1833; this may have been retailed to Donndorf by
Heine, who visited Chevalier in Sainte-Pélagie.

interesting reading; whilst the *Morgenblatt*, whose Paris correspondent, G. Depping[1], treated the Saint-Simonians with merry unconcern, printed a series of articles breathing fire and fury when the Saint-Simonians visited Strassburg[2].

At the other end of the scale from the *Allgemeine Zeitung* stands the *Allgemeine Kirchenzeitung*; and it is amusing to observe the intense and angry interest with which this little paper followed the history of the Saint-Simonians. Its severely Protestant leanings, its learned pretensions and its theological colouring would lead one to expect a more dignified attitude. But far from the *Allgemeine Kirchenzeitung* was any policy of restraint. It pounced with equal alacrity on Poupot, who won the prize for the best refutation of Saint-Simonian doctrines offered by the *Société de la morale chrétienne*[3], and on the criminal lunatic of Narbonne who turned out to be a Saint-Simonian[4]. It even sidled up to the Catholic Church and reprinted the pastoral letter of the Archbishop of Treves[5]. It retailed frivolous scandals from other papers[6]; vicariously perhaps, but none the less triumphantly, it stood by the grave of Talabot[7], and supervised d'Eichthal as he washed the plates at Ménilmontant[8]. It peered over the shoulder of the judge at the trial[9], and a faint far voice from Constantinople proclaimed the arrival in the East[10]. Hampered by its debts to other papers[11] it lagged behind the rest, but it never abandoned the chase; indeed it was a veritable sleuth-hound, toiling protesting and scandalised but ever *poursuivant* in the tracks of the unconscious Saint-Simonians, nose to the ground, picking up many an unsavoury morsel on its way and thirsting for blood.

The chief characteristic of the attitude of public opinion in Germany towards the Saint-Simonians is the note of actual fear.

---

[1] Cf. *Zeitung für die elegante Welt*, April 28, 1835.
[2] *Morgenblatt*, October 5–8, 1831.
[3] *A.K.Z.* December 20, 1831, and August 2, 1832.
[4] April 21, 1832.   [5] March 8, 1832.
[6] May 3, 1832 = *A.Z.* March 27, 1832.
[7] August 14, 1832.   [8] September 15, 1832.
[9] September 29, 1832.
[10] May 23, 1833 = *A.Z.* May 16, 1833.
[11] Most of the articles and notices in this paper are borrowed, generally without acknowledgments, from other papers, notably from the *A.Z.*

In considering the Saint-Simonians absurd and potentially mischievous, Germany did little more than echo the opinion current
in France and elsewhere; but the real alarm in the German
papers, especially noticeable when the Saint-Simonians approached Germany, is peculiarly their own. To the French
journalists the Saint-Simonians were an undoubted boon, an
inexhaustible topic for wit, an invaluable silly-season subject.
The *Morgenblatt* alone betrays a similar attitude, but it made
haste to change it when the Saint-Simonians came to Strassburg,
and the *Morgenblatt* addressed itself to the *gebildete Stände*; a
certain detachment, a tone of unshocked amusement is to be
expected from a paper with the courage to bear such a title.
But otherwise the voices upraised in the press from all parts of
Germany have the same strident quality of fear. Subdued at
first, or masked by an uneasy mockery, then rising to the pitch
of panic and dying away finally in nervous mutterings, they
put one in mind of those listeners trembling in the quiet town
whilst the djinns swept through it and away.

(b) PUBLIC OPINION ON SAINT-SIMONISM

A glance at the list of German writers on Saint-Simonism
between 1830 and 1835 and the sources they quote will give a
fair impression of the attention paid to the doctrine in Germany
and the extent of the authors' knowledge; and on the whole it
would seem that Saint-Simonism was surprisingly well-known
in Germany, in spite of gaps here and there, misunderstandings
and mistakes. The lists of sources added together cover the
whole ground of the doctrine, and the number of authors and
newspapers who felt themselves drawn to comment on that doctrine was by no means inconsiderable; and yet these critics one
and all protested that the movement could never become important in Germany; making these protests with an engaging
lack of humour in those very publications which helped to spread
its fame[1]. They maintained however that they were invul-
nerable, clad in the shining armour of Protestantism, and girt

---

[1] Cf. *Morgenblatt*, October 8, 1831; Kapff, p. 78; Matter, p. 83; *Allge-
meine Literaturzeitung*, June 1832, No. 112; *Theologisches Literaturblatt*,
June 18, 1832; Bretschneider, pp. 57, 113, 118–119; *Blätter für literarische
Unterhaltung*, March 3, 1834.

with the sword of philosophy; one cannot help reflecting to-day
on the dramatic irony of the situation, for they were shortly to
be confronted with a special German version of a system which
they condemned in no uncertain tones[1].

For on the whole it cannot be said that Saint-Simonism had
a sympathetic reception in Germany. Such sympathy as was
accorded went chiefly to the negative side of the doctrine; and
here the Saint-Simonians were praised either at the expense of
France or in the teeth of Rome; they were not loved for themselves alone. The positive side of their doctrine received but
scanty praise. Their attack on property aroused angry alarm;
their pantheism was pooh-poohed by the philosophers and en-
raged the theologians; the theory of the 'rehabilitation of the
flesh' and all that it involved was regarded with horror and
disgust; the emancipation of women called forth a storm of
ridicule, the Supreme Father mockery and dislike. Moreover
the most gratifying unanimity was everywhere apparent. Philosophers, theologians, journalists, authors and pamphleteers,
usually the most quarrelsome of folk, drew together in a veritable
entente cordiale of a defensive nature against the common foe,
raising in particular a unanimous chorus in which the words
plagiarism and lack of originality were an ever-recurrent refrain.

Die *neue* Lehre der Saintsimonisten wird es kaum für Deutschland
seyn; die Geschichte der Deutschen Philosophie seit Kant hat alle
die Ideen hervorgebracht, welche dem System der...Schule zu
Grunde liegen....Wir finden Ansichten und Behauptungen von Kant,
Hugo, Schelling und vielen andern Naturphilosophen auf eine ganz
sonderbare Weise mit einander vermischt und zu einem *religiös-
politischen* Systeme verbunden....[2]

I have quoted this last extract, because the Saint-Simonians,
who, on the whole, paid very little attention to the flood of
criticism pouring out from these German pens, were acquainted
with Warnkönig's article, and were moved to make the obvious
retort:

---

[1] Cf. Veit, pp. 189–190; Bretschneider, p. 212; Wiedenfeld, pp. 31–32.
[2] Warnkönig, pp. 79–80. Cf. also Veit, pp. 118–121; Kapff, p. 1; Bretschneider, pp. 97–98; Carové, pp. 196–197; *Ausland*, July 10, 1832; *A.Z.*
June 7, 1831; *Blätter für literarische Unterhaltung*, May 6, 1831; *Evangelische Kirchenzeitung*, March 23, 1831.

M. Warnkoenig dit ailleurs que la doctrine Saint-Simonienne n'a rien à enseigner de nouveau à la nation allemande, parce que la plupart des idées qu'elle professe ont déjà été senties et exprimées par Kant, Hugo, Schelling, Hegel, etc. Cette coïncidence remarquable une fois constatée, deux conclusions différentes étaient à en tirer: la première était une accusation de plagiat, la seconde une forte présomption de vérité en faveur d'une doctrine qui dans son appréciation du monde et de l'histoire embrasse spontanément toutes les idées élevées des plus grands penseurs d'un pays auquel ses fondateurs sont demeurés étrangers[1].

The Saint-Simonians were represented by these authors as battering unavailingly at the gates of Germany and demanding an audience. This purpose, they loudly declared, was never accomplished. Germany was far too staunchly Protestant, far too highly trained philosophically to pay any attention to such criminal absurdities. So they protested. Meanwhile much Saint-Simonian literature found its way into the country; book after book crept into the press, and was reviewed in one journal after another; leaders, articles and notices flooded the papers and were devoured by a seemingly insatiable public; translations were prepared and accepted; no German tourist in Paris omitted to attend at least one meeting in the *salle* Taitbout and to publish his impressions on his return. Germany had not consented to grant an interview forsooth, yet she seemed to be listening at the door.

But she listened with anger and disgust; and when the Young Germans appeared in her midst, like a band of incendiaries with dishevelled hair and eyes ablaze, spreading the wild-fire from France and calling strange watch-words to each other, public opinion, with clumsy haste and leaking hose, directed a stream of coldest water on the flames they fanned, whereat an angry hiss arose and stifling smoke and stench.

(c) ENLIGHTENED OPINION

Midway between the main body of public opinion and the Young Germans there was a small group of men and women who were interested in Saint-Simonism and expressed this

[1] *Globe*, January 16, 1832.

interest in an independent and enlightened way[1]. Ludwig Börne was one of these, a typical exponent of the liberal opinion current at the time, for he was the most liberal German alive.

It is with regret that I find myself forced to omit this interesting figure from the main portion of this book; the more so since Young Germany was born under the sign of Börne and was only baptised later into the Saint-Simonian church. But Börne remained outside, and there is nothing to be gained by saying this at any length. There was something noble and austere in his nature, something rigid and uncompromising in his moral outlook against which the doctrine of the 'emancipation of the flesh' would be powerless to prevail. He never mentioned this doctrine, nor are there many references to the Saint-Simonians in his *Letters from Paris*; but such as there are reflect his independent opinions, which were not altogether unfavourable to the Saint-Simonian school. He began with a jesting reference to the equal distribution of riches which he imagined to be one of their principles[2]; but more than a year later he confessed regretfully that he knew very little about the movement. He had never heard a Saint-Simonian sermon, partly because their hall was always crowded, and partly because he had felt antagonistic towards the doctrine on account of the hierarchical constitution of their church:

Sie haben einen Papst; vor solchem kreuze ich mich, wie vor dem Satan. Sie haben eine Autorität; die fürchte ich noch mehr, als den Räuber im finstern Walde[3].

Enfantin's powers were never measured against the rock-like resistance of this freedom-loving mind; but they would inevitably have met with a complete check. Börne was neither very sensitive to personal charm, nor capable of making the slightest concession where the principle of freedom was involved. And since he was already half a convert to the Christianity of

---

[1] Goethe, although he took the *Globe*, is not amongst this group; he even warned Carlyle against the dangers of Saint-Simonism: 'Von der Société St-Simonienne bitte sich fernzuhalten,' *Briefe*, Weimarer Ausgabe, XLVII, p. 300, dated October 17, 1830.

[2] Ludwig Börne, *Gesammelte Schriften*, Hamburg, 1862, VIII, p. 60, dated October 1, 1830.

[3] *Ibid.* x, p. 114, dated December 30, 1831.

a Lamennais, the Saint-Simonian religion was not likely to appeal to him; Heine truly described him later as a 'Nazarene' by temperament; and for such the church of Saint-Simon opened her arms in vain.

He contented himself on this occasion with a rapid review of the mottoes printed as a heading to each number of the *Globe*: 'Les institutions sociales doivent avoir pour but l'amélioration du sort moral, physique et intellectuel de la classe la plus nombreuse et la plus pauvre. Tous les privilèges de la naissance, sans exception, seront abolis. A chacun selon sa capacité, à chaque capacité selon ses œuvres.' Börne was in complete agreement with the first motto, but he made the scrupulous addition that it entails the tacit assumption that the fortunate by birth need neither the protection nor the assistance of civil laws. He was also of the opinion, indeed it had ever been his strongest belief, that the privileges of birth should be abolished; but he was impatient with the Saint-Simonian proclamation, for it seemed to him that the time for words had passed, and that it was too late in the day to be stating self-evident truths. It is not surprising that Börne, who had an acutely sensitive feeling for justice, should have been outraged by the dictum 'A chacun selon sa capacité, à chaque capacité selon ses œuvres'; for the fundamental unfairness of such an arrangement lies very near to hand. But he was led to draw the false conclusion that the Saint-Simonians advocated communism, a theory for which he also expressed great dislike. He then went on to state that the abolition of marriage was supposed to be on their programme. This reproach he found difficult to believe, since no new religion had ever yet been founded on immorality, although destructive principles were often later adopted during periods of decay. It is clear from the term immorality that Börne would not have been in sympathy with the theory of the constant, the inconstant and the 'calm'; whilst his views on the emancipation of women were of a completely conservative character[1]; even in marriage and family life he denied the possibility of independence to women.

Now if ever there were a disinterested foe of every kind of

---

[1] Cf. Börne, x, p. 120.

oppression, bondage and tyranny; if ever there were an impartial administrator of justice; if ever there were a fearless fighter against the forces of tradition and convention, that man was Ludwig Börne. Single-minded and incorruptible, he lived, wrote and thought solely for the welfare of humanity; and for one essential condition, the principle of liberty. And yet he unhesitatingly condemned one half of mankind to remain in the state of modified bondage which was the lot of women in 1830. In a man so consistent and so uncompromising this inconsistency is startling enough. Possibly it was a legacy from the deep-seated oriental instincts of his race; possibly an unconscious tribute to the mighty god of tradition; it is certainly the one slender yet unbreakable bond which held him captive to the past.

On the occasion of the government intervention against the Saint-Simonians Börne noted with delight the generous attitude of the French press and notably of the *Figaro*[1]; and the last time he mentioned this subject in his letters, he gave a very favourable account of a Saint-Simonian *soirée*, by far the most sympathetic notice of such a function to be found from any German pen[2]; for these receptions were generally considered extremely absurd. So that this testimony from Börne, whose stinging wit made him the scourge of his enemies and the terror of governments, is a remarkable tribute to the 'magnetic spirit of faith' which animated the Saint-Simonians in 1832. For all his fierce asceticism he felt the beauty in Saint-Simonism which is not easy to define. 'It was something from a foreign clime, from a lovelier season than we know.'

It is often stated that the Varnhagens, who took a great interest in Saint-Simonism, first introduced the Young Germans to the new doctrine; but this theory will not stand the test of examination; for the influence of the Varnhagens here is doubtful in some cases and entirely out of the question in others. Wienbarg knew neither husband nor wife; Laube first met Varnhagen in 1834, a year after Rahel's death, by which time he had been under the influence of Saint-Simonism for more than two years;

[1] Börne, x, pp. 232–233, dated February 4, 1832.
[2] *Ibid.* x, pp. 257–258, dated February 10, 1832.

but his interest had been partly aroused by Karl Schall, who had been in Berlin in 1832, when Saint-Simonism had been eagerly canvassed between himself and Rahel. Here therefore an indirect influence was partly in play. Gutzkow entered into correspondence with Varnhagen in 1835, whereas his references to Saint-Simonism had begun in 1832. Mundt on the other hand opened relations with Varnhagen in 1833 and was probably swayed to some extent by the appreciation of Saint-Simonian ideas contained in *Das Buch Rahel*. But this is far from being a clear case of primary influence as will be seen in the section on Mundt.

The most doubtful and interesting problem is presented by Heine here. He alone of the Young Germans knew both Rahel and Varnhagen, indeed their friendship had dated from the year 1824. He had spent the first half of 1829 in Berlin and Potsdam and had seen something of his friends; but it is unlikely that anything should have transpired about Saint-Simonism in Germany at such an early date, when it was hardly known in Paris itself. Heine spent the year 1830 in Hamburg, Wandsbeck and Heligoland, and in 1831 he was again in Hamburg. Here, on February 10, 1831, he made his first discoverable reference to Saint-Simonism, quoting indeed from the *Exposition de la doctrine de Saint-Simon*[1]. A few weeks later he wrote to Varnhagen that his 'new religion' was beckoning him to Paris, rather in the tone of one who supposed his correspondent to be *au fait*, although it is the first allusion of its kind[2]. Varnhagen's letters to Heine and Rahel's also of this period were destroyed in a fire so that it is impossible to say whether or not he owed his knowledge of Saint-Simonism to them; but the phrase 'meine neue Religion' looks to me as if he had become acquainted with it independently. This supposition is further strengthened by the letter which Rahel wrote to Heine on June 5, 1832, where she speaks of Saint-Simonism as of a subject not hitherto broached between them, regretting emphatically that they could not have half an hour's conversation about it[3]. The first of her allusions to the new religion which I have been

---

[1] F. Hirth, *Heinrich Heines Briefwechsel*, I, p. 640.
[2] *Ibid.* I, p. 642, dated April 1, 1831.   [3] *Ibid.* II, p. 23.

able to trace was made on January 18, 1832[1], after which they
followed each other rapidly until her death; it seems therefore
reasonable to assume that she was not keenly interested until
1832, or we should find traces of such a preoccupation in *Das
Buch Rahel*. Heine on the other hand had expressed himself
with great enthusiasm nearly a year earlier. In view of these
facts I incline to think that he obtained his information elsewhere; and it is even possible that he first roused the interest
of the Varnhagens. But this postulates some lost letters from
Heine since he was not in Berlin after 1829; and as Varnhagen
was an indefatigable and scrupulous collector of every kind of
autograph, this theory seems difficult to believe. And all the
more so since it appears from the correspondence with Pückler-
Muskau that the fount of knowledge and certainly the purveyor
of Saint-Simonian literature was a 'junger nicht hübscher, aber
gescheidter Amerikaner'[2] called Albert Brisbane[3].

Rahel welcomed the new doctrine with extravagant ardour
curiously blended with discrimination. For new ideas brought
from this strange woman an emotional and a mental response.
Her mind was like an alchemist's cauldron, transmuting base
metal to gold, and seeking as eagerly for universal truth as ever
mediaeval visionary sought the philosopher's stone; whilst beneath the surge of ideas and thoughts the flames of an ardent
temperament burned fiercely, burned despairingly, but never
burned away. Rahel becomes increasingly difficult to understand as time bears us ever farther from the days when this frail
and fervent Jewess dominated the society of Berlin. And the
book which was to perpetuate her genius and to keep her
memory green fails in this task to-day. It is a difficult book to
read; wearisome rather than stimulating, distressful rather than
delightful; confused, obscure, chaotic; painful to a sympathetic
mind. Heine called Hoffmann's *Tales* 'a terrible cry of fear in
twenty volumes'; and in the same way these three closely
printed tomes of letters and diaries might fittingly be likened
to one long cry of despair.

[1] *Rahel, ein Buch des Andenkens für ihre Freunde*, Berlin, 1834, III, p. 550.
[2] *Ibid.* III, p. 418.
[3] Cf. *Briefwechsel und Tagebücher des Fürsten Hermann von Pückler-
Muskau*, Berlin, 1874, III, pp. 91–92, 95, 104–105, 106, 110, 113–114.

Rahel was born to suffering, even had circumstances been kinder to her than they were. Her sensitive and highly-strung temperament responded to the smallest mental or emotional disturbance as accurately as her nervous system registered the slightest variations in temperature. But not enough that she should be cursed with this dangerous sensibility, she was born the daughter of a despised and persecuted race; born the child of hard, unloving parents; born a woman with gifts and aims which fretted against the barrier of her sex; born with an all-too-passionate heart, humiliated often and cruelly disdained. And yet in reading *Das Buch Rahel* it is an effort to maintain the high level of passionate sympathy which the writer, the now unconscious writer, demands. For this admirable friend, this self-sacrificing lover, appears in her confessions shrouded within herself and drowning in an ocean of self-pity. She tears open her heart, she exposes her wounds; again and yet again she utters an exceeding bitter cry: 'I am a virtuoso in suffering; none other has endured so much; I have been tortured and martyred beyond the common lot of men.' But these piteous vociferations have not the tragic ring. Universal pain and eternal woe must re-echo an agonised human cry before tragedy is born; and they guard most sternly those austere proportions which dignify the individual fate. So that tragedy escapes from Rahel, and leaves her bereft indeed.

Complete and unquestioning sympathy is therefore not present in the reader's mind, and complete comprehension is even further removed. Rahel's tortured metaphysical style, her jerky and aphoristic utterances are far from doing justice to her obscure and visionary but undoubtedly creative thought. There are occasional phrases of real beauty, and moments of intuition so deep and daring that a feeling akin to awe accompanies these glimpses into her mind; for her intellect was a noble instrument, but ruthlessly played upon by her temperament, which sets the strings jarring, wailing, vibrating until our nerves cry out for surcease. Part mystic, part sceptic, her great desire for truth was her most admirable intellectual quality, the one which ensures respect even in her most extravagant moods.

And to Rahel there was something in Saint-Simonism which

seemed like a clear and triumphant answer to the dark and
difficult questions which had tormented her during her life; for
there are many passages in her letters and diaries which show
that she was already a Saint-Simonian before Enfantin was
breeched. Naturally enough she was a feminist, she suffered
cruelly in her youth from the conventional attitude towards
women which was adopted in her own home[1]; but the social side
of the question tormented her less than the moral aspect[2]; whilst
a deep and abiding dissatisfaction with marriage, even after
her own happy union with Varnhagen, is often apparent in this
book[3]. Quite unmistakably too Rahel foreshadowed the Saint-
Simonian conception of Christianity, too much attuned, they
felt, to the spirit of self-sacrifice and denial of life to be of per-
manent benefit to humanity[4]; and closely connected with this
opinion of Christianity we find the Saint-Simonian attitude towards history, the same prophecy that a new period is at hand,
inspired and directed by new beliefs[5].

It would need many pages of quotations to show the mysterious affinity existing between the brooding thoughts of this
very unusual woman and the clear-cut logical ideas which the
Saint-Simonians presented to the world in 1830; but there is a
remarkable passage which throws a strange light on this affinity:

Du weisst wie ich das Volk liebe: bloss weil es die Meisten sind,
und die Ärmsten; es muss ohn' Unterlass für die Menge, für's Ganze
geschehen. An mir ist ein Gesetzgeber, ein Pestalozzi, ein Moses
untergegangen....[6]

The spirit of the times, enmeshed in these words, stares at us
here with questioning eyes; that strange composite spirit, born
of the desires and ideals of the men who were living then, seeking
a law-giver for humanity, and whispering into the ears of
Saint-Simon, Rahel and Enfantin the same bewildering words:
'La classe la plus nombreuse et la plus pauvre...un homme
revêtu d'un grand pouvoir...Jésus, Moïse, Enfantin.... Die

[1] *Rahel*, I, pp. 55 56, dated April 2, 1793.
[2] *Ibid.* I, p. 312, dated February 15, 1807; III, p. 19, dated May 17, 1820.
[3] *Ibid.* I, p. 259, dated March 8, 1803.
[4] *Ibid.* I, pp. 262–263, dated December 12, 1804.
[5] Cf. *ibid.* II, p. 382, dated February 5, 1816; III, pp. 20–21, dated
May 20, 1820.
[6] *Ibid.* II, p. 472, dated August 9, 1817.

Meisten und die Ärmsten...Pestalozzi, Moses, Rahel....' Meanwhile Fourier dreamt in Paris of an 'omniarque pivotal,' and Lady Hester Stanhope prophesied in the East; the Red Indians of America awaited the coming of a god, whilst Joanna Southcott in England made her fantastic claims. So the spirit of those times went ranging over the world, seeking but seeking in vain.

We are prepared now for the enthusiasm with which Rahel heralded the advent of Saint-Simonism. 'Aber Glück auf! Die alte Erde muss sich erhellen; und die kommenden Menschen besser und glücklicher sein'[1]; it was in an almost exalted frame of mind that she greeted the new doctrine[2], and poured out her opinions to Heinrich Heine:

Schade! dass uns nicht eine halbe Stunde mündlichen Gesprächs über den St Simonismus geschenkt ist. Mich dünkt, wir sind über manches davon nicht einer Meinung. Er ist das neue, grosserfundene Instrument, welches die grosse alte Wunde, die Geschichte der Menschen auf der Erde, endlich berührt. Er operiert und sähet; und unumstössliche Wahrheiten hat er ans Licht gefördert. Die wahren Fragen in Reihe und Glied gestellt: viele, wichtige beantwortet: die Religionsfrage mir nicht zur Gnüge, und hierüber müssten wir streiten, sprechen. Den ganzen Winter waren diese Schriften, besonders der Globe meine Nahrung, Unterhaltung, Beschäftigung: sein Ankommen meine ganze Erwartung. Die Erde verschönern. Mein altes Thema. Freyheit zu jeder menschlichen Entwickelung: ebenso....Hieraus kann jedes Verhältniss deduziert werden, also auch Ehe[3].

There can be no doubt, although she never said so, that Rahel was in complete accord with the feminist theories of the Saint-Simonians; indeed such an agreement is implicit in her acceptance of the principle of freedom 'for every kind of human development.' Whether she cared for the final consequence is open to doubt; she made no reference to the 'supreme mother.' On the other hand, whilst accepting the doctrine as a whole with something like rapture, she could not bring herself to consider it as a religion[4], for Rahel, although her intelligence was of the sceptical kind, had had too many spiritual experiences to be

[1] *Rahel*, III, p. 557, dated February 18, 1832, to Pückler-Muskau.
[2] Cf. *ibid.* III, p. 568, dated April 25, 1832, to Adolph von Willisen; and *ibid.* III, p. 570, dated May 5, 1832, to Karl Schall.
[3] Hirth, II, pp. 23–24, dated June 5, 1832.
[4] *Rahel*, III, pp. 555–556, dated February 8, 1832.

deceived for a moment by the mystical colouring of the new
school of thought; and she saw without difficulty the error which
underlay their pretensions, the substitution of deduction for
revelation. Nor was she satisfied with the theory of marriage
propounded by Enfantin; when 'A' rushed into her room
babbling of the new state of marriage which should not preclude
freedom and change, she reacted rather violently against such
a proposal[1]; the compromise between matrimony and freedom
did not appeal to Rahel, for she justly considered it typical
of all the unsatisfactory marriages which she saw around her.
She preferred the voluntary subjection to the institution as it
stood, a subjection brought about by disciplining the affections
and the mind.

She also condemned as unsound and superficial Enfantin's
famous division of mankind into the faithful and the inconstant; and the part to be played by the Saint-Simonian priest
between them received very short shrift: 'Unnütz: und unthun-
lich.'[2] But when she proceeded to develop her own hopes for
the future of marriage she lost herself in obscurity and vagueness, shedding no light into darkness here.

The words 'emancipation of the flesh' do not occur in these
various references. But in welcoming the doctrine as she did,
Rahel must have meant to include this fundamental clause, or
she would surely have expressly omitted it. Her criticisms were
levelled against the religious pretensions of the school, against
the theory of free marriage and against the absurd but useful
category of changeable and constant natures. Otherwise it was
all eager approval and constant exclamations of delight: 'Gründ-
licheres, Rechtschaffeneres, Klareres, Einfacheres, Unwider-
sprechlicheres ist wohl nicht gedruckt.'[3] High praise from
Rahel, one of the great intellectuals of her age.

But this epithet fits more closely when applied to her husband
Karl August Varnhagen von Ense; Rahel was an intellectual
and an emotional at one and the same time; and this frequently
obscures her judgments; Varnhagen is easier to understand.

[1] *Rahel*, III, pp. 550–551, dated January 20, 1832.
[2] Cf. *ibid.* III, pp. 557–559, dated Spring 1832, for the whole of this
passage.
[3] *Ibid.* III, p. 561, dated 1832, to Pückler-Muskau.

For the intelligentsia of any age react towards the ideas around them through their heads rather than through their hearts. They are not hampered for the most part by obscure instincts, by unacknowledged fears, by those deep atavistic tendencies which drag humanity backwards; they are not often faced by confused issues, by perplexing dilemmas, in which the mind may approve what temperament and tradition condemn. They are not afraid of words, they do not fight with shadows; they think clearly and their intellectual courage is high. And Varnhagen von Ense, cold, reserved, buttoned-up rather too tightly in his official uniform, perhaps a little acid and petty-minded, yet had the quality of disinterested intelligence which is the hall-mark of his kind. His undoubtedly liberal leanings, the result of fair-mindedness and straight thinking, led him to view the Saint-Simonian doctrine with favour; but it was also his almost slavish admiration for the genius and temperament of his wife which made him so strong a supporter of this cause, and which kept his interest and appreciation alive after the companion who had inspired them was dead.

His partner in the correspondence which reflects most clearly his interest in Saint-Simonism was the prince Hermann von Pückler-Muskau; and never perhaps did a couple more dissimilar combine to tread a more stately, a more formal and a more enchanting measure.

It is the fascinating figure of the prince Pückler-Muskau which gives to this volume of letters its entrancing quality of romance, and it seems almost as if he had been created to prove that legends can be true. He was of noble birth; handsome, strong, daring and courageous as any hero of antiquity; nature in an extravagant mood threw in the virtues of another age and a later civilisation, making him honourable, generous and chivalrous; she added the humbler but no less attractive attributes of warmheartedness and modesty; finally, to suit the modern taste, impulsiveness and charm. Then she sent him off on his travels and turned her mind elsewhere. He travelled far, as is the right of legendary heroes, and as is their no less inalienable right, he was irresistible to women. He freed no captive princesses, you say? But he brought home a dusky mistress from the

East, and saved her from the fate of a slave; he slew no fabulous monsters, to be sure, but he was a hunter of big game, and broke in a giraffe on the banks of the Nile. He did not ride forth to liberate the oppressed perhaps, but he extended his protection and patronage to a hunted wretch after the manner of a by-gone age[1]; and if he did not enter the lists in helmet of bronze, he broke a gallant lance in defence of a persecuted poet whom his relatives were doing to death[2].

A fantastic figure, I admit, this globe-trotter through life on the beautiful steed romance; but whether he were making his park at Muskau to blossom like the rose, or seeking Daniel O'Connell through the storm of an Irish night, or bestriding an Arab mare to the terror of those who watched, or listening at the feet of Lady Stanhope whilst she read him the riddle of the stars, he was surrounded by that indefinable glamour of legendary days.

Now a man who is adventurous by nature rarely refuses adventures of the mind; and Pückler-Muskau, initiated by Rahel, chiefly in private conversations, was soon amongst the Saint-Simonian adepts. He was 'delighted' by his first perusal of Saint-Simonian literature, so delighted that he could not forbear to exclaim:

Dies ist wahrlich eine neue Lehre, und die klare Erkenntniss einer beginnenden neuen Zeit, wenn auch diese nur ganz langsam sich entfalten sollte in Jahrhunderten. Uebrigens steht sie *uns* noch weiter, und bleibt blos als ein fernes Meteor zu beschauen, wenn man nicht nach Spandau wandern will[3].

For all his receptivity to new ideas and impressions the prince, it will be remarked, was far from losing his head. It is characteristic of Rahel that she seized upon his eager appreciation; and of Varnhagen that he warmly seconded the statement that centuries must elapse before the new times would be ripe[4].

---

[1] He offered the shelter of Muskau to Heinrich Laube, who passed eighteen months of his captivity on the prince's estate.

[2] He tendered his services to Heinrich Heine during the feud over Salomon Heine's will; cf. Hirth, II, pp. 571–572, 577–578, 580.

[3] *Briefwechsel und Tagebücher des Fürsten Hermann von Pückler-Muskau*, III, p. 91, dated February 5, 1832, Pückler to Varnhagen.

[4] Cf. *ibid.* III, pp. 92–93, dated February 6, 1832, Rahel to Pückler; pp. 93–94, dated February 7, 1832, Varnhagen to Pückler.

The Saint-Simonian conversations between the three were in full swing during the months of February, March and April, but Pückler-Muskau left for his estates towards the end of the month; and from now onwards until 1834 hardly a letter passed between the two men which did not contain some appreciative reference to the absorbing topic[1].

Rahel, Varnhagen and Pückler-Muskau are not the main objects of the present study, but enough has been said to show that these three, and there were others, independently of the Young Germans but contemporaneously with them, welcomed the Saint-Simonian doctrine as one that held the secret of the future; differing from them only in this, that they saw clearly and expressed emphatically that the time to say this publicly was not yet. Rahel indeed made no such reserve, but as she was not a writer of books she had no need to do so; whilst both Varnhagen and Pückler-Muskau refrained from published propaganda; for if Varnhagen were the author of certain articles in the *Allgemeine Zeitung*, the fact that they were dated from the Rhine would prove that he was anxious to preserve his anonymity.

But they all three expressed their enthusiasm in private more warmly and more whole-heartedly than the five unlucky Young Germans ever felt moved to testify in print. And if three such different and in their different ways such admirable human beings could all so fervently acclaim the doctrine of Saint-Simon, it was because it came at the psychological moment; and, more than this, because it held a germ of progress which the more enlightened of that age were privileged to recognise. But it is not always these who have the management of states.

(d) THE YOUNG GERMAN WOMEN

The prominence given by the Young German historians to Rahel, Bettina and Charlotte diminishes considerably when they are looked at through Saint-Simonian spectacles. It is true that the Young Germans hailed *Das Buch Rahel* and *Goethe's Briefwechsel mit einem Kinde* with a very particular enthusiasm; it

---

[1] Cf. *ibid.* III, pp. 102, 105, 106–107, 110, 113–114, 125–126, 128, 179, 182.

is true that they appeared in the critical years 1834 and 1835, and were reviled as Young German literature by an angry press; and it is also true that they contained Saint-Simonian elements; but in so far as any vital influence is concerned they came *post festum*. For nearly all the typical books of the men we are considering had already been published, with the exception of *Wally die Zweiflerin* by Gutzkow and *Madonna* by Theodor Mundt. Although Gutzkow was interested in these three women and referred to them in his novel, the interest was not directed towards their Saint-Simonian views, for he had already made up his mind about Saint-Simonism. Mundt on the other hand was particularly preoccupied with Rahel's pronouncements on this subject[1], but only, I believe, because he was already thinking on the same lines. And this is probably one of the reasons why the Young Germans were so much affected by these two books; it was the delightful feeling of surprise with which we are wont to greet a fellow-countryman in a far and alien land, or with which, surrounded by uncongenial companions, we welcome a spirit of our own kind.

Charlotte Stieglitz, on the other hand, influenced Theodor Mundt during her life-time, but only indirectly and involuntarily towards Saint-Simonian beliefs. Her untimely death found an echo in Gutzkow's breast which gave the first impetus to his novel and resulted in Mundt's best book, his Memoir of this unhappy woman. But Charlotte's death had nothing to do with Saint-Simonism, which is a strong affirmation of life, and in particular banished self-sacrifice to the limbo of outworn ideals.

On the other hand it must not be forgotten that the Young Germans were entangled in feminist ideas and theories of social reform; therefore amidst all the talk about women and love swelling against the banks of custom towards a periodic flood, they could do no less than pay an eager attention to the outstanding women of their day; and this was probably the second reason why Rahel, Bettina and Charlotte were given a place in the sun. But there is no need to follow the fashion set by Gutzkow and Kühne, who would have us believe that these three women were mysterious portents in the Young German

[1] Cf. *Jahrbücher für wissenschaftliche Kritik*, June 1835, Nos. 112–114.

sky; nor is there much to be learnt from the phrases: Rahel's 'Thought,' Bettina's 'Poem' and Charlotte's 'Deed.'

Bettina von Arnim, like Rahel Varnhagen, belonged by birth rather to the romantic age than to the period of 1830, for she was fifty years old when she published her correspondence with Goethe and took the hearts of the Young Germans by storm. It is not difficult to account for this triumph, for it is a delightful book; mere 'Dichtung und Lüge' to the 'Goethe-Forscher' and the Goethe-worshipper, it commends itself to other readers by its charm and its emotional truth. There are weaknesses in it certainly; it is too long; and the theme of adoring love becomes monotonous and definitely wearisome in the third part, producing almost the same impression as a protracted solo on the harp; inexorably beautiful, hauntingly melodious, almost suffocatingly sweet. But this effect is transitory; there is poetry, wit, daring and grace to be found in these pages; there are charming stories, lively thumbnail sketches of enemies and friends; musical rhapsodies which seem almost to tremble on the brink of revelation; whilst the romantic passion which the authoress felt for Goethe, and which was not returned in kind, lends an emotional value of unfulfilled desire to her passionate protestations of love.

But her descriptions of nature, animate and inanimate, show her most completely and most delightfully herself. She was called 'dämonisch' and 'hexenartig' by her contemporaries, but these epithets seem misapplied, for they suggest something sinister, eerie and uncanny, whereas Bettina was endowed rather with those half-human, half-ethereal qualities which we attribute to dryads and nymphs, and with a madcap grace of her own. She was as happy in natural surroundings as any child at play; climbing trees and moonlit towers, or sleeping under the stars; bathing in casual pools and streams, or sunning herself on the banks; watching the squirrels and stealing their nuts, marshalling a flock of butterflies before her, or lighting the moths to bed. Now to-day, when the cry of the 'Wandervogel' is heard in the land, such antics are not uncommon, although possibly less gracefully performed; but in Bettina's youth it was a most unheard-of thing for a girl to run wild in this way.

But there was no holding Bettina; nature had but to beckon, and off she danced.

To search for Saint-Simonian elements in this book is rather like looking at a rose through a microscope to discover the reason why it is red. It seems a trifle foolish to start analysing love-letters, or to deduce opinions from lyrical improvisations where pure fancy plays hide-and-seek with thought. Besides, if Bettina were a Saint-Simonian, she was an unconscious member of that clan; for her letters were written between 1807 and 1811, and although she altered them for publication, it is of all things most unlikely that she had a Saint-Simonian end in view. But undoubtedly any intelligent follower of Enfantin would have claimed her as his kin; for not only did she hold a fair balance between the spiritual and sensual elements in her love for Goethe, which was a passion both of body and mind, she also believed most fervently in the divinity of the passion of love[1].

She was therefore one of the faith, whether she knew it or not, and she has this title to originality that she was a musical Saint-Simonian, or rather a Saint-Simonian musician; for she was constantly seeking for harmony, and she found it in music, the absolute expression of love[2].

And that this harmony was the Saint-Simonian harmony, the fusion of spirit and flesh, is clear from many passages both about music and love: '...das Blut ist geheiligt; es entzündet den Leib, dass er mit dem Geist zusammen dasselbe wolle.'[3]

There is a real temptation to linger over this book, but it would be out of place to do so here; it is too well-known in the first place, and in the second Bettina, for all the admiration she inspired, did not alter the Young German course, which was set before her fairy bark appeared bobbing and curtseying on the waves. In truth they were all in the grip of the same current which ran near a dangerous coast; but whereas the Young Germans were dashed on to the rocks, Bettina von Arnim escaped.

[1] *Goethe's Briefwechsel mit einem Kinde*, 3rd ed. Berlin, 1849, I, pp. 38–39, to Goethe's mother, May 1808.
[2] *Ibid.* I, pp. 189–190, to Goethe, dated November 11, 1808.
[3] *Ibid.* I, p. 310, to Goethe, dated August 7, 1808.

The tragic death of Charlotte Stieglitz, who stabbed herself to the heart on December 29, 1834, will be considered in greater detail in connection with the story of Mundt's literary career. It was a suicide perpetrated for the strangest reason surely that has ever led to such an act. The instinct towards self-sacrifice, reaching in this deed its rare but logical conclusion, is unhappily common enough, but Charlotte's special motive has no parallel in history. She hoped to quicken the feeble flame of inspiration which wavered in her husband's languid spirit; and also to cure him of his mysterious melancholia which the physicians could not heal. This at least is the generally accepted interpretation of her last letter to Stieglitz; but it seems almost certain that there must have been an element of personal despair in her magnanimous choice of death. If it were a sacrifice brought to the altar of genius, then the sacrifice was vain, for the altar was empty. The melancholy minor poet called Heinrich Stieglitz remained a minor poet to the end; and although he was over-whelmed with sorrow, it was the sorrow of a small and be-wildered mind. He strained every nerve to reach the height of her sacrifice, for he naïvely accepted it as such, but even in this he failed. It was rumoured that he wrote a poem before the week was out; if Charlotte died for him, she was betrayed.

There is something in this story and in the characters of Charlotte and Heinrich which puts one in mind of the anguished realism in Dostoevski's tales. And indeed the spirit which lives in Dostoevski's novels was abroad in Germany at that time; born perhaps of the grinding oppression and tyranny which filled the prisons and fortresses, but could not altogether crush the soul of a people; quickened perhaps by the plague which arose in the East and swept over Europe with its grim companion death. The religious exaltation which mastered Karl Sand when he murdered Kotzebue; the spiritual fervour which upheld a Börne and a Büchner on their dangerous and persecuted paths; the courage which sustained Charlotte Stieglitz in her final hour; they are all signs of that selfless love of humanity, the very spirit of Christianity, which dies that others may live and which loses itself that others may be saved.

The profound and shattering impression produced throughout

Germany by Charlotte's death is another sign that the minds of men were attuned to a deed which would have no such result to-day; but it is a strange feature of the case that both those who decried and exalted her act considered that Saint-Simonism had played its part in her fate. 'This comes of being a Saint-Simonian' was in effect the conservative cry; whilst Mundt and others hinted plainly that she had been forced to abandon life because the world was not Saint-Simonian enough.

The first suggestion is absurd; Charlotte was no Saint-Simonian; her only point of contact with this doctrine was a gentle and unchallenging feminism, for she felt keenly at times the passive part which the world demanded of women[1]; but otherwise her self-sacrificing relations with her husband, and her over-spiritual conception of marriage make it difficult to believe that this philosophy of life would have met with her approval. Moreover if we accept the testimony of Heinrich Stieglitz, and there seems no reason to doubt it, Charlotte, far from being swayed by these ideas, was definitely antagonistic towards them[2]; whilst the motive for her death is not susceptible of a Saint-Simonian interpretation; it was a private tragedy, and the spirit in which it was accomplished was one before which Saint-Simonism would veil its face in horror and regret.

The three books which bore the names of Rahel, Bettina and Charlotte were not prohibited in Germany in spite of the outcry of the press; and this symbolises the minor part played by women in the Young German movement. Rahel's intellect, Bettina's poetical gifts and Charlotte's character make them at least the equals of a Gutzkow, a Laube and a Mundt. But even allowing for the personal influence of Rahel on Heine and Charlotte on Mundt, they played a less important part than the men. Two of them died before the movement was well on the way, but it is unlikely that events would have taken a different course if they had remained alive. They were too much withdrawn within themselves, leading the absorbing life of personal emotions or the mysterious and exacting life of the nerves; they glided away from real events; sorrowing, loving, sacrificing;

---

[1] Cf. *Charlotte Stieglitz, ein Denkmal*, Berlin, 1835, pp. 78, 81, 96.
[2] H. Stieglitz, *Eine Selbstbiographie*, Gotha, 1865, pp. 179–182.

unassailable, remote. But the men, disciplined in a harder school, directed their energies outwards; and so it befell that events followed each other thick and fast round the figures of these young men, but they were events of a most disastrous kind.

(e) THE DISASTER

When one reads to-day the books which gave rise to the Prussian and Federal Edicts against the Young Germans, the feeling uppermost in one's mind is surprise that the governments involved could bring themselves to take this literature so seriously. It is not difficult to see why these books should have been forbidden in Prussia on their appearance, considering the state of the censorship of the press and the dead and crushing weight of the reaction. The fact that they all make more or less definite attacks on Christianity, and allow themselves criticisms on the marriage laws, however vague and immature these criticisms may be, is quite sufficient to explain the gruff 'Verboten' with which each insignificant pawn was swept from the board. But between the negative policy which automatically refused publication to any book of a character which could be called revolutionary in any sense, and the positive alarm which created a dangerous conspiracy from the slight material offered by the works of the Young Germans there is an interesting and important difference. Much has been written and much has been said to account historically for the tremendous machinery brought to bear to crush this literature, which ironically enough only persists to-day because of the pains taken to exterminate it then. Later generations return to the tombs in which these young men were buried alive, and stand puzzled before the forbidding monument which once denied all entrance; but the spirit of life has escaped to fight new battles, and the tombs have become tombs indeed[1].

Saint-Simonism certainly played its part in precipitating the

---

[1] The text of the Prussian Edicts is given by Houben, *Jungdeutscher Sturm und Drang*, Leipzig, 1911, pp. 43–44. J. Proelss in *Das junge Deutschland*, Stuttgart, 1892, pp. 612 ff., gives a portion of the Federal Edicts; cf. also L. Geiger, *Das junge Deutschland und die preussische Censur*, Berlin, 1900, pp. 33–34; K. Fischer, *Die Nation und der Bundestag*, Leipzig, 1880, pp. 423–424.

catastrophe of 1835. It will become clear I hope in the ensuing chapters that the only real resemblance between these five very different men was their preoccupation with Saint-Simonian theories, and in particular their luckless academic efforts to 'emancipate the flesh.' The omens were not propitious to the leaders of so hazardous an enterprise in Germany. The entrails of public opinion showed most disquieting signs; and no priestess, howsoever cautious, but would have felt constrained to utter: 'Saint-Simonism shall be their doom.' And indeed this prophecy would have proved no idle warning, although it was accomplished in a strange and unexpected way according to the fashion of oracles. For the press, which had been on the whole well-informed on the subject of Saint-Simonism and strongly antagonistic towards it, now fell tooth and nail on the Young Germans, and was yet for the most part blind to the obvious connection, whilst the Prussian government was in a state of even greater ignorance.

I have told elsewhere the manner in which this ignorance was dispelled[1]; how Hengstenberg in the *Evangelische Kirchenzeitung* laid bare the tendency of the school; how Menzel, from less disinterested motives, came forward to denounce Gutzkow and Wienbarg; how the affair came to the ears of Metternich and the steps he took in consequence; how Prussia eagerly if clumsily obeyed his orders; how a vast anabaptistical system was erected by the governments from the immature theories of these young men; how the supposed conspiracy was triumphantly crushed and order reigned once more in the fatherland.

The tragic disharmony at the root of the quarrel between the Young Germans and their detractors is the same which divides this work-a-day world from poetry, and which so often makes of practice the relentless murderer of gallant theories. The tragic guilt, which was shared by both sides equally, lay in the fact that they were not aware of this disharmony, and that each side persisted in treating the language of the other as if it were their own. It is because the Young Germans miscalculated the extent of the gulf fixed between the two worlds,

[1] *The Persecution of the Young Germans, Mod. Lang. Review*, January 1924.

one is tempted to add, that they hoped to span it by that curious bridge called 'Tendenzdichtung.' The means were miserably inadequate, the effort remained abortive; it resulted neither in true poetry nor yet in social reform. The gulf was wider than they thought, and like a famous prototype, it proved not averse from human sacrifice.

PART III
HEINE AND SAINT-SIMONISM

CHAPTER V

HEINE AND THE SAINT-SIMONIANS

(a) A CONSPIRACY OF SILENCE

Heine left Germany for Paris in 1831, and it is a well-established fact that he entered almost immediately into personal relations with Enfantin and the Saint-Simonians. The history of these relations, although by no means easy to reconstruct, is of fundamental importance, and also a most absorbingly interesting study.

One aspect of Heine's problematical character, an aspect which adds to its great complexity, is the way in which his judgment, even in literary matters, was swayed by his personal relations, or his personal feelings. That his genius was almost entirely subjective is a commonplace of criticism which needs no further emphasis. His intensely personal attitude towards life, towards people, books, politics and religion was further complicated by an abnormal sensitiveness, which caused him to be up in arms at the slightest alarm, and which developed with failing health and shattered nerves into an irritability of which he himself was painfully conscious. This sensitiveness and irritability were responsible for many actions which would be inexcusable in a person of robuster nerves, and for many a line which his admirers would gladly pass over in silence, but they are necessary to the better understanding of Heine, and cannot be disregarded. He became excessively suspicious in later years, and imagined himself the victim of intrigues and persecutions, some of which were non-existent, but which his stormy and unhappy life gave him but too many reasons to expect. It is a distressing experience to turn over the pages of his letters, to read the story of many fine friendships ruined, and to see frantic suspicion and distrust take the place of the happy confidence of former days. Heine became all too quick to believe evil of his friends, and in many of his quarrels he bears the greater blame, but he was often most cruelly hurt. His nature was an affectionate and grateful one, and his trust, where he placed it, was absolute. But so small a thing could destroy that trust, and then gratitude and affection changed in the twinkling of an eye into the most virulent hatred. At the bottom of it all lay that curiously personal attitude of mind. There is scarcely one detached judgment among all his writings on contemporary persons, literature and events. This does not mean that some of his judgments are not extremely sound, for Heine was possessed to an unusual degree of that rare quality, common sense; many of them are of an intuitive brilliance which borders on the prophetic, but all are coloured by his personal sympathies and antipathies. And since his judgments were so largely the reflection of his personal relations and feelings, and these were subject to change, it is no longer a matter of surprise that he should have contradicted himself not infrequently, and occasionally performed a complete and startling *volte-face*. He underrated his enemies, he overrated his friends; he felt the spell of personality and allowed it to sway his thoughts; so that, to take a typical example, the undying impression made by Napoleon on his boyish fancy, and a personal feeling of loyalty to that memory, struggle in his mind for mastery with a just appreciation of the great evils of the Napoleonic *régime*.

If, then, Heine's judgments were so often at the mercy of the incalculable human factor, it is clear why the problem of his dealings with the Saint-Simonians must precede the study of the influence of their doctrine on his mind. And here we are brought up short by a surprising scarcity of documentary evidence on which to base such an investigation. Heine is the chief conspirator in what appears almost like a conspiracy of silence. There are hardly more than a dozen references to the new church and its members in his works, whilst his letters, adequately edited at last[1], although bringing a good deal that is both new and illuminating, are not by any means a mine of information

---

[1] Cf. F. Hirth, *Heinrich Heines Briefwechsel*, Munich and Berlin, 1914–1920; an excellent edition containing many new letters and all that have been hitherto published, with the exception of those in *Heine-Reliquien*, ed. Heine-Geldern and Karpeles, Berlin, 1911.

on the subject. There are two letters to Michel Chevalier (1855)[1], one to Duveyrier (1835), and none to Emile Pereire, although two at least were written to him. Alfred Pereire, who is in possession of the Pereire Archives, has assured Hirth that there are no letters from Heine to either of the brothers in this collection. Hirth comforts himself with the reflection that any lost letters of Heine's to Paris notabilities consisted probably of unimportant notes, invitations and the like, since all serious discussions would take place in personal interviews. Nevertheless the total absence of any letters to the Saint-Simonians during the critical period 1831–1833 must be regarded as a serious loss. Not only this, but neither in his articles for the *Allgemeine Zeitung*[2], nor in his private correspondence do we find any account of the meetings in the *salle* Taitbout and elsewhere, which Heine attended constantly. Now as the *Allgemeine Zeitung* was interested in the Saint-Simonian church and printed many articles and notices on this subject, it would seem that Heine's reticence needs some special explanation. The question of his private letters is a different one, it raises the point of Heine as a letter-writer; and Hirth's edition of the correspondence provides the material to form a judgment on this subject. The impression left on the mind after reading these letters is that only in the rarest cases were any of them written for pleasure, or in obedience to the inward necessity for confessions and outpourings, which makes Hebbel's letters psychological documents of the first importance. In Heine's voluminous correspondence there are few such letters to be found after his first youth; they cease almost completely on his arrival in Paris. In some letters to Varnhagen von Ense, August Lewald, Madame Jaubert, the Princess Belgiojoso, and Prince Pückler-Muskau we catch a glimpse of the poet Heine; the letters to his mother and his sister show the man his mother and sister knew, shorn of all his stinging sharpness, harmless and simple as a child, deeply affectionate, grateful and considerate; but as he kept the torments of his body hidden from his mother, so too the turnings

[1] I print below a note from Heine to Chevalier from the year 1832, by kind permission of the Administrator of the *Bibliothèque de l'Arsenal*. It is not included in Hirth's edition, and now appears for the first time.

[2] *Französische Zustände*, December 28, 1831–October 10, 1832.

and twistings of his mind. His letters to his wife, written at the
fever heat of a jealous passion, reveal nothing but that passion
itself; and it is not till his last days, in his letters to Camille
Selden, that we get an idea of what a letter-writer Heine might
have been had he ever possessed a completely sympathetic
correspondent. The great body of the correspondence is made up
of business letters addressed chiefly to his publisher Campe, and
which are relieved only by the yet more painful ones dealing with
those intrigues, literary and other, in which Heine again and again
became involved, and the tortuous ramifications of which draw
out their unending length through the second and third volumes
of the correspondence. These are even more distressing than
the business letters because they so often show Heine stooping
to unworthy methods in order to defeat unworthy adversaries;
unable to leave the mud-flinging to his enemies, and presenting
a piteously undignified spectacle to a censorious world. In his
letters to Campe, however, Heine has the *beau rôle*, and Campe
is seen now, in this first complete reproduction of the correspondence, to be the villain of the piece. These letters, as well as
those of intrigue, denunciation, exculpation, explanation and
insinuation were all written under the pressure of immediate
necessity, and a feverish note of haste is common to them all.
Heine seems to have taken up the pen only when he was driven
to do so; the majority of his letters contain excuses for not
writing sooner, or at greater length, the hall-mark of an unwilling
correspondent. It is very disappointing to find no detailed
descriptions of the Saint-Simonian doings here, but the reason
lies in the nature of Heine's correspondence, and it would be
idle to complain. But a certain feeling of injury accompanies
the discovery that Heine's published works contain remarkably
few allusions to the Saint-Simonians. Fate has had her share
in this rather unaccountable phenomenon; for in 1832 Heine
announced to Varnhagen that he was going to write a book on
Saint-Simonism[1]; the scheme was allowed to drop however and
the book was never written. Nevertheless Heine did write a
book which probably contained the history of his relations with
the Saint-Simonian school, but this mysterious book has mys-

[1] Hirth, II, p. 22, delivered in Hamburg on May 22, 1832.

teriously disappeared. I refer to the famous Memoirs of which
only a fragment remains. The vicissitudes of the Memoirs make
a fascinating tale[1], but at this distance of time it is becoming
more and more unlikely that any portion of them will ever be
found; and no one who studies Heine can be indifferent to their
loss, for in these pages he told the story of his own life, and the
truth as he saw it about his contemporaries. We can only
surmise that the Saint-Simonians would play a not insignificant
part in any description of Heine's life, and the following extract
from a letter to Campe shows fairly clearly that he would not
have overlooked them entirely:

Doch habe ich noch einige Briefe, die sie[2] mir über den St Simonismus hierher schrieb, und die das Bedeutendste sind, was je aus
ihrer Feder geflossen. Ich denke für meine Lebensbeschreibung
davon Gebrauch zu machen, wo ich überhaupt dieses merkwürdige
Weib plastisch darstelle[3].

The Memoirs have been destroyed or scattered to the four
winds, and Heine's connection with the new church must be
studied without the brilliant light these pages would probably have shed. It might not have been a becoming light to
the Saint-Simonians, for his attitude towards them changed very
greatly just before his death, and the Memoirs were written in
an extremely polemical spirit, if we are to believe Camille
Selden[4]. But conjectures, if fascinating, are vain; the net result
obtained from a study of Heine's works is the appearance of a
rather puzzling silence on the subject of the Saint-Simonians,
a silence which seems to call for interpretation, whilst lost letters
and an undiscovered manuscript play their baffling part in a
situation full of possibilities but very ill-defined.

For if Heine showed a curious reticence about Enfantin and
his colleagues, we find the same quality even more conspicuously
present in the works of the Saint-Simonians themselves. The

---

[1] Cf. Hirth, i, pp. 45–66; E. Engel, *Heinrich Heines Memoiren*, Hamburg,
1884; E. Elster, *Heinrich Heines Sämtliche Werke*, Leipzig and Vienna,
1890, vii, pp. 453–458; F. Kohn-Abrest, *Les coulisses d'un livre. A propos
des Mémoires de Henri Heine*, Paris, 1884.

[2] Rahel Varnhagen von Ense.

[3] Hirth, ii, p. 161, dated May 3, 1837.

[4] Camille Selden, the *Mouche* of the correspondence, Heine's companion
and friend during the last months of his life.

author of the *Notice Historique* does not mention Heine's name
in any of the long and voluminous reports of public and private
meetings which go largely to fill up the thirteen volumes of the
life of Enfantin. They are compiled from the original documents, and the reader is often struck by the extreme conscien-
tiousness of the editors; for no fact would seem too trivial to be
mentioned, no names too obscure to be transcribed. And yet
Heine's name occurs in all four times only in the *Notice Historique*, and in each case the reference to him is of the slightest[1].
Yet we know from his own casual allusions, as well as from the
testimony of eye-witnesses, that he was a constant attendant
at the open meetings, at the *soirées*, and at the sermons. Although he was not a member in the strict sense of the word,
he seems to have been more intimate with the leaders of the
new church, with Enfantin, Rodrigues, and Michel Chevalier
who indeed remained his friend until death, than most of the
visitors and spectators:

Die St Simonisten bemüheten sich ihn für ihre Interesse zu gewinnen. Man sah ihn in ihren Soireen, die sie in der Rue Taitbout
gaben, wo er sich sehr amüsirte und er hörte gern die Reden, die bei
ihrem sogenannten Gottesdienste gehalten wurden. Olinde Rodrigues
und den Père Enfantin die er persönlich kannte, schätzte er, ohne
sich jedoch ihren Wünschen hinzugeben[2].

Irre ich nicht, so habe ich zur Zeit, als ich im Stillen den Predigten
der Saint-Simonisten mit vielen anderen folgte...irre ich nicht, so
habe ich dazumal aus der Ferne Sie, den berühmten Dichter, vor-
dringen sehen bis in das Sanctuarium....[3]

The silence of the author of the *Notice Historique* is therefore
hard to account for, the more so since Heine was a well-known
figure almost from his first arrival in Paris, and a European

---

[1] (a) *Œuvres de Saint-Simon et d'Enfantin*, VI, p. 108. In a footnote:
'Cette correspondance a été attribuée à Henri Heine'; i.e. an article in the
A.Z., see pp. 60–61.

(b) *Ibid.* x, p. 108. Before reproducing Enfantin's letter to Heine; the
editor is under the impression that it was written in answer to a letter
from the poet. It was an acknowledgment of his book, *De l'Allemagne*,
containing a dedication to Enfantin.

(c) *Ibid.* x, p. 140: 'Mais le jour même j'écrivais ma lettre à Heine....'

(d) *Ibid.* XI, p. 109: 'Duguet m'a violé en imprimant à mon insu ma
lettre à Heine....' The two last references occur in letters from Enfantin.

[2] A. Lewald, *Aquarelle aus dem Leben*, Mannheim, 1836, II, p. 118.

[3] F. Liszt, *Gesammelte Werke*, Leipzig, 1880–1883, II, pp. 200–201, letter
to Heine, dated April 15, 1838.

celebrity by the time Enfantin's life was compiled. It is one of those curious facts which seem to have no imaginable cause behind them.

But if Heine's reticence is interesting, and the silence of the Saint-Simonians inexplicable at most, there is some real irritation to be faced when the French and German memoirs about Heine come to be studied. For none of them give an adequate account of the years 1831–1833; and this, considering the gaps the correspondence shows during this period, is exceedingly disappointing. The French memoirs are for the most part late, and there is a general tendency amongst all those who wrote about the poet to describe his last unhappy, tormented years in great detail, and to omit the first years in Paris almost completely; the later studies, on the other hand, neglect the personal factor in the problem, and have no words to waste on the rather remarkable silence of the chief characters in the tale.

(b) 1831–1833

Heine's first reference to Saint-Simonism is to be found in an interesting letter first published by Hirth in 1914. It is dated from Hamburg on February 10, 1831, and addressed to a certain Hartwig Hesse, a Hamburg philanthropist, and a patron of men of letters and science. It opens with a quotation from the first year of the *Exposition de la doctrine de Saint-Simon*, published, it will be remembered, in 1830. It is unlikely that he also possessed a copy of the second year of the *Exposition*, considering that it did not appear until the end of 1830, and that the methods of transport were dilatory and slow in those days; but the perusal of the first volume had the effect of firing his imagination and enlisting his sympathies. The extract which Heine thought suitable to communicate to Hartwig Hesse was an eloquent apology for the begging letters which Saint-Simon constantly addressed to the great men of his day; and it proved to be the preface to a graceful begging letter from Heine to his correspondent. This appeal was made in the interests of his 'new gospel,' and was inspired by a self-confidence akin, so he maintained, to religious pride:

...die Zukunft mag Ihnen beweisen, dass letzterer Ausdruck[1] mein
tiefster Ernst ist, die Zukunft wird Ihnen zeigen, wie gross die
Interessen waren, die mich bewegen, Sie jetzt zur schleunigsten
Hülfleistung aufzufordern....[2]

This letter has some interesting points. In the first place it is
written in a mood of uncritical and generous enthusiasm for the
new doctrine of which we shall never again be witness. Secondly
it seems more than probable from the context that the great
interests which constrained him to apply to Hesse for money
were none other than the interests of his new gospel, and that
therefore amongst the many motives which induced Heine to
leave Germany for Paris the lure of the Saint-Simonian religion
played an important part. When compared with the following
extract from a letter to Varnhagen, this probability becomes a
certainty:

...und träume jede Nacht, ich packe meinen Koffer und reise nach
Paris, um frische Luft zu schöpfen, ganz den heiligen Gefühlen meiner
neuen Religion mich hinzugeben, und vielleicht als Priester derselben
die letzten Weihen zu empfangen[3].

Heine's voluntary exile from Germany in his early manhood
altered the whole trend of his career; his literary projects, his
philosophy of life, his mode of living, his very style were all
profoundly modified by his sojourn in the French capital, which
continued with occasional interruptions until the day of his
death. Saint-Simonism, it would appear, was one of the forces
which drew him away from his native land, and therefore even
indirectly it assumed the proportion of destiny shaping his
future.

'Ich war noch keine 24 Stunden in Paris, als ich schon mitten
unter den Saint-Simonisten sass,'[4] Heine declared to Karl Grün
in 1845; he had doubtless little to complain of in his reception.
The Saint-Simonians were anxious for proselytes, and Enfantin
was not the man to disdain enthusiasm and eagerness. Nor
were the Saint-Simonians unaware of Heine's importance and
true to their creed that the artists should play the *rôle* of priests
and teachers in the hierarchy, they early began to angle for the

[1] 'Neues Evangelium.' [2] Hirth, I, p. 640.
[3] Hirth, I, p. 642, dated April 1, 1831.
[4] Karl Grün, *Die soziale Bewegung in Frankreich und Belgien*, Darm-
stadt, 1845, p. 80.

support of the brilliant and receptive poet. In the *Globe* of December 5, 1831, there is an anonymous review with long extracts translated into French from the *Vorrede zu Kahldorf über den Adel*; and on January 2, 1832, another on the *Gemäldeausstellung in Paris*; neither of these works had then been translated into French. In each case the language is most flattering and the proselytising note is clearly heard:

Si, comme nous le croyons, le temps est proche où l'Allemagne et la France se donneront la main pour réaliser la *sainte-alliance des peuples*, une belle mission est réservée à M. Heine dans ce grand œuvre[1].

And more insistently:

Il existe des hommes qui, par un heureux privilège, tiennent à la fois des artistes et des penseurs; en même temps qu'ils savent comprendre une idée progressive, ils possèdent le don de la vivifier en l'exprimant comme ils la sentent, avec enthousiasme, avec poésie. De tels hommes sont faits pour apprécier les premiers toute la grandeur des vues Saint-Simoniennes sur l'avenir de l'art. C'est avec une vive satisfaction que nous venons aujourd'hui enregistrer un de ces cas vraiment exceptionnel. L'écrivain qui nous a si bien compris est un Allemand; son nom est connu de nos lecteurs: c'est M. Heine[2].

To these amiable insinuations, Heine made no response in print and the letters which have been preserved are equally uncommunicative. Yet the *Globe* was almost the first French newspaper to acclaim Heine in Paris[3]. It is possible that his critical faculty had already been aroused.

Meanwhile the year 1831 had been a shattering and eventful one for the Saint-Simonians, for they had just come through the great crisis of the schism with Bazard on the question of divorce, and had lost some of their ablest members, amongst them Leroux, and Carnot, both of whom were friends of Heine's. One of the stormy meetings was open to the public[4], and

---

[1] *Globe*, December 25, 1831. Heine accepted this mission, but without acknowledgment to the Saint-Simonians; cf. Elster, v, pp. 11–12.

[2] *Globe*, January 2, 1832. The *Gemäldeausstellung in Paris* shows many traces of Saint-Simonian influence.

[3] The *Revue des deux Mondes* published the first article on Heine on June 1, 1832. Before that date only the *Nouvelle revue germanique* had mentioned his name. Heine refers to a garbled translation of *Französische Zustände* in the *Tribune des Mouvements*, Hirth, II, p. 11.

[4] November 27, 1831.

Béranger (not yet a disciple) was present at it; also the admiring words of Felix R — (a stranger) were quoted, but of Heine never a word; and no word from him[1]. It was reported in the *Globe* of November 28, 1831, so that if Heine were not present at it, he would almost certainly have read about it; yet the whole question of the schism was passed over by him in the most resolute silence. It is perhaps not too fanciful to imagine that he saw that common sense at least was on Bazard's side, but that his sympathies were with Enfantin and his religious doctrines, and that a personal sense of loyalty kept him dumb. It is difficult to believe that he would not have given voice to his approval of Enfantin's views, had he really approved of them[2].

There followed the government intervention which drew a comment from Heine; for on January 25, 1832, he wrote to Cotta:

Ich war just im Saal der St Simonisten, als der königl. Prokurator ihn schliessen liess, und kam noch zeitig zu Dondorf, [*sic*] der solches in der Allg. anzeigt. Herr v. Kersdorf aus München ist hier und wüthet gegen seine Tochter, welche St Simonistin werden will oder schon ist[3].

That Heine took the part of the Saint-Simonians against the government on this occasion is proved by the sympathetic tone of Donndorf's communication to the *Allgemeine Zeitung* which was inspired by him; but nothing could be more indifferent and detached than the lines quoted above. And yet he was so far from being indifferent to the non-delivery of the *Globe* that he called specially on Chevalier to remind him that he wished it to be continued:

Je suis venu pour demander votre pardon que j'ai manqué au rendezvous du mercredi et puis je voudrais vous ressouvenir que vous m'avez promis la continuation du Globe qu'on ne m'apporte plus depuis 14 jours. Votre dévoué Heine[4].

[1] There is a gap in his correspondence here, from October 31, 1831, to January 20, 1832.

[2] Heine seems to have had only the slightest acquaintance with Bazard. He never mentions him either in his letters or in his works. There was probably nothing in Bazard's personality which appealed to Heine's temperament.

[3] Hirth, II, p. 13. The incident occurred on January 22, 1832.

[4] *Fonds Enfantin, Bibliothèque de l'Arsenal*, written in 1832.

Whether he always read it with respect is another question. There is one allusion in *Französische Zustände* which shows that his sense of humour was not asleep, however carefully it might be controlled:

Die Saint-Simonisten rechnen zu den Vorzügen ihrer Religion, dass kein Saint-Simonist an der herrschenden Krankheit sterben könne; denn da der Fortschritt ein Naturgesetz sei und der sociale Fortschritt im Saint-Simonismus liege, so dürfe, so lange die Zahl seiner Apostel noch unzureichend ist, keiner von denselben sterben[1].

This is the first hint of an ironical attitude towards the members of the new church, and although the irony is gentle, the statement consists of one of those ingenious perversions of fact in which Heine was a past master. The Saint-Simonians did consider that progress was a law of nature, and that social progress was bound up in Saint-Simonism; they had also made the following statement in an article in the *Globe* entitled: 'Fin du choléra par un coup d'état':

Il n'est qu'une manière d'écarter le choléra, c'est d'agir sur le moral des masses. Toute personne dont la situation morale est satisfaisante n'a rien à craindre du fléau. C'est ainsi que nous, qui avons une foi et qui contemplons l'avenir d'un œil calme, nous ne pouvons en être atteints[2].

Heine altered this statement slightly, and something latently childish in it became positively absurd. It is characteristic of his later attitude towards the school that he should attack them where they were strongest. These articles on the cholera were sensible and far-seeing and written on sound hygienic principles. The plan of rendering Paris more sanitary by means of the better distribution of water was partially realised by Haussmann during the Second Empire. But Heine had no sympathy with the practical ideals and reforms of the new church; and the foregoing extract is typical of the way he was to belittle their great practical achievements.

On April 12, 1832, took place the sensational retreat of the apostles to monastic seclusion at Ménilmontant, and a month later, on May 22, 1832, in a letter to Varnhagen von Ense, we

---

[1] Elster, v, p. 103, dated April 19, 1832. I use Elster's edition of Heine's works for reference, whilst retaining the original spelling.

[2] *Globe*, April 11, 1832, written by M. Chevalier.

get the first really satisfactory revelation of Heine's attitude of mind towards the whole question:

Ich beschäftige mich jetzt viel mit der französischen Revoluzions-geschichte und dem Saintsimonismus. Ueber beide werde ich Bücher schreiben. Ich muss aber noch viel studieren. Habe jedoch im letzten Jahre durch die Anschauung des Partheytreibens und der saintsimo-nistischen Erscheinungen sehr vieles verstehen gelernt: z. B. den 'Moniteur' von 1793 und die Bibel....Was Sie mir in Betreff des St Simonismus schreiben[1] ist ganz meine Ansicht. Michel Chevallier[2] ist mein sehr lieber Freund, einer der edelsten Menschen, die ich kenne. Dass sich die St Simonisten zurückgezogen, ist vielleicht der Doktrin selbst sehr nützlich; sie kommt in klügere Hände. Besonders der politische Theil, die Eigenthumslehre, wird besser verarbeitet werden. Was mich betrifft, ich interessire mich eigentlich nur für die reli-giösen Ideen, die nur ausgesprochen zu werden brauchten, um früh oder spät ins Leben zu treten. Deutschland wird am kräftigsten für seinen Spiritualismus kämpfen; mais l'avenir est à nous[3].

The importance of this letter hardly needs emphasis. Heine was sufficiently interested in the religious doctrines of Saint-Simonism to contemplate writing a book on the subject; but the fate of the apostles at Ménilmontant left him completely cold; far from understanding the policy which dictated this movement, he looked upon it rather as a final retirement and prophesied that the doctrine would fall into wiser hands. The excesses of Enfantin and his followers were thus slightly touched upon in that cool, dry little sentence; but his affection for Michel Chevalier, Enfantin's Benjamin, and amongst the forty apostles now awaiting the taking of vows, remained as warm as before.

The 'prise d'habit' took place on June 6, 1832, but Heine appeared far too much occupied in writing up the report of the battle raging in Paris on the occasion of the funeral of General Lamarque to spare a thought for his friends now dressed in the famous costume, and helping each other to button the symbolic waistcoat; a later statement would seem to prove however that

[1] I have not been able to trace this letter in Varnhagen's published correspondence.

[2] He appears to have known the Varnhagens, for in a later letter he sends them greetings; cf. Hirth, II, p. 40.

[3] Hirth, II, p. 22.

he was not as unaware of their activities as his silence would seem to suggest:

Es war doch etwas Grosses [he said to Grün in 1845]; unten in den Strassen wurde der verzweiflungsvolle Kampf der Republikaner gekämpft, während oben in stiller Sammlung bereits der neue Glaube gepredigt wurde[1].

Whether or not he were amongst the crowd who flocked to the 'Ouverture des travaux du temple' and similar functions, we have no means of knowing. He was not a witness of their thwarted attempt to figure at Bazard's funeral, nor was he present at their trial[2]; he was in Normandy at the time so that he missed one of the most curious acts of the drama. But he paid the sect a great compliment in the article he wrote from Dieppe on the death of the Duke of Reichstadt, by declaring that Napoleon had been in a certain sense a Saint-Simonian emperor; for he had favoured government by capacity and had aimed at the physical and moral well-being of the more numerous and poorer classes; whilst his army had been a hierarchy where rank could be obtained only by personal merit and capacity[3].

These sparse gleanings are all that can be gathered from the year 1832, and the result is a negative one; the experiment of the apostles at Ménilmontant, the trial and condemnation of Enfantin, Duveyrier and Chevalier, the subsequent dispersal of the apostles, and the imprisonment of the leaders were passed over in the same non-committal silence as the schism of the year 1831.

This silence is broken to very little effect in *Zur Geschichte der neueren schönen Literatur in Deutschland*, 1833, and in *Zur Geschichte der Religion und Philosophie in Deutschland*, 1835. Both these works are instinct with the criticism of Christianity and the doctrine of the 'rehabilitation of the flesh' as expounded by Bazard and Enfantin, but the allusions to the Saint-Simonian school and its members are short and unilluminating. There is

---

[1] K. Grün, *op. cit.* p. 118.

[2] W. Stigand in *Life, Works, and Opinions of Heinrich Heine*, London. 1875, II, p. 136, states that Heine was present on this occasion; he quotes no authority, and I imagine that he mistook the trial for the descent of the government on the *salle* Taitbout. There are many inaccuracies in his chapter on the history of the Saint-Simonians.

[3] Elster, v, p. 194, dated August 20, 1832.

a complimentary reference to the Saint-Simonian conception of pantheism in both books[1], and he adds, after the second reference, that the school had been working on unfavourable soil, and that the surrounding materialism had crushed them, at least for a time. In Germany they had been better understood[2]. He mentions E. Rodrigues' translation of Lessing's fragment *Ueber die Erziehung des Menschengeschlechts*[3], and quotes a sentence from one of Barrault's sermons[4]; he also gave a gently mocking account of an incident which occurred on January 15, 1832, and which was reported in the *Globe* of January 16, 1832:

> Wenigstens beim Saint-Simonismus, welcher die neueste Religion, ist gar kein Wunder vorgefallen, ausgenommen etwa, dass eine alte Schneiderrechnung, die Saint-Simon auf Erden schuldig geblieben, zehn Jahr' nach seinem Tode von seinen Schülern bar bezahlt worden ist[5]. Noch sehe ich, wie der vortreffliche Père Olinde in der Salle Taitbout begeistrungsvoll sich erhebt und der erstaunten Gemeinde die quittierte Schneiderrechnung vorhält. Junge Epiciers stutzen ob solchem übernatürlichen Zeugnis. Die Schneider aber fingen schon an zu glauben![6]

This ironical tone in a book written under the influence of Saint-Simonian theories suggests that Heine was but little edified by the practice of the school, and reserved his admiration for a certain aspect of the doctrine. More than a year after the last letter to Varnhagen, there is another allusion to the fortunes of the school in a letter to the same correspondent:

> Poley sitzt hier wegen Schulden in St Pelagie.—Mit Michel Chevalier, der Sie tief sinnigst grüssen lässt, habe ich Stundenlange Berathungen über Religion.—In drey Wochen reise ich ins Bad.—Nächstes Jahr reise ich vielleicht nach dem Orient. Mich befriedigen nicht die Obelisken, die man mir nach Paris bringt[7].

The thought-associations in this letter are amusingly clear. Sainte-Pélagie at once suggests Michel Chevalier to Heine's mind; for Chevalier was still in prison at this date, although he

---

[1] Elster, v, p. 253, *Die Romantische Schule*; IV, p. 224, *Zur Geschichte der Religion und Philosophie in Deutschland.*

[2] *Ibid.* IV, p. 224.   [3] *Ibid.* v, p. 229.

[4] *Ibid.* v, p. 300: 'Mit Recht sagte einst Barrault: "Die Jesuiten konnten die Erde nicht zum Himmel erheben, und sie zogen den Himmel herab zur Erde."'

[5] The amount of the bill was 1460 francs.

[6] Elster, IV, pp. 192–193.

[7] Hirth, II, p. 40, dated July 16, 1833.

and Enfantin were to be released on August 1. Since April 4, 1833, when Chevalier and Enfantin had once more appeared before the court of assizes (Enfantin in a velvet cloak trimmed with ermine, and answering and instructing his judge in *vers libres*)[1], there had been a coldness between the two prisoners, a coldness due it seems to Chevalier rather than to Enfantin. Heine's long conversations on religious subjects with Michel must therefore have been peculiarly interesting, since Chevalier was in a condition of apostasy at the time. But Heine was still not uninfluenced by the Saint-Simonians, as is shown by his desire to go to the East, whither all those who had not forsworn the doctrines were then drifting[2]; but he breathed no word of the two great missions which drew them thither. He ignored the mystic mother and the Suez Canal as utterly as the tragi-comedy of Bazard's schism and the farce of Ménil-montant. This mystifying and obstinate silence on all the burning questions of the strange new church has a challenging quality that seems to demand a solution, or at least an explana-tion; and this is perhaps the most suitable point to attempt to define the problem, since we have come nearly to the end of the year 1833, that is to say to an end of the extravagances of the Saint-Simonian church.

As one turns over the pages of the *Notice Historique* and the *Globe* and reads the *verbatim* accounts of meetings in the *salle* Taitbout, of *Réunions* and *Communions Générales de la Famille Saint-Simonienne*, of the sermons, of the private and public meetings during the 'affaire Bazard,' of the ceremonies during the Ménilmontant retreat, of the trials in the courts of justice, in all of which one figure maintains an awe-inspiring predomin-ance, it is impossible not to remember that Heine was there at the time.

Heine was there, not only in Paris, but actually an attendant at the meetings, a personal acquaintance of Enfantin and a

---

[1] There is nothing to show whether Heine was at this second trial or not. He wrote his first letter to Laube from Paris on April 8, 1833, in which there is no reference to Saint-Simonism; but only a part of the letter has been preserved; cf. Hirth, II, pp. 34–35.

[2] Cf. also Hirth, II, p. 45, a playful threat to his mother, that he would be off to Egypt if she insisted on coming to see him.

friend of Chevalier; so that it is not too rash to assume that what he did not see himself, and what was not published in the *Globe*, would reach him by private channels. But even assuming that he knew no more than the general public who flocked to the *salle* Taitbout, there is sufficient food for thought.

He was present at many a meeting presided over by the divine couple Bazard-Enfantin, and attended by a crowd of perfervid adorers. He witnessed the adoration setting in a steady stream towards Enfantin, and its remarkable effect on the prophet's mind. He attended Barrault's eloquent and very emotional sermons; and though he was doubtless not privy to the murmurings and mutterings swelling to recriminations and ravings which preceded Bazard's secession on the question of divorce, yet it is at least extremely likely that he was present on November 27, 1831, when Reynaud in his capacity of Protestant brought a wasp's nest of argument round Enfantin's ears, and Baud delivered his tribute to the father's physical and moral beauty, whilst Rodrigues proclaimed him to be the most moral man of the age, a declaration which he was shortly to regret.

He saw all this and maintained his silence. He must have seen the empty chair by Enfantin's side, an outward and visible symbol of the appeal to woman. He witnessed the quest for the 'femme libre' as it became a more and more urgent one, ending in Barrault's almost incredible journey to Constantinople, and in all the hysterical excitement of the 'year of the mother.' Heine was in Paris on the occasion of the funeral of Enfantin's mother, and of the sensational retreat to Ménilmontant; he may have been a spectator of the fantastic ceremonies which brightened the apostles' lives during this retreat, he will certainly have heard all about them. In a word he was in a privileged position to observe Enfantin and all his works; and yet seeing he remained silent and did not speak his thoughts.

(c) HEINE AND ENFANTIN

The friendship between Enfantin and Heine is perhaps the strangest feature of this remarkable story, and the most difficult to reconstruct. According to the testimony of contemporaries, they were friends, but Enfantin never dwelt on his feelings for the poet; and although Heine made some sort of statement at the end of his life, it was in circumstances which make his confession, if not entirely worthless, at least rather unreliable. It does not appear that they were ever really intimate, but the fact that there should have been a friendly understanding between two natures so fundamentally different is a tribute to Enfantin's vaunted power of being all things to all men.

It is not difficult to see why he should have liked and admired the brilliant poet all afire with the new gospel; but that Heine, whose sense of humour was almost too keen, should have reciprocated the liking and admiration proves that Enfantin's charm must have been really compelling, and that his magnetic power was no vain boast. There is no doubt however that Heine maintained his independence of judgment towards this portentous figure; and was never among those who worshipped at that bizarre shrine. Yet he seems to have felt that he owed him some allegiance, for he dedicated *De l'Allemagne*[1] to Enfantin in 1835. The dedicatory epistle is couched in respectful but sober and formal terms, and runs as follows:

A PROSPER ENFANTIN

EN EGYPTE,

Vous avez désiré connaître la marche des idées en Allemagne, dans ces derniers temps, et les rapports qui rattachent le mouvement intellectuel de ce pays à la synthèse de la doctrine.

Je vous remercie de l'honneur que vous m'avez fait en me demandant de vous édifier sur ce sujet, et je suis heureux de trouver cette occasion de communier avec vous à travers l'espace.

Permettez-moi de vous offrir ce livre; je voudrais croire qu'il pourra répondre au besoin de votre pensée. Quoi qu'il en puisse être, je vous prie de vouloir bien l'accepter comme un témoignage de sympathie respectueuse.

HENRI HEINE[2].

The book with the dedication reached Enfantin in Egypt at the moment when Hoart, one of the most ardent and indefatigable apostles, was lying on his death-bed, and when Enfantin was despairing of the success of the venture which had already

---

[1] This edition of *De l'Allemagne* contained: *Romantische Schule*, *Zur Geschichte der Religion und Philosophie in Deutschland* and the first part of *Elementargeister*.

[2] Elster, IV, p. 568.

cost the Saint-Simonians so dear. There is reason to suppose that this tribute from the German poet did something towards heartening the disconsolate prophet, and helped him towards the conception of the new *rôle* he felt himself called upon to play in the 'apostolat royal':

> Lorsque notre brave Hoart mourait dans nos bras...Bruneau me dit à l'instant: *l'apostolat est fini*, et il avait à moitié raison, il l'aurait eu tout à fait s'il avait dit: notre apostolat *populaire*, notre appel au peuple est fini; mais le jour même j'ecrivais ma lettre à Heine; ce même jour, je le sentais, *l'apostolat royal*, *l'appel aux grands, aux princes du monde, commençait*[1].

It is something to learn that Enfantin recognised in Heine one of the princes of the world, and that he hoped to use him as his mouthpiece in Germany; but the letter adds little to our scanty knowledge of the personal relationship between these two remarkable men. It is much warmer in tone than Heine's dedication; but after a few rather touching expressions of thanks for this public testimony of sympathy at a time when he was still pursued 'par le retentissement des injures que le monde européen m'a prodiguées,'[2] he hastens to a criticism of Heine's book from the Saint-Simonian standpoint, and to rather incoherent if lofty instructions on the direction his next work should take. He further begged Heine almost passionately to abstain from profane pleasantries on religious subjects, and from mocking at his fellow-men:

> Croyez-en, mon cher monsieur Heine, un homme qui a reçu de tous injures et mépris, pour ses travaux, pour sa vie, et qui attend toutefois avec calme la justice du monde; croyez-moi, vous qui êtes un des premiers organes de cette justice, et qui êtes venu guérir une des innombrables blessures de mon cœur; croyez-moi, rien de plus sacré pour l'homme que l'homme lui-même; or, sur les choses sacrées, abstenons-nous de la plaisanterie profane.
>
> L'homme qui met au pilori voltairien son semblable remplit les fonctions de bourreau, non d'enseigneur, de prêtre, de père de l'humanité....[3]

---

[1] *Œuvres de Saint-Simon et d'Enfantin*, x, pp. 139–140.

[2] *Ibid.* x, p. 108, dated October 11, 1835.

[3] *Ibid.* x, p. 129; this letter is reproduced in full in the *Notice Historique*, x, pp. 108–136; and a German translation is given by Strodtmann in his life of Heine.

We can imagine the wry smile with which Heine will have read this serious moral snub, it reflects the fatuousness of the prophet who would prevent the wayward poet from indulging his wit.

'A travers l'espace, je vous serre bien affectueusement la main'; these are the parting words of this incoherent and wordy epistle, weakened however by a postscript in praise of the *Préface* to the French edition of the *Reisebilder*[1].

Enfantin's solemn epistle and grandiloquent instructions seem to have caused Heine a certain amount of satisfaction and it is clear from the following extract that he was inclined to regard the mission deputed to him seriously:

> Wer das Losungswort der Zukunft kennt [he wrote to Laube], gegen den vermögen die Schächer der Gegenwart sehr wenig. Ich weiss, wer ich bin. Jüngsthin hat einer meiner saint-simonistischen Freunde ein Wort gesagt, welches mich lachen machte, aber doch sehr ernsthaften Sinn hatte, er sagte, ich sei der erste Kirchenvater der Deutschen.
>
> Dieser Kirchenvater hat in diesem Augenblick sehr viele Dinge um die Ohren, die ihn in Frankreich sehr andrängend beschäftigen und es ihm unmöglich machen, in Deutschland das neue Evangelium zu vertreten. Wird die Noth gross, so werde ich doch ins Geschirr gehen[2].

And he wrote to Campe making arrangements for the publication of Enfantin's letter:

> Ich schicke Ihnen diese Tage auch Ex. des Briefes von Enfantin, und wünsche, dass Sie denselben so verbreiten, dass sie im Publikum etwas Aufsehen erregen[3].

The flattery of Enfantin's high opinion was not without its effect; but it was a bold step to have the letter published at a time when the government prohibition of the works of the Young Germans was already public property; for the prohibition was definitely aimed at those tendencies in their writings

---

[1] Cf. Elster, III, pp. 508–509; this French preface praising the phrase 'l'exploitation de l'homme par l'homme,' 'que nous devons ainsi que beaucoup d'excellentes choses, aux Saint-Simoniens,' was certainly well calculated to commend itself to Enfantin.

[2] Hirth, II, p. 87, dated November 23, 1835; although Enfantin does not actually call Heine the first father of the new church in Germany, he certainly delegates to him the duties of such an office; it is also possible however that the epithet was bestowed on him by another Saint-Simonian.

[3] Hirth, II, p. 99, postmark January 30, 1836.

which were identical with the Saint-Simonian ideals[1]. At a very critical moment therefore Heine, far from denying Enfantin, made it clear that he gloried in the mission with which the latter had entrusted him. It seems rather inexplicable that the relationship between them, now at its closest and most interesting, should have broken off abruptly at this point; but the correspondence in which Enfantin had seen such possibilities was not continued, and we hear no more about the supreme father from Heine for many years.

With the exception of a note to Duveyrier in which he addressed him as 'poète de Dieu,' and which shows that there had been some talk of dramatising the Gumpelino scenes in the *Reisebilder*[2], there are only two more references to the Saint-Simonians to be considered during the period 1831–1835; and both of them are denials that Heine was a member of this sect. The first occurs in the preface to *Zur Geschichte der neueren schönen Literatur in Deutschland*, where he justified his use of those terms defining the nature of God with which the French had already become familiar owing to the apostolic zeal of the Saint-Simonians, and which he was retaining in the German version because they expressed his meaning clearly:

> Junker und Pfaffen...mögen immerhin jene Ausdrücke missbrauchen, um mich mit einigem Schein des Materialismus oder gar des Atheismus zu beschuldigen; Sie mögen mich immerhin zum Juden machen oder zum Saint-Simonisten...keine feigen Rücksichten sollen mich jedoch verleiten, meine Ansicht von den göttlichen Dingen mit den gebräuchlichen zweideutigen Worten zu verschleyern[3].

This protest was repeated more emphatically in the sketch of his life which he wrote for Philarète Chasles on January 11, 1835, and which appeared in the *Revue de Paris* in February of the same year:

> Des compatriots mal instruits ou malveillants ont depuis longtemps répandu la nouvelle que j'ai endossé la casaque saint-simo-

---

[1] Cf. *The Persecution of the Young Germans*, Mod. Lang. Review, January 1924.

[2] Hirth, ii, pp. 77–78, dated July 6, 1835; Heine concludes with a request to Duveyrier to send on the *Reisebilder* to Lerminier, also a former Saint-Simonian.

[3] Elster, v, pp. 527–528, dated April 2, 1833.

nienne; d'autres me gratifient du judaïsme. Je regrette de n'être pas toujours en état de récompenser de tels services[1].

In so slight a sketch this very determined and public denial is significant, as is also the fact that in both these protests Heine bracketed Judaism and Saint-Simonism together as equally damaging terms of reproach. He had been baptised in 1825 for convenience rather than from conviction; but at this time he was no more a Jew than a Christian, and since the Platen episode he had always considered the term Jew applied to him by his enemies as the insult it was intended to be. By placing Saint-Simonism in the same category he threw a revealing light on his opinion of the sect as a whole. But most significant of all is the fact that this protest appeared after the publication of 'De l'Allemagne depuis Luther'[2] in the *Revue des deux Mondes* (March 1, November 15 and December 15, 1834), and that it preceded the appearance of the book *De l'Allemagne*, with its dedication, by a few months. The two books, therefore, which show the clearest traces of Saint-Simonian influence, *Zur Geschichte der neueren schönen Literatur in Deutschland*, and *Zur Geschichte der Religion und Philosophie in Deutschland*, were both accompanied by a definite denial that Heine was a member of that church.

He had set off for Paris already an enthusiastic convert to the new religion and dreaming of a future priesthood; but there is no trace of this uncritical enthusiasm after his arrival in Paris. During the years 1831–1835 his references to the Saint-Simonians were aloof and detached in tone; he reserved his appreciation for certain points of their doctrine, and permitted himself an occasional jest at their expense. In an expansive letter to Varnhagen he drew a very decided line between the doctrine and its exponents, expressing a hope that the doctrine might fall into wiser hands. He had no opinion to offer on the differences between Bazard and Enfantin, nor did he come forward openly to champion the Saint-Simonians during the government persecutions. Their later excesses he passed over in silence, and his dedication of *De l'Allemagne* came at a time when they were

[1] Elster, VII, p. 300.
[2] I.e. *Zur Geschichte der Religion und Philosophie in Deutschland*.

already dispersed and sinking into obscurity. But during these years he was engaged in writing two books, the whole conception and treatment of which were profoundly influenced by the religious doctrine of the new church, of which however he declared that he was not a member. And yet in 1835 he seemed for a moment willing to undertake the part of an apostle of Saint-Simonism in Germany. There are many inconsistencies here; but the most immediate problem is Heine's baffling silence on the subject of Enfantin and the Saint-Simonian manifestations. During the whole of his life he spared neither praise for his friends nor blame for his enemies, and it seems that he must have had a strong reason for his reticence during these years on a subject which interested him deeply. If he did not praise the Saint-Simonians and champion them, then he cannot entirely have approved of them; and since, on the other hand, his criticisms are gentle and restrained, it is possible at least that a sense of gratitude and loyalty kept him silent.

The Saint-Simonians had received Heine with open arms; some of them were his personal friends, and his relations with Enfantin were friendly ones. And it is safe to assume that in an atmosphere so saturated with love and trust as were the Saint-Simonian reunions, nothing would be said or done to wound the poet's sensibilities. More than this the artist within him perceived the poetry in the conception of the 'emancipation of the flesh'; this catch-word became an open-sesame for Heine, disclosing riches, beauties and wonders beyond the dreams of the *Arabian Nights*. I think this debt was present in his mind during the ensuing years, for if he never forgot an injury, he was also slow to forget a benefit; and the silent acknowledgment he tendered to the school was perhaps the most impressive tribute this wayward genius was ever known to bestow.

For it is impossible to deny that the situation during the years 1831–1833 was big with absurdities, and that Enfantin was a ridiculous figure to the cold eye of reason, as he solemnly presided over religious rites, over balls, and funerals, or appeared in fancy dress in courts of justice; it must be granted that his claims were preposterous, couched in bombastic language, and accepted with an exaltation that bordered on madness; whilst the search for the mystic mother was full of possibilities for a satirist. Yet in the general chorus of mockery and ridicule that followed on these various antics, Heine's voice, the voice of the greatest wit of the age, is strangely silent. And yet his wit[1] had for its basis that sound common sense which he inherited from his mother, and which made him so merciless a mocker of those manifestations of his day which threatened to cross the frontier dividing what is natural, sane and normal from the abnormal, the unnatural and the unbalanced. But it must be remembered as well that nearly all his wittiest pages were written under the stimulus of anger; and that it was generally in response to some personal attack that he girt his loins for the fray, except in the cause of freedom. Then indeed his brilliant wit was brought into the service of a principle to which he remained true throughout his life. But the Saint-Simonians he considered were on the side of freedom, and here was one reason why he should respect them[2]. Further, he had no quarrel with them personally, and so an important motive for satire was lacking; lastly he had a double reason for gratitude towards them, as a man and as an artist, and he let them go free. It would be impossible to believe that he was blind to all that was ridiculous in their behaviour, knowing that he was Heine, and we have evidence that he was not so blind:

Wie viel hat Gott schon gethan, um das Weltübel zu heilen! Zu Mosis Zeit that er Wunder über Wunder, später in der Gestalt Christi liess er sich sogar geisseln und kreuzigen, endlich in der Gestalt Enfantin's that er das Ungeheuerste, um die Welt zu retten: er machte sich lächerlich—aber vergebens! Am Ende erfasst ihn vielleicht der Wahnsinn der Verzweiflung, und er zerschellt sein Haupt an der Welt, und er und die Welt zertrümmern[3].

But he let them go free, thus showing the benevolent side of that personal attitude towards life which often led him along such doubtful paths, and whose terrible malevolence threatens balefully in the sinister warning:

---

[1] Most aptly described in his own admirable definition of *Ideenwitz*: 'Eine wilde Ehe zwischen Scherz und Weisheit'; Elster, VII, p. 248.
[2] 'Le parti le plus avancé de l'émancipation humaine,' Elster, IV, p. 569.
[3] Elster, VII, p. 408.

Beleid'ge lebendige Dichter nicht,
Sie haben Flammen und Waffen,
Die furchtbarer sind als Jovis Blitz,
Den ja der Poet erschaffen.

   *   *   *   *

Kennst du die Hölle des Dante nicht,
Die schrecklichen Terzetten?
Wen da der Dichter hineingesperrt,
Den kann kein Gott mehr retten[1].

If anything, Heine overrated the annihilating power of his pen, and the scruples which this vanity engendered may have played their part in his gentle treatment of the Saint-Simonians. His satire, though often mischievous in the worst sense, unscrupulous, wanton and cruel, was never, if we care to adopt Heine's point of view, unprovoked. And so we may imagine him watching Enfantin and his disciples with impish delight, whilst his sensitive lips began to twitch with the curious daemonic smile which so impressed his contemporaries. But the smile was repressed, and the imps were banished from his eyes when the pen was in his hand. His ideals were too nearly akin to theirs, he was too much involved with them, he owed them too much. This silence must have cost Heine some sacrifice, and posterity is the poorer for his restraint; but the gain is greater than the loss; for it is a striking proof of the fact that the poet who could be so bitter and unrelenting an enemy was also a very generous friend.

So furchtbar treu er in Feindschaft war, so liebenswürdig treu war er in Freundschaft[2].

(d) THE MIDDLE YEARS

The last public notice of Heine's during the period 1831–1835 on the subject of Saint-Simonism, was his protest against being considered a Saint-Simonian[3]. His last private communication was a letter to Campe requesting him to print copies of Enfantin's missive in Germany, and to distribute them in a manner to

---

[1] Elster, II, p. 494.

[2] G. Karpeles, *Heinrich Laube über Heinrich Heine, Deutsche Rundschau*, Berlin, 1887. The most witty, and at the same time the most unpardonable satire Heine ever wrote, the attack on Platen in the *Bäder von Lucca*, was written rather in defence of Immermann than in his own.

[3] January 11, 1835.

attract some attention[1]. After this there fell a silence of over four years, except for a passage on the Saint-Simonian theory of art, in which he advocated art for art's sake in opposition to Enfantin's view that the artist should be the priest of the community[2].

In this passage he called the Saint-Simonian church 'the invisible church which is everywhere and nowhere,' and indeed by this time the school had completely dispersed and had disintegrated into a number of private individuals who were for the most part putting the industrial principles of their religion into practice.

During the period 1836–1844 Heine was involved in the quarrel with the *Schwäbische Dichterschule*, which resulted in his *Schwabenspiegel*; in recriminations against Gutzkow, Wihl and Campe, which resulted in *Schriftstellernöthen*, and in answering as best he might the general chorus of disapproval and hatred which greeted his book on Börne. His insinuations on the subject of the Börne-Strauss *ménage* led to a duel between Heine and Strauss in September 1841, and before it took place the poet made Mathilde his lawful wife. Meanwhile the never-ending struggle with Campe on the question of fees became more bitter than before, and his cousin Karl Heine began to make mischief between the poet and his rich uncle Salomon, Karl's father. Also Heine's eyes were beginning to cause him considerable anxiety. Nearly all the letters of this period were written in self-defence of one kind or another, and in no way reflect his life in Paris, since all his troubles and all his enemies came to him from beyond the Rhine. It is not surprising therefore that the Saint-Simonians should enjoy an almost complete obscurity in his correspondence now.

In 1840 Heine wrote a cordial letter of recommendation for Carnot to Varnhagen von Ense:

...wir kennen uns schon seit zehn Jahren, wo ich ihn im sacré collège der Saint-Simonisten fand; das waren brillante Zeiten—jetzt ist Herr Carnot nur Mitglied der Deputiertenkammer[3].

---

[1] January 30, 1836.
[2] Elster, IV, pp. 524–525, *Ueber die französische Bühne*, 1837.
[3] Hirth, II, p. 326, dated July 3, 1840.

The episode was fading into the background of Heine's mind, but it was still a pleasing memory.

In 1845 there is a similar letter to Laube introducing Félicien David, the great composer, as Heine calls him, and the only artist whom the Saint-Simonians managed to bend to their will. He was among the forty apostles at Ménilmontant, and there composed many Saint-Simonian songs. Later he followed them to Egypt, and this resulted in his most famous composition, *The Desert*. This was the moment of his greatest popularity in Paris, and Heine, in another letter to Laube a few weeks later, confessed that he only knew David slightly, but that he, Tom Thumb and the railway shares are the topic of the hour in Paris[1]. The first letter, however, closes with a much more interesting statement:

David kommt wahrscheinlich in Gesellschaft eines Mannes zu Ihnen, den Sie gewiss genau kennen—es ist der Vater Enfantin, das ehemalige Oberhaupt der Saint-Simonisten—der bedeutendste Geist der Gegenwart[2].

Enfantin may or may not have accompanied David to Germany, but the fact that he contemplated such a visit is something to be grateful for, since it drew from Heine the surprising characterisation quoted above; the supreme father of the Saint-Simonians was 'the foremost mind of the age.' And this statement increases in significance because Heine was writing to Laube, a fellow Young German, to whom he always spoke openly and with complete frankness.

A few months later in a letter to Campe, whilst protesting against a rumour that he was gambling on the Stock Exchange, Heine adds the following rather important piece of information:

...aber das Eisenbahnwesen, dem meine Freunde (z. B. alle ehemaligen Saint-Simonisten, mit Enfantin an der Spitze) die merkwürdigste Thätigkeit widmen, hat auch mich in finanzieller wie geistiger Hinsicht interessirt und beschäftigt. Für die Folge erwarte ich grosse Vortheile davon, in der Gegenwart sind sie aber noch nicht realisirt[3].

At this date then the Saint-Simonians were still his friends, and Enfantin was still held by him in high esteem; he was

[1] Hirth, II, p. 555, dated May 24, 1845.
[2] *Ibid.* II, p. 554, dated May 5, 1845.
[3] *Ibid.* II, pp. 560–561, dated October 31, 1845.

following their activities on the railways with some eagerness, and was already financially interested in these ventures; indeed Grün reported in 1845: 'Und noch jetzt spricht Heine mit wahrer Sympathie vom St Simonismus, er, den man so gern als keiner Sympathie fähig darstellt.'[1]

There are further a certain number of references both to Saint-Simonism itself and to various former members in *Lutetia* (1842–1843): '...aber um mit Saint-Simon zu reden, auf allen Werften Englands gibt es keine einzige grosse Idee.'[2] Heine had once before quoted the Saint-Simonian opinion of England[3]; this extract is noteworthy because it is the only quotation from Saint-Simon himself which Heine ever made, with the exception of the phrase 'l'avenir est à nous,' which Saint-Simon used on his death-bed, and which became one of the catch-words of the school.

In a short and favourable notice of Duveyrier's *Lettres Politiques*, Heine made a few playful references to Duveyrier's rather varied career, which illustrated to his mind the adaptability of Frenchmen:

Ein merkwürdiges Beispiel der Art bieten die Transformationen unsres lieben Charles Duveyrier, der einer der erleuchtetsten Dignitare der Saint-Simonistischen Kirche war, und, als diese aufgehoben wurde, von der geistlichen Bühne zur weltlichen überging. Dieser Charles Duveyrier sass in der Salle Taitbout auf der Bischofsbank, zur Seite des Vaters, nämlich Enfantin's; er zeichnete sich aus durch einen gotterleuchteten Prophetenton, und auch in der Stunde der Prüfung gab er als Martyrer Zeugnis für die neue Religion[4].

This is probably an allusion to the dramatic speech which Charles Duveyrier made before his judges at the trial.

In the 'Anhang' to the second part of *Lutetia* entitled 'Kommunismus, Philosophie und Klerisei,' which contains a sympathetic character-sketch of Leroux, Heine gave his opinion of

[1] H. Grün, *op. cit.* p. 118.

[2] Elster, VI, p. 329, dated September 17, 1842; Saint-Simon's dictum ran thus: 'J'en reviens avec la certitude qu'ils n'avaient sur le chantier aucune idée capitale neuve'; this has a rather different meaning from the one Heine adopts.

[3] Elster, V, p. 58, *Französische Zustände*, dated March 1, 1832: 'Mit Recht sagen die St Simonisten, England sei die Hand und Frankreich das Herz der Welt.'

[4] Elster, VI, pp. 340–341, dated February 2, 1843.

Saint-Simonism as a social doctrine; and it is not a favourable one[1]. He considered the Saint-Simonians at best to be very dilettante socialists; he exalted Fourierism above Saint-Simonism, and voiced what was to the end of his life a never-ceasing wonder, in some sort an impersonal grievance against the Saint-Simonians, apparent in the sentence: 'seine Bekenner unter seltsamen Aushängeschildern sind noch immer am Leben.' Heine could never quite conquer the feeling that the Saint-Simonians, in leading ordinary and prosperous lives, were being untrue to their principles. In this he profoundly misunderstood them, nor was he alone to do so[2].

Heine's biographical references to Leroux furnish some further proof of his regular attendance in the *salle* Taitbout and of his intimate knowledge of events at that time:

...Pierre Leroux, den wir vor elf Jahren in der Salle-Taitbout als einen der Bischöfe des Saint-Simonismus kennen lernten. Ein vortrefflicher Mann, der nur den Fehler hatte, für seinen damaligen Stand viel zu trübsinnig zu sein. Auch hat ihm Enfantin das sarkastische Lob ertheilt: 'Das ist der tugendhafteste Mensch nach den Begriffen der Vergangenheit.'[3]

Enfantin made this statement in answer to the violent protestations of Leroux during the family meeting of November 19, 1831, when Bazard finally seceded[4]; and although it is unlikely that Heine would have been permitted to attend this private meeting, his quotation of Enfantin's words throws considerable light on the authoritative knowledge which he undoubtedly possessed, and which caused him to add drily:

Seine Tugend hat allerdings Etwas vom alten Sauerteig der Entsagungsperiode, Etwas verschollen Stoisches, das in unsrer Zeit ein fast befremdlicher Anachronismus ist und gar den heitern Richtungen einer pantheistischen Genussreligion gegenüber als eine honorable Lächerlichkeit erscheinen musste[5].

He went on to tell how Leroux was the first to protest against the new morality, and to withdraw from the gay assemblies[6].

---

[1] Elster, VI, p. 409, dated June 15, 1843.
[2] Cf. F. Liszt, *Gesammelte Werke*, II, p. 200.
[3] Elster, VI, pp. 409–410, dated June 15, 1843.
[4] Cf. *Œuvres de Saint-Simon et d'Enfantin*, IV, p. 159.
[5] Elster, VI, p. 410.
[6] Leroux left with Carnot and many others after the meeting of November 19, 1831, and went over to Fourierism for a time.

In spite of his asceticism, Heine held him in great respect; he did full justice to the nobility of his mind, and the zeal with which he worked for the amelioration of the poorer classes. There is a fine paragraph on the poverty of Leroux, Saint-Simon and Fourier towards the end of this chapter: 'Ja Armuth ist das Loos der grossen Menschheitshelfer, der heilenden Denker in Frankreich'[1]; such was Heine's conclusion, another instance of his attitude towards philosophy and wealth. And although it is not quite reasonable to admire socialistic thinkers in proportion to their poverty, nor fair to despise them in proportion to their wealth, yet there is just enough inconsistency between great possessions and selfless ideals to give him some appearance of right.

Altogether, Heine adopted a definitely ironical attitude towards Saint-Simonism and its former members in *Lutetia*. The term 'pantheistische Genussreligion' is not a complimentary one; particularly with the addition that many gold pheasants and eagles, but still more sparrows were fluttering about this shining cage[2].

His grievance against them lay, I think, in the fact that he viewed their material prosperity with distrust. He had also grown away from them during the last years, and was growing beyond the doctrines which had fascinated him at an earlier date. His personal relations with them, however, although probably extremely slight, seem to have remained unruffled. On the whole his chief praise was accorded to those members of the school, Carnot, Leroux and Reynaud, who had seceded from Saint-Simonism on the retirement of Bazard; and although he paid Enfantin a magnificent compliment in his letter to Laube in 1845 and spoke of him as a friend to Campe in the same year, it is a noteworthy fact that when in the winter of 1839–1840 Heine introduced Laube to all his Paris friends, and to the notabilities of the day, the Saint-Simonians do not appear to have figured on either list. We may conclude, I think, that the ties had become very slack, but that no personal ill-will was as

[1] Elster, VI, p. 417.
[2] Elster, VI, p. 410; cf. also p. 431; a reference to their theories of criminal punishment, in which he awards them the epithet 'schwärmerische Naturen.'

yet felt by Heine; at the most he nursed an intellectual grievance against them which might in favouring circumstances disappear, but which might also, if combined with a sense of personal injury, become acute.

(e) HOME TRUTHS

It is a coincidence, though certainly a striking one, that Heine's pronouncement upon Enfantin, 'the foremost mind of the age,' should have preceded a silence of nearly ten years on the subject of Saint-Simonism and all its works and that this silence was broken in 1855 on a very different note. The intervening years were of such cataclysmic importance for Heine, and altered the trend of his mind so completely, that some of the outstanding events must be briefly considered.

Salomon Heine, Heinrich's millionaire uncle, died on December 23, 1844, and to the amazement and fury of the poet his will contained no reference to the pension of 4800 francs which he had allowed his nephew, and promised that it would continue during the latter's life, and revert to his wife. He left him the sum of 8000 francs, and preserved a non-committal silence on the subject of the pension. It has been argued with some plausibility that Salomon instructed his son Karl to continue the pension, and did not think it necessary to mention this in his will. It is even more likely that Karl Heine, who was always stirring up strife between the wilful poet and his eccentric and irascible relative, was responsible for the omission. For Karl behaved extremely badly in the matter, he refused to acknowledge any obligation towards Heine and made humiliating conditions for the continuance of financial support. When at last he was shamed into paying, he did so in a grudging and ungenerous manner, sometimes withholding help when it was most needed, sometimes certainly increasing the payment greatly, but never letting Heine feel for one moment that its continuance could be counted on, and always making it quite clear that he was giving alms to a beggar. It seems odd indeed that so proud a spirit as Heine's should have stooped to accept such ungracious charity, but his financial position was in more than its usual precarious condition, and he could not afford to refuse it; nay, more, he intrigued feverishly and desperately to secure it. It is painful to read those pages in which the agile and inventive brain of a great imaginative poet is seen hunting for the mean motives which will cause his cousin to pay up. He was not above playing on the base strings of flattery, cajolery and threats; and although by turns insulted, angry, despairing and hurt, he never lost his quarry from sight. He was extravagant and generous by nature and he had never had enough money for his needs. His affairs would have been less involved however had it not been for his wife, Mathilde, who is called 'die Verbrengerin'[1] in his letters. Heine was reduced to having as little as possible in the house, for he seems to have been incapable of refusing her anything. Campe paid him at a low rate for his works, and then only after the most wearing process of haggling, so that the threatened loss of his pension was in the nature of a catastrophe. This distressing family quarrel certainly hastened the disease which was already menacing Heine, and occasioned a stroke in January 1845. From this stroke he never completely recovered; he was bed-ridden from 1848 onwards, enduring the most terrible agony, and almost complete loss of sight for an uninterrupted period of eight years. When the pains became unendurable, the doctor would order opium to be rubbed into a wound kept open for the purpose, and this was the only relief he knew. Too much has already been written on the subject of the 'mattress-grave,' nor is there any temptation to dwell on it; but it played an important part in his financial difficulties, for the expenses of this long and incurable illness were great. To add to the discomforts of the situation the February Revolution of 1848 brought about a sudden fall in the value of railway shares which affected Heine considerably, for his interest in railways had ceased to be a Platonic one since 1845. He also lost his secret pension from the French government, which had been paid to him since 1835; and was involved in a terrible scandal when the *Revue Rétrospective* published a list of such pensioners in 1848. There were cries of 'traitor!' accompanied by statements that he had sold his pen to Guizot. Heine denied

[1] A slang term of the time meaning extravagant, wasteful.

this emphatically[1], and indeed the whole tone of his writings during the period 1835–1848 invalidates such a suggestion. The pension was in the nature of a tribute to the exiled poet; but the publication of his name on the list was exceedingly detrimental to his reputation.

The terrible illness which had declared itself fully by 1848 also played an important part in his so-called conversion, although there had been earlier signs that the pantheistic 'Genussreligion' no longer satisfied his needs. There is hardly a page of Heine's letters from 1848 onwards which does not contain some allusion to the change which had taken place in his attitude towards religious subjects. Some of these allusions are witty in tone, and he often indulged in half-playful, half-reproachful blasphemies, as for instance that he is thinking of reporting God to the Society for the Prevention of Cruelty to Animals[2]. But in all of them there is the same clear-eyed recognition of the reason which had led to his acceptance of a personal God, the need for a spar to cling to in the shipwreck of his life.

Heine's nature was an honest one; it led him to make no less than three confessions of his change of faith embodying a restatement of his former views—the *Nachwort zum Romancero*, 1851; the preface to the second edition of *Zur Geschichte der Religion und Philosophie in Deutschland*, 1852; and the *Geständnisse*, 1853–1854, written originally to form an integral part of the second edition of *De l'Allemagne*, 1855, and first published in the *Revue des deux Mondes*, 1854.

What concerns us here in these various confessions of faith which give the history of Heine's religious life is the complete absence of any allusion to the Saint-Simonians. Heine ascribed his pantheistic views to Hegel and Hegel alone, while his paganism appeared as the natural outcome of good health, high spirits, love of beauty and love of life. This tacit denial of the Saint-Simonian influence here, although it has its parallel in the past, is strange at least in those frank and open confessions with which he sought to atone for errors he had now outgrown.

But most significant of all is the fact that he now declared

---

[1] Cf. Elster, VI, pp. 373–391; *Retrospektive Aufklärung*, August 1854.
[2] Hirth, III, p. 558, November 1855.

the whole tendency of *De l'Allemagne* to have been a polemical one directed against Mme de Staël[1]. He owned indeed to having championed German sensualism against German spiritualism, which the French authoress had glorified and magnified; but that the book was written almost at the request of Enfantin and certainly under the influence of his religious views, he neither acknowledged nor denied. He maintained his baffling silence.

The second edition of *De l'Allemagne* appeared in Paris early in 1855 and contained the French version of the *Geständnisse*; whilst in the stead of the dedicatory epistle to Enfantin which had preceded the first edition there stood a startling preface in which Heine made his first and last public attack against the Saint-Simonians. That part of the preface which embodies the attack must now be quoted in full:

Je m'abstiens de toute observation au sujet des éliminations que mon livre a subies. J'évite du moins ainsi le danger de me rendre coupable d'un manque de tact. J'ai supprimé des diatribes émanées autrefois d'une malice juvénile et injuste, et j'ai fait de même pour les hommages dédicatoires, qui seraient un anachronisme aujourd'hui, et dont la forme intempestive produirait surtout dans ce moment un effet tout contraire à celui où l'auteur visait lorsque parut la première édition de son livre. A cette époque, le nom auquel j'adressais ces hommages était pour ainsi dire un schibolet, et désignait le parti le plus avancé de l'émancipation humaine, qui venait d'être terrassé par les gendarmes et les courtisans de la vieille société. En patronisant les vaincus, je lançais un superbe défi à leurs adversaires, et je manifestais ouvertement mes sympathies pour les martyrs qu'on outrageait alors, et qu'on bafouait sans merci dans les journaux et dans le monde. Je ne craignais pas de m'exposer au ridicule, dont leur bonne cause était, il faut l'avouer, un peu entachée. Les choses ont changé depuis: les martyrs d'autrefois ne sont plus honnis ni persécutés, ils ne portent plus la croix, si ce n'est par hasard la croix de la Légion d'honneur; ils ne parcourent plus nu-pieds les déserts de l'Arabie pour y chercher la femme libre;—ces émancipateurs des liens conjugaux, ces briseurs de chaînes matrimoniales, à leur retour de l'Orient ils se sont mariés et sont devenus les épouseurs les plus intrépides de l'Occident, et ils ont des bottes. La plupart de ces martyrs sont à présent dans la prospérité; plusieurs d'entre eux sont néo-millionnaires, et plus d'un est arrivé aux places les plus honorifiques et les plus lucratives—on va vite avec les chemins de fer. Ces ci-devant apôtres qui ont rêvé l'âge d'or pour toute l'humanité, se sont contentés de propager l'âge de l'argent, le règne de ce dieu-

[1] Elster, VI, p. 22, *Geständnisse*, 1853–1854.

argent, qui est le père et la mère de tous et de toutes—c'est peut-être le même dieu qu'on a prêché en disant: Tout est en lui, rien n'est hors de lui, sans lui on n'est rien—Mais ce n'est pas le dieu qu'adore l'auteur de ces lignes, je lui préfère même ce pauvre Dieu nazaréen qui n'avait pas le sou, et qui était le Dieu des gueux et des souffrants. Comme j'appartiens un peu à cette dernière catégorie, je ferais un acte de grande niaiserie, si je voulais préconiser par des compliments surannés les hautains triomphateurs, les heureux du jour, qui peuvent bien s'en passer[1].

This declaration of war must have come to the astonished Saint-Simonians like thunder from a clear sky. And indeed, if we had not the solution to the riddle in Heine's letters, it would be matter for much surprised conjecture as to why he should have broken so long and so determined a silence in so startling a manner. For the prosperity of the former Saint-Simonians did not date from yesterday, it was not a new and monstrous fact which had suddenly thrust itself upon Heine's notice; it was an old story, and does not account for this sudden leap into angry and fiery life on a subject on which he had been shamming dead for so many years. And it seems rather curious that the manner in which Heine revoked the dedication has never been the cause of any comment, although this preface has often been quoted to show his indifference to Saint-Simonism. The author himself however felt that it called for an explanation, and one cannot help speculating on Michel Chevalier's feelings when he received this edition of De l'Allemagne with a half-apologetic letter from his old friend:

Je vous envoie la nouvelle édition de mon livre de l'Allemagne.... Je n'ai pas besoin de vous dire que la préface n'est pas à votre adresse; je me repens presque aujourd'hui de l'avoir écrite; mais j'étais dans un moment de juste indignation. Il ne s'agit pas ici d'Enfantin, qui n'était jamais pour moi autre chose qu'un mythe; lui aussi ne s'est guère préoccupé de moi, pas plus que si je m'appelais Osiris—quoiqu'il ait bien su que ce pauvre Osiris était très souffrant, depuis qu'il a été déchiré en morceaux par le méchant Typhon. Je lui ai écrit une fois, non au Dieu Typhon, mais au divin Enfantin; cependant, depuis sa missive datée des bords du Nil, il ne m'a honoré d'aucune ligne. C'est un Dieu et il peut dire: prosternez-vous ou reniez-moi! Ce que je viens de faire, c'était mon droit, et il ne peut pas m'en vouloir. J'en ai renié bien d'autres qui valaient mieux. Ce

[1] Elster, IV, p. 569, dated January 15, 1855.

n'est donc pas d'un Dieu que je me plains: les griefs m'arrivent de plus bas.—Mon cher Michel, mon engouement à réclamer les droits de la matière a cessé depuis que je vois combien cette matière devient envahissante, après s'être vue un peu réhabilitée; elle ne se contente plus d'être établie sur un pied d'égalité avec l'esprit, non, d'usurpation en usurpation elle va jusqu'à insulter l'Esprit. Ah, Madame la matière, c'est très bête à vous, et vous êtes une sotte!

Je me tais car ce que j'allais dire devient très mesquin de ma part. D'ailleurs, il n'y a rien de plus niais que de se plaindre par le temps qui court. Je devrais même m'abstenir de me plaindre de ma santé![1]

So much at least is clear; Heine had written the preface in a moment of anger, not with Chevalier and not with Enfantin, but with someone who had insulted him, one of the prosperous band, since he typified matter insulting mind. He also had an uneasy feeling that the cause of his anger was a petty one, and was half regretting the preface already. Beyond this it is plainly apparent that Enfantin had hurt Heine's feelings by neglecting him; and since he speaks now of denying his godhead, this would seem to suggest that he had at one time taken his claims more seriously, even if it is true that he appeared to him rather as a mythical being than a real person. The one letter which he refers to may well be the dedicatory epistle, as has always been assumed. It is also possible, however, and indeed rather more likely from the context, that it was a letter subsequent to the missive from the Nile. For if Heine had never answered this he could not very well complain of Enfantin's silence[2].

By a great stroke of good luck Chevalier's answer to this letter has been preserved, although in a German translation. The editor, Julia, then in possession of some of Heine's unpublished papers, asserts that they included many letters from Chevalier to Heine. Unfortunately these letters seem to have disappeared. They are not in the possession of Professor Hans Meyer in Leipzig who purchased Julia's papers, and who assured me that no such letters were among them. They would have been a most valuable addition to this study; but the following lines at least show the part which Chevalier played in the imbroglio:

Also denkend, finde ich Ihre Sendung und Ihren prächtigen Brief.

---

[1] Hirth, III, pp. 509–510, dated February 18, 1855.
[2] There is no trace of such a letter in the *Fonds Enfantin, Bibliothèque de l'Arsenal.*

Das Wenigste was ich thue, mein Lieber, ist dass ich Sie heut besuche, und das thue ich sicherlich. Ich habe Ihr 'Vorwort' gelesen und wünschte, es wäre nicht vorhanden. Enfantin hat viele Fehler, unter anderen den, dass er an Sie auf Ihrem Schmerzenslager nicht mehr denkt. Aber er hat die alte Devise nicht vergessen: 'alle sozialen Einrichtungen müssen zum Zwecke haben, u.s.w.'

Er ist der herrlichsten Freundschaft untreu geworden, aber er ist es unserer alten Liebe, dem mittelländischen Meere nicht geworden: er wird den grossen Suezkanal beginnen. Was die Neu-Millionäre anbetrifft, so kenne ich deren nur zwei, die beiden Pereire; ich kann Ihnen jedoch versichern, dass sie einen sehr guten Gebrauch von ihrem Reichthum machen. Seien Sie, mein lieber Deutscher, nur nicht undankbar gegen sie, gegenwärtig sind sie ja Deutschlands Wohlthäter. Wer die, welche hohe Staatsämter bekleiden, sein mögen, weiss ich nicht; ich kann sie also nicht vor Ihrem hohen und mächtigen Tribunal verteidigen. Auf baldiges Wiedersehn. Von ganzem Herzen Ihr Michel Chevalier[1].

This letter, eminently reasonable and almost kinder in tone than Heine had deserved, is a tribute to the friendship between the two men and to Chevalier's goodness of heart. It is interesting to hear his version of the relationship between the prophet and the poet: 'the most beautiful friendship.' The epithet may sound exaggerated, and neither Heine nor Enfantin might have subscribed to it, yet Chevalier's opinion in this matter is of weight[2]. It is something of a relief to realise that Heine was not alone in his opinion that Enfantin had treated him badly by neglecting him in his illness.

Michel, then, went to see his friend on the same day. The whole story was poured out to him, and he offered his help to the outraged poet; but it seems more than doubtful that he was successful in what steps he may have taken. Heine wrote a second long letter to Chevalier a few days later; and this, although it is not without obscurities, gives the main facts of the situation, and is worth an attentive perusal[3].

The essentials of the situation seem to have been as follows. Heine had written to Emile Pereire, probably in the name of their old acquaintanceship, and asked him for financial aid, in

[1] H. Julia, 'Heinrich Heine. Erinnerungen,' *Deutsche Revue*, Breslau, 1884, III, dated February 20, 1854, obviously a mistake for 1855.

[2] It is just possible however that this remark applies to Enfantin's friendship with Chevalier.

[3] Cf. Hirth, III, pp. 512–514, dated February 24, 1855.

order to give him a breathing-space in which to finish his
Memoirs and to release him from the necessity of wasting his
time and his energies in turning out inferior work to satisfy the
needs of existence. He asked in fact to be allotted a hundred
shares in one of the industrial companies, either in railways or
in Austrian mines, which Pereire was floating at the moment.
To this 'first' letter Pereire did not reply, but sent him twenty
shares. This is the 'procédé blessant' of which Heine complained so bitterly that it wounded him in his two most vulnerable spots, his self-respect, and his financial interests. He felt
that he had committed a base action, and worse still a base
action to no purpose, in appealing for sympathy, he, one of the
martyrs of the spirit, to one of the great lords of matter. This
anger had led him to commit the 'folly' of writing the preface,
which he regretted already and hoped to atone for sooner or
later in an honourable manner.

The least pleasant part in this rather unpleasant affair is
Heine's tenacity of purpose. He still hoped, through Michel's
good offices, to squeeze some more shares out of Pereire; in fact,
though he does not actually say so, the honourable amends were
probably dependent on the heaping of more coals of fire on his
resigned and guilty head. Although the joke is a good one, it
produces a painful impression.

In fact it is altogether with a feeling of discomfort that we
see Heine's cards on the table at last, for certainly the motive
which caused him, if not to revoke his dedication, then at least
to write so scornful and in many ways so unjust a preface, was
not a very worthy one. It would, however, be less than fair to
Heine to assume that it was only his failure to make money
out of Pereire that went to its composition. The fact that his
letter received no answer bore at least as great a share; the
hot and bitter feeling that he had abased himself before someone
whom he obviously considered his inferior in all but wealth,
only to receive such cool and contemptuous treatment, must
have been hard to bear. And Heine had been dying in agony
for six years, and the state of his nerves is something that can
only be guessed at. Moreover, he was by no means turning
traitor in speaking as he did. He was only voicing at long last

opinions that he had held for years. He had never understood
the industrial ideals of the Saint-Simonians, and he had a deep
and rooted distrust of the combination religion and wealth,
which was one of the corner-stones of their philosophy. He was
temperamentally incapable of sympathising with their feminist
views, and their search for the 'free woman' can never have
appeared to him as anything but absurd. Finally, he had
abjured his former religious beliefs and thus severed the one
bond that bound him to them, and his personal relations with
them had well-nigh ceased. Also he wrote at once to Chevalier,
the only former Saint-Simonian with whom he was still on terms
of friendship, and affectionately assured him that the preface
was not aimed at him nor yet at Enfantin. And yet his action
remains regrettable, because of the fine and generous quality
of the silence he had shattered[1]; but I think that Heine was
telling the truth when he wrote it, and that apart from the
angry excitement which led him to overstate his case, his
opinions even before the Pereire incident were what he now
declared them to be.

It was the insult he had received from Pereire that provided
a motive strong enough to break an almost life-long silence on
the actual facts of Saint-Simonism as he had observed them.
The motive for his silence has been sufficiently discussed. It is
to be noticed however that it still restrained him from ridiculing
Enfantin's peculiarities, or the excesses of the school in general.
A side thrust was delivered at their feminist views with which
he had never associated himself; otherwise he took his stand
on what he considered to be the glaring inconsistency of their
early theories and their later practice; and here it must be remembered that philosophy and poverty had always appeared
to him inseparable.

But he certainly exaggerated rather wildly both the tone and
the importance of his dedication to Enfantin. It seems curious
to hear this formal and soberly written epistle being criticised
for its 'forme intempestive,' and being hailed as a 'superbe défi'

---

[1] Cf. Hirth, iii, pp. 534, 561 and 566 for further references to the
'affaire Pereire.' All these letters are addressed to members of the Rothschild family, who had always treated Heine generously and courteously
in similar transactions.

launched at the adversaries of the Saint-Simonians; especially
when we consider that at that date (1835) they had practically
ceased to exist in France and that their worst enemy was the
plague. But the reason he gave for this championship is, I think,
the right one: they were the most advanced party in the cause
of the emancipation of humanity; and we can also assume with
some degree of certainty that this reason was an important
factor in his protective silence. It is perhaps open to doubt that
his personal relations with them put a bridle on his tongue, but
it was certainly a personal reason which turned him against
them in a later hour. And yet if everything be taken into
account—his natural dislike and distrust of industrialism, his
unsuccessful attempts to profit by the railways, his extremely
unstable financial position aggravated by the failure of his
speculations, the loss of the government pension, and the terms
of his uncle's will—it is hardly surprising that the Saint-Simonian
golden age appeared to him now in a very unpleasant light; the
wealthy and successful among the former Saint-Simonians must
have been objects of greater contempt to his mind than any
other among the heroes of industry whom he observed around
him; they were guilty of what was to him the unpardonable
sin of attempting to combine philosophy and wealth; and he
interpreted this in his own way as the denial of their former
beliefs. He must have viewed with a very bitter twist of the
lips the gradual overshadowing of Rothschild by Pereire, and
we can imagine that it was not without an inward struggle that
he set himself to write to the latter, and beg him to grant him
a hundred shares in one of his great industrial enterprises. When
all this is taken into account the *Préface* appears perhaps in a
less unforgivable light, and Heine may even have exercised some
self-control whilst he was writing it. To my mind the surprising
feature in the case is not that he wrote it, but that he wrote it
so late. The inhibitions to free speech had been gradually removed; the new religion meant so little to him since his
conversion, that he had not even troubled to mention it in
his confessions, and with the exception of Chevalier he held no
intercourse with any former member of the school. If a sense
of loyalty kept him silent, it was loyalty of an almost quixotic

character; I am inclined to think that it was not the gratitude
for what he owed them in the past; but rather, since 1842, the
gratitude which has been defined as a lively sense of favours
to come. For, indeed, his silence in the confessions squares ill
with the theory that the memory of a spiritual or intellectual
debt was still fresh in his mind. Rather, as he said in his letter
to Chevalier, the cup of bitterness was full. He hated Saint-
Simonian industrialism, yet he still desperately hoped to profit
by it. The contemptuous treatment which his begging letter
had received was the last drop in this cup. It overflowed into
the *Préface*.

The silence having once been broken, it is only natural to
suppose that the Saint-Simonians figured to some extent in his
memoirs; and it is impossible not to speculate on the treatment
they received; for the 'affaire Pereire' played a great part in
his dying thoughts; and he wrote the last pages of his last book,
we are told, in a very fury of vindictiveness:

Que de fois j'ai trouvé Heine couvrant les grandes feuilles de papier
blanc, eparsées devant lui, de ces vigoureux caractères dont la forme
seule trahissait l'audace et la netteté de sa pensée! Le crayon qui
courait avec une activité fébrile sur les blancheurs de la page, prenait,
entre les doigts effilés du malade, l'inflexibilité d'une arme meurtrière,
et semblait raturer des réputations intactes. Un jour, le bruit du
crayon fut remplacé par celui d'un rire cruel, un rire de vengeance
assouvie. Je regardai Henri Heine. 'Je les tiens, fit-il. Morts ou vifs,
ils ne m'échapperont plus. Gare à qui lira ces lignes, s'il a osé s'at-
taquer à moi! Heine ne meurt pas comme le premier venu, et les
griffes du tigre survivront au tigre lui-même.'[1]

As the later memoirs were written in this spirit of merciless
revenge, the Saint-Simonians may have been the recipients of
some very unpleasant home-truths on the lines laid down in the
Préface. But during this process some unknown facts must
surely have emerged relating to the part they played in his life,
and it is a matter for keen regret that they should have so un-
accountably disappeared.

For the story of Heine and the Saint-Simonians still remains
to be told, and will probably never be unfolded in its entirety.
Nothing has been done in these pages but to interpret a most

[1] Camille Selden, *Les derniers jours de Henri Heine*, Paris, 1884, pp. 66–67.

obstinate and unyielding silence. Heine, the Saint-Simonians, the memoir-writers and the biographers have all, as it were, played their part in a dumb-show full of ambiguous and misleading gestures. And if a solution has been found for the protective silence of the early years; and a suggestion offered for the wary criticisms of the middle period, the silence in the various confessions of faith must remain unsolved for the present. It will be part of the task of a following chapter to attempt to account for it.

CHAPTER VI

COMING EVENTS

(a) 'ENFANT PERDU'

Heine embraced the Saint-Simonian faith with great ardour after his perusal of the first year of the *Exposition de la doctrine de Saint-Simon*, and the reasons for this sudden conversion were mainly psychological; indeed any attempt to read the riddle of Heine's nature lays bare an element which made him peculiarly susceptible to their interpretation of the universe.

There was a tragic lack of harmony in his personality, which expressed itself in his outer life and most insistently in his writings. He was rarely at one with himself; he was often at variance with others; much oppressed by outward circumstances; taking many a humiliating tumble in the dusty arena of life, and striving in vain for that detachment and calm, which was never to be his portion. And in his unsettled and unstable life he had no strong principles to support him; nor was he capable of finding in his inner nature the consolation which the circumstances of his life denied him. Had he been more harmoniously balanced, or less sensitive to outside influences, he might have achieved happiness. As it was, he has truly described himself as the 'enfant perdu' of the age. And it is difficult to imagine any time and any country in which he would have been completely at home; for he was bound up of contradictions: romanticism and reason, sentimentality and wit, scepticism and religious longings, idealism and materialism in love, small wonder that he was restless, dissatisfied, and ill at ease. This lack of harmony in himself made him sensitively aware of it in the world around him: wherever he looked he saw antitheses, and more particularly in the passion of love, with its limitless desires and its ephemeral nature. He was early the victim of disappointments here, but, beyond his personal unhappiness, he felt the greater unhappiness of the ever recurring disillusion; the ideal swamped by the real, love 'insensible of mortality, and desperately mortal':

Die Nachtigall sang: 'O schöne Sphinx!
O Liebe! was soll es bedeuten,
Dass du vermischest mit Todesqual
All' deine Seligkeiten?'[1]

This conception of the disillusion lying in wait for the lover is
the keynote of his lyric poetry; it was sometimes expressed with
the most poignant sadness, sometimes by means of that much-
abused irony, that wilful destruction of the illusion, which became a mannerism, but whose first cause was undoubtedly the
realisation of the irony of life and love. But the antithesis
between the ideal and the real in love, its infinite aspirations,
and its finite achievements, is but one aspect of the eternal
dualism of man, his soul at odds with his body, his spirit warring
with his senses, a problem which has at all times preoccupied
philosophers and priests, and which the Saint-Simonians were
once more attempting to solve. Now Heine could not be indifferent to a problem which concerned himself so closely; for
two inimical principles were ever at war within him. He
was at one and the same time an ardent spiritualist, and an
exuberant sensualist[2]: his love poems show him in both aspects.
He responded with enthusiasm to the call of the spirit, and to
the lure of the flesh, but he had at first no philosophy that
could 'moralise' them both, they seemed to him mutually incompatible; and in these earlier years his youthful love of life
and women, his undisciplined temperament and sceptical habit
of mind, triumphed for the most part over his religious longings
and spiritual aspirations; so that he appeared as the declared
enemy of Christianity and asceticism, and as a vague apologist
of pagan classicism. He experienced all this before he came
under the Saint-Simonian influence, although the coincidences
between their religious doctrine and his hedonism are so remarkable, sometimes even textually, that it seems as if they
must both have had a common origin. It is possible that this

---

[1] Elster, I, p. 9, 1839.
[2] Cf. Elster, II, p. 13:

> Himmlisch war's, wenn ich bezwang
> Meine sündige Begier;
> Aber, wenn's mir nicht gelang
> Hatt' ich doch ein gross Plaisir.

was Hegel, whose influence on Heine's thought is generally
assumed, for Enfantin mentions him as one of the philosophers
studied by the school[1].

(b) SAINT-SIMONIAN THOUGHTS

It is no light task to disentangle Heine's religious opinions
from his many and varied statements before 1831; for he approached the subject frequently and from different angles; but
only those views which show a predisposition toward Saint-
Simonism need emphasis here; it should perhaps be noticed
that on the whole he condemned the Catholics and particularly
the Jesuits on social rather than on religious grounds; and that
although he championed the Jews socially he spared them no
criticisms from the religious point of view. He became a Protestant for social reasons (no public appointments were then
open to Jews in Germany) and he interpreted Protestantism
etymologically as the right to protest; but although his reason
approved of this form of Christianity as a social institution,
emotionally it left him completely cold. He cherished something
in the nature of hero-worship for Luther, but he considered that
Protestantism had already fulfilled its religious mission, and
here he coincided with the opinion of the Saint-Simonians.

But his criticism of Christianity shows an even more striking
similarity with the views of Bazard and Enfantin; and we find
it expressed as early as 1821 in the tragedy *Almansor*. The
tragic conflict in this play depends on the contrast of Christianity
with Mohammedanism; the one inspired by a spirit of self-sacrifice,
renunciation, sadness and asceticism; the other interpreted by
Heine as a frank and happy paganism. Socially the Mohammedans
were mere pseudonyms for the Jews, and the play contains a
veiled protest against the treatment of the Jews by the Christians
in Heine's day; but the criticism of Christianity as a religion is
written rather by Heine the pagan than by Heine the Jew, and

[1] *Œuvres de Saint-Simon et d'Enfantin*, XVII, p. 27. The possible influence
of Hegel on Saint-Simonism would be a study in itself, and the influence
of Hegel on Heine might well call for deeper consideration than it has
hitherto received. Brandes in his book on Young Germany considers that
Hegel was the originator of Heine's pagan Hellenism, and observes that
in his philosophy we can detect the spirit which might evolve such a watch-
word as 'emancipation of the flesh.'

is certainly the finest part of the play; for the poet was able
to feel and to express the beauty of a religion whose social
manifestations he regarded with pity and scorn. Almansor, a
Mohammedan, and Zuleima, a converted Christian, lovers once
and separated now by their differing faiths, are the two mouth-
pieces chosen by Heine to represent pagan joyfulness and
Christian sorrow. Almansor, returning after many years to the
garden where he had played with Zuleima and later loved her,
finds the myrtle tree dead and in its place the mournful cypress,
the pomegranate tree has been cut down, the red rose has
perished in a storm, her lover the nightingale is gone. And
brooding over this desolate scene is the crucified figure of Christ:

> Doch sprich, mein Lieb, dort steht ein fremdes Bild,
> Das schaut mich an so mild, und doch so traurig,
> Und eine bittre Thräne lässt es fallen
> In meinen schönen, goldnen Freudenkelch[1].

Then Almansor remembered what he had heard and seen in a
Christian church. The heavy muffled boom of bells, and the
gloomy giant tones of the organ had seemed to drag him into
the building, where the hoarse singing of the monks sounded
like a song of death; and look where he would, he saw the same
figure staring at him from every niche, pale, agonised and sad
and crowned with thorns....And then he heard a sharp and
piercing voice: 'This is his blood,' and, turning, he shuddered
to behold a man in the act of raising a cup to his lips.

You were in the house of Love, replied Zuleima, and it was
Love whom you saw lying dead in the bosom of his mother; but
when Almansor, vanquished by the word love 'which creates
worlds and unites them,' is ready to declare the whole earth a
temple of love, she interrupts him: 'Die Erde ist ein grosses
Golgotha, Wo zwar die Liebe siegt, doch auch verblutet.'[2]
Heine already saw in Christianity that austerity and sadness
which he came to hate so bitterly; and throughout this scene
his sympathies were with Almansor the pagan, rather than
with Zuleima the Christian. But he was also fated to be swayed
by the beauty of the Christian conception of love, and he never
quite escaped from the shadow of the crucifix; this symbol had

---

[1] Elster, II, pp. 283–284.   [2] *Ibid.* II, p. 287.

made an undying impression on his mind when he was a little
boy at school, and it remained with him throughout his life:

> In den dumpfen Bogengängen des Franziskanerklosters, unfern der
> Schulstube, hing damals ein grosser gekreuzigter Christus von grauem
> Holze, ein wüstes Bild, das noch jetzt zuweilen des Nachts durch
> meine Träume schreitet und mich traurig ansieht mit starren, blutigen
> Augen.... [1]

It was a natural enough reaction against such an impression
that made him sing the pagan gods, wandering exiled as clouds
in the heavens; and a terrible longing mastered his heart for the
unquenchable laughter of the gods which has long since died
away:

> Und wenn ich bedenke, wie feig und windig
> Die Götter sind, die euch besiegten,
> Die neuen, herrschenden, tristen Götter,
> Die Schadenfrohen im Schafspelz der Demuth—
> O, da fasst mich ein düsterer Groll,
> Und brechen mocht' ich die neuen Tempel,
> Und kämpfen für euch, ihr alten Götter,
> Für euch und eur gutes ambrosisches Recht.... [2]

And although he might turn from the past to the future and
prophesy the return of a natural religion under the aegis of
mysticism, such happier moments were rare[3]. For in truth
Heine was in a painful dilemma between paganism and Christianity, strikingly reflected in the famous passage in Chapter VI
of the *Stadt Lucca* which is prefaced by an extract from the
first book of the *Iliad*[4]. With dramatic suddenness Heine
describes the overthrow of the happy gods; a pale Jew, dripping
with blood, a crown of thorns on his head, a great wooden cross
on his shoulders, came panting into the assembly, and threw
the cross on to the tall table, so that the golden bowls trembled,
and the gods fell silent and became ever paler, until they dissolved in mist. And now followed a sad time; the world was
grey and dark, the laughter of the gods was heard no more;
Olympus became a hospital where gods who had been flayed

---

[1] Elster, III, p. 151, *Das Buch Le Grand*, 1826; cf. also *ibid.* II, pp. 456–457,
Deutschland, ein Wintermärchen, 1844.

[2] *Ibid.* I, p. 189, 1826.   [3] *Ibid.* VII, pp. 251–252.

[4] Lang, Leaf and Myers' translation, ll. 597–604; Heine used Voss's
translation. Elster in the footnote gives the reference as Book IX of the
Iliad; probably a printer's error (IX = I in Greek capital numbers).

and burnt at the stake slunk about, dressed their wounds, and sang depressing songs. For there was no joy in this new religion, though it might bring comfort to the sad; it was a mournful religion for the use of sinners, and it was stained with blood. Thus far Heine speaks as a pure pagan, one who might have sung with Swinburne: 'Thou hast conquered, oh pale Galilean; the world has grown grey from thy breath'; but the romantic in him, the sentimentalist, the sorrowful son of a sorrowful age, doubts and hesitates, and adds finally:

War sie vielleicht nöthig für die erkrankte und zertretene Menschheit? Wer seinen Gott leiden sieht, trägt leichter die eignen Schmerzen.... Um so ganz von ganzem Herzen geliebt zu werden—muss man leidend sein. Das Mitleid ist die letzte Weihe der Liebe, vielleicht die Liebe selbst. Von allen Göttern, die jemals geliebt haben, ist daher Christus derjenige Gott, der am meisten geliebt worden, besonders von den Frauen[1].

Thus Heine stands wavering between paganism and Christianity on the threshold of his acquaintance with Saint-Simonism. For although, when considering Schelling's natural philosophy, he prophesied the return of better and happier days in which men shall be as the gods, he in no way attempted to define this new religion; and unlike the Saint-Simonians, who saw in Christianity hardly more than a necessary antidote against the unspiritualised sensualism of paganism, he was sensitively aware of its beauty; he felt the appeal of its message to the sorrowful, and the pitiful quality of Christian love touched him intimately. This attitude is in its nature romantic; but it also reflects the instinctive need of a poetical temperament, labouring under the mysterious curse which pursues the Jewish race. Amidst all his blasphemies against Christianity, and they are legion during this period, varying from whimsical jokes to bitter invective, he never denied the beauty of Christian love, the universal brotherhood of man[2]. Yet for all his Christian velleities, it may truly be said that on the whole he hated Christianity more than he loved it; and this hatred was chiefly directed against its one-sided spiritualism resulting in hypocrisy and lies. His tirade against the 'Gothic lie,' which tolerated only secret pleasures and in-

---

[1] Elster, III, p. 395. Cf. Heine's picture of Christ the Saviour; *ibid.* I, pp. 177–178, *Nordsee I*, 1825.

[2] Cf. Elster, VII, p. 199; and III, p. 280.

sulted all free feelings with a hypocritical fig-leaf[1], shows how
much he disliked the restrictions imposed by Christianity on
the relations between men and women, and this is even more
clearly apparent in the passage, purely romantic in tone, in
which he saluted the new day on the battlefield of Marengo:

Ja, es wird ein schöner Tag werden, die Freiheitssonne wird die
Erde glücklicher wärmen als die Aristokratie sämmtlicher Sterne;
emporblühen wird ein neues Geschlecht, das erzeugt worden in freier
Wahlumarmung, nicht im Zwangsbette und unter der Kontrolle geist-
licher Zöllner; mit der freien Geburt werden auch in den Menschen
freie Gedanken und Gefühle zur Welt kommen, wovon wir geborenen
Knechte keine Ahnung haben[2].

The free love which Heine glorified in this passage is the free
love of the German romantic poets, and the 'freie Wahlumarmung' leads straight back to Goethe's 'Wahlverwandtschaften.'
It was, however, another point in common between Heine and
the Saint-Simonians, who by their demand for divorce were
gradually working towards free marriages. 'Freie Wahlumarmung' is vague in tone, and indeed there was a certain turgid
vagueness about the whole attitude of the German romantics
towards this question. The Saint-Simonians on the other hand
had a definite programme to offer; the difference between them
is the difference between individualists and socialists, but the
underlying theory is the same[3].

(c) CONFLICT

Any attempt to characterise Heine as a thinker before 1831
is rendered vain by the incoherence of his views; the reproach
of inconsistency, one of the standing accusations of his enemies,
is certainly justified when applied to the author of the *Reisebilder*. The apostle of freedom, who worshipped Napoleon, and
at one moment even acclaimed Russia as the land of liberty;
the ardent patriot, who made such cruel fun of Germany; the
enemy of the nobility and the defender of the people, who yet

[1] Elster, III, p. 318, *Die Bäder von Lucca*, 1820.
[2] Elster, III, pp. 280–281, *Reise von München nach Genua*, 1829.
[3] Cf. also the following passages for resemblances between Heine's ideas
and those expressed in the *Doctrine de Saint-Simon*:
(a) Elster, III, pp. 92 and 304, 'époques organiques.'
(b) *Ibid.* III, pp. 175, 189, 404, 418, 421, substitution of the earthly for
the heavenly paradise.

showed all the aristocrat's disdain for the common herd; this is all so much grist to the mill of those who, like Börne, would deny that Heine was a serious political thinker at all. And yet it is only fair to add that even at this period he had one great principle which gave a kind of fantastic unity to his incoherent views. This principle was liberty. It was his eternal preoccupation, and although it may be true that he espoused this cause in the first place because as a Jew he was one of the oppressed, nevertheless it was the great disinterested passion of his life. During this period he called it his religion, and declared that it deserved that name more truly than the hollow, withered, spiritual ghost which still usurped the title. His finest pages, perhaps the only pages which ring quite true in the *Reisebilder*, were dedicated to its service, and all the political and religious manifestations of his day were tried by that fiery test, and found wanting.

But if his political opinions were mutually irreconcilable, his religious views were in a state of chaos; sudden flashes of pure reason would be overwhelmed next moment by his impressionability; a fine and virile anger would be softened in the course of a paragraph into sorrow; so that we find 'the born enemy of all positive religions'[1] singing the praises of Mary, the mother of God[2]; whilst he literally seems doubtful whether to hate Christianity or to love it; to despise the Jews or to admire them; to sing the joys of paganism or to condemn the pagan gods. One thing alone seems clear; he longed for the solace of religion, but could not find in any of its revealed aspects that which would satisfy his dual nature; Christianity starved his senses, and paganism starved his soul. And although in the character of his much-loved sister Charlotte he recognised a nature in which body and spirit were harmoniously balanced[3], the idea that a religion might arise which would recognise and establish such a harmony had not yet occurred to his mind.

This discordant condition of mind is reflected in those remarkable changes of mood, which form one of the outstanding

[1] Hirth, I, pp. 243–244, letter to Moses Moser, dated August 23, 1823.
[2] Elster, I, pp. 146 ff., *Die Wallfahrt nach Kevlaar*, 1822.
[3] Hirth, I, pp. 199–200, letter to Moritz Emden, his future brother-in-law, dated February 2, 1823.

features of the *Reisebilder*. These changes are amusing and stimulating at first, but they end by being wearisome; and the attempt to read the whole volume at a sitting leaves one restless and almost dazed. Heine plays too many parts in the *Reisebilder*. There are moods of bitter pessimism, alternating with moods of impish gaiety; there are moments of almost maudlin sentiment, and we learn to dread any reference to the 'kleine Veronika' or to the 'todte Maria.' And although these are relieved by delicate and charming passages, yet the impression that remains is that there are too many nightingales, too many red roses and blue violets, too many tears, too many dreams, too many lovely maidens, and that Heine swaggers through Europe altogether too much of a fop. Then, although his wit is often delightful, and nearly always refreshing, it is not free at times from an ugly cynicism which forms a peculiarly unholy combination with his romantic sentimentality[1]. This fickleness of mood mirrors with painful clearness the mental and moral lack of poise which partly occasioned it. Heine's mind was the battle-ground of so many conflicting opinions because his unstable temperament drew him this way and that, unconsciously seeking a centre of rest which perpetually seemed to change.

Altogether, although, partly owing to the influence of German romanticism and Schelling, partly owing to Hegel, but largely, I think, owing to his own temperament, he was already speaking almost with the voice of Bazard in the *Exposition, Deuxième année*; yet he was profoundly unlike the Saint-Simonians in this, that he had no idea of co-ordinating his various opinions into a combined whole. There was no philosophy at the root of his criticism of Christianity, as there was in the case of the Saint-Simonians, only the fret occasioned by the strife between soul and senses within him, which could find no healing balm in religious faith[2].

[1] He was reading Sterne at the time.

[2] It is extremely unlikely that Heine was acquainted with the religious doctrine of the Saint-Simonians before his arrival in Paris. The First Year of the *Doctrine* dealt almost exclusively with the industrial and social views of the school, so that Heine would learn very little about the religious side from the copy he had in his hands in 1831. And the Second Year which dealt with this subject, published in December 1830, was little known in Germany; Carové, Bretschneider and Schiebler, who were the first to print books on Saint-Simonism, were in ignorance of its contents.

CHAPTER VII

THE SAINT-SIMONIAN PERIOD

(a) THE CONFLICT RESOLVED

Auf diesen Felsen bauen wir
Die Kirche von dem dritten,
Dem dritten neuen Testament;
Das Leid ist ausgelitten.

Vernichtet ist das Zweierlei,
Das uns so lang' bethöret;
Die dumme Leiberquälerei
Hat endlich aufgehöret.

Hörst du den Gott im finstern Meer?
Mit tausend Stimmen spricht er.
Und siehst du über unserm Haupt
Die tausend Gotteslichter?

Der heil'ge Gott, Der ist im Licht
Wie in den Finsternissen;
Und Gott ist Alles, was da ist;
Er ist in unsern Küssen[1].

The very metre of this gay and impudent confession of faith tells its own story; but Heine, although bubbling over with fun, was not giving vent to pure nonsense. He was expressing his sense of escape from the prison of his own temperament; and during the early period of the Saint-Simonian influence this happy, care-free mood predominates in his writings. His conflict seemed to be solved, and his religious longings were assuaged for a time. For if we analyse the pessimism which is so painfully apparent in his early writings, it always resolves itself into the unhappiness occasioned by the deep cleft between his spiritual and sensual natures; ennobled, but also rendered more tormenting by the realisation that the whole world was suffering in the same way. He himself justified his so-called 'Byronic pessimism' in a very illuminating page in the *Reisebilder*.

The world, he says, is rent in twain, and since the poet's heart is the centre of the world, it must suffer the same fate; his own

[1] Elster, i, p. 228, *Das dritte Evangelium*, 1831.

has been completely torn asunder, for the great gods have considered him worthy to bear the martyrdom of the poet. And he
makes the following reflection which shows that 'der grosse
Weltriss' is nothing less than the bankruptcy of Christianity,
after the bankruptcy of paganism:

> Einst war die Welt ganz, im Alterthum und im Mittelalter; trotz
> der äusseren Kämpfe gab's doch noch immer eine Welteinheit, und
> es gab ganze Dichter. Wir wollen diese Dichter ehren und uns an
> ihnen erfreuen; aber jede Nachahmung ihrer Ganzheit ist eine Lüge,
> eine Lüge, die jedes gesunde Auge durchschaut, und die dem Hohne
> dann nicht entgeht[1].

Another sign of the discord in Heine's breast is the presence
of those almost unbearably sentimental moods, which mar the
artistic effect of the *Reisebilder*. Sentimentality is a sure
symptom of mental lack of health; and perhaps no one has
analysed it more satisfactorily than Heine himself in a passage,
which is obviously dictated by personal experience, and which
reveals clearly the secret of his mental torment:

> Die Sentimentalität ist ein Produkt des Materialismus. Der Ma-
> terialist trägt nämlich in der Seele das dämmernde Bewusstsein, dass
> dennoch in der Welt nicht Alles Materie ist; wenn ihm sein kurzer
> Verstand die Materialität aller Dinge noch so bündig demonstriert,
> so sträubt sich doch dagegen sein Gefühl; es beschleicht ihn zuweilen
> das geheime Bedürfnis, in den Dingen auch etwas Urgeistiges anzuer-
> kennen; und dieses unklare Sehnen und Bedürfen erzeugt jene unklare
> Empfindsamkeit, welche wir Sentimentalität nennen. Sentimentalität
> ist die Verzweiflung der Materie, die sich selber nicht genügt und nach
> etwas Besserem, ins unbestimmte Gefühl hinausschwärmt[2].

And this glimpse of the despair which accompanies materialism
is balanced by Heine's confession that, in a world lying sick with
the spiritualism of Christianity, he was the sickest of all[3].

There is yet another symptom of Heine's temperamental conflict. He was a great dreamer, and a true romantic poet in his
eternal preoccupation with dreams. It cannot, of course, be
assumed that all the phantasies he presents to us in this form

---

[1] Elster, III, p. 304, *Die Bäder von Lucca*, 1829. The resemblance to the
Saint-Simonian 'époques organiques' is very striking here.

[2] Elster, IV, p. 512, *Ueber die französische Bühne*, 1837.

[3] Cf. Elster, IV, p. 249, *ibid.* VI, p. 19, and Hirth, II, p. 567: the two last
passages throw a revealing light on his romanticism, a product of the same
mixed feeling.

were really dreamt. The introduction 'mir träumte' became
almost as much of a mannerism as his romantic irony; nevertheless it had a foundation in fact, and since we have come to
believe to-day that those whose inner life is ill-balanced and
inharmonious will find an expression of their thwarted desires
and tendencies in their dreams, we can the more readily believe
of Heine that the constant nightmares and symbolic phantasies
with which he regales us, were not all poetic fictions[1]. And here
again he divined with unerring instinct the psychological factor
in dreams and foreshadowed the theories of the psycho-analysts
in a truly remarkable way[2].

His definition of sleep: 'a life full of the terrors of that divorce
between body and soul, which we have arbitrarily decreed' is a
revealing phrase here, and the hag-ridden nights he describes
were undoubtedly his own; but on the other hand he also knew
the consolation of beautiful dreams, when the scent of the
trampled roses and the song of the banished nightingales fled
for sanctuary into his unconscious mind.

The same conflict is apparent in another of Heine's most
striking characteristics, his brilliant and searching wit. In a
very interesting study Freud[3] establishes a suggestive parallel
between the technique of wit and the technique of dreams, and
shows further how both are adapted for the purpose of evading
the inhibiting censor. He comes to the conclusion that all the
great tendencies and instincts of the mind use wit for this
purpose in the same way as they use dreams; whilst all strong
tendencies which extend into the unconscious are a great in-
citement to wit. This, he concludes, may furnish an explanation for the fact that the subjective conditions favourable to
wit are so often found in neurotic and ill-balanced persons. It
goes far to furnish a solution of the riddle of Heine's many-sided
personality; for an analysis of his wit entirely justifies Freud's
thesis[4]. Throughout his work witticisms are to be met with based

[1] Cf. particularly Elster, III, pp. 21–23, 41–42; also *ibid*. IV, p. 505.
[2] *Ibid*. IV, p. 132, *Schnabelewopski*, 1833.
[3] S. Freud, *Der Witz und seine Beziehungen zum Unbewussten*, Leipzig
and Vienna, 1905.
[4] This has been admirably done by E. Eckertz, 'Heine und sein Witz,'
Literarhistorische Forschungen, Berlin, 1908, XXXVI; but he ignores the
Saint-Simonian influence.

HEINRICH HEINE

on the contrast between Hellenism and Nazarenism, Greek objec-
tivism and Christian spiritualism, that is to say the terms which
symbolised the two warring tendencies within him. These two
worlds are brought into witty contrast or united in his imagination in comparisons, enumerations, and various other combina-
tions. A typical example is the appellation 'Unsere liebe Frau
von Milo.'[1] But whereas before and after the Saint-Simonian
period the whole tone and tenor of his mind was imbued with
this sense of contrast, during the period we are now considering,
it was coloured with the conviction that in the glorious future
the two worlds would be as one.

Enough has probably been said to show how the discord in
Heine's nature, a discord which was never completely solved,
which pursued him into his dreams, and troubled his waking
hours, apparent moreover both in his sentimentality and in his
wit, must have made him peculiarly sensible of the beauty
underlying the Saint-Simonian conception of harmony between
flesh and spirit in man, between sensualism and spiritualism in
the world; a harmony which, far from being the abstract result
of an abstract philosophy, was presented to him under the guise
of a religion with a practical programme of reforms. It must
have seemed to him as if he had found at last what he had
been seeking for so long, as if indeed this religion were provi-
dentially revealed in answer to the needs of the whole world
lying sick of a one-sided spiritualism or clogged by a base
materialism. He owed to Enfantin in fact nothing more definite,
yet nothing less great than the hope of a solution of his personal
conflict and the great conflict of mankind.

So much for his spiritual debt. Intellectually, too, he owed the
Saint-Simonians much. Not that they presented him with anything fundamentally new. He had arrived independently at a
point of view which was almost identical with their doctrine; but
by the study of their completer philosophy, order was evolved out
of the chaos of his hitherto seemingly contradictory ideas. From
now onwards, Heine was in possession of the key to his puzzle,
and it is really remarkable to see how the odd pieces which lay
jumbled on the board slipped into their appropriate places and

---

[1] Elster, I, p. 487, *Nachwort zum Romancero*, 1851.

were combined into a coherent whole. The Saint-Simonians helped him to something in the nature of a complete philosophy of life; which, when it emerged from his mind, was not entirely theirs, although it bore a striking resemblance to theirs; Heine in fact remained independent; yet it is extremely doubtful whether he would ever have arrived at his synthesis without their help. He entered into his own kingdom, but it was the Saint-Simonians who unbarred the gates.

(b) ORDER OUT OF CHAOS

It is not my intention to quote once more all those passages in the *Romantische Schule*, and *Zur Geschichte der Religion und Philosophie in Deutschland*, which Strodtmann, Stigand and Lichtenberger have already used in their chapters on Heine and Saint-Simonism and which form conclusive evidence of the extent of the influence of Saint-Simonism on Heine's mind. This is old ground, and needs no working over. With German thoroughness and French acuteness[1] they have said between them everything that is worth saying on this subject, and Lichtenberger especially has brought the two doctrines face to face, and established interesting textual resemblances; rather I shall attempt to show how what before was undeveloped and incoherent in Heine's mind was combined into a logical synthesis, and to decide how far the new religion which Heine preached was or was not Saint-Simonism.

In the first place Heine accepted from the Saint-Simonians their philosophy of history. As early as 1826 he characterised the Middle Ages as an organic period, though he did not use the term, and in 1829 he came sensibly nearer to this conception, speaking of antiquity and the Middle Ages as periods in which humanity was whole and at one. He now adopted their idea of progress, and therefore the critical period from which he suffered so greatly fell into its proper place; he no longer looked back to antiquity and the Middle Ages with ill-defined longing, he looked forward to the golden age on earth[2]. Like

[1] Stigand's chapter on Saint-Simonism itself bristles with inaccuracies; and that portion of it which deals with Heine and Saint-Simonism is merely an abbreviated version of Strodtmann.

[2] Cf. Elster, VII, pp. 294–296, *Verschiedenartige Geschichtsauffassung*, about 1832.

the Saint-Simonians, he was unwilling to relegate this golden
age into the far-distant future; he wished to establish it here
and now by means of the fundamental principle, 'le pain est le
droit du peuple,' which he would alter to 'le pain est le droit
divin de l'homme.'[1] Here again an old dislike of the substitution
of heavenly for earthly joys found a complete justification[2].
But it is in the application of the doctrine of progress to the
religious history of the world that his former confusion of mind
most conspicuously disappears, and this without the rejection
of a single one of those views whose inconsistency had tormented him so greatly in earlier years. For he now felt that
Christianity had been a wholesome reaction against the overweening pride of the flesh in pagan times[3]; but also that it had
long ago fulfilled its mission, and that the spirit had become
overbold. Thus two strangely opposite tendencies in his mind,
his love and hatred of Christianity, found their solution. He
will still respond to the beauty of Christianity as an artist and
as a romantic; and he will do this with a good conscience, since
history has proved to him the divine mission of this religion;
on the other hand his hatred of Christianity has now become
the noble hatred of the man of progress; it is a reasoned impulse,
and not a purely destructive one, since it is combined with the
acceptance of a new religion in which all that is beautiful in
Christian spirituality shall be retained and united with all that
is beautiful in pagan sensualism[4]. And there follows a repetition
of the prophecy on the battlefield of Marengo: happier and more
beautiful generations will arise 'durch freie Wahlumarmung.'
But whereas in the earlier prophecy the emphasis was on liberty,
it is now on the happiness to be tasted in the future by means
of the religion of joy. Further, by adopting the Saint-Simonian
use of the terms spiritualism and sensualism, he arrived at the
definition of these two philosophies of life, and thus crystallised
his ideas once and for all on this subject. He had felt the antithesis before both in himself and in the world around him, but
from now onwards they became for him the only two possible

---

[1] Cf. Elster, VII, p. 296; IV, p. 223.
[2] Cf. *ibid.* V, pp. 217, 261; IV, p. 170.
[3] *Ibid.* V, p. 218.
[4] Cf. *ibid.* V, p. 327; IV, p. 170.

attitudes towards life. It should be noticed here however that sensualism meant to him during this period the philosophy which harmonised flesh and spirit. He used the term more loosely than the Saint-Simonians who took sensualism and spiritualism as the two aspects of their religion which combined both[1]. Later he was to see once more in sensualism the antithesis of spiritualism.

Heine had forestalled the attitude of the Saint-Simonians towards Christianity in 1821, for his criticism of its sadness, austerity and renunciation was formulated in *Almansor*, four years before the appearance of the *Nouveau Christianisme*. Nevertheless, the analysis of the Christian dualism, by which good and evil seemed impersonated in spirit and flesh, was like a light switched on in a dark room. Whereas he had groped blindly before, fumbling and reconnoitring, he now saw everything in its place and in its true proportions; a revelation all the more dazzling and perhaps all the more surprising because he had known it all beforehand, but by touch and not by sight, by his feelings and not by his reason. So that when he now asks, 'What is the idea of Christianity?' he no longer answers, as both he and Saint-Simon had answered before: 'brotherly love'; he re-writes whole pages from the *Exposition*. *Deuxième année* to prove that the root idea of Christianity lay in the dualism between flesh and spirit[2].

Last but not least the phrases 'anathema against the flesh,' 'rehabilitation of matter,' appealed to the sensationalist in Heine; and though it may sound frivolous, yet I believe it to be true that these convenient, symbolical catch-words did almost more than anything else to crystallise his views.

(c) *DIE ROMANTISCHE SCHULE*

The historical attitude towards religion generally and Christianity in particular affected profoundly Heine's theory of art, which found expression in *Die Romantische Schule*[3]. His in-

---

[1] Cf. Elster, IV, p. 208. Cf. also *ibid.* IV, pp. 185 and 187–188 for Heine's defence of spiritualism.

[2] Elster, IV, pp. 168 ff., 220.

[3] First published under the title *Zur Geschichte der neueren schönen Literatur in Deutschland*, Paris and Leipzig, 1833; and republished under the title *Romantische Schule*, Hamburg, 1835, augmented by about a third.

stinctive dislike of the mediaevalism and Catholicism of the
German romantic poets had been expressed in 1820 in his essay
Die Romantik; but he had only the vaguest notions of the
characteristics of mediaeval art, and probably but the slightest
acquaintance with its monuments. The journey to Italy had
increased his knowledge, and when he came to review his impressions in 1833, with the revealing phrase 'anathema against
the flesh' sounding in his ears, he found in the whole field of
mediaeval art the enduring expression of that anathema. The
works of art of that period expressed in his view the domination
of matter by mind, and to do this was often, he maintained,
their whole task[1]. From this angle he proceeded to an analysis
of German epic poetry during the Middle Ages[2], and showed
that the fundamental difference between classicism and romanticism lay in the symbolism of the latter, which wished to
represent the infinite, spiritual relationships and truths, and
was therefore forced to seek refuge in parables and symbols[3].
This might still pass in the recitative arts which are spiritual
in their nature, but the plastic arts had a most unnatural task
to fulfil, since they must represent the conquest of matter by
means of matter itself. There follows an eloquent page on the
martyrdom of sculpture during the Middle Ages, and the pictures
which seem to have been painted for the galleries of an execu-
tioner. He recognised the beauty in the pictures of the Madonna;
but this was because the painters did homage to beauty at the
cost of spiritualism. Architecture showed the same character
as the other arts; and Heine illustrated this thesis by the famous
description of the Gothic cathedral, an elaboration of Almansor's
speech, but much more poetical; for his whole conception of
Christianity had deepened and become more convincing, established as it now was on the revelation of the Christian dualism
which found an echo in his own nature[4].

And this is the kind of art which the romantic poets wish to
revive; so runs the moral of the book, and although Heine was
not stinting of praise for some amongst them, yet he condemned

---

[1] Elster, v, p. 219. [2] *Ibid.* v, pp. 220 ff.
[3] Cf. Elster, v, p. 224.
[4] Elster, v, p. 226. Cf. also *ibid.* iv, p. 171.

the movement as a whole; like Goethe he considered that
romanticism and sickness were almost the same thing[1]. And he
was particularly incensed with those members of the school
who had gone over to Catholicism, to the party of lies; the
myrmidons of despotism, who wished to revive the misery, the
horrors and the foolishness of the past[2]. The tendency of the
book as a whole lies in this characterisation of romanticism as
reactionary, and German Catholicism as the political instrument
of that reaction, the hoary warder who would force Germany
back into the prison from which she has escaped. Hence his
praise of Protestantism[3], because it favours freedom of thought.
Hence his exaggerated appreciation of the Young Germans,
whom he regarded as artists, tribunes and apostles, fighting in
the good cause[4]. It is interesting to notice that in this book,
Heine adopted the Saint-Simonian theory of the artist priest.
He was putting it into practice by the whole tendency of *Die
Romantische Schule*, and he further made his adherence to it
perfectly clear, by his strictures on Goethe's artistic aloofness
from the great questions of his day[5]. Saint-Simonism may be
said to have affected Heine's theory of art in three ways. Firstly
it supplied him with a very suggestive interpretation of the art
of the Middle Ages and of its romantic revival[6]. Secondly it
hardened in him the tendency already noticeable in his earlier
writings to regard art as a pulpit from which to proclaim his
social and religious theories[7]; and lastly it supplied him with
an historical background against which the history of German
literature appeared to him as a series of successive religious
reactions[8].

[1] Elster, v, p. 302.
[2] *Ibid.* v, p. 355. Heine was careful to distinguish German from French
Catholicism in this piece of invective.
[3] *Ibid.* v, pp. 240–241.
[4] *Ibid.* v, pp. 328–330.
[5] *Ibid.* v, pp. 251–252, 254.
[6] He saw in the *Faust* saga an attempt at the 'rehabilitation of the
flesh' (Elster, v, p. 261) and in *Don Quixote* an allegory of the strife between spirit and flesh (Elster, v, p. 292).
[7] This tendency is particularly noticeable in *Französische Maler*, 1831.
[8] Elster, v, pp. 238–239.

(d) ZUR GESCHICHTE DER RELIGION UND PHILOSOPHIE IN DEUTSCHLAND

Heine saw in the history of German literature a succession of religious reactions: Christianity against paganism, the Renaissance against Christianity, mediaeval romanticism against the imitation of the classical writers, and finally the Young German movement against Catholic romanticism. In the history of religion and philosophy in Germany he saw a never-ending struggle between spiritualism and sensualism, in which sensualism, so far almost continually vanquished, was now on the eve of victory. He opened his argument with the exposition of the Christian dualism, borrowed from the *Doctrine de Saint-Simon*, but in the description of the influence of this dualism on Mediaeval Europe his deepened comprehension of the nature of Christianity affected the theme of the banishment of the gods which had early attracted him; and his interest in goblins, elves, and spirits inherited from the romantic school took on a philosophical colouring. In particular he reproached Christianity for having converted the old Germanic pantheism into pandaemonism[1]. Though Heine had constantly recurred in his earlier writings to the theme of the disappearance of the gods, or the exile of the gods on the appearance of Christ, this is the first time that he spoke of their transformation into devils, and whereas until now it was the Olympian gods whose loss he lamented, somewhat after the manner of Schiller and purely as a poet, the relics of old Germanic pantheism are now the chief subject of his study, whilst his attitude is less romantic and more philosophical. In *Elementargeister* he was to give a more detailed account of mediaeval German daemonology, but the conception and treatment differ not at all from the corresponding pages of this earlier book[2].

This, then, was the first stage in the victory of spiritualism, the old gods were banished to hell, and Christianity reigned in Europe. But the idea of Christianity, the destruction of sen-

---

[1] Cf. Elster, IV, pp. 173–174, 182.
[2] Elster, IV, pp. 172–183. In 1830 Heine was planning a book on witchcraft (VII, pp. 54–55); the clearer realisation of the Christian dualism gave him the necessary impetus.

sualism, was altogether too much in contradiction with human
nature ever to be completely carried out. Catholicism was clear-
sighted enough to perceive this; it established a compromise
between flesh and spirit, a concordat between God and the devil.
The supremacy of the spirit was proclaimed in theory; but in
practice the flesh was allowed its rights[1]. It was the wisdom of
this compromise which Luther was unable to understand; the
selling of indulgences was not an abuse, it was a consequence
of the whole system; and in attacking it, he did really attack
the Church itself, and the Pope was right, from his point of view,
in proclaiming Luther a heretic. The Reformation therefore in
the first instance was spiritualism attacking sensualism; in its
result, it was the temporary liberation and triumph of sensualism[2]. But the result was not of long duration. Spiritualism
came forth again as conqueror in the north, but it was nourishing
a viper in its bosom, which would sting it to death. This was
the freedom of thought which the Reformation had established
in Germany, and which was to prove of such world-wide importance. For the finest flower of freedom of thought was
German philosophy[3]. This gave the sanction of logic to Heine's
championship of the spirit of Protestantism[4], and to his hero-
worship of Luther[5], which before this date had been vague and
unreasoned enthusiasms.

Having defined the religious revolution in terms of sensualism
and spiritualism, he then reviewed the philosophical revolution
in the same way; and here, in the second part of the book, he
acclaimed the advent of pantheism, already, he affirmed, the
secret religion of Germany; and prepared the ground for the
annihilation of deism by the hand of Kant. This, from our
point of view, is the nucleus of the book, for in these pages
Heine joined forces with the Saint-Simonians in demanding the
'rehabilitation of the flesh'; and he did this in language which
puts their prosaic eloquence completely into the shade. His

---

[1] In this connection Heine develops an earlier theme of the *Reisebilder*:
the literary satires to which this compromise gave rise in France, ending
with *Tartufe* and Voltaire. Elster, IV, pp. 186–187; cf. *ibid.* III, pp. 386–387.
[2] Elster, IV, p. 188.   [3] *Ibid.* IV, p. 194.
[4] *Ibid.* IV, p. 230; cf. *ibid.* V, p. 240.
[5] *Ibid.* IV, pp. 190–191, 196.

pantheism however, based on the pantheism of Spinoza, is rather different from theirs; it is more eloquently exposed, more nearly akin to Schelling's *Naturphilosophie* and shows no trace of their philosophical trinity, nor of the curious modification, by which it came much closer to deism, the theory of the material manifestation of God in male and female form. He had declared in the *Romantische Schule* that the great law of progress in nature, by which God manifests himself in all things, but not in all things equally, and by which every creature carries within itself the desire to attain to a higher degree of godliness, had been most profoundly understood and most clearly revealed by the Saint-Simonians[1]. He now acknowledged briefly that they had wished to increase the material happiness of people and to fight for the divine rights of mankind; they were unfavourably placed however and the surrounding materialism had crushed them[2]. Otherwise he did not touch on their pantheistic views. Enfantin, in his letter to Heine, criticised the system of Spinoza as too theoretical, too philosophical and not sufficiently religious. In the *Exposition*, Bazard had seen between Saint-Simonism and Spinozism the difference between harmony and homogeneity. To similar systems he gave the name 'confusion panthéistique.' They did not therefore see eye to eye on this subject, yet there is much in Heine's pantheism which is Saint-Simonian:

'Gott,' welcher von Spinoza die eine Substanz und von den deutschen Philosophen das Absolute genannt wird, 'ist Alles, was da ist,' er ist sowohl Materie wie Geist, Beides ist gleich göttlich, und wer die heilige Materie beleidigt, ist eben so sündhaft, wie Der, welcher sündigt gegen den heiligen Geist[3].

This led him to inveigh against the disastrous results of the Christian dualism, and to conclude that great sacrifices ought to be offered to the flesh to compensate for the oppression to which it has been subjected; and that feasts should be ordained to help mankind back to moral health:

Der nächste Zweck aller unserer neuen Institutionen ist solcher massen die Rehabilitation der Materie, die Wiedereinsetzung derselben in ihre Würde, ihre moralische Anerkennung, ihre religiöse

---

[1] Elster, v, pp. 252–253. [2] *Ibid.* iv, p. 224.
[3] *Ibid.* iv, p. 219.

Heiligung, ihre Versöhnung mit dem Geiste....Durch ihre gewaltsame Trennung...entstand die grosse Weltzerrissenheit, das Übel[1].

For evil in the world is the result of this terrible blasphemy
against matter, which becomes evil only when it must conspire
in secret against the usurpation of the spirit, or prostitutes itself
because the spirit has branded it, or revenges itself on the spirit
in the hatred of despair.

And indeed matter cannot be evil, for God resides in matter.
He is identical with the world[2]; he manifests himself in plants
and stones, in the animal kingdom, and most gloriously of all
in man; not in single men or through a single man, but in mankind; every man conceives and represents only a part of the
God-universe, but mankind together conceives and represents
the God-universe in idea and in reality[3]. God therefore is the
great hero of the history of the world, and it can be said with
truth of humanity as a whole that it is the incarnation of God[4].
This pantheism is an open secret in Germany. Indeed, we have
outgrown deism. We are free, and want no thundering tyrants.
We are of age, and need no father's care. Nor are we the
bungling work of a great mechanic. Deism is a religion for
serfs, for children, for Genevans and for watchmakers[5].

The destruction of deism by Kant has made the establishment of pantheism inevitable in Germany; but it is not to be
expected that this will take place peacefully. Kant is the
Robespierre, and Fichte the Napoleon of the German revolution,
but the end will not be as bloodless as the beginning, and
Kantians, Fichtians and pantheists will combine to establish the
German republic. And the pantheists will be the most terrible
of all, for they are at one with the forces of nature and can
conjure up the old Germanic pantheism; the same lust of battle

---

[1] Elster, IV, pp. 221–222. Enfantin in the *Enseignements* had also proclaimed the necessity of feasts, and indeed had put this theory into practice
in the balls and *soirées* which the Saint-Simonians gave to the Parisian
public during the winter of 1832, and which Heine attended.

[2] Elster, IV, p. 222; cf. p. 285 and V, pp. 293–294.

[3] The Saint-Simonians held that God manifested himself especially in
the 'hommes providentiels.' Although Heine adopts this term, and uses
it as they do, e.g. of Luther, he does not appear to have accepted their
theory of the personal divinity of great men.

[4] Elster, IV, pp. 222–223.   [5] *Ibid.* IV, p. 224.

will awake in them which we find in the old Germans, who did
not fight to destroy, or to win, but simply to fight:

Das Christentum—und Das ist sein schönstes Verdienst—hat jene
brutale germanische Kampflust einigermassen besänftigt, konnte sie
jedoch nicht zerstören, und wenn einst der zähmende Talisman, das
Kreuz, zerbricht, dann rasselt wieder empor die Wildheit der alten
Kämpfer, die unsinnige Berserkerwuth, wovon die nordischen Dichter
so viel singen und sagen. Jener Talisman ist morsch, und kommen
wird der Tag, wo er kläglich zusammenbricht. Die alten steinernen
Götter erheben sich dann aus dem verschollenen Schutt and reiben
sich den tausendjährigen Staub aus den Augen, und Thor mit dem
Riesenhammer springt endlich empor und zerschlägt die gothischen
Dome[1].

The tendency of this history of German religion and philosophy
is now clear. It was the proclamation of the gospel of pantheism,
ending with a fine terroristic prophecy. This pantheism, though
it owed much to the Saint-Simonian system, was in its essence
peculiarly German; and Heine was careful to connect it with the
old Germanic pantheism which Christianity had perverted to
pandaemonism, but which still formed part of the life of the
people.

But in the proclamation of the 'rehabilitation of the flesh'
Heine spoke as a Saint-Simonian, with greater eloquence, certainly, and less practically, but still as they were wont to speak.
There is however no mention of the position of women, or of
the relations between men and women, unless we except the
repetition of the phrase 'freie Wahlumarmung,' which has lost
none of its vagueness. Nor did Heine seem much concerned for
the rehabilitation of industry[2], although he was undoubtedly at
one with the Saint-Simonians in his wish to rehabilitate the
people.

He took their catch-word in a narrower sense, but in that sense
it probably meant more to him than it did to them, for he was
profoundly convinced that he was aiming at nothing less than
the rehabilitation of beauty, and this made a far greater and more
intimate appeal to his artistic nature than to their more philosophical minds; however earnestly they might praise beauty

---

[1] Elster, IV, p. 294.
[2] He mentions it once however: 'und die Industrie wird der alten
Schmach entlastet,' Elster, IV, p. 221.

and though they placed it at the head of their trinity, BEAUTY, *truth* and *usefulness*, it was to them rather an abstract conception than a living force.

(e) HEINE'S INTERPRETATION OF THE DOCTRINE

Heine is an eloquent pleader, and many an imaginative mind may have been dazzled by the riches which these two books promise to mankind in the fair pantheistic future he foresees. Certainly they were the most brilliant advertisement for Saint-Simonism, their only fault in this respect being that they came too late, when the Saint-Simonians as a religious fraternity had already ceased to exist. Enfantin on the whole showed himself but moderately pleased with *De l'Allemagne*, and found a good deal more in it to blame than to praise: it was not so much points of doctrine, except in the case of Spinozism, which offended him, as Heine's belligerent attitude towards Catholicism and his polemical prophecy of the German revolution, which shocked and startled him profoundly. The Saint-Simonians had spent much breath in calling the artists to their aid, and no one but Félicien David had responded. When Heine espoused their cause, or a cause that was nearly theirs, he made it his own, and spoke independently and passionately, according to his nature, caring little whether he expressed their views, Spinoza's, Schelling's, Hegel's or his own, so long as he obtained a hearing and unburdened his soul of the message which oppressed him. This, however, was not exactly the *rôle* which the Saint-Simonians assigned to the artists, and which is best illustrated by the following story:

Duveyrier, l'un des coreligionnaires de David, le pria un jour de composer une symphonie sur la devise Saint-Simonienne: 'A chacun suivant sa capacité, à chaque capacité suivant ses œuvres,' thème peu susceptible de développements musicaux et qui heureusement demeura stérile.[1]

The Saint-Simonians must indeed have looked at Heine with startled eyes if they were capable of such an interpretation of the functions of art. Although Enfantin by no means despaired of him, and even assigned him an honourable position in the

[1] R. Brancour, *Félicien David*, Paris, 1910, p. 21, footnote 2.

'Apostolat Royal,' he yet regarded him with some of the feelings of that unfortunate individual who loosed the genie from the bottle, and was then chiefly concerned with the problem how best to coax it back. Heine, for his part, was not only far removed from the eager, submissive discipleship of a Félicien David, he did not consider himself a disciple at all, but rather the servant of an idea:

> Die Leute glauben, unser Thun und Schaffen sei eitel Wahl, aus dem Vorrath der neuen Ideen griffen wir eine heraus, für die wir sprechen und wirken, streiten und leiden wollten, wie etwa sonst ein Philolog sich seinen Klassiker auswählte, mit dessen Kommentierung er sich sein ganzes Leben hindurch beschäftigte—nein, wir ergreifen keine Idee, sondern die Idee ergreift uns, und knechtet uns, und peitscht uns in die Arena hinein, dass wir, wie gezwungene Gladiatoren, für sie kämpfen[1].

Heine went on to define the idea which had seized and enslaved him; it is his apology for those poems which were included in *Salon I* between *Französische Maler* and *Schnabelewopski*[2]; the hypocrites of all colours will once more sigh very deeply over many a poem in the book, he declared, but it will avail them little:

> Ein zweites 'nachwachsendes Geschlecht' hat eingesehen, dass all mein Wort und Lied aus einer grossen, gottfreudigen Frühlingsidee emporblühte, die, wo nicht besser, doch wenigstens eben so respektabel ist, wie jene triste, modrige Aschermittwochsidee, die unser schönes Europa trübselig entblumt und mit Gespenstern und Tartüffen bevölkert hat[3].

This 'grosse, gottfreudige Frühlingsidee' had now become the only master he acknowledged, the only cause to which undivided loyalty was due. And that he was in fact a true servant of this idea is proved by the letter he wrote to Laube, after Menzel had opened fire on the religious and political views of the Young Germans:

> Ich beschwöre Sie bey allem, was Sie lieben, in dem Kriege, den das junge Deutschland jetzt führt, wo nicht Parthey zu fassen, doch wenigstens eine sehr *schützende* Neutralität zu behaupten, auch mit

[1] Elster, IV, p. 14, *Vorrede zu Salon I*, dated October 17, 1833.

[2] Chiefly the poems entitled *Verschiedene*, in which Heine sings the 'niedere Minne'; and including the poem quoted above.

[3] Elster, IV, pp. 13–14; cf. also *Zur Geschichte der neueren schönen Literatur in Deutschland*, Elster, V, p. 528, dated April 2, 1833.

keinem Worte diese Jugend anzutasten. Machen Sie eine genaue Scheidung zwischen politischen und religiösen Fragen. In den politischen Fragen können Sie so viel Concessionen machen, als Sie nur immer wollen, denn die politischen Staatsformen und Regierungen sind nur Mittel.... Ich sage das religiöse Prinzip und Moral, obgleich beides Speck und Schweinefleisch ist, eins und dasselbe. Die Moral ist nur eine in die Sitten übergangene Religion (Sittlichkeit). Ist aber die Religion der Vergangenheit verfault, so wird auch die Moral stinkisch. Wir wollen eine gesunde Religion, damit die Sitten wieder gesunden, damit sie besser basirt werden als jetzt, wo sie nur Unglauben und abgestandene Heucheley zur Basis haben[1].

This letter is an eloquent testimony to the fact that Heine was deeply in earnest on the subject of his religious views. Nothing was to stand in the way of the establishment of a healthy religion, which would react on morality, and to which end political institutions were but means. That is why he had always proclaimed his Protestantism, that is why he would not even disdain the help of the Philistines. And he concluded the letter by adopting, if with a half-humorous reservation, the title of the first father of the Saint-Simonian church in Germany. He might laugh at the title, because he was not a root-and-branch Saint-Simonian; but he did not actually reject it, because he knew how intimately connected were his ideas and theirs. The original revelation of the possibility of a harmony between senses and spirit he owed, I think, to the Saint-Simonians[2]; but it was a debt that was easy to overlook, since we have seen that he came to Paris already speaking their language and thinking most of their thoughts. These thoughts now became co-ordinated and coherent; their relative value was enhanced, but they remained the same, and were moreover the thoughts which his temperament compelled him to think. The question of influence in a case like this is a peculiarly delicate one to decide, and Heine's position in this matter is not without ambiguity. He preached their doctrine; he described himself as the slave of an idea which is in effect the union of the Christian dualism spirit *v.* flesh in the Saint-Simonian trinity LOVE =

---

[1] Hirth, II, pp. 86–87, dated November 23, 1835.

[2] Cf. here an article in the *Modern Language Review*, January 1923, on *The Date of the Letters from Heligoland*; in which I have given reasons for supposing that they were re-written in 1840, more particularly those passages which seem to be proclaiming such a harmony as early as 1830.

spirit + flesh, an idea which we seek for vainly in his earlier writings; he adopted their philosophy of history and their analysis of the nature of Christianity; he repeated their very catch-words, and dedicated the completed work to their supreme chief; yet he proclaimed his independence emphatically, and was silent on the subject of debt. So that, if I said before that he reserved his appreciation for their religious doctrine, I must qualify that statement now, and add that his expression of that appreciation is on the whole guarded, and to be sought for rather in the trend of *De l'Allemagne* than in the few definite statements he made on the subject of Saint-Simonism.

An attempt to summarise Heine's interpretation of the Saint-Simonian doctrine ends in some sort in a characterisation of Heine himself, for he interpreted their views according to the dictates of his nature, and therefore of his fate. Their breadth of vision was denied to him, and where they were most emphatically men of progress, they walked their ways without him. Not for Heine the optimism which could confidently foresee vast benefits to mankind by means of industrial progress, a belief that was not shaken whilst trains were wrecked and fortunes lost and won on the stock exchange; a faith which he abandoned to join the ranks of the timid and the conventionalists, of the romantics who dream their way back to the glories of the past, while humanity steps over them to the unseen golden future. Not for him either the courage to see the potential greatness of one half of mankind, and to salute in woman the equal of man, a faith which was not weakened though the women proved unequal to the first imperious demands, and the mystic mother remained deaf to their prayers. The idealism that underlay their industrialism and their feminism was a closed book to Heine. But it must not be forgotten that he was far too great an idealist in love to follow Enfantin along those winding paths which led the prophet of progress back to a primitive promiscuousness, which had not even the simplicity of savage customs to recommend it, since it was combined with a religious mysticism which made it more repellent. Nor should it be forgotten that his sound common sense protected him from any association with their many absurdities and excesses; whilst

his innate good taste never suffered contamination from the less
pleasant side of their views. And yet it might seem that in his
demand for the 'rehabilitation of the flesh,' and in his prophecy
of pantheism and harmony between senses and soul he was
committed to the whole of their programme. It might be argued,
and argued plausibly, that the tendency of *De l'Allemagne* is
an immoral one, yet this immorality would never be granted by
those who love beauty. The rehabilitation of beauty which
Heine dreamt of in these two books is perhaps impracticable and
might well end in immorality: but he was unaware, I think, of
the snares and pitfalls which surrounded his feet. For Heine this
doctrine was encircled by the girdle of Aphrodite which lends
beauty and grace to the wearer. It would be a carping critic
indeed who could read these books to-day, and feel none of the
inspiration and intoxication which dictated them; and an uncompromising moralist alone could attribute this inspiration to
impure sources. Heine was not a thinker, and it is because of
its very vagueness and beauty that the doctrine expounded by
Heine is more dangerous than the *Enseignements d'Enfantin*.
He was an artist intoxicated by no unworthy ideal; he dreamt
dreams and saw visions which may be for ever unreal, whose
attempted realisation might even end in the grossest immorality;
and yet which in themselves, and taken as visions and dreams,
are not without beauty, and not without truth.

The difficult task of attempting to balance his doctrine
against theirs ends with the scales almost equally poised. Theirs
was the broader vision, the surer feeling for progress; his the
saving sense of beauty, the poet's secret which kept him from
their mistakes; but his also the romantic lack of courage which
evaded the practical issue and was contented with words for
deeds.

CHAPTER VIII

DISILLUSION

(a) 1836–1848

There is nothing to be gained by composing a list of all those passages in Heine's works after 1835 which still show traces of Saint-Simonian influence, although there are innumerable traces to be found. He never really returned to the charge. The first and obvious reason was that his books would not have been published if he had done so; as a political and religious writer he was gagged until the Edicts were revoked in 1842. Another reason lay in the fact that he had exhausted the vein. He had nothing to add to *De l'Allemagne*; he had said what he had to say about the spiritualism of Christianity, and had hurled his alarming prophecy of pantheism in the teeth of an angry fatherland. How to establish it, he knew no more than the Saint-Simonians, who at least had made great efforts to be practical and constructive. Prophecy was the utmost Heine could achieve in the way of constructive policy, and he could not easily improve on what he had already done in that line. The third reason is to be found in an ever-increasing personal disillusionment on the subject. There is first-hand evidence of this disappointment in a letter to the Princess Belgiojoso in which he is to be found dallying with the idea of making an 'ignoble peace' with the authorities beyond the Rhine. He was ill with jaundice at the time, and suffering in spirit as well as in purse as a result of the Prussian and Federal Edicts; indeed writing to Moser a week later he called this period 'die schmerzlichste Passionszeit meines Lebens.'[1] His letter to the princess further illustrates his state of mind:

Vous auriez une juste idée du triste état de ma santé morale, si vous saviez quelle réaction se fait depuis peu dans mon esprit par rapport aux doctrines religieuses dont on me connaît l'adversaire. Mes opinions sont en contradiction d'avec mes sentiments; je porte un chapelet de roses sur la tête et la douleur dans mon cœur. J'ai soif d'unité morale, de faire harmoniser mes opinions avec mes senti-

[1] Hirth, II, p. 126, dated November 8, 1836.

ments; il faut que j'arrache toutes les feuilles roses de mon chapelet, afin qu'il ne reste qu'une couronne d'épines, ou que j'anéantisse toutes les souffrances de mon cœur, et que je les remplace par de nouvelles joies. Mais hélas! je les combats en vain, ces douleurs; elles sont cuirassées, et les armes les plus acérées de la raison s'émoussent contre elles[1].

Heine was early discovering that it is one thing to declare that one ought to be happy, and that happiness can be obtained by harmonising the senses and the soul, and another thing to establish that harmony. He was suffering in body and in mind, and it is difficult to see how the 'rehabilitation of the flesh' was to benefit a sick man, or a harmonious balance between spirit and senses to assuage the pangs of home-sickness or to fill his purse. He was already aware of the canker in the Saint-Simonian rose; and during the period 1836–1848 we shall find him ever less enthusiastic about the 'emancipation of the flesh' and the gospel of harmony and joy.

There are four main tendencies to be observed in Heine's prose writings during these years. He first returned to the *Reisebilder* style[2]; then he became involved in personal polemics to which he devoted all his energies for several years[3]; later he turned once more to the political journalism of the *Französische Zustände* of 1832[4]. The fourth and most interesting tendency is the deflection of his religious interests into the channel of daemonology apparent in the *Elementargeister*, 1836, the *Göttin Diana*, 1846, and the *Faustballet*, 1847; all these books deal

---

[1] Hirth, II, pp. 122–123, dated October 30, 1836.

[2] *Florentinische Nächte*, 1835–1836. *Die Memoiren des Herrn von Schnabelewopski*, written in 1833, are in the same vein; they continue under the guise of mockery the theme of the destruction of deism.

[3] (a) *Vorrede zu Salon III: Ueber den Denuncianten*, 1837; an attack against Menzel.

(b) *Schwabenspiegel*, 1838; directed against the Suabian school who had attacked him, notably G. Pfizer, in his article *Heine's Schriften und Tendenz*, 1838, which embodies an able and weighty criticism on his religious views, with a very undiscriminating attack on the quality of his prose.

(c) *Schriftstellernöthen*, 1839; directed against Campe, Gutzkow and especially Wihl on the occasion of the mutilated publication of *Schwabenspiegel*.

(d) *Heinrich Heine über Ludwig Börne*, 1840; also partly political and religious in tendency.

[4] *Lutetia*, 1840–1843; *Atta Troll*, 1842; and *Deutschland, ein Wintermärchen*, 1844, are a mixture of personal, political and religious polemics.

with the theme of the banished and wandering gods which
recurs also in *Atta Troll*[1] and in the book on Börne[2]. Under
this poetical guise he continued his criticism of Christian spiritualism, contrasted it with the joyousness of paganism, and left
his readers to draw their own conclusions. Of these three books
the *Elementargeister* alone is polemical in tone, and shows a close
connection with *Zur Geschichte der Religion und Philosophie in
Deutschland*; it is here that Heine first used the terms Judaism
and Nazarenism for Christian spiritualism in a passage on the
neo-Platonic philosophers[3]. But there is an elegiac note running
through the *Elementargeister*; the pessimism peculiar to Heine
came creeping back and found an expression in the legend of
Tannhäuser:

> Aber der Mensch ist nicht immer aufgelegt zum Lachen, er wird
> manchmal still und ernst und denkt zurück in die Vergangenheit;
> denn die Vergangenheit ist die eigentliche Heimat seiner Seele, und
> es erfasst ihn ein Heimweh nach den Gefühlen, die er einst empfunden
> hat, und seien es auch Gefühle des Schmerzes[4].

During the preceding period the emphasis lay on the harmony
to be established between the two philosophies of life, but during
the period we are now considering, Heine was chiefly preoccupied
with the antithesis between them, gradually slipping back to his
former point of view that they are irreconcilable. He did not
hesitate in his choice between them, but it is significant that it
was now rather a case of choosing than of uniting. In his book
on Börne he crowned his Hellenism as the 'greater philosophy,'
by implication the one which will harmonise the sensual and
spiritual natures of man, but at the same time he saw between
Hellenism and Judaism an eternal and never-ending duel[5]. The
Saint-Simonians would have considered this a grave confusion
of thought, since Hellenism, used in this sense for harmony,
should find room for Judaism and paganism and unite them
both. Heine however, by intuition a sounder psychologist than
the Saint-Simonians, was discovering with painful clearness all
the difficulty of striking a fair balance between these two ten-

---

[1] Elster, II, pp. 391 ff., *Die Wilde Jagd*.
[2] *Ibid.* VII, pp. 144–146.   [3] *Ibid.* IV, p. 423.
[4] *Ibid.* IV, p. 429; cf. also for his pessimism *ibid.* IV, p. 421, although
the passage ends on a robuster note.   [5] *Ibid.* VII, p. 23.

dencies within himself, and this led him to despair of such a balance for humanity. Hence many hasty generalisations in his amusing division of men into the fat and the lean kinds[1]. During these years he placed himself in the former category and his enemies in the latter, or perhaps it is truer to say that he looked upon the lean kind as his natural enemies. Börne is the typical example, but he was far from being the only one: Hengstenberg[2], the Communists[3], Liszt[4], Leroux[5], Michelet[6], Quinet[7], Lamennais[8], and Bocage[9]; he characterised all these men from this point of view, and placed them in one category or the other. The story which the indefatigable Karpeles extracted from Laube of the visit to George Sand in the winter of 1839, and which he collated with Laube's shorter version in the *Erinnerungen*, is a precious document here. For we are privileged to witness Heine defending sensualism against Lamennais with an eloquence and command of the French language which left Laube open-mouthed with admiration, and completely nonplussed Lamennais, who was quite unable to meet the torrent of wit and wisdom which poured from Heine's lips: 'Er herrschte bei diesem Lever wie ein Imperator des Geistes,' Laube reported in hushed accents, and Karpeles concludes:

Bei diesem Symposion hatte allerdings zum erstenmal vielleicht ein Deutscher in Paris das grosse Wort geführt und vielleicht auch zum erstenmal der Sensualismus den Spiritualismus, in der Debatte wenigstens, überwunden[10].

Again, Heine's enthusiasm for Hebbel's *Judith* is very characteristic; it was a theme after his own heart, since it presented the tragic conflict between Judaism and paganism. We owe to Hebbel's inveterate diary-habit the transcription of the very words which Heine used in his discussion of the play with the author on October 14, 1843:

Auch Holofernes in seiner Selbstvergötterung sei sehr tief angelegt, und ich hätte ihm, dem blassen jüdischen Spiritualismus gegenüber, gern noch mehr kecke Lebenslust geben können[11].

[1] Elster, VII, p. 39.   [2] *Ibid.* IV, p. 500.   [3] *Ibid.* VI, p. 409.
[4] *Ibid.* IV, p. 558.   [5] *Ibid.* VI, pp. 410, 414, 416.   [6] *Ibid.* VI, p. 401.
[7] *Ibid.* V, p. 403.   [8] *Ibid.* IV, p. 558 and VII, p. 24.
[9] *Ibid.* IV, pp. 529–530.
[10] G. Karpeles, *Heinrich Heine, aus seinem Leben und aus seiner Zeit*, p. 241.   [11] *Hebbels Werke*, ed. Poppe, IX, p. 366.

During this period then Heine showed a reactionary tendency towards paganism, rather than an attempt at harmony between paganism and Christianity, and this perhaps was because this now seemed the shortest way to happiness. Thus in the *Göttin Diana*, a ballet in which, to quote the libretto, 'griechisch heidnische Götterlust mit der germanisch spiritualistischen Haustugend einen Zweikampf tanzt,'[1] paganism triumphs in the end in all the glory of transfiguration; while the tragedy of the *Faustballet* lies in the victory of the Christian philosophy, the same tragedy which underlies the *Elementargeister* and the mythological dream at the end of the book on Börne. Yet he never actually denied the earlier ideal, and often used the term Hellenism to express it; moreover, he proclaimed it once more definitely in his book on Börne, declaring proudly that he could not help the latter in the storm that wrecked him, for he dared not deliver the treasures confided to his care to certain ruin: 'Ich trug an Bord meines Schiffes die Götter der Zukunft.'[2]

'Wer sind jene Götter?'[3] he asked seven years later in his introduction to A. Weill's *Sittengemälde*, almost as if he were writing a postscript to the first chapter of the book on Börne, and there follows a prophecy of the religion of the future, which reads like a page from the *Romantische Schule* or *Zur Geschichte der Religion und Philosophie in Deutschland*:

Ich weiss nicht, wie sie heissen, jedoch die grossen Dichter und Weisen aller Jahrhunderte haben sie längst verkündigt. Sie sind jetzt noch geheimnissvoll verhüllt; aber in ahnenden Träumen wage ich es zuweilen, ihren Schleier zu lüften, und alsdann erblicke ich....Ich kann es nicht aussprechen, denn bei diesem Anblick durchzuckt mich immer ein stolzer Schreck, und er lähmt meine Zunge. Ach! ich bin ja noch ein Kind der Vergangenheit, ich bin noch nicht geheilt von jener knechtischen Demuth, jener knirschenden Selbstverachtung, woran das Menschengeschlecht seit anderthalb Jahrtausenden siechte, und die wir mit der abergläubischen Muttermilch eingesogen....Ich darf nicht aussagen, was ich geschaut....Aber unsere gesünderen Nachkommen werden in freudigster Ruhe ihre Göttlichkeit betrachten, bekennen und behaupten. Sie werden die Krankheit ihrer Väter kaum begreifen können....[4]

---

[1] Elster, VI, p. 106.   [2] *Ibid.* VII, p. 41.   [3] *Ibid.* VII, p 375.
[4] Elster, VII, pp. 375–376; cf. *ibid.* VII, pp. 251–252, 1827; III, p. 281, 1829; IV, p. 170, 1834.

It is with a certain feeling of pity that we read this echo from
the past, and with no little disappointment, for there is no trace
of progress here; Heine is repeating, in words which have a
strangely familiar sound, a prophecy which by now we have
heard at least once too often. It was vaguely worded at first as
a 'Naturreligion,' and slightly modified to suit his religion of
freedom on the battlefield of Marengo; it was thundered forth
with real conviction in the pages of *De l'Allemagne*, and grandilo-
quently implied rather than clearly expressed in the book on
Börne; but here the prophetic vein has become hardly more
than a mannerism; for when he wished to recapture the conviction of the past, he was forced to use phrases which had
already seen service. We can only conclude that the Saint-
Simonian synthesis had become a lifeless and sterile conception
to Heine, that he had no gods to proclaim, and that in order
to hide his religious bankruptcy he was forced to help himself
out with such obvious tricks as: 'Ich darf nicht aussagen, was
ich geschaut'; all that remains of the vaunted new religion is
the criticism of Christianity, which still rings true, but no truer
than the unhappy confession that he himself was a child of the
past and had been suckled with humility and superstition.

But an even more revealing phrase is to be found in a fragment written in 1844, which was not published until after his
death, and which he used very largely in the *Geständnisse*. It is
part of a proposed book *Briefe über Deutschland*, probably something in the nature of a continuation of the *Romantische Schule*
and *Zur Geschichte der Religion und Philosophie in Deutschland*.
The first letter, the only one found among his papers, opened
with a consideration of *De l'Allemagne*; but we hear no more of
pantheism; the emphasis was on the destruction of deism:

> Man hat mir von mancher Seite gezürnt, dass ich den Vorhang
> fortriss von dem deutschen Himmel und Jedem zeigte, dass alle
> Gottheiten des alten Glaubens daraus verschwunden, und dass dort
> nur eine alte Jungfer sitzt mit bleiernen Händen und traurigem
> Herzen: die Nothwendigkeit[1].

I think it not unlikely that it was because he realised that he
had nothing now to put in the place of the 'alte Jungfer' that

---

[1] Elster, vi, p. 535.

Heine went no further with the *Briefe über Deutschland*. He was a prophet without a message, or with a message which he no longer believed.

(b) THE CONVERSION

If Heine's much-discussed conversion is seen in its true light, the idea of a sudden change of heart cannot be entertained for a moment. It was the logical outcome of his bitter disappointment in Saint-Simonism. Before 1848 he may seem at times, if not to have advanced beyond 1834, at least to be true to the broader vision, the 'gottfreudige Frühlingsidee' which had seemed to him then the key to a golden future. But if we look closer we shall find that such prophetic passages have a polemical purpose behind them, or else that the author is merely hypnotised by the rhythm of remembered phrases. It was no more than a mood, sometimes recaptured in the swing of composition, sometimes no doubt in the presence of congenial friends:

...Heine ist immer noch starker Pantheist, er schwärmt seiner dichterischen Natur gemäss in der Weltseele umher[1].

In reality however, almost since 1836, he had ceased to respond to this vision; and saving from the wreck of the larger ideal the conception of the two worlds which he had once hoped to unite, he joined the ranks of the pagans in a determined and bitter warfare against Jewish-Christian spiritualism.

Then came his terrible illness, and he changed sides in the battle in 1848. No one can blame him for doing this, but it is clear that his adoption of deism in his physical and mental agony was on the principle of 'any port in a storm' rather than the result of spiritual conviction.

It would be impossible to state more clearly than Heine has done himself how he created his God to minister to his personal need[2]; impossible too to state more poignantly than in the

---

[1] K. Grün, *Die soziale Bewegung in Frankreich und Belgien*, p. 119. He is speaking of the year 1845.
[2] Elster, I, pp. 485–486, *Nachwort zum Romancero*, September 30, 1857; his deism was not Christianity; he died neither a Protestant nor a Catholic, but a Jew, who was however as far from being orthodox as he was far from being a 'fromme Seele.' As a poet he felt no need for such orthodoxy; cf. Hirth, III, p. 222.

following lines the underlying tragedy of his rejection of paganism:

Es war im Mai 1848, an dem Tage, wo ich zum letzten Male ausging, als ich Abschied nahm von den holden Idolen, die ich angebetet in den Zeiten meines Glücks. Nur mit Mühe schleppte ich mich bis zum Louvre, und ich brach fast zusammen, als ich in den erhabenen Saal trat, wo die hochgebenedeite Göttin der Schönheit, Unsere liebe Frau von Milo, auf ihrem Postamente steht. Zu ihren Füssen lag ich lange und ich weinte so heftig, dass sich dessen ein Stein erbarmen musste. Auch schaute die Göttin mitleidig auf mich herab, doch zugleich so trostlos, als wollte sie sagen: Siehst du denn nicht, dass ich keine Arme habe und also nicht helfen kann?[1]

But Heine's conversion was not only the outward act of a hunted and persecuted man seeking sanctuary; it was infinitely more than this, the victory of one side of his nature; Nazarenism and Hellenism had fought in Heine during his whole life. We have seen how uncertain was the victory of Hellenism before 1831, how eagerly he grasped at the hope of uniting them during the Saint-Simonian period; how later, when he became convinced that the two tendencies were irreconcilable, his natural love of life asserted itself, and he strove to be happy in the victory of what was then the stronger element. But the loss of his bodily health altered this precarious balance; pain and grief were cast into the scales, and the spirit mounted higher, whilst the flesh sank down towards the grave[2].

Heine's conflict was not resolved by the victory of the Nazarene principle. There are many poems written during his last years which show that he still knew thwarted desires and unattainable aspirations[3]. And in the last dream which he communicated to the world, *Für die Mouche*, the conviction that the life-long struggle within him would only cease with death found a poignant symbolical expression[4].

---

[1] Elster, I, p. 487. The impression of this description is heightened rather than diminished by the gallant spirit which causes Heine to add: 'I will break off here, for I am getting maudlin.'

[2] Cf. Hirth, III, p. 78; Elster, I, pp. 452 and 483.

[3] Cf. Elster, II, pp. 105, 110, 1853; 90–91, 91–92, 97–98, 1854; 41, 85, 1855, etc.

[4] Elster, II, pp. 45–49, 1856; in spite of Andler's interesting contention that *Für die Mouche* was written by Meissner and not by Heine, I am

Nevertheless he was in bitter earnest about his conversion, and he felt it incumbent on him to neutralise as far as possible the effect of his former sceptical and blasphemous utterances. Thus he wrote to Campe that he had destroyed all those still unpublished poems and prose writings, 'those beautiful poison flowers,' whose publication would now be treason to God, the sin against the Holy Ghost. And when a new French edition of the *Reisebilder* came out, without Heine's knowledge or permission he wrote:

J'ai eu l'intention de purifier ce livre par une nouvelle édition, en en retranchant les passages scabreux, ou en les neutralisant par des notes réfutatives, et un aveu sincère, comme je l'ai fait dans des éditions récentes de mes livres en Allemagne. Vous comprenez alors quel tort m'a fait la réimpression des 'Reisebilder,' qui a été faite à mon insu et sans ma participation. C'est un tort irréparable, et qui me compromet autant dans le ciel que sur la terre[1].

When it came to this 'purification' however Heine's honesty would not let him undertake it. His artist's conscience could not brook such 'cowardly fig-leaves.' Nor could he suppress these books. What he had written he had written, and he stated this clearly:

Aber der Pfeil gehört nicht mehr dem Schützen, sobald er von der Sehne des Bogens fortfliegt, und das Wort gehört nicht mehr dem Sprecher, sobald es seiner Lippe entsprungen und gar durch die Presse vervielfältigt worden[2].

In this dilemma he had recourse to those confessions of faith to which I have already alluded in an earlier chapter; the *Nachwort zum Romancero*, 1851, the *Vorrede zu Salon II*, 1852, and the *Geständnisse*, 1853–1854. And the problem which was left unsolved in the first section confronts us now and demands a closer attention. Why is it that whilst condemning his earlier heretical opinions, Heine maintained so complete a silence on the subject of Saint-Simonism? There is no doubt of the sincerity of his purpose. He wished to tell the truth about his

convinced that the dream itself was Heine's, although it may well be, in view of Andler's searching textual criticism, that Meissner wrote the poem; cf. Ch. Andler, *D'un faux dans l'œuvre littéraire de Heine*, *Revue Germanique*, Paris, May–June 1906.

[1] Hirth, III, p. 331, letter to Armand Bertin, dated January 10, 1853.

[2] Elster, IV, p. 155, *Vorrede zur zweite Auflage des Salon II*, dated May 1852.

conversion, and the truth about himself as far as it is ever
humanly possible to do this[1]. He set himself to make an open
confession in the course of which it becomes apparent that he
attributed his former opinions entirely to the influence of Hegel[2];
and his private letters reflect the same conviction[3]. He seems
sincerely convinced himself that *De l'Allemagne* was inspired by
Hegel, and written to confute Mme de Staël; the truth perhaps,
but only half the truth; for we know that it was also inspired
by Saint-Simonism and written partly at the request of Enfantin;
its avowed purpose being, according to the dedication, to edify
Enfantin by an analysis of the progress of thought in Germany,
and of the connection between the intellectual movement of
that country and the Saint-Simonian synthesis[4].

Are we then to believe that Heine had completely forgotten the
part the Saint-Simonians had played in his thought? And if we
are to believe this, must we not also conclude that he had learned
nothing from them, that at the most they had helped him to
formulate his views? On the other hand, if he was ignoring them
purposely in these various confessions of faith, we are under
the unpleasant necessity of assuming that these are not the
sincere and unvarnished records which they purport to be.
I think myself that the truth lies midway between these two
views, and points to nothing more than a pardonable confusion
on Heine's part, a mistake in dates. To my mind the key to
the problem lies in the sentence: 'Ehrlich gesagt, selten verstand
ich ihn (Hegel), und erst durch späteres Nachdenken gelangte
ich zum Verständniss seiner Worte.'[5]

Heine attended Hegel's lectures in Berlin from 1821 to 1823,
yet I think it almost safe to assume that although they influenced
his style and his technique, they did not modify his ideas. There
is certainly no trace of such an influence in his writings during
that period, or indeed before he came to Paris. His references
to Hegel are generally mocking or depreciating[6]; they are rare

---

[1] Cf. Elster, VI, pp. 20–22, *Geständnisse*, 1854.
[2] Elster, I, p. 485; IV, pp. 156, 158; VI, pp. 47–48.
[3] Cf. Hirth, III, pp. 78, 99–100, 220.
[4] Elster, IV, p. 568.   [5] *Ibid.* VI, p. 46.
[6] Cf. Elster, I, p. 255, 1823; I, p. 192, 1826; Hirth, I, p. 219, 1823; and
Elster, III, pp. 381–383, 1829.

and always slight, and though he occasionally used the term
'Identitätslehre,' he did not attempt to define it. During this
period, Schelling seems undoubtedly to have influenced him
more than Hegel. Later however when he came to study German
philosophy more deeply in the light of the Saint-Simonian synthesis, he became keenly aware of the fact that Hegel was an
intellectual giant who threw such puny weaklings as the Saint-
Simonians and Schelling completely into the shade. But even
then he probably only saw in Hegel what the Saint-Simonians
had helped him to see, and it is certain that he begged the whole
question of the Hegelian system in *Salon II*, although he had
advanced far enough to perceive that it was a magnificent
exposition of the pantheism he had set out to proclaim. Later
still he studied Hegel more deeply, but at a time when his
religious convictions were already tottering[1]; and the painful
impression of what he then, in 1848, and now, in 1854, considered
the godlessness of Hegelianism was still fresh in his mind when
he came to write the confessions; indeed according to his own
account it led him to destroy the book he had written on Hegel
and his sytem[2].

It is unfortunate that Heine should not have continued the
Briefe über Deutschland, and that he should have burnt his book
on Hegel, since these works would have been documentary
evidence of the intensity of the influence of Hegel on Heine's
mind, an influence which is only latent in his book on German
philosophy. But when he began his recantations, Hegel had
been in the ascendant for a long time; the German philosopher
now towered above the Saint-Simonians, blocking them from
Heine's sight; and the poet was probably a half-unconscious
confederate in this optical delusion. He held French philosophy
in light esteem and might prefer to father his errors upon a
worthy sire; or again, he might not wish to pay railway magnates
the compliment of suggesting that they had led him astray.
Half pardonable confusion, half self-suggestion, and that suggestion again half-conscious and half-unconscious, the omission
of Saint-Simonism from the pages of the confessions is a problem
which can find no rough and ready solution; and indeed the

---

[1] Elster, vi, pp. 47–48.   [2] Cf. Elster, vi, p. 48.

whole subject of Heine and Saint-Simonism is one so full of contradictions and complications, of half-shades and half-answered questions, haunted by the ghosts of so many lost letters and elusive manuscripts, that the whole truth of their inter-relations is never likely to be revealed.

(c) EXTENT OF THE SAINT-SIMONIAN INFLUENCE

The psychological relations between Heine and Saint-Simonism may still present some doubtful points, but the influence of this philosophy stands out clearly when we cease from a detailed study of Heine's works, and look at them from a greater distance and as a whole. During the Saint-Simonian period Heine attained to something in the nature of a complete philosophy, expounded in *De l'Allemagne,* and rightly characterised by Lichtenberger as a 'vaste synthèse.' It has been already sufficiently emphasised that no such synthesis was his before he came to Paris, but it is also clear from his later works that as he lost his feeling for this doctrine, his philosophy crumbled into ruins. He wrote nothing after 1834 that can be placed beside *De l'Allemagne* for unity of conception, and certainly nothing of any constructive value from the philosophical point of view. I have tried to evoke the psychological reasons which made his acceptance of the doctrine a foregone conclusion, and to show how the temporary release from his inner conflict disposed him to foresee a future in which the dominant note should be harmony; whereas before and after the Saint-Simonian period, the *leitmotif* of his writings was the conflict of spiritualism and sensualism. Hegel later came to be the dominant influence on his thought, but it was an influence which bore no literary fruit, for he interpreted Hegelianism as a doctrine of negation and destruction, and therefore it was doomed to sterility. Saint-Simonism on the other hand certainly gave the impulse to the conception of *De l'Allemagne*; although when Heine came to complete it, he was already on the road which was to lead him away from Saint-Simonism towards Hegelianism. In a natural reaction from the conclusions of the Hegelians of the Left, unbearable to a man of his temperament, he ended by embracing a Judaic deism, which was not very different from the religion he had been taught in his childhood, but which, even at the last, did not completely satisfy him.

Had Saint-Simonism been able to fulfil the dazzling promise which it held out to Heine in 1831, there is little doubt that he would have adhered to this doctrine throughout his life, but it was an illusory ideal. In the first flush of his hope and belief however he wrote two books which hold a high place amongst his literary achievements, and a unique place in the history of his thought. Nor was this all. However great the influence of Grimm may have been on Heine's books on daemonology, the Saint-Simonian conception of the Christian dualism gave to *Elementargeister* in 1836 and to *Götter im Exil* in 1853 their artistic value and unity, their appealing and haunting sadness. The influence of the Saint-Simonians in this direction made itself felt from the day he knew them until the day he died.

Heine owed the Saint-Simonians a greater debt than has generally been realised, and their influence on the whole trend of his life and thought was far greater than his biographers and critics have hitherto acknowledged. Consciously and unconsciously the chief actor created a good deal of dust round the subject, and his earlier predisposition towards Saint-Simonism tends to confuse the issue. For good or for ill it was the outstanding religious adventure of his life; it was further the only intellectual experience which resulted in creative thought; and lastly its psychological effect was almost incalculably great. It is not too much to say that he was in some definite relationship towards Saint-Simonism during the whole of his life. Like a castaway on an alien island he waited and longed for it until 1831; he hailed it with rapture when it materialised with its promise of speedy salvation, and embarked upon it with spirits almost deliriously high. But on the deep sea of life the ship began to founder and to sink; yet he was powerless to leave it for no other help was in sight; and at the last, almost too late, he hastily constructed a raft from the wreckage of his former ideals, and, clinging desperately to the belief in a personal God, he left the ship to its fate and died on the open sea. But it remains the proudest title of that unseaworthy craft that it was the only hope of salvation which Heine ever knew.

PART IV

LAUBE AND SAINT-SIMONISM

CHAPTER IX

LAUBE'S INTEREST IN SAINT-SIMONISM

(a) HIS KNOWLEDGE AND SOURCES

The interest which Heinrich Laube felt in Saint-Simonism was vivid enough to suggest that it was reflected in his correspondence; but his letters during the early thirties were for the most part destroyed in a fire, and there is little evidence of this interest to be found in those letters which remain.

The biographical details in this chapter are therefore based on Laube's *Erinnerungen*, 1869–1875, and more particularly on the *Nachträge*, 1883. Laube was sixty-three years of age when he began these memoirs and seventy-seven when death completed them; so that one needs to be on one's guard against anachronisms and mistakes[1].

It is more difficult to make up one's mind as to how far his memory served him faithfully in detailing the impressions and in estimating the influences of thirty and forty years ago; wherever possible the memoirs have been collated with earlier allusions; but the references to Saint-Simonism are not very numerous during the thirties, partly owing to the lost letters, partly to other reasons. But there is comfort in the reflection that the memoirs were written for the most part in a spirit of sincerity and that the author's memory was remarkably good. Laube went into greater detail about Saint-Simonism in the *Nachträge* than he did in the *Erinnerungen*, although the facts are essentially the same. He had dived into the past when he wrote the first instalments, and the waters thus disturbed sent up bubbles to the surface of his consciousness from depths which had long remained asleep.

It is impossible to be certain of the extent of Saint-Simonian

---

[1] For example, his pardonable confusion between Veit's articles (1832) and Veit's book (1834); he states that he read the latter at Jäschkowitz in 1832.

literature which Laube was able to command. He read Veit,
first his articles and later his book[1]; he was also acquainted with
Bretschneider's treatise, for he mentioned it in the *Zeitung für
die elegante Welt*[2]. He almost certainly read the articles in the
Allgemeine Zeitung, for he saw this paper daily from 1832 onwards if not before[3]. And it is more than likely that he followed
the fortunes of the Saint-Simonians in the *Breslauer Zeitung*;
or if he did not read such items of news, Karl Schall certainly
detailed them to him[4]. Besides this he reports that Biedenfeld
would arrive at Jäschkowitz, his pockets stuffed with books
about Saint-Simonism[5], but what these books were he does
not disclose. There is a charming description in the *Nachträge*
of this eccentric figure with his one arm and his fabulous stories,
who had a warm regard for Laube and even proposed to adopt
the young writer. The dramatic fire with which he retailed the
doings of the Saint-Simonians was not without its effect on his
hearers, and the whole household was soon taking sides.

Karl Schall, a lovable and almost Falstaffian character of
whom Laube has given a lively portrait in the *Moderne Charakteristiken*, reprinted from the *Zeitung für die elegante Welt*, was
one of those born pagans to whom Saint-Simonism must have
made an intimate appeal. He had been living in Berlin and
associating with the Varnhagens from 1830 to 1832, and had
been drawn into this circle of ideas by Rahel. She wrote him
a letter on May 5, 1832, promising to send him all the essential
literature on the subject[6]; and as she took in the *Globe* and the
Revue Encyclopédique, and had a copy of the *Enseignements
d'Enfantin*, it is possible that Laube saw some numbers of these
journals and even read the *Enseignements*. The fact that he
showed himself particularly *au fait* on the subject of the constant
and the inconstant, together with certain passages in the *Poeten*,
rather bears out this latter supposition, but generally speaking
his knowledge might just as well have been gleaned from German

---

[1] *Z. f. d. e. W.* October 17, 1833.   [2] *Ibid.* January 4, 1833.
[3] Heinrich Laube, *Gesammelte Werke*, Leipzig, 1908, xL, p. 156. Wherever possible I use this edition of Houben's, referring to it by the number
of the volume; but I have adhered to the spelling of the first editions.
[4] xLI, p. 288.   [5] xLI, p. 289.
[6] *Rahel, ein Buch des Andenkens für ihre Freunde*, III, p. 570.

books and articles, and from conversations with well-informed
and interested people like Biedenfeld and Schall, as from the
study of Saint-Simonian literature.

Indeed he made some mistakes which point to information
not received at first hand. Thus the schism with Bazard on the
question of divorce he believed to have been due to Enfantin's
appeal to the 'femme libre,'[1] and he further committed the not
inconsiderable blunder of asserting that Madame de Staël, who
died in 1817, was the first to receive an invitation to accept this
high office[2]. Allowances must be made for the memory of a
man of seventy-seven; he might not have made these mistakes
in 1832, but it looks as if his knowledge had been to a certain
extent from hearsay[3].

(b) AN INTERRUPTED JOURNEY

Laube was twenty-five years of age when in July 1831 he
accepted his second post as private tutor in a family of the name
of Nimptsch who lived at Jäschkowitz, a property situated some
miles from Breslau. It was here that he first became acquainted
with the doings and the doctrines of the Saint-Simonians through
the offices of Karl Schall and Freiherr von Biedenfeld. The
result was immediate: enthusiastic appreciation and a burning
desire to know more. Now what manner of young man was
this who found himself in such striking accord with the teachings
of the *salle* Taitbout?

'Er war der Haudegen, der Lärmmacher, der Stabstrompeter
...dieser literarischen Armee,'[4] a contemporary declared, and
indeed when one reads Laube's early writings, the predominant
sensation is not one of perusing printed matter now sadly out
of date, but rather that of listening to a fresh young voice
calling out a challenge to God and man in clarion tones. It is
impossible to come into contact with anyone so fearless, so
healthy and so ebullient as Laube was in the early thirties, and

---

[1] XLI, p. 287.

[2] XLI, p. 340. He was probably thinking of Saint-Simon's proposal of
marriage.

[3] In the year of his death he read Maxime Du Camp, *Souvenirs littéraires*,
and quoted from him in the *Nachträge* (XLI, pp. 337–339).

[4] F. Wehl, *Das junge Deutschland*, Hamburg, p. 93, 1886.

not to feel refreshed, stimulated, amused and finally affectionate. Then when one considers his straitened circumstances, the struggle he had had to support himself at the universities of Halle and Breslau, and the shadow of the church, which still lay along the path of this most unsuitable theological candidate, admiration for his youthful high spirits will not be denied.

Laube was a young man who was glad to be alive and determined that the world should profit by this fortunate accident. Traces of the peasant class from which he had sprung manifested themselves in a certain predisposition towards bluntness, downrightness and roughness; his temperament supplied him with a buoyant and spirited energy, and education and aspiration added something of smartness and elegance, which makes a peculiarly attractive combination with his native simplicity of manners.

There is no doubt that his contemporaries felt this charm. One of Laube's most outstanding characteristics was his happy knack of getting on with all sorts and conditions of men. He approached them frankly, and very few resisted him. He numbered some of the most eminent men of his day among his intimate friends. Wagner, Heine, Pückler-Muskau, Varnhagen von Ense, they all found something in Laube to which they responded with affection, and they were men of very different calibre. Indeed it is especially interesting to notice the real affection with which Varnhagen regarded Laube, for the other three were men of temperament; whereas this cold and cautious diplomat might well have been pardoned for treating such an outspoken child of nature with wary aloofness. But he befriended him warmly on all occasions, tried unavailingly to soften Metternich's heart towards him whilst he was in prison, and when Laube fell into general disrepute for dissociating himself from the Young Germans in their hour of need, Varnhagen understood and pardoned this action, and wrote a letter in his defence, showing the keenest insight into his young friend's character and the warmest sympathy and admiration[1]. There were dissentient voices; Laube's personality was challenging enough to ensure him enemies; he was to meet a very

---

[1] Houben, *Jungdeutscher Sturm und Drang*, pp. 386–387.

bitter one in Hebbel in later life, but in these early years especially he was rich and happy in many a pleasant friendship.

There was a strong sensual element in Laube's nature which coloured his attitude towards love and women during his youth. The spiritual side of love held no appeal for him; it was all plain unvarnished physical attraction which he felt and described with fervour and conviction in the *Poeten* and the *Krieger*, but *ad nauseam* (as his enemies maintain not unjustly) in the *Reisenovellen*. This was the outcome of high animal spirits and in itself normal enough; the insistence and the reiteration however sometimes produce an unpleasant impression in spite of his frankness and absence of cant.

Curiously enough Laube was occasionally a victim to acute attacks of hypochondria. This would seem to harmonise with nothing else in his nature, but the inappropriate malady was his, and facts must be faced. This dashing figure may not always meet events as courageously as might have been expected. It is the only enigmatic, and one might therefore say the only romantic element in a nature whose transparent simplicity is otherwise its greatest charm.

When an ardent and generous-minded young man begins to look around him and to think, there are always ten chances to one that he will espouse liberal ideals. In the Germany of 1830 there was hardly even the one chance in ten for reactionary principles. The youth of that period was born to liberalism as the sparks fly upward, and our hero went up like a sky rocket. Calling the name of Börne and brandishing the sword of freedom, he had already entered the lists for Poland in the literary tourney of his day. Such was the soil on which the seed of the Saint-Simonian gospel fell in the summer of 1831.

Like Heine, Laube overlooked the complete negation of individual liberty inherent in the powers of the supreme priest and bracketed Saint-Simonism and freedom together:

Die Nachrichten über den in Paris aufstehenden St Simonismus erweckten mir wieder jenen Gedanken an Freiheit. Sie sprachen von einer ganz neuen Organisation des Begriffes von Freiheit, sie verbreiteten ihn auf alle Theile der Gesellschaft, auf Familie, Kirche, auf den ganzen Staat. Auch von einer neuen Stellung des Weibes war die Rede. Es war der Beginn des Socialismus in ausgedehntestem Sinn[1].

He followed their socialistic teachings with appreciation and interest and rejected with scorn the academic criticisms of German philosophers and theologians who were blind to the spirit of progress in these teachings:

Diese geniale Sekte ist bis jetzt bei uns immer nur aus unserer Schulphilosophie, Schultheorie und Schulpolitik heraus beurtheilt worden, der Schultheologie gar nicht zu gedenken. Es wird vom Pantheismus und Materialismus gefaselt und vornehm von halber Kenntniss deutscher philosophischer Schätze und Sätze gesprochen, aber das historische Genie, der steile Gipfel des ganzen neuern Weges, auf dem die Simonisten so eifrig vorausgejagt sind, dass sie in Früh-reife und jäher Laufbahn den Hals zu brechen befürchten müssen, wird unbeachtet gelassen[2].

Laube was not long to remain vitally interested in the social-istic aspect of the Saint-Simonian doctrine, although he praised it more than once. The theory of inheritance by capacity he called 'Eine der schönsten Foderungen der Simonisten,'[3] and it is not difficult to see why a clever young man with his way to make in the world should have found this doctrine an attractive one. He also prophesied that the 'sociale Vortrefflichkeiten' would find recognition in the future[4], but on the whole, as time went on, he was inclined to leave the future to look after itself and to give up the problem with a sigh:

Ich wohne natürlich auf der schlechteren Seite, denn die Wohn-ungen sind heidnisch theuer—alles Schöne und Reiche wohnt drüben jenseits des Flusses wie die schöne Zukunft der Simonisten[5].

'Mich interessirten gerade die religiös-kirchlichen Ideen, ja die Frage um die Frauen in bezug auf die Ehe interessirte mich besonders.'[6] Laube made this statement at the end of his life, but it needs a comment. The unwilling student of theology hailed the new Christianity with delight, but less because it taught him new truths than because it liberated him from old ones. Fired by the liberal ideal of a practical religion based on

---

[1] XLI, p. 284.   [2] *Bl. f. lit. Unt.* April 29, 1832, article on Veit.
[3] *Ibid.* March 24, 1832.
[4] *Politische Briefe*, Leipzig, 1833, p. 360.
[5] *Ibid.* p. 225.   [6] XLI, p. 292.

the command 'Thou shalt love thy neighbour as thyself,' he
felt at length the courage to abandon the church as a profession[1] in order to become the apostle of a creed in which he
thought to recognise the liberalism of his hero Börne[2]. This
sudden release from strain, this sudden removal of the inhibitive
effects of material difficulties, he owed to the Saint-Simonian
religion, and it is an almost incalculable benefit. We can further
believe him when he adds that a reform of the Protestant
church along Saint-Simonian lines occupied his mind during a
long period of his life[3]. For it was in this way that he accepted
their gospel, rather as a disciple of Saint-Simon than as a Saint-
Simonian. He repeated many of their criticisms of Christianity,
but he blamed the priests and not the founder. Indeed, in so
far as he had any religion at all, he might best be classified as a
free-thinking Christian.

But the religious element was almost entirely lacking in
Laube's nature. No more striking proof of this could be offered
than the fact that he was able to contemplate embracing a
preacher's life for no better reasons than material ones. He
took an intelligent interest in dogma, but religion as a quickening
force, a spiritual revelation, or even as an emotional experience,
was beyond his ken. Further, and more important here, the
dualism inherent in the nature of man never led to strife and
struggle in Laube; it resulted in a cheerful compromise, in which
the rights of the senses were certainly not disregarded; so that
the Saint-Simonian solution of this conflict held no message of
dazzling hope for him as it did for Heine, although he was willing
enough to help, in his own robust way, towards the 'emancipation of the flesh.'

The more mystical side of the Saint-Simonian religion caused
this healthy and normal young man a certain uneasiness, as the
following passage shows:

Und dies ist auch das Unglück des Simonismus, dass er aufge-
treten ist zur Zeit des Kampfes—aber das Unglück des Simonismus

---

[1] Cf. xl, pp. 153–154 and xli, p. 282. In the *Erinnerungen* this change
of programme is ascribed vaguely to the influence of liberalism; in the
Nachträge definitely (and I think correctly) to the influence of Saint-
Simonism.

[2] Cf. *Bl. f. lit. Unt.* June 26, 1832.   [3] xli, p. 301.

wird der Welt Glück werden, denn seine socialen Vortrefflichkeiten werden sich Bahn brechen, weil sie offne Arme im Streben unserer Tage finden, seine transcendenten Ansichten werden zu keinem Despotismus gelangen. Sie wissen, wie sehr ich gegen positiven Glauben bin—seine Fratzen und Auswüchse werden zertrümmert werden.'[1]

But if Laube's benevolent interest in the socialistic theories of the Saint-Simonians was a more or less Platonic one, and if he was by temperament debarred from sympathising with the whole extent of their religious dreams, yet they had brought forward a topic to which he was not likely to turn a deaf ear, the topic of women. Nothing relating to the sex which so incessantly preoccupied him could fail to arouse his instant attention, and the demand for greater freedom in love was bound to find an enthusiastic response in a young man who was still at the fickle stage of his career, when every pretty girl seemed an earnest of prettier girls to come[2], and so it befell that at the age of twenty-five he pitched his bonnet over the mill and raced after the Saint-Simonians. At first he contented himself with planning an account of Saint-Simonism, which he offered as part of a general liberal potpourri to the publisher Brockhaus in Leipzig[3]. This book was not accepted, but during the year 1832 Laube was a regular contributor to the *Blätter für literarische Unterhaltung*, and besides the review on Veit's articles on Saint-Simonism, there are several references to the absorbing theme[4]. But this could not satisfy him. The newspaper reports of the Saint-Simonians became daily more exciting, the last news was of the retreat to Ménilmontant, and Laube, unable to bear this waiting and watching from a distance, packed up his trunks, made his farewells, and set off for Paris by way of Leipzig on June 29, 1832, two days before the 'Ouverture des travaux du Temple,' accompanied as far as the Breslau mail coach by that enthusiastic supporter, Freiherr von Biedenfeld.

It was not a sudden decision; he had been contemplating this journey for several months, hesitating on account of the cholera

---

[1] *Politische Briefe*, p. 360.   [2] Cf. XLI, p. 284.

[3] Houben, *op. cit.* p. 348, letter dated March 4, 1832, the first reference to Saint-Simonism from Laube's pen which I have been able to find. The scheme for this book is clearly recognisable in *Das neue Jahrhundert*.

[4] *Bl. f. lit. Unt.* March 24, April 29, June 3, June 26, Dec. 8, 1832.

and passport difficulties[1], but he did not reach Paris. An attack of hypochondria forced him to Carlsbad, where a long and depressing cure left him for the moment too languid and too spiritless to attempt the difficult journey on a slender purse:

Die Welt und meine Zukunft hatten ein aschgraues Ansehen, als ich mich zur Abreise rüsten musste, weil der Geldbeutel zu schlank wurde... und weil die Genesung doch unerreichbar schien. Paris und die Saint-Simonisten zerflossen wie Nebelbilder vor meinen nächsten Sorgen, und Leipzig erschien als einziger Anhaltspunkt[2].

And when, back in Leipzig, with returning health and spirits, he once more turned his eyes towards Paris, the news of the trial and of the dispersion of the Saint-Simonians put an end to all hopes of playing a practical part in their lives:

Meine Lockung nach Paris war hiermit verschwunden. Ich blieb nachdenklich in Leipzig[3].

So ended the frustrated attempt to establish a personal contact with this sect, and Laube was keenly disappointed. But he was not one to sit down and grieve overlong for what might have been. His appointment as editor of the *Zeitung für die elegante Welt* did much to console him for the lost opportunity of playing the priest of progress: 'Und die Saint-Simonisten?' he says airily when recounting the history of this appointment: 'Sie fielen mir wohl auf der Stelle ein, aber ich war jetzt schon mehr auf Schriftstellerei gestellt als auf eine Religionsbahn.'[4]

(c) UNCOMPLETED SCHEMES

But Laube did not abandon his interest in Saint-Simonism. He had planned an article on the subject in March 1832, and when the two volumes of *Das neue Jahrhundert* (*Polen* and *Politische Briefe*) appeared in January 1833 he stated in the preface that the third volume was to contain an account of Saint-Simonism:

Mit meinen jüngsten Lesern spräche ich nun am liebsten noch ein ungenirtes Wort über den neuen Gottes- oder Götzendienst zu Paris, denn wo Götter oder Götzen sind, da bleibt auch der Dienst nicht aus—über den Simonismus....Ich denke, im Anfange des III. Bandes einige vergnügliche Unterredungen über das äussere Leben und Treiben der Simonisten anknüpfen zu können, wenn sich

---

[1] Houben, *op. cit.* p. 348, letter to Brockhaus, dated May 1, 1832.
[2] XL, p. 179.   [3] XLI, p. 300.   [4] XL, p. 185.

nicht alle gute Christen von meinem ersten Capitel, und meinen lieben Simonisten, abgewendet haben. Es sind wirklich liebe, charmante Leute, und ich denke und hoffe, es werden mich auch schlechte Christen lesen—und was werden nun erst die Weiber sagen, wenn wir mit einander zu St Simons in die Kirche, d.h. auf den Ball gehen, wo Pater Enfantin die Honneurs macht, den Cotillon aufführt, seidne carirte Strümpfe trägt, jedem Fragenden Auskunft giebt über den oder jenen Lebersatz, 'chassez à gauche' dazwischen spricht, und mit der äussersten Linken noch nicht zufrieden ist. Was werden die Weiber sagen wenn sie in dieser Kirche Klavier spielen und sonstige Künste treiben, und die fashionablste Gesellschaft beschäftigt sehen, wenn sie erfahren, man theile jetzt die Weiber in bewegliche und unbewegliche, und gebe ihnen entsprechende Ehemänner, und die beweglichen könnten wechseln, so viel sie wollten, und die Priester könnten sie alle nebenbei iieben— — —

—Aber wie höre ich meine jüngsten Leser jauchzen, und wie höre ich die alten brummen. Ach, es ist auch eine böse Welt, die sich's gar zu bequem machen will![1]

It seems highly probable that this description of a Saint-Simonian ball was inspired by an article in the *Allgemeine Zeitung* of March 9, 1832, for there is a certain resemblance of detail, and the same amusement is noticeable in both accounts. It is not the first, although it is the most striking instance of a critical attitude on Laube's part. He had sounded a warning note in the *Blätter für literarische Unterhaltung* in 1832, declaring that the Saint-Simonians were rushing so fast towards the steep summit of progress that they must fear to break their necks, and in the *Politische Briefe*, the second volume of the series to which the above is a preface, he spoke of the 'Fratzen und Auswüchse' of their religious views. But the tone of deliberate persiflage is heard here for the first time, in connection too with the first appearance of the name of Enfantin, and yet those views on morality, which were especially Enfantin's, were just what avowedly interested Laube most. There are two facts which explain this seeming inconsistency. In the first place, Enfantin was also more particularly associated with the mystical aspect of the Saint-Simonian religion, which made Laube definitely uneasy and restive. In the second place, he saw this strange figure through the eyes of his contemporaries, and adopted the normal view current at the time, not only in

[1] *Polen*, Fürth, 1833, pp. xiv–xv.

Germany but in France as well, and which has been more or
less sanctioned by posterity. With the exception of the elect,
most sympathisers of the movement draw the line at Enfantin
and consider him fair game for satire, and Laube was no exception to this rule. In the *Zeitung für die elegante Welt* for
example he alluded to Saint-Simonism as 'dies kühne Gebäude,
in welches sich materielle Narren wie Narciss-Enfantin und seine
Genossen gelagert,'[1] a rather unfair comment, since none had
a greater right to occupy the building than those who had
raised it aloft. In 1883 Laube returned to this subject and voiced
his grievance against the supreme priest:

> Dieser gedankenreiche, aber leichtfertige Mann hat die ruhige
> Entwicklung der Reform übereilt und durch seine dreisten Einführ-
> ungen gestört, wohl gar zerstört...mit einem Worte das einzuführen,
> was so grell Emancipation des Fleisches genannt wird, das musste in
> solcher Grellheit abschrecken...und wie nun gar Enfantin bei der
> Einführung seiner Grundsätze zu Werke ging, das musste Scandal
> erregen. Das Suchen und Ausstellen der Offenbarungsfrau war für
> die Polizei die ganz geeignete Veranlassung zum Einschreiten ge-
> wesen; im Predigtsaale der Rue Taitbout hatte er Julie Fanfernaut
> zum leeren Sessel geführt, und fast ohne Bekleidung hatte sie ihr
> Bekenntnis abgelegt. Alle Welt hatte es gebilligt, dass nun die
> Municipalgarde den Saal geräumt hatte[2].

It is perhaps not altogether idle to wonder whether Laube might
have thought and written differently, if in his impressionable
youth he had come to Paris as he wished to do, and had known
Enfantin personally. Heine, for all his satirical wit, seems to
have been not completely immune to the charm radiating
from this fantastic figure. But Heine's nature was emotionally
and spiritually a rich one. Laube remained in a state of ele-
mentary spiritual development all his life, and his emotions
were strong rather than deep, simple rather than complex. His
sturdy sense of humour and his fundamental sanity of outlook
might have withstood the enchantment, those clear but short-
sighted blue eyes might not have been dazzled, but wiser heads
than his were being turned in Paris, and had circumstances
not kept him in 'paper Leipzig' he might one day have been
seen in the famous costume and washing the plates at Ménilmontant; for there would have been no half measures with this

---

[1] *Z. f. d. e. W.* October 17, 1833.   [2] XLI, p. 292.

young hothead, and no paralysing fear of making himself ridiculous.

The third volume of *Das neue Jahrhundert*, of which such a titillating sketch had been given in the preface to the first, never appeared in print, and was probably never written, since Laube was now fully occupied with the first volume of *Das junge Europa*, published in July 1833, and with his editorship of the *Zeitung für die elegante Welt*, interrupted by a journey to Italy in company with Gutzkow during the summer of 1833, which resulted in the *Reisenovellen*, published in April 1834. The book, or at least the chapters on Saint-Simonism, was allowed to lapse for the moment, but Laube did not forget the Saint-Simonians, and indeed during this period the influence of their doctrines is most clearly apparent, not only in *Die Poeten* and the *Reisenovellen*, but also in the *Zeitung für die elegante Welt*. It was no exaggeration when Laube confessed in 1883 that the Saint-Simonian philosophy of life 'pulsirte in jedem meiner Artikel.'[1] The actual references are few but interesting, since they occur in the periodic reviews of the *Messkatalog*, in each case implying or expressing reproach that this most important movement figures so slightly in the new lists of books[2].

In marked contrast with the serious and respectful tone of these considerations is a flippant remark in the *Reisenovellen*, which is strongly reminiscent of the preface to *Das neue Jahrhundert*[3], and which is interesting because it shows that Laube was following the acts of the Saint-Simonians in the East. On August 9, 1833, he had indeed printed a correspondence from Paris in the *Elegante Welt* to the effect that a Saint-Simonian had written from Constantinople to proclaim that he had found the 'free woman' among the sultan's houris.

But Laube's days of light-hearted jesting were numbered. His more than liberal writings, appearing in the reactionary Germany of 1830, and preaching as they did subversive principles anent church, state and morality, had for some time pre-

[1] XLI, p. 300.
[2] Cf. Z. f. d. e. W. January 4, 1833, October 10, 1833, October 17, 1833, references to Bretschneider's and Veit's books on the subject.
[3] *Reisenovellen*, Leipzig, 1834, I, p. 81.

occupied the mighty in their seats, and the manner of his entry into the literary world was not calculated to reassure them.

He had been giving a spirited rendering of Daniel in the den of lions. But this is not an exhibition which even Daniel would care to prolong unduly, and Laube had been performing for two years; the lions were becoming restive. They had growled ominously on the appearance of *Das neue Jahrhundert*; the growl had swelled alarmingly when the *Zeitung für die elegante Welt* and *Die Poeten* came under their notice, and now they crouched to spring.

Tzschoppe, the life and soul of the Prussian anti-liberal persecutions, prepared himself for action. Early in May 1834 Laube, who had remained a Prussian subject, was notified by the Leipzig police that a decree of banishment had gone forth at the bidding of the neighbouring state, and that he must quit Leipzig within the month. It was the first move in a cruel game, a game which Prussia always won. The object was to shepherd the victim either into Prussia, where he could be caught and dealt with, or across the frontier to Switzerland or to France, where he became comparatively harmless, and might drag out the rest of his life in exile and more than probable poverty. The unhappy wretch would fly from one place to another, but Prussia was for ever at his heels, and in the end he must either throw himself on the mercy of a merciless government, or say farewell to his native land. Laube chose the former alternative and left Leipzig for Berlin on May 10, 1834. At first he was ignored by the authorities, wandered through the streets of Berlin in liberty, and cultivated the acquaintance of Varnhagen von Ense with whom he had long conversations on Christianity and marriage, on which subjects they found themselves in complete accord. That the Saint-Simonian religion must have come under discussion is a matter of deduction rather than guess-work, since Varnhagen was still keenly interested in this movement. The elder man advised Laube to leave Berlin as fast as he might, this warning was not without effect, and Laube left Berlin for Gräfenberg by way of Sprottau, Glogau and Breslau, the scenes of his childhood and youth. Gräfenberg in Austrian Silesia was famous then for a particularly strenuous water-cure inaugurated under the auspices of Priessnitz, a cross between a genius and a crank, to whom Laube has done full justice both in the memoirs and in the *Reisenovellen*.

He underwent the cure, but, warned that papers were out for his arrest on the Prussian frontier, and realising that he was caught between Prussia and Austria, he fled to Dresden, thence to Leipzig, and once more hounded from Leipzig, he reappeared in Berlin on July 10. Varnhagen was horrified at this step, and persuaded the fugitive to write to Pückler-Muskau, then in Paris on his way to the East, and beg for permission to accompany him. But before the prince's answer arrived (a not very formidable negative, which might have been coaxed into an affirmative) the heavy hand of the Berlin police fell on our hero's shoulder, and he was marched off to prison on July 26.

Saint-Simonism was much in Laube's thoughts during these weeks of flight from a pursuit which it would be cynical to call justice. At the very outset, when he was debating the alternatives between capture and exile, he chose the former; '...die Saint-Simonisten waren in Frankreich, waren für mich untergegangen,'[1] so runs the reason he gave for this choice in later years. It was a dark world for Laube in May 1834, and the darkness deepened when he considered the joyful plans of 1832, and how they now lay shattered: the Saint-Simonians were dispersed, and he himself was brandmarked as a political criminal.

But his long-delayed article on Saint-Simonism once more took shape in his mind, possibly an outcome of the stimulus supplied by the conversations with Varnhagen, and he wrote the following lines to Schlesier, deputy editor of his paper, from Berlin:

In den nächsten Tagen erhältst Du 'Ludwig Rellstab 1812,' d.h. Recension, dann 'Simonismus,' dann Kleinigkeiten, dann Bulwer mit freiem Thema; es werden aber Wochen vergehen[2].

And again from Gräfenberg:

Mit vieler Mühe hab ich zwei Hauptartikel für's Lit.Bl. gearbeitet, zwei 'Bulwer u. Simonism.' werd ich noch—dabei den ersten Artikel einer Correspond.—man hat gar keine Zeit hier[3].

[1] XL, p. 217.   [2] Houben, *op. cit.* p. 365, dated May 1834.
[3] *Ibid.* p. 369, dated June 15, 1834.

It is a curious instance of the fate which dogged the would-be critic of Saint-Simonism that this article did not appear in the *Zeitung für die elegante Welt*, although both the others are to be found there. Possibly Schlesier was afraid to print it and it was lost; but it is more likely that it was never written. Laube's time was running short, and the article on Bulwer Lytton was still unwritten on July 15. But when he was arrested in Berlin Veit's book on Saint-Simonism was found among his papers. Then fell the long and tragic silence.

(d) AN ENFORCED SILENCE

Alas, poor Laube! Would that he could have turned back into the past or have taken a long leap into his happy and successful future. He was so entirely unsuited to the trial which awaited him as he took his last walk through the streets of Berlin by the side of the police magistrate Duncker, characteristically abandoning the idea of flight because he was on parole.

The six weeks 'honeymoon' in the 'Stadtvogtei' were bad enough, but here at least he was allowed exercise, books and writing-materials. Also Duncker's cross-examinations were conducted on such humane and sometimes even humorous lines, were carried on with such an air of not being taken seriously, that Laube could not but flatter himself with dreams of speedy release. And a certain amount of female society was to be enjoyed in the mornings, when some fellow prisoner, always young and often pretty, was engaged in sweeping out his room. Our incorrigible philanderer listened to confidences and responded to advances in the spirit in which they were made. Among his many stories of tender conquests none rings so true, none has such poignancy and touching charm, as the uncompleted idyll of the little light of love, heading straight for a house of correction, who slipped up to his room one night, only to find that, although her own door had been left open, the key to his had been duly turned. Whilst she whispered through the door that he could surely find a way, the turnkey's step was heard, and off she fled. Laube saw her no more, but even in the penitentiary, he thought, she would sometimes laugh and be happier than he.

Meanwhile his connection with the 'Burschenschaft' in Halle and Breslau had come to light; the 'Stadtvogtei' knew him no more, he was taken across to the 'Hausvogtei' and left to the mercies of Dambach, the Prussian rhyme for Hambach, as the prisoners had it. And here the dark waters washed over his soul. Brimful of energy, he was confined to one obscure and narrow cell, where the sunlight of that riotous summer of 1834 never came, whilst the incalculable blessing of an hour's exercise round the prison yard was for months denied him. A social and gregarious nature, he was to know the horrors of solitary confinement. Intellectually alert and alive and fresh from all the bustle of his editorship, he was to fight his way through the never-ending hours without one page of printed matter to distract him; a writer by profession and from choice, he was to feel the accumulated misery of unuttered thoughts, and yet be forbidden the immeasurable relief of literary expression. And that his cup might be full, his temperamental optimism forsook him, merged in an attack of hypochondria which turned the whole world dark and brought him down to the very gates of madness. Thus the only weapon with which he might have fought the giants of solitude and despair was snatched from his hand. He was not born to be a martyr; he lacked that passionate yet steadfast devotion to principle which can even welcome personal sufferings in a great cause. Börne, in a like situation, would have been upheld by such a spirit, but Börne was a true reformer and Laube was not. Moreover Laube had been growing less and less interested in the questions of liberal reform; he had outlived most of the enthusiasms which went to the making of *Polen* and *Politische Briefe*, and those were the books on which he was most often cross-examined. He had outlived even more completely those old student ideals which had made him a member of the 'Burschenschaft' in Halle and an honorary member in Breslau. And this was the capital charge against him. What dreams of glorious martyrdom could help him here? He was suffering solely for the light-hearted incautiousness of his youth, since he could no longer identify himself with the extravagant aims of 'Turnvater Jahn,' nor with that delightfully innocent programme which began with a spiritually united

Germany and ended with a stern injunction to chastity. Truly
Laube must have sometimes thought that he heard the laughter
of the gods when he considered this last piece of irony. For the
ideals which were nearest his heart when he went to prison were
in direct antagonism with the purity commanded by the 'Burschenschaft.' And, that nothing might be lacking, they were
ideals which could in no wise harmonise with dreams of the
stake and of the martyr's crown. Enfantin indeed had very
calmly endured imprisonment in the cause of the freedom of
love and the triumph of the flesh, but Enfantin's imprisonment
was child's play compared with Laube's, and Enfantin was a
religious fanatic.

But when the world will have none of us, when the pleasures
of the flesh are beyond our reach, and when even the devil
proves hard of hearing, the least religious amongst us, the very
atheist himself, will attempt to come to terms with God. Now
Laube was no atheist, nor was he what could be fairly called
an irreligious man; it was rather that his spiritual needs were
too slight to make religion a necessary part of his life. But in
the agonies of an eight months' imprisonment which, as far as
he knew, might extend for years, or even for the rest of his life,
bereft of any kind of mental or physical occupation, he turned
his thoughts towards religion and wrestled with the spirit of
God[1]. This is the only time that he ever came near to anything
like a spiritual vision of life. It needed the long drawn-out
torture of his months in prison to force from him an inarticulate
prayer, and even then a certain stubborn honesty, a not unworthy pride, rebelled against this betrayal of his essential self.
But the effort resulted at least in a more positive attitude towards this vital question than had yet been his, the conception
of the spirit of God manifest in the world and answering him
from his own inner consciousness, a conception of Saint-
Simonian design.

Yet the picture of Laube trying to pray in prison remains a
painful one, since it hints at the disintegration of his personality;
it was writhing in the melting pot, and had the process continued
much longer, he might have left the 'Hausvogtei' a being essen-

[1] Cf. III, pp. 67–68.

tially different from the one who went in. But human nature is tough, and the sentry within us, who is for ever zealously guarding the integrity of our secret selves from foreign incursions, saved Laube from such a fate.

He left his prison, altered indeed in many ways; sobered, broken, but for the time only, in health and spirits, matured rather too suddenly in that cruel forcing-house, but along the lines of his logical development, grown cautious and even timid, so ready to fly the white flag of peace in the face of the authorities, that we can sympathise with those of his contemporaries who took it for the white feather, but still essentially the same. He had not grown pious, his love of life had not deserted him; and if, with the sentence still unpronounced hanging over his head, he proclaimed a change of heart rather too often and rather too loudly, let those who have been through a like experience throw the first stone. Not if he could help it should he be dragged back again into the horrors from which he had just escaped. What did a few compromises signify, what did anything signify, so long as he could breathe the air and see the sun and mix with his fellow-men? It was not a noble attitude, but it was a perfectly natural one, and might even have been consistent with dignity, if Laube had been content to lie low and say nothing until the danger was passed. But in the first place he had to make his living by the pen, and this could only be done by conciliating the government, and in the second place he found to his horror that his early sins were once more pursuing him in the shape of the Prussian and Federal Edicts against the Young Germans. This cruel pursuit he attempted to evade by successive denials. He had crawled from the lions' den badly mauled, and nothing would induce him voluntarily to enter their presence again.

(c) THE LOSS OF INTEREST

Laube's imprisonment played its part in the history of his relations with Saint-Simonism. On September 7, 1834, he was taken from the 'Stadtvogtei' to the 'Hausvogtei,' and on September 11, after a five days' experience of the evils of this much severer captivity, he was brought before the formidable

Dambach, and dictated an autobiography, which first Geiger and later Houben have disinterred from the Prussian archives[1]. It is hardly a matter for surprise, although it is of great interest to find that no mention of the proposed journey to Paris, or of the reason which inspired it, figures in this sketch of his life. Laube stated simply that he left Jäschkowitz for Leipzig because he wished to embrace a literary career. and to establish more closely his connection with Brockhaus and the *Blätter für literarische Unterhaltung*. This was true as far as it went, and if it was only half the truth, no one can blame him for not dragging in a journey which was never made, or for omitting a confession of incriminating sympathies to his inquisitor.

The omission is interesting because it is a sign that Laube was very well aware that his Saint-Simonian leanings would only aggravate a position already grave enough. Henceforward Saint-Simonism spelt danger to him, and his interest in this movement began to wane. We hear no more of a book or an essay on this subject; and he made haste to retire from all the positions he had adopted under the influence of Saint-Simonism, as will become apparent later. Meanwhile, writing to Pückler-Muskau in 1836, he showed himself determined to abandon the pantheistic conception of the universe which had done something towards comforting him in prison[2]. But the chivalrous German prince, to whom Laube's apostasy smelt strongly of treachery, answered this letter rather grimly:

Sie thun gut, sich einzubilden, Ihre Meinung geändert zu haben, weil sie *einsehen*, nicht damit durchzukommen.... Wenn Sie mir aber sagen, dass der Spinozismus noch nichts Organisches gestaltet, muss ich widersprechen. Sie vergessen den Saint-Simonismus, der, seine französischen Narrheiten abgerechnet, die erste Eröffnung dazu gemacht. Er hat das Saamenkorn in die Erde gelegt, und der organische Wuchs wird schon kommen, wenn *wir* auch noch zu dürrer Boden sind, um dass er gleich daraus emporkeimen könne. Klassisch und polizeilich gewordenes junges Deutschland, klage mich wegen dieser Ketzerei nicht an[3].

---

[1] Geiger, *Das junge Deutschland und die preussische Censur*, pp. 78–89. XLI, pp. 445–456.

[2] *Briefwechsel und Tagebücher des Fürsten Hermann von Pückler-Muskau*, VI, pp. 14–15, dated January 8, 1836.

[3] *Ibid*. pp. 15–16, dated April 1836.

This thrust probably went home, and Laube may sometimes have heard in his ears the reproachful words 'Sie vergessen den Saint-Simonismus.'

Before this letter reached him he had had another reminder. He had received a published copy of that strange letter which Enfantin wrote to Heine from the banks of the Nile; the old allegiance stirred within him, and the *Mitternachtzeitung*, the pale and languid ghost of the *Elegante Welt*, published an article entitled *Pabst Enfantin*, in which Laube quoted at some length from the letter, with an introduction which shows with melancholy clearness that Enfantin was now nothing more to the author of *Die Poeten* than a voice from the past:

Wir leben so schnell, dass jener Name fast vergessen ist. Wie lange dünkt es uns, dass Paris das auffallende Schauspiel einer neu entstehenden Religionsgesellschaft gab, jener blauen Simonisten mit den wunderlichen Dingen, wie lange! Und es sind ein Paar kurze Jahre! Ich wurde in diesen Tagen daran erinnert; eine jener kleinen Broschüren, die auf wenig Seiten eine neue Welt zu extemporiren pflegten, verirrte sich wieder einmal in ihrem simonistisch-blauen Umschlage zu mir. Das wird Manchem gemahnen, dachte ich, wie ein altes Seidenband, das der Wind in sein Fenster führt, er weiss nicht von wannen es kommt, aber er erkennt die Farbe, welche jenes interessante Mädchen mit wunderbar sinnlichen Augen trug[1].

But if he could not completely forget, neither would he clearly remember, and for the next few years his printed references to Saint-Simonism were carefully guarded and aloof[2]. But by this time the universal lover was married and happily married[3]. He had found contentment in those very limits which had once seemed to him a blasphemy against the liberty of love. The champion of the 'free woman' had now the interests of a husband to guard. The only strong tie which had held him to the Saint-Simonians was snapped.

When therefore in the calm of the Muskau forests, where from 1837 to 1839 Laube was allowed to serve the sentence which a gracious government had commuted provisionally from seven years to eighteen months, he came to consider the part which

[1] *Mitternachtzeitung für gebildete Stände*, Brunswick and Leipzig, Feb. 29, 1836.
[2] Cf. XLIX, pp. 253–254; III, pp. 114–115; L, p. 42; *Reisenovellen*, Mannheim, III, p. 5; *Neue Reisenovellen*, Mannheim, I, p. 300.
[3] On November 10, 1836.

Saint-Simonism had played in the Young German movement, he was able to dismiss it in two short sentences:

Der Simonismus selbst ward eben so wenig ein eigentliches Vorbild; im Weben der Phantasie zu nüchtern, in der praktischen Ausführbarkeit zu phantastisch, ward er nicht mehr als ein Reiz für derartige Spekulation. Als solcher allerdings von grosser Bedeutung, denn es ist eine vorlaute Unbescheidenheit, ihm grosse Kühnheit und ein seltenes Vermögen in der Formation abzusprechen[1].

A certain real impartiality is noticeable here. Theoretically, he was once more able to do the Saint-Simonians something like justice, but their ideas had ceased to interest him as a practical proposition.

To the end of his life, however, he kept a sincere if sporadic personal interest in their doings. One of the first questions he put to Heine when he met him in Paris in the winter of 1839 was about his relations with this sect[2]. But Heine would do nothing but laugh and tell him funny stories: how Mathilde had wished to present herself as a candidate for the post of the mystic mother; how he had stifled this ambition by telling her that she would have to learn philosophy, and wear one garment only, and that an inadequate one; how all Paris had mocked at the famous costume adopted at Ménilmontant.

So Heine talked, and the strange destructive smile of which Meissner speaks in his *Erinnerungen* played over his face, while Laube listened eagerly to the ruthless comments, and the ghost of a renounced allegiance made a silent but not a negligible third. In the crucible of that fierce mockery, the measure of Heine's bitter disappointment, but which to Laube seemed all delightful humour and wit, what little remained to him of serious appreciation melted into jests and evaporated into laughter.

Hereafter the references to Saint-Simonism are few and far between[3]. It is with a quickening of the pulses that one reads Heine's letter to Laube introducing Félicien David, and mentioning the possibility that he might be accompanied by Enfantin[4]. But if David came to Leipzig, he must have come

---

[1] *Geschichte der deutschen Literatur*, Stuttgart, 1839–1840, IV, p. 199.

[2] XLI, pp. 336–337.

[3] 1841, *Gans und Immermann*, L, pp. 117–121; 1843, *Gräfin Chateaubriand*, X, pp. 94–95; 1845, *Einleitung zu Monaldeschi*, XXIII, p. 39.

[4] Hirth, II, p. 554, dated May 5, 1845.

alone, for there is no reference to any such meeting in Laube's letters or in his memoirs, whence it would certainly not have been omitted. Meanwhile in describing his second visit to Paris in 1847, Laube had something to say in praise of Fourier and Fourierism[1], but the Saint-Simonians were passed over in silence.

One reference remains to be considered. In defending his political opinions during the third revolution at the expense of the ideas of 1848, Laube wrote not without a certain bitterness to Heine:

Ja ich finde jetzt noch, dass der Simonismus unvergleichlich geist-voller und poëtischer war als das jetzige schwammige Zeug[2].

But the theme did not recur. In the hustle and bustle of an increasingly successful and satisfying life, Saint-Simonism vanished over the horizon of his mind, a ship on which he had once thought to sail to the enchanted isles, but which now, a derelict on uncharted seas, drifted hither and thither at the mercy of unknown currents.

When he came to write the *Erinnerungen*, it swam, ghost-like, into his ken, and he viewed it from the great distance of a secure and comfortable haven. But he was becoming an old man, and beginning to live more and more in the past; the ship came slowly nearer. He was able to discern details which had long remained forgotten, and in the *Nachträge* he sketched lightly but surely the bold and gallant ship, with the eager young sailor on board. It was perhaps with a sigh for those hopes of high adventure, that he laid down the pen, and turned to read of Enfantin and the Saint-Simonians in the *Souvenirs littéraires* of Maxime Du Camp.

(f) INHIBITIONS

The story of Laube and Saint-Simonism is one of continually baffled enterprise. His first desire to express his opinions in print was baulked by Brockhaus, who looked coldly on the scheme. He then set off for Paris, and circumstances stopped him on the way. He once more determined to write an account

---

[1] xxxv, p. 57.

[2] *Deutsche Rundschau*, Berlin, 1908, cxxxvi, p. 448, dated February 12, 1850.

of the Saint-Simonians, but other books and other ventures
thrust themselves forward. Finally, the subject, which was
clamouring to him to be written, forced the pen into his hands
in Berlin and again in Gräfenberg; but fate was too much for
him; at her imperious bidding he pushed aside the paper and
retired into solitary confinement.

Yet these divers and sundry prohibitions were not perhaps as
external as they appear. Brockhaus was not the only publisher
in Germany as Laube soon discovered; the difficulties in the
way of the journey to Paris in 1832 were far from being insuperable; there was nothing to prevent Laube from writing
the third volume of *Das neue Jahrhundert* instead of *Die Poeten*
or instead of the *Reisenovellen*. And again, why did he leave
the article on Saint-Simonism so late in 1834? It was intended
to precede the one on Bulwer Lytton in the first instance, but it
dropped to the second place and then was heard of no more.
What led to all this hesitation and procrastination in one as
impulsive and as cock-sure as Laube was then?

It is a question which cannot be answered with any finality,
but I am inclined to seek the key to this riddle in the attack of
hypochondria in July 1832. On the face of it, it looks as if
Laube missed the psychological moment for going to Paris because this malady put him out of action. But it is at least
possible that he was put out of action because he was going to
Paris to join the Saint-Simonians. This strange disease appears,
we are told, 'on the advent of an exciting cause.' Unknown to
Laube, something within him may have rebelled against the
projected journey and shammed sick rather than be dragged
along a road which it did not wish to tread. The same unconscious resistance may account for the mystery of the unwritten book. If this theory is true, it would seem that the
saner part of Laube's nature was putting up a determined fight
against an influence whose far-reaching consequences may have
been dimly felt. Indeed, he would have cut a strange figure
as one of Enfantin's disciples. He lacked the vision which led
them into such curious situations, but which was responsible
for the hold of a possibly unpracticable ideal over their minds.
Take away that vision, and absurdity remains. Force it upon
an unfit subject, make him accept it by the strength of a mag-

netic personality, and his own individuality will be submerged, the continuity of his development will be broken; there will be loss of balance, there may be worse. Faced with such a dilemma, common sense rejects the absurd, sanity will have nothing to say to the abnormal. Laube remained in Leipzig.

But the fact that he was dallying with the idea of giving an account of the Saint-Simonians during the years 1832–1834 provides a fairly satisfactory explanation for the scarcity and the brevity of his references during the years of his most intense preoccupation with their teachings and adventures. He was holding himself in reserve for the book which was never written.

Heine also contemplated writing such a book in 1832. And indeed, although the account of Laube's interest in Saint-Simonism may seem a bald one when contrasted with the subtleties of Heine's mental experiences, yet there is a strange resemblance between them. Both greeted the first news of the doctrine with great enthusiasm, and set out for Paris to become the apostles of a new creed. Heine indeed was a year earlier than Laube, and accomplished the journey, but neither of them was destined to become a Saint-Simonian. The religious gospel expounded in the *salle* Taitbout had a liberating effect on both their minds. Heine, for a time at least, was freed from the wearing struggle between his spiritual and his sensual self; Laube escaped the more concrete trials of a clergyman's life. For both therefore the Saint-Simonian religion spelt release. Both again, quite independently of each other, set out to write a book on Saint-Simonism, and neither of them wrote that book. But both, almost simultaneously, produced works written under the influence of Enfantin's teachings, although approached from a different angle. Both, finally, fell out of love with Saint-Simonism, ultimately because life was too much for them.

But here the resemblance ends. It was Heine's tragedy that the Saint-Simonian synthesis failed him when he put it to the test of reality; while the light-hearted laughter of comedy greets Laube's desertion of the 'free woman' and his entry into the bonds of matrimony. Thus the same theme has been played but in different keys; ending in one case with the triumphant clash of a wedding march, in the other with the arresting effect of broken melody, of an unresolved discord, an unsatisfied desire.

CHAPTER X

LAUBE AND BÖRNE

Laube opened his literary career in 1829 by becoming the president of a students' society in Breslau and the editor of their paper, the *Aurora*, to which he contributed literary and dramatic criticisms, *Xenien*, and lyrical effusions. Incidentally he also wrote dramatic criticisms for the *Breslauer Zeitung*, the *Schlesische Zeitung*, the *Komet* and the *Planet*. He had further composed a farce, *Nicolo Zaganini*, and a tragedy, *Gustav Adolph* (both had the unusual fortune to cross the boards), and had abandoned another tragedy, *Moritz von Sachsen*, before its completion. Thus the July Revolution found him keenly interested in the stage, and with the invaluable experience of a six months' editorship behind him.

The upheaval in France had a sobering effect on this versatile young man. He began to read the newspapers intelligently, and to feel the need for serious study. He therefore left Breslau and entered the household of Dr Rupricht of Kottwitz as a private tutor to his children in the summer of 1830. His principal was keenly interested in politics; Laube learnt a great deal at his table and began to take an active share in the political discussions; he also applied himself seriously to the study of history, and when the news of the revolution in Warsaw spread like wild-fire over Germany, he was able to conquer his initial prejudice against the Polish nation and to sympathise heart and soul with their cause. For Laube was born to be a partisan, as he owned himself, and by this time he had already taken sides in the new world of politics and had become an eager champion of liberalism. As an immediate result he fell under the spell of Börne and for a time Laube was as enthusiastic a disciple as the heart of man could wish. He took up the pen which he had hitherto devoted to lighter uses in the name of those ideals which Börne was transforming into a living force.

There is no need to linger over his first book, *Polen*, a badly written and ill-conceived production, in which the note of extravagant sympathy with the Polish nation is unconvincing and often irritating. Laube was simulating a personal enthusiasm which he was in reality far from feeling[1]; and this disharmony is apparent in the book, in its exaggerated sentimentality and in its confused composition no less than in its inequalities of style.

The same verdict might be passed on *Politische Briefe*, although the sentimental note is less frequent and less jarring. In its place there is a certain sprightliness and wit, modelled on Börne, whose *Briefe aus Paris* provided the inspiration and suggested the form of this second volume of *Das neue Jahrhundert*[2]. The composition again leaves much to be desired. The two correspondents of the first part, the moderate conservative and the ardent liberal, men of straw with no individual characteristics, are elbowed to one side without explanation, and a series of one-sided letters from Laube to some unspecified lady completes the first part. There follows a 'Zwischenspiel,' an amusing satire on Jarcke's *Politisches Wochenblatt*, which has no particular connection with the rest of the book; and the second part contains letters from Laube written from Carlsbad, Brunswick and Leipzig in 1832 of an undisguised autobiographical character.

'Es giebt einen Gott, denn es giebt den Gedanken der Freiheit —Freiheit Dich bet' ich an.' This is the motto which Laube placed at the head of the book, an expression of the vitalising influence of the July Revolution which is apparent in the letters of the liberal correspondent[3]; for Laube realised clearly the promise underlying the upheavals and changes of his age:

> Wir haben Eilposten, unsre Zeit reis't schnell.... Es ist mir immer an jedem Abend, als müsse die Blume am andern Morgen aufgesprungen sein; als sei's eine Aloe, der Grossvater habe uns die Zeit ihrer Blüthe falsch gesagt, um uns zu überraschen, die hundert Jahre seien morgen um, und der Knall ihrer Lichtgeburt werde uns heut Nacht wecken. Ach, das würde ein Freuen sein, das nie gesehene Gewächs, dessen Schönheit man nur ahnte, in voller Blüthe zu sehen![4]

---

[1] Cf. XL, p. 139.
[2] *Polen* was the first volume of this series.
[3] Cf. *Politische Briefe*, Leipzig, 1833, p. 90.
[4] *Ibid.* p. 134.

There is also an impassioned appeal to the more hesitating friend to fight for the new ideas with the pen, which shows that Laube took his present task seriously[1]. 'Lehre Jeder, was er kann'[2]; this is the refrain, this is the didactic purpose underlying the book. Laube was behaving like a true disciple of Börne. Like Börne, too, he made a great parade of his hatred and contempt for the nobility. There is a passage in the first part, which seems to hint that life was not altogether a bed of roses for the tutor at Jäschkowitz[3], and there is another in which Pückler-Muskau was rather severely chastised for writing against Börne, and which may have caused the author some retrospective discomfort in later years, when that gallant and quixotic figure had become his patron and his friend[4].

There are other elements in this book, but Börne's influence is the outstanding feature. We have seen that it contains two direct references to Saint-Simonism, notably to the future which lay in store for these social ideas[5], and there are other indications that Laube was willing to believe that the adoption of Saint-Simonism would lead to the freedom of the world. His definition of the ideal behind his present liberalism reads like a paraphrase of the formula 'à chacun selon sa capacité, à chaque capacité selon ses œuvres':

Das Befugniss zu allem Glücke zu aller Ehre wird jedem Kinde in der ersten Nahrung gereicht, die Räume sind offen und keine Schranke hemmt[6].

Further his reference to Christianity as 'der Grundstein der Demokratie,' followed by the revealing phrase 'Die neue demokratische Zeit ist seine zeitgemässe neue Auflage,'[7] shows how near he was to the conception of the new Christianity. Nevertheless the rather startling assertion: '...wir sind lange nicht frei, wenn wir eine Constitution oder eine Republik haben, so lange es noch eine Kirche giebt,'[8] underlines the difference which

---

[1] *Politische Briefe*, pp. 80 ff.   [2] *Ibid*. p. 86.   [3] *Ibid*. p. 30.
[4] *Ibid*. pp. 240–241; Gutzkow in *Der jüngste Anacharsis* also made a violent attack on Pückler-Muskau on account of the same article in the *Morgenblatt*, only to discover later that the author was L. Robert.
[5] *Ibid*. p. 360; cf. also p. 225.
[6] *Ibid*. pp. 198–199.   [7] *Ibid*. p. 273; cf. also p. 247.
[8] *Ibid*. p. 306.

lay between Laube and the Saint-Simonians and which led to
his condemnation of their transcendental views[1].

There is also a hasty review of the history of the world very
much on Saint-Simonian lines[2], and a half timid adoption of
the attitude of the school towards industry, which he calls 'der
fruchtbar bewässernde Strom der Civilisation,'[3] but against which
he feels it incumbent upon himself to sound a warning note.

But there is no word of the Saint-Simonian theories on love
and marriage, although there is a very energetic protest against
marriage itself:

Heirathen soll ich? Doch wohl nur, um das Maul zu halten und
solide zu werden; lieber Gott, als ob mir's eben nur auf der Zunge sässe,
um herunter geküsst zu werden—ihr lieben Weiber, seid mir drum
nicht böse, aber ihr mögt manchen frischen Burschen im Wege sein[4].

Anything more unlike the high opinion which the Saint-
Simonians held of women than the attitude betrayed in this
angry, brutal little outburst it would be hard to imagine. It
may be too fanciful to suppose on such slight evidence that the
self-appointed champion of liberalism was trying to do without
women altogether in order to keep all his energies for the cause.
I think it possible at least that he felt the incompatibility of
frivolous behaviour with lofty ideals, and that even here Börne
may have had a temporary but surprising effect.

If *Polen* is an irritating book, *Politische Briefe* is a wearisome
one. We have heard almost everything that Laube says much
better said by Börne. The strictures on Goethe, the admiration
of Jean Paul, even the satire on the *Politisches Wochenblatt*,
they all read like pale imitations of that fierce and gifted writer,
whilst a large portion of the first part is given up to a discussion
of *Briefe aus Paris*. In so far as the book lives at all, it lives
with an alien life. The very letter form reminds the reader,
greatly to Laube's disadvantage, of those intensely real letters
which Börne wrote to Jeannette Wohl, and which were only
published as an afterthought. The fervent convictions reflected
in a brilliant, picturesque and nervous style, the stinging wit,
the mordant satire, the sunny gleams of humour; all this poured
out from a real correspondent to a real recipient, makes of each

---

[1] *Politische Briefe*, p. 360.　　　[2] *Ibid.* pp. 167 ff.
[3] *Ibid.* pp. 281–282.　　　[4] *Ibid.* p. 35.

letter a masterpiece in its special style, and of the whole book something so enthralling, that it is difficult to put it down.

Politische Briefe has none of these qualities, and shows little or no promise. Yet there was promise in Laube. Nor can it be plausibly advanced that his youth was responsible for this incoherent and chaotic book. If a man of twenty-six in the grip of a great enthusiasm cannot produce something worth reading, there can be only two conclusions to be drawn. Either he is incapable of literary expression, or he is following after alien gods. Laube was not incapable of literary expression, as his next book and his subsequent life were to prove; it seems therefore as if, in making himself the exponent of liberal and revolutionary ideals, he had mistaken his true vocation. And this I believe to have been the case.

He took freedom for his god, and Börne for his prophet. But freedom in the widest sense was not destined to be his life-long divinity, and indeed the time for his preoccupation with a rather more questionable ideal was already at hand, although he was doubtless able to persuade himself that here too he was seeking after freedom. The lofty beauty of Börne's ideal, its austerity and purity, although it could impress him for a time, could not touch him closely. He lacked Börne's passionate and selfless intensity. His love of life could not keep pace for long with the fiery asceticism of his master. It is this disharmony, I think, which is to blame for the failure of the book. Laube was urging his flagging steps in the wake of one who was too mighty for him to follow; and it was perhaps not only his hypochondria which was responsible for the note of weariness and discouragement in the second part. Luckily for himself, he shortly abandoned the effort, much to the improvement of his style and his composition.

The articles which Laube wrote for the *Blätter für literarische Unterhaltung* reflect the same trains of thought and the same interests as *Das neue Jahrhundert*. They consist almost entirely of reviews of historical and political books; whilst three long articles were consecrated to R. O. Spazier's account of the Polish Revolution, and here again Laube's enthusiasm was boundless and unfettered.

But if the waves of liberalism and revolution clamour and clash on the stormy surface of Laube's mind, the undertow, if less tumultuous, is by no means negligible, and there are many signs in these articles that Laube's preoccupation with Saint-Simonism was growing apace. He reviewed Veit's articles in the *Magazin* in a way very favourable to the Saint-Simonians[1], he applauded the doctrine of inheritance by capacity[2], and declared the importance of the new gospel with its implied scorn of old-fashioned theology[3], whilst one or two other references, unimportant in themselves, show that it was a subject much in his mind.

Nevertheless it is a matter for some surprise that the references are so few, and, with the exception of the review of Veit's articles, so slight. Laube was so much interested in Saint-Simonism during this period, that he was contemplating a journey to Paris, with the object of becoming a member of this sect. There is no hint that he ever thought of flying off to Poland to fight with the revolutionaries, or even to observe them at close quarters. Yet the enthusiasm for Poland seems to outweigh the interest in Saint-Simonism, not only in these articles, but also in *Das neue Jahrhundert*. I have offered the explanation that he meant to write a book on the subject, and was holding himself in reserve. Yet it should be noticed that he was actually writing a book on Poland and still could not stay his pen on this theme. The more fanciful suggestion therefore may possibly be nearer the mark; but whatever inhibitions Laube may have felt in the matter, some of his interest escaped into these articles.

Apart from his praise of the socialistic doctrines of the Saint-Simonians, Laube identified himself broadly with their criticism of Christianity in the *Blätter für literarische Unterhaltung*; exclaiming joyfully for instance in connection with one of those *Erbauungsbücher*, which generally called forth his unmitigated scorn:

Es ist ein sonniges, wärmeres, schöneres Christenthum, was nicht im Kerker wohnt, wohinein man es gern sperren möchte[4].

---

[1] *Bl. f. lit. Unt.* April 29, 1832.
[3] *Ibid.* June 26, 1832.
[2] *Ibid.* March 24, 1832.
[4] *Ibid.* June 26, 1832.

There is further an interesting paragraph in a review of some
books on the strange story of Kaspar Hauser, which shows with
what uneasy feelings Laube approached anything in the nature
of mysticism, and how strongly his common sense and his
healthiness of mind revolted from all forms of religious char-
latanism. Here again the fundamental difference between Enfantin and Laube makes itself felt[1].

The Saint-Simonian conception of the relations between men
and women does not come under consideration in these articles,
but a scornful little notice of a book called *Das Tagebuch eines
Neuvermählten* is perhaps worthy of quotation, for it shows a
picture of Laube protesting with all his healthy if unsubtle
instincts against such a task undertaken at such a time:

> Dass ein Neuvermählter ein Tagebuch schreibt, ist an sich schon
> ein philisterhafter Gedanke; ein Neuvermählter hat Besseres zu
> thun....Am schlimmsten aber ist jedenfalls die junge Frau daran,
> die in den ersten Tagen der Ehe ihren Mann unaufhörlich schreiben
> sehen muss; wer interessante Notizen eines Neuvermählten dem Titel
> nach vermuthet, der irrt sich gewaltig, Alles ist zu finden, auch einige
> Verlobungsgeschichten, aber die Notizen nicht[2].

There is altogether a fresh and lively tone in these articles, much
wit and spirit, much youthful enthusiasm, courage and light-
heartedness. As a successful journalist Laube has already made
his mark. But there was more in him than this, as his first novel
was to show.

---

[1] *Bl. f. lit. Unt.* May 21, 1832; cf. June 22, 1832, where he mocks at the
' Seherin von Prevorst.'
[2] *Ibid.* May 25, 1832.

CHAPTER XI

A SAINT-SIMONIAN SOCIETY

(a) THE PLOT

The scene of *Die Poeten* is mainly 'Grünschloss,' the property of an eccentric count called Topf, who has assembled round him a small society of poets remarkable for their advanced views. Valerius is the hero of a novel in which the number of principal characters is somewhat embarrassing. Laube obviously gave an idealised portrait of himself in Valerius, and if other elements entered as well, this is not the moment to divulge whence they came. He was loved and respected by all who knew him; wise, tolerant and sympathetic; a free-thinker in religious matters and an ardent liberal in politics; he was also an enthusiastic lover, determined to free the poetry and beauty of love from the shackles of convention. He arrived at 'Grünschloss' pale and pensive after the consummation of an unhappy *liaison* with the devoted and beautiful Clara—whose father had promised her to another—and to whom he had sworn an oath of fealty in a night of rapture, although he himself was no believer in rigid faithfulness: 'Der Begriff von Untreue existirt zudem bei mir nicht.... Ich bin der Liebe treu, nicht aber der Geliebten.'[1] But he felt that he could not break his oath without endangering Clara's life. Valerius' air of interesting melancholy straightway touched the heart of Camilla, a gay and lovely maiden, Alberta's best friend, and the affianced of one Ludovico, who was not amongst the guests at 'Grünschloss.'

William was of very different kidney; a stern and rigid moralist, a puritanical Christian, an upholder of tradition and authority; he was moreover a dry and unpleasing fellow who cut a poor figure in the society of poets but was nevertheless greatly admired for his talent. Leopold, a half-fantastic, half-romantic figure, the type of the light lover, is introduced paying airy attentions to Alberta, the daughter of Count Topf.

Constantin, a young man of aristocratic birth but of some-

---

[1] I, p. 38.

what unsteady character, never appeared at 'Grünschloss,' but
he was invaluable to the plot, for he was the chief correspondent
of Count Topf's guests; indeed he opened the story in a series
of letters recounting an unsuccessful intrigue with an actress
named Rosa, in pursuit of which he removed to Berlin, only to
be deceived and abandoned in favour of an officer in the guards.
He then fell into a mood of great pessimism heightened by
Byronic despair; and finally on receipt of loans from his friends
he transported himself to Paris, after the fashion of the day,
not however before having opened relations with Julia, the
charming and virtuous friend and correspondent of Camilla.

Meanwhile affairs at 'Grünschloss' had been moving peacefully but fairly rapidly. William had cast a favourable eye on
Alberta, who responded kindly; Leopold had gone fluttering off
after humbler loves in the neighbouring village; and Camilla and
Valerius had progressed quite as far together as an engaged
young lady and a young man who had taken a vow of constancy
to another could have any right to expect. But the calm of the
life in this castle, where love-making went on side by side with
religious, political and moral arguments, occasionally varied by
games of shuttle-cock, was rudely shattered by the advent of
Hippolyt[1].

If Valerius is the hero of *Die Poeten*, Hippolyt plays the part
of super-hero, and for a time he almost elbowed Valerius off
the stage. Laube took great pains to make Hippolyt an attractive figure, and there is an impressive description of this young
half-god who was also half-beast, dowered with magnificent
physical beauty and irresistible grace, gifted with reckless
courage, but cursed with untamed passions and ruthless self-
will. This spirited lover disdained the virtues of resignation
and self-sacrifice; he was impatient of all restraints and incapable
of dragging behind him the chain of a dead affection.

He appeared among the others on the conclusion of two love-
affairs which he had been carrying on simultaneously to the
disaster of one of the women. The gentle and clinging Desdemona, a tragic actress of great gifts and a romantic tempera-

---

[1] Laube spelt this name Hyppolit in the first edition, and shocked Gutzkow profoundly by this piece of ignorance.

ment, had been obliged to resign her position in the caste and
to leave the town, owing to the machinations of the princess
Constantie, Hippolyt's discarded mistress, a proud and noble
lady, gallant in love and generous with her favours, fearless and
highly intelligent, but of a jealous and revengeful nature. In this
dilemma, Hippolyt pressed a last kiss on the lips of the swooning
Desdemona, mounted his steed and made off for fresh fields and
pastures new.

His coming had all the effect of a stick poked into a beehive.
He began by making love to Alberta, who was transported to
the seventh heaven of bliss, and flung herself on Valerius' bosom
in a moment of emotional delight. Camilla, an invisible witness
to this scene, drew the natural conclusion, and began to avoid
Valerius, at the same time writing to break off her engagement
to Ludovico.

On this brooding atmosphere of emotional tension the news
of the July Revolution, hymned by Constantin, burst like a
liberating clap of thunder. Valerius forgot the unhappiness
Camilla was causing him in the glory of the rebirth of freedom;
and Hippolyt, calling wildly for his horse, was preparing to set
off for Paris to play his part among the barricades, when Julia's
carriage came thundering into the courtyard. One glance was
enough; he saw her, forgot the July Revolution, forgot Alberta
even more completely and remained. Now Julia was pretty but
she was a prude, and she would have none of Hippolyt, who now
knew the tortures of unrequited love for the first time in his
conquering career. He ran through the whole gamut of frustrated passion; he roared like a lion; he sighed like a furnace;
he raved like a madman, but it availed him nothing.

There was not one happy person in 'Grünschloss' now.
Camilla and Valerius were estranged; Alberta's heart was
broken; Hippolyt was in despair; Julia was suffering under an
emotional pressure too great for her nature; William raged at
Alberta's indifference; and even the irresponsible Leopold had
fallen on evil times, for the course of his airy loves with two
village beauties was cruelly interrupted by their angry fathers.

The unwelcome arrival of the princess Constantie added to
the general discomfort; she and Hippolyt were at daggers drawn,

and the news of the madness and probable death of Desdemona
did nothing to reconcile them. To make confusion worse con-
founded, an anonymous challenge forced Valerius on to the
duelling ground. Camilla caught sight of the unknown enemy,
packed up her things and fled. Valerius was dangerously
wounded by his antagonist who proved to be Ludovico, Camilla's
lover and the outraged brother of Clara. Valerius' critical condition for a time drew all the circle together round his bed; but
things had gone too far to hope that they could be righted now.
Julia sought refuge from Hippolyt by flight to Paris; he made
off in pursuit, and they met for a moment in a hotel in Vienna;
but he was forced from her side to assist at the death-bed scene
of Desdemona which took place under the same roof. He saw
her die; then, deeply shattered, continued his hopeless pursuit.
Constantin, who had lost faith in the July Revolution, and had
experienced a complete revulsion towards the old order of things,
cut out Hippolyt with Julia, and the last that is heard of that
titanic figure is that his hat and coat have been found in the
Seine. But the reader agrees with Valerius who feels convinced
that Hippolyt is not dead yet.

The princess had left 'Grünschloss' for her own castle, taking
Leopold and William with her. Leopold absconded on his
wedding-day, leaving his shadowy bride, Amelie, in the lurch,
and made for Belgium, where he joined the revolutionary army
in the character of a regimental surgeon. William, in the grip
of a devastating passion for Constantie, forced his way into her
room, stabbed her brother-in-law who attempted to oppose him,
and was now erring, a fugitive from justice; his virtue was lost,
his principles were abandoned.

Camilla meanwhile had returned to 'Grünschloss' and the
cloud that separated her from Valerius had vanished. In spite
of the perpetual presence of Alberta, who now also loved Valerius, but in a romantic and innocent way, they had come to
an understanding, and had laid their plans for a future life together, a free union, which time might confirm or dissolve at
its pleasure. Camilla was not heart and soul with so precarious
an arrangement, but she loved Valerius too well to protest.

The Polish Revolution swept all such considerations aside,

for Valerius decided to throw in his lot with the revolutionaries. Returning from the neighbouring town where he had been making his preparations for departure, he found that Clara, who was also one of Camilla's best friends, had joined the party at 'Grünschloss.' The situation was delicate in the extreme, for he was still convinced that Clara would not long survive the knowledge of his unfaithfulness. But he managed to conceal it from her, and both women behaved with such sweetness and tact that his last day was spent in complete harmony with all three, for Alberta never left his side. On his departure he called up to the window, from which she had happily withdrawn, 'Ade, meine Liebe, in einer freieren Welt wieder.' Both Clara and Camilla took this promise personally, and fell into each other's arms. Valerius rode away, and the book ends with the unsubstantiated rumour that he had fallen in action at Grochow.

(b) THE CONSTANT, THE INCONSTANT AND THE 'CALM'

In this novel eight correspondents detail the complicated adventures and love-affairs of six men and seven women, counting the more important characters only. Not one narrator but eight narrators; not one story but seven at least; not one hero, but half a dozen heroes and heroines. Judged as a work of art the book would seem foredoomed to failure. As a work of art *Die Poeten* certainly does not rank very high, but it has one of the essential conditions; there is unity underlying the plot, it is a whole and complete in itself. And it is built up on a rather unusual pattern, for the apparent disorder is, or so it seems to me, the paradoxical result of the unity of conception underlying *Die Poeten*:

> Warum finden unsere jungen Schriftsteller, welche die Fortschritte der Gesellschaft lehren wollen, diesen Weg nicht auf? Statt neue Lehren zu predigen, welche die Censur streicht, sollen sie Gestalten aus neuem Odem, sollen sie neue Menschen schaffen und auf neue Weise in den Romanen handeln lassen. Solche Contrebande-Atome entgehen dem scharfsinnigsten Mauthbeamten[1].

When Laube daringly communicated this new set of rules for the popular game of fooling the censor, he was, with charac-

[1] *Z. f. d. e. W.* May 23, 1833.

teristic recklessness, outlining the programme of the novel he
had just completed and which, I believe, was nothing more nor
less than an attempt to translate Enfantin's theory of the constant and the inconstant into terms of real life, and to see how
it worked.

It was a task which might have given the boldest pause, since
it pre-supposed the creation of that mythical being who united
in harmonious balance the attributes of constancy and inconstancy within himself, and whom Enfantin called 'calm,'
pointing as he did so to his own breast. But Laube, no whit dismayed, undertook to play the part himself. He drew a rather
flattering likeness, to be sure, but that was the part of wisdom.
He was careful to give Valerius his own beautiful eyes, though
they were modestly called grey, he further presented him with
his own past, his own friends, his own opinions and enthusiasms,
his own popularity and his own warm-heartedness. But there
are signs that another figure also sat for this portrait; many of
Valerius' outstanding qualities were borrowed rather from the
high priest of the Saint-Simonian religion than from the author
of the book.

First and foremost was that outward calm, symbol of the 'calm'
within, which Enfantin possessed in a marked degree, but which
emphatically was not innate in this eager, headstrong young
man, who went at everything like a bull at a gate, and was at
this moment filling Leipzig with the clamorous noise of his
editorship.

'Du bist wirklich ein fataler Mensch mit Deiner Ruhe,' said
Leopold, who also made use of the epithet 'kühl'[1]; and Valerius
himself mentioned his 'ruhiges Gleichgewicht,'[2] whilst Camilla
called him 'der ruhige Valer,'[3] and Julia praised his moderation[4].

The second point to be considered is the effect which Valerius
produced on those who surrounded him. Laube undoubtedly
had a gift for friendship; women smiled on him, older and abler
men treated him with indulgent tolerance, whilst his own contemporaries liked him and ragged him after the fashion of their

[1] I, pp. 22, 23.   [2] I, p. 28.
[3] I, p. 44.   [4] I, p. 173.

kind, but did not give proof of overwhelming respect[1]. How different from the characters in *Die Poeten*. Constantin, in his unregenerate days, confessed to an insurmountable awe of this paragon; he could not bring himself to confide in Valerius the story of his amorous intrigues:

Aber ich sehe seine grossen klaren Augen dabei centnerschwer auf mich fallen und mit erdrückender Wehmuth auf mich verweilen—das ertrag' ich nicht. Ich weiss, er gestattet eine rein subjective Sittlichkeit, aber sein wenn auch wohlwollender Blick dringt so schonungslos in alle Ritze meines Wesens, dass ich immer zu fühlen glaube, es beginne ein murmelndes Bröckeln und Lösen meiner innern Wände[2].

It is difficult to believe that Laube, whose life in Breslau was sufficiently gay, and who was shortly to publish in the *Reisenovellen* adventures supposed to be his own, and which read quite as loosely as Constantin's affair with Rosa, ever inspired such a feeling in the bosom of a friend. But there was a man in Paris to whom a simple workman had addressed much the same language:

J'ai pour v o u s une admiration si grande qu'un seul de vos regards, s'il exprimait le reproche, serait, en quelque sorte, capable de m'anéantir[3].

Again, when Valerius was lying dangerously ill after his duel with Ludovico, Hippolyt wrote thus to Constantin:

Es würde mich ein Todtenfieber schütteln, wenn mir der liebe Mann von meinem Feinde, dem Tode, entrissen würde. Ihr seid alle Trabanten, er ist ein Planet mit eignem Lichte; ich bin sein Komet. Sein Anblick, ein Wort aus seinem Munde, eine Zeile von seiner Hand sind mein Polastern [*sic*] auf meiner grossen Seereise, ich würde mich den Wogen überlassen, ginge mir dieser Stern unter[4].

The metaphor is certainly mixed; but mixed or not, Laube

---

[1] Curiously enough Gutzkow alone drew a picture of Laube which harmonises to a certain extent with the Valerius of *Die Poeten*: 'Heinrich Laube besass die Kunst...enthusiastische Freunde zu gewinnen. Wer je mit ihm eine Cigarre geraucht, oder...seinen massgebenden Aussprüchen gelauscht hatte, ging für ihn durchs Feuer.' Karl Gutzkow, *Ausgewählte Werke*, Leipzig, XI, p. 19.

[2] I, p. 7.

[3] *Œuvres de Saint-Simon et d'Enfantin*, XVI, p. 122, Clouet to Enfantin. Laube may have read this in the *Enseignements*.

[4] I, p. 134.

never inspired it. If Valerius was to call forth this hero-worship, he must look elsewhere for a model:

O mon père! je suis autour de toi comme le satellite auprès de sa planète....Et quand tu verses, sur le monde que Dieu t'a donné, les flots de lumière qui t'inondent, ton fils brillant à tes côtés, se réjouit aussi de son modeste éclat[1].

So wrote a disciple to Enfantin on January 1, 1831, in language no less impassioned. The model lived beyond the Rhine.

On the outbreak of the July Revolution Constantin wrote to Hippolyt: 'Frage den Valer, ob er Präsident werden will, ich werd' ihm meine Stimme geben.'[2] This suggestion was not perhaps meant to be taken seriously, but neither was it meant to be greeted with the Homeric laughter with which Laube's boon companions would have hailed such an idea. Yet Michel Chevalier once wrote an article in the *Globe* suggesting that Louis-Philippe would do well to resign his throne in favour of Enfantin, and whatever Paris may have done, the Saint-Simonians did not laugh.

These instances of hyperbolical language on the part of the characters in *Die Poeten* are the measure of the extraordinary influence which Valerius exerted over those who came into contact with him; an influence always wielded for good, and the mainspring of which was love. The wayward Leopold, the unstable Constantin, Hippolyt the fierce, William the prig, they all listened to him and looked up to him, they all turned to him in their troubles. During the Julia crisis, Hippolyt would speak with no one but Valerius; when Constantin deserted into the ranks of the reactionaries he wrote to Valerius to save him if he could; William confided his crime to him, and trusted in his honour. He alone stood upright, we are told, all the others leaned on him[3]. Indeed the only two men who knew him and did not love him were Fips, a purely lay-figure, and Ludovico; and Fips, an irreclaimable fool, at least stood in awe of him, whilst Ludovico had the strongest private reasons to aggravate an already brutal nature.

---

[1] *Œuvres de Saint-Simon et d'Enfantin*, III, p. 79. This letter was not published until 1865, so that the resemblance of metaphor is a pure coincidence.

[2] I, p. 97; cf. also I, p. 43, and I, p. 140.   [3] I, p. 125.

But if Valerius was admired and loved by his fellow-men, he had what can only be described as a *succès fou* with the women. Clara loved him so passionately that she counted the world well lost for his sake; Camilla so selflessly that she was ready to condone past, present and future infidelities; Julia was lyrical in his praise; Constantie admired him and regarded him with awe (indeed she too was to love him passionately in the future); Alberta gave him a dreamy, romantic and clinging affection, to which he responded with caresses. His relationship with Alberta was indeed a peculiarly Saint-Simonian one:

Es ist, als ob er mit Alberta in magnetischem Rapport stände, so wie er zu ihr tritt, schliesst sich die Blume ihres Schmerzes mit ihren Thränen, und das liebe Mädchen ist mild, sanft, ja manchmal sogar heiter[1].

Of all the women in the book, Desdemona and Rosa alone did not love him, but then, unhappy ones, they did not know him. The others were all around him, like flies round honey:

Ist so was in Arabien erhört worden? Wie barmherzige Samaritanerinnen sitzen die Weiber um sein Lager herum und sprechen und lesen ihm vor....Der Graf hat dem armen Kranken einen weichen seidnen Patientenanzug geschenkt, in diesem nun liegt Valer wie ein verwundeter Emir, dem die verrückten Kreuzfahrer hart zugesetzt, auf seiner Ottomane und lässt die Houris um sich tändeln[2].

Laube fancied himself particularly in the *rôle* of lady killer, as the *Reisenovellen* were to prove. Here therefore he would feel at no loss for a model, and indeed it is unlikely that he consciously made Enfantin and not Laube the hero of this book, for his infrequent references to the ' père suprême ' were on the whole not reverent ones. But however great a favourite he may have been among his friends, and however attractive this lively young novelist may have been to women, there is yet a solemnity about Valerius with his power to experience and to inspire an almost universal love, which will not square at all with what we know of the author from his own confessions and from the testimony of contemporaries, but which does square completely with what we know of Enfantin.

When Laube cast himself for the part of 'calm,' it was but

---

[1] I, p. 125; cf. also p. 141.   [2] I, p. 141.

natural that his eyes should stray ever and anon towards the
prototype; and as we watch this radiant centre of love, this
ever flowing fount of wisdom sitting among his intimates,
leading the discussions to higher planes, moderating the ardours
of Hippolyt, steadying the steps of Constantin, calming the
sorrows of Alberta, softening the hardness of William, educating
and 'moralising' one after another, we hardly know whether to
exclaim because Laube is behaving so unlike himself, or to
protest because Enfantin has been shorn of his priesthood.

The other parts were not so difficult to fill; and here again
Laube drew largely from life, although he typified his friends
of the 'literarischer Verein' to suit his needs. It is clear from
the outset where his sympathies lay. William was to stand for
the constant[1]; he is the only perfectly unamiable character in
the book, if we except the shadowy but sinister figure of Constantie's brother-in-law, and Ludovico, who is very lightly
sketched, but who certainly stood for the old order, and of whom
we hear nothing but evil.

Constantin started with the most modern ideas, and entered
into his relationship with Rosa from the lightest of motives;
but if his character was unsteady, his nature seems to have
been rather constant than otherwise. The bottom fell out of
his world when Rosa deceived him, and he took a long time to
get over it. He was to settle down later and marry Julia; we
meet him here in the effervescent stage, but he was born to
marry and to settle down. Not perfectly constant, but rather
on this side than the other, he occupies a position midway between William and Valerius, and it should be noticed that he
does not play a sympathetic part in the story.

The inconstant were represented by Leopold and Hippolyt.
Leopold's loves are so rapid and numerous that no one tries to
count them; but even if he is not taken seriously by the poets
themselves, he is treated by nearly everyone with affectionate
indulgence, and Laube obviously tried to invest him and his
affairs with a certain poetic grace, a certain romantic charm.

---

[1] There was a break in the composition later, when William is made to
fall in love with Constantie; probably in order to show of what little avail
his principles were.

In the same way he surrounded the more seriously conceived figure of Hippolyt with all the glamour which high courage, great strength, irresistible beauty and a passionate temperament could bestow.

Constant		CALM	Inconstant	
William	Constantin	VALERIUS	Leopold	Hippolyt

When it came to the women a difficulty arose. As a man, and a young one, Laube might preach the beauties of inconstancy and take some trouble to show that the inconstant are on the whole more pleasant than the constant, although only the 'calm' are completely admirable; as a man also, and an exuberant one, he might sing the praises of the woman who could interpret love freely, give herself freely, and sympathise with his desire for change; but as a man also, and a very normal one, he found some difficulty in persuading himself of the real amiability of the inconstant woman. He struggled gamely against this prejudice, but his sympathies tended the other way.

Clara, as constant as the polar star, may be blamed for being one-sided and for laming Valerius for life, but she is compact of charm. Desdemona, who dies for love, is treated throughout with the greatest tenderness. Julia combines virtue and amiability in a high degree. Camilla, who is thought worthy to become Valerius' temporary mate, certainly has the strength of mind to break with Ludovico, and to own that her feelings have changed, but shows signs that in the future she also may become almost embarrassingly constant. Rosa, the light little actress, is not drawn with a very sympathetic pencil, and Constantie produces the impression of a beautiful but dangerous tigress turned loose among innocent lambs in a field. And Alberta, although she sways from Leopold to William, from William to Hippolyt and from Hippolyt to Valerius without losing one jot of feminine charm, never becomes inconstant of her own initiative. Abandoned by one, she turns to the other, for she must love someone, and what adamant heart will blame her for that?

Constant			Inconstant			
Clara	Desdemona	Julia	Camilla	Rosa	Alberta	Constantie

The scheme was complete. It was time to get to work.

Constant		CALM	Inconstant	
William	Constantin	VALERIUS	Leopold	Hippolyt
Clara	Desdemona	Julia	Camilla	Rosa	Alberta	Constantie
	Constant			Inconstant	

Judged by Enfantin's standard, there are grave faults in this scheme. To begin with, there is the lack of fairness. In spite of their different natures, no moral condemnation should have been attached to either class. Each should have been shown as one aspect of the divine nature working in man, each therefore equally worthy of respect. But Laube started with a bias in favour of the inconstant men and the constant women, and before he was through with the story, he was scattering moral condemnations right and left.

Then, although Camilla occupies the centre of the group of women, I have not been able to write her name in capital letters. She figures opposite to Valerius as the most harmoniously balanced, but she has no other attributes to make her a central figure, and there seems to be no likelihood that she will enter on a constant union with Valerius, and vary this with inconstant unions of her own, thus playing the part of 'mère suprême.' Valerius has made no such proposal. Valerius is constant to love only, and if he seems to intend that his union with Clara shall be a constant one, and that Camilla shall be one of the episodes, this is because he fears that Clara might die if he deserted her; for she is all hopeless constancy; she has broken off the engagement her father made for her and will live and die for her lover. There is therefore an empty chair beside Valerius, just as there was an empty chair beside Enfantin, but with the interesting difference that Laube had no intention of filling it. Some may consider that Constantie has a claim to this seat, for is she not a free woman? But Constantie, far from being harmoniously balanced, is all feverish inconstancy, and loves when and where the spirit moves her; her constancy to the husband whose name she bears is fictitious only, not the Saint-Simonian constancy of the 'couple prêtre.'

Now Enfantin had definitely proclaimed that the society of the future, based on his engaging theory, could not be organised until the 'free woman' came forward to sit by his side and to elaborate the new moral laws; but Laube had no such scruples; he felt perfectly adequate to tackle the situation unaided, and embarked on his novel in the lightest of moods.

But there is another and a graver omission of which this frivolous young man was capable. The religious synthesis which underlay, and to a certain extent justified, the theory of the constant and the inconstant, was utterly disregarded by him. What Enfantin hoped to achieve in the name of the God 'who is all that there is,' and who dwells in our souls and our senses, Laube set out to perform in the name of quite another god; Cupid grown to manhood, shall we say, striding lustily through a startled world, and armed with his bow and his arrows.

Laube translated Enfantin's theory into terms of real life; that is to say, he presented it to the reading public of 1833 shorn of its religious justification, bereft of the high ideal behind its fantastic feminism, with a man of the world to perform the functions of the priest; but with real men and women to undertake the parts which had hitherto been filled by the shadowy abstractions of a morality play; instead of theorising, he worked it out in practice, and had the courage or the recklessness to place the action in the present, instead of waiting, as Enfantin waited, for an extremely problematical future.

(c) THE 'SOCIAL REVOLUTION'

The theory did not work completely, a result which Laube may have foreseen when he started to write *Die Poeten*, but which probably imposed itself on him during the composition of the novel. From the purely human point of view it has indeed a grave stumbling-block which Enfantin never frankly acknowledged.

If the constant always loved the constant, and the inconstant their own kind, then this theory would have been a great advance on the actual marriage laws. But human nature is not so accommodating, and when the inconstant fall out of love with the constant, the latter must always suffer severely; a theory which ignores these sufferings and concentrates on the progressive nature of the dissolution of such unions is just as one-sided and unfair as the theory which ignores the sufferings of the inconstant chained for life to a perpetual partner; and since marriage is the basis of the family, enforced constancy has a powerful argument in its favour.

Laube was not concerned with the next generation, but he was clear-sighted enough to perceive the other stumbling-block. The amount of suffering he managed to compress into some one hundred and eighty pages speaks eloquently here, and if we look at his scheme again we shall see how far he was from holding the optimistic theory that like would attract like. For in a well-ordered Saint-Simonian society the lines of affection or attraction uniting the different men and women in *Die Poeten* would have been something like this:

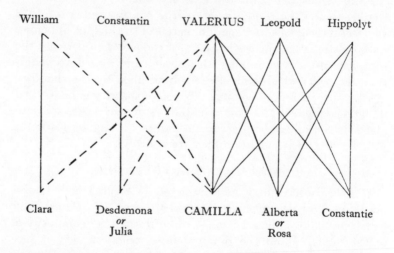

Leopold and Alberta might have performed a *chassez-croisez* with Hippolyt and Constantie, or progressed to further unions outside this immediate circle; whilst Valerius and Camilla would have had threads of sympathy connecting them with all the rest, and although remaining constant to each other, would have contracted passing *liaisons* with the inconstant, Leopold and Hippolyt, or Alberta (Rosa) and Constantie. But Laube was dealing with real life, and what really happened was this:

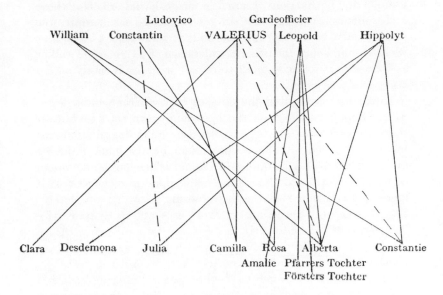

A lamentable lack of symmetry is apparent here. Valerius alone is playing his preconceived part properly.

An analysis of the various actions and reactions of the characters in this novel proves clearly that most of the trouble springs from the pain which the constant and the inconstant cause one another, and results at the end in a scene of wreckage. Desdemona is dead. William is a murderer in intention if not in fact. Hippolyt has disappeared under disquieting circumstances which point to suicide. Constantin has survived his crisis at the expense of his principles. Leopold is becoming more and more an irresponsible buffoon. And Laube, who by now had rather lost control, tried to account for all this by blaming one person after another and society most of all. Then hastily he girt up his loins to save something from the wreck.

If all else failed him, Valerius must still remain. We are therefore called upon to witness the final scene: Valerius spending his last hours in 'Grünschloss' in an atmosphere of harmonious love, with Clara on one side, Camilla on the other, and Alberta, we suppose, at his feet.—Valerius the 'calm,' Camilla the harmonious, Clara the faithful, and Alberta whose affections are *vives* rather than *profondes*. It is an impressive performance, but even Valerius finds it somewhat of a strain; we are reminded of the precarious balance of a tight-rope walker as we watch it uneasily, and we rejoice when he is safely on his horse and away.

Laube had attempted the difficult task of stage-managing a Saint-Simonian society on the lines laid down by Enfantin in the *Enseignements*. He began with characters drawn from real life, but typified for the purpose, and neatly labelled in his mind: constant, inconstant and 'calm.' Then he set to work; but as he wrote, and the characters gripped him, he saw with increasing clearness that the theory would not work completely; that it was only successful in rare cases and with unusually dowered temperaments. He saw the constant in love with the inconstant, and fleeing from their own kind. He saw the inconstant living according to their natures with devastating results. He saw that even the 'calm' caused suffering in others and might know uneasiness themselves. But if the characters had hold of him, the idea gripped him still more, and with increasing grimness he worked it out to the end.

Complicated situations might arise, and, worse still, situations almost absurd. Heroines might lose their reason and die; duels might be fought, murder might be attempted, suicide contemplated, treachery consummated, but Laube went on directing operations, until it would almost seem that the social revolution had failed, that society and not the revolutionaries held the field. But with a triumphant nod into the wings, this intrepid stage-manager summoned on to the almost deserted stage the figure of his hero, and the final words are left to him: 'In einer freieren Welt wieder.'

A good curtain, one must allow. The rebels are not beaten yet. They have retired for a time, but let society look to itself. Freedom is at hand.

(d) OTHER SAINT-SIMONIAN IDEAS

It has very generally been admitted by Laube's biographers and commentators that the influence of Saint-Simonism is clearly apparent in the social and religious theories advocated by the various characters in this book, and especially by Valerius, who more particularly represents the opinions of the author.

The Saint-Simonian criticism of the one-sidedness of Christianity, to begin with, is implicit in the following passage, although it should be noted that the criticism is levelled at the deterioration of Christianity in the hands of the priests and not at its essential nature:

...das mit tausend Zungen zu predigende und zu preisende Gute, was Christus gebracht und durch seinen Tod besiegelt hat, ist durch die Handwerker entstellt worden. Sein Opfer, wodurch er einen unschätzbaren Schatz von Wahrheiten beglaubigt und der Welt ans Herz gelegt hat, dieses Opfer ist zu einer erdrückenden Kreuz- und Wundertheorie verdreht worden. Man muss sich schämen, wenn man einen Zeisig lustig zwitschern hört—die ganze Erde ist durch die schwarzblütigen Leute zu einem Sarge eingesegnet worden; Sonne, Mond und Sterne sind Todtenfackeln, der Himmel ist ein grosses schwarzes Leichentuch, die Menschen sind lauter Todte oder Todesreife und tragen alle Leid. Es schickt sich nicht zu lachen, wenn man an Gott denkt—o Du fröhlicher Gott, der so viel Freude ausgegossen. Das nennen sie Christenthum. Grosser Christus, was würdest Du zur Ausgeburt Deiner menschenfreundlichen Gedanken sagen![1]

The criticism is the same, if the blame is laid at a different door; and in the following lines Laube spoke almost as Bazard had spoken in the second volume of the *Doctrine de Saint-Simon*:

Es wird nicht leicht Jemand die unendlichen Segnungen, die das Christenthum der Erde gebracht, die jede positive Religion mehr oder minder der Gesellschaft sich erst entwickelnder Menschen bringt, so preisen als ich; aber sobald man nicht eine tägliche Perfectibilität dieser Lehren annimmt, sobald man ihren Dienst nicht auf grenzenlose Freiheit gründet, unterküsst man das Gute, zerstört man das Beste, so lange trägt ihr Segen an den Schwingen unendlich viel Elend.... Es muss die positive Religion vervollkomnet werden können, wenn sie Nutzen haben soll—kann man denn etwa leugnen,

---

[1] *Die Poeten*, Leipzig, 1833, II, p. 125. Not included in the later edition.

dass ein Dritttheil unserer jetzigen Welt ein andres Christenthum als das der Pfaffen braucht?[1]

And Laube's appeal for the recognition of the beauty under-lying the life of the roué is worthy to be placed beside a passage in the *Cinquième Enseignement*, in which Enfantin made an im-passioned apology for the life of light women[2].

But if Laube was ready enough to give his vote to the 'emancipation of the flesh,' he was less concerned with the hypothetical harmony between spirit and senses, which the Saint-Simonians considered the corner-stone of the new Chris-tianity. On this subject he maintained an indifferent silence. It was the practical outcome of the new theories, the social revo-lution, which interested him most. Thus we find him giving his meed of praise to the abolition of aristocracy by birth, and speaking as a true disciple of Saint-Simon[3]. But even here, though he could praise, he could not linger. His chief concern lay in the problems dealing with women, love and marriage, and the various arguments on this theme form the background to the book. There are eloquent disquisitions on the beauty of free love, and the petty restraints to which society subjects it[4]; there are scornful repudiations of 'das traurige Einmal Eins der Ehe,'[5] and of 'die sentimentale *eine* Jugendliebe'[6]; faithfulness is defined as the crutches of love, which must be thrown aside if we are to walk independently. Then when Valerius settled down to formulate a positive theory, the words were borrowed from Enfantin, although the manner of delivery was Laube's:

Valer, welcher die Frauen selbstständiger gestellt sehen will, und wunderlich genug von den neuen verwirrenden Zeitbewegungen Viel für uns erwartet, opponirte der Fürstin in vielen Dingen. Er machte sie darauf aufmerksam, wie gerade jetzt das äussere Leben der Frauen in der Luft schwebe, wenn sie ihren einzigen Haltpunkt, die Ehe, aufgäben; wie nur die stärksten und edelsten Weiber einen Übergang zu besserem freierem Gesellschaftsleben dadurch bilden

---

[1] *Die Poeten*, Leipzig, 1833, II, pp. 129–131. Not included in the later edition; cf. *Œuvres de Saint-Simon et d'Enfantin*, XLII, pp. 266–267: 'Rendons un dernier hommage à ce grand système...Mais...tournons nos regards vers l'avenir.'

[2] *Die Poeten*, Leipzig, 1833, II, pp. 110–112. Not included in the later edition; cf. *Œuvres de Saint-Simon et d'Enfantin*, XIV, pp. 151–152.

[3] I, p. 114.   [4] I, pp. 63 ff. and 162.
[5] I, pp. 105–106; cf. also I, p. 110.   [6] I, p. 65.

könnten, dass sie sich der Ehe nicht unterwürfen, die neuen Begriffe
aber auf alle Weise unterstützten, weil nach der politischen Revolution die sociale vor den Thoren läge, durch welche das Weib eine
gesellschaftliche Stellung erlangen würde. Das Christenthum habe
das Weib nur zur Hälfte frei gemacht, es müsse es ganz werden[1]; der
jetzige Durchgangspunkt aber bringe wie jedes Ringen nach neuen
Zuständen, wie alles Halbe sehr viel Unglück, und die Frauen
müssten sehr auf ihrer Hut sein, da die öffentliche Meinung keineswegs
so weit gebracht sei, Toleranz gegen sie zu üben. Die alten Verhältnisse seien wie die alte Kirche in Auflösung begriffen, die Rettung
sei nahe, aber die Gefahr doppelt gross[2].

Both Enfantin and Laube were agreed in sounding this warning
note, and indeed both stated emphatically that the old order
should be respected until the new order was revealed[3]; but
underlying these resemblances there is the striking difference
in their feminist attitude.

Laube's advocacy of freedom for woman was restricted to
the emotional aspect; she was to be free to love freely[4]; there
is no hint of the amazing mission to which Enfantin had called
her, or of the powers with which he wished to endow her. It is
significant also that Laube did not mention the 'social couple.'
His feminism was of a very different nature from Enfantin's;
it is doubtful indeed whether it could be called feminism at all.
He delighted in the beauty and the youth of women: Clara,
Camilla, Rosa, Alberta, Julia, Constantie, Desdemona, they are
all the most lovely creatures, and their physical perfections are
dwelt on at great length, but we hear very little of their minds;
they have temperament in abundance, allied to a most conspicuous lack of character. Julia certainly gives proof of
stubbornness in her resistance to Hippolyt, otherwise they seem
to be there to be made love to and to respond, or to be abandoned
and to break their hearts. The part they play is an almost
entirely passive one; the men initiate the action, and the women
are caught up and swept along. But there is one outstanding

---

[1] Cf. Œuvres de Saint-Simon et d'Enfantin, IV, p. 123. 'Le christianisme
a tiré les femmes de la servitude, mais il les a condamnées pourtant à la
subalternité....Les saint-simoniens viennent annoncer leur affranchissement définitif, leur complète émancipation.'
[2] I, p. 126; cf. Œuvres de Saint-Simon et d'Enfantin, XVI, p. 126.
[3] I, pp. 105–106; cf. Œuvres de Saint-Simon et d'Enfantin, IV, pp. 161–162.
[4] Cf. I, pp. 26 and 105.

exception, the princess Constantie, in whom some have seen
Laube's ideal of the free woman. She has both intelligence and
character, she initiates the love-affair with Hippolyt, and has
some influence on the incidents in the book. But this influence
is mostly for ill, the judgments that are passed on her generally
take the shape of condemnations; Laube himself does not seem
to approve of her entirely, and had she ever entered for the
competition to become 'mère suprême,' Enfantin would have
blackballed her immediately. She is indeed much more what
the world means by an emancipated woman, or what melodrama
means by an adventuress, than what the Saint-Simonians meant
by 'femme libre.'

CHAPTER XII

THE INFLUENCE OF HEINE

(a) THE *REISENOVELLEN*

The influence of Laube's literary enthusiasm for Heine in the early thirties, pleasantly apparent in their correspondence[1], is symbolised in the very title of the book we are now considering, in the fact that he wrote these *Reisenovellen* at all. Yet I should like to vindicate for the author a certain originality of conception. He approached his task as an historian rather than as a poet; as a student of manners and customs rather than as an artist. He tried, not without some success, to reproduce the atmosphere and the associations of the various places through which he passed, showing both skill and insight in the choice of the stories which he used as illustrations of national characteristics. He gave an amusing and lively account of the methods of travel in his day, and some passages in the *Reisenovellen* are almost worthy to be placed besides Börne's monograph on the *Deutsche Postschnecke*. Further, he never failed to devote a chapter or at the least some pages to the famous men connected with the towns he visited, and these character-sketches or appreciations, for all their cock-sure blunders, show him possessed of a considerable journalistic *flair*.

But if the conception of the *Reisenovellen* owes little to the *Reisebilder* beyond the common denominator of travel, the technique is almost entirely Heine's. Like Heine Laube aimed at giving impressions, and he adopted for the purpose that impressionist style, which Heine had invented, one might almost say, and which he bequeathed to posterity, a legacy more often a curse than a blessing:

Bei dem Worte Chateaubriand denke ich auch immer an Heinrich Heine, und wenn ich an Heine denke, so sehe ich eine indisch wollüstige Welt, welche ein kleiner Despot regiert, der all seinen bezaubernden und peinigenden Launen den Zügel schiessen lässt, und dem

---

[1] Cf. Ernst Elster, *Deutsche Rundschau*, Berlin, CXXXIII–CXXXVI, 1907–1908.

ein schönes Wort mehr gilt als ein gutes, und der deshalb die Monar-
chie liebt. Alles in jener Welt spricht aber in stolzversigen Worten,
an allen Wegen blühen Lotosblumen, und unter den Palmen und
Cedern liegen purpurne und goldne Gewänder, und auf diesen die
reizendsten Bajaderen, welche Goethesche Lieder singen und die
Cymbel spielen, und das Tamburin schlagen[1].

So Laube wrote of Heine who throughout the *Romantische
Schule* made play with this symbolical constructive criticism,
and had even used very much the same imagery when speaking
of the *Westöstlicher Divan*[2]. This impressionism, in which Heine
showed great skill, nevertheless made of his literary criticisms
something hybrid, since even constructive criticism should deal
with books and not with arbitrary symbols. It became extremely
popular in France, and Théophile Gautier in comparing the
muse of *Les Fleurs du Mal* with the heroine of one of Poe's tales,
has given the perfect type of this kind of criticism, embodying
all its beauties and all its dangers. But Heine and many of his
imitators had the gift of poetic divination, whereas Laube had
not, nor had he sufficient knowledge to make these impressions real; they often seem faked.

Again Heine would reproduce the impressions he received
from places, men and books by describing the moods with which
they inspired him; a dangerous method, but which he generally
used successfully, for his moods were real, so that he achieved
poetic truth, and varied enough to be interesting. Laube's imitations were not so successful; for he was obliged to simulate
appropriate moods—at least they strike the reader as artificial;
further they are monotonous, and all too often sentimental.

Laube was completely under Heine's spell in 1833, a fact
which is even more manifest in his altered interpretation of
Saint-Simonism than in his literary technique[3].

They had been attracted to this religion independently, as a
result of their feeling for sensuous beauty, and both had accepted the doctrine of the 'rehabilitation of the flesh.' Broadly

---

[1] *Reisenovellen*, Leipzig, 1834, I, p. 389.
[2] Elster, v, pp. 262–263.
[3] It is apparent in the correspondence, although the actual term does
not occur during this period, and also in the *Z. f. d. e. W.*, that Saint-
Simonism was the magnet which drew Laube to Heine in the first instance.

speaking, the one interpreted this beauty from the point of view of the poet, the other from the point of view of the lover, but they were both inspired by the same ideal. Then they drew together in 1833 and Laube saw all the beauty of Heine's conception and attempted to graft it on to his own; it is the task of this chapter to determine how far he succeeded.

Hitherto Saint-Simonism had come to Laube directly, and he had accepted it according to his nature; he had seen in it only what his mental equipment had taught him to see. It now came to him through Heine, modified by a poetical temperament, more beautiful, much vaguer, but with the same message of future hope and joy. Laube looked through Heine's eyes and transcribed faithfully what he saw. And he saw much the same things undoubtedly, but not in the same way.

Heine's description of a Gothic cathedral in the *Romantische Schule* gave rise to a similar passage in the *Reisenovellen* in which is to be found typified once and for all the interesting likeness and the great difference between Laube looking through Heine's eyes, and Heine looking through his own[1].

For Heine taught Laube to look at a cathedral as a symbol of Christian asceticism. Laube looked and saw, saw something new, learnt something stimulating, and repeated his lesson well and vividly; but he could not see the beauty Heine saw and worshipped, even while he rejected it. Heine taught Laube to seek for the symbol behind the reality, one of the tricks of the poet's trade; he could not teach him to feel with the poet's heart.

Laube also learnt from Heine to approach Saint-Simonism from the religious point of view. The intense preoccupation with Christianity and especially with Catholicism, which is so leading a feature of the *Reisebilder* and of the *Romantische Schule*, is everywhere apparent in the *Reisenovellen*. It is the intensity of the interest which is new. Laube had responded gladly enough to the doctrine of religious progress preached by the new church, but his intimate interests lay elsewhere; he abandoned his theological career with a sigh of relief and expressed

---

[1] Cf. Elster, v, p. 226; and *Reisenovellen*, i, p. 11; also ii, pp. 44–45.

himself once or twice on the gloominess of present-day Christianity, but there the matter ended; it was an intellectual position, there were no deeper feelings involved. But now there is an emotional colouring in his strictures on the asceticism of Christianity, and the emotion was an echo of Heine's:

So kam ich mit dem Monde zu gleicher Zeit auf dem Dreikreuzberge an. Der Herr Christus, leider Gottes einziger Sohn, hängt dort zwischen den beiden Schächern. Ich, ein dritter Schächer, setzte mich auf die Bank an den Kreuzen, und dachte an mein Kreuz, und der Mond blies seine lichten Backen heller auf—an das Kreuz der Menschen, die da unten in den Thälern und auf den Bergen wohnten, und fragte den schwarzen Himmel: 'warum Kreuze? Sind die Sterne, das heisst die Glückssterne, nicht eben so wohlfeil?'[1]

This is a new note for Laube to strike, but newer still is the sentimental attitude adopted towards Christianity in the following passage, entirely reminiscent of the sorrowful and pitying eyes with which Heine was wont to regard the crucifix:

Wie jenes Krippelkind lag Karlsbad in christlicher Mondbeleuchtung unten, und die Tepel war die weisse Strasse von Küchensand, und die Menschenbilder mit den schuldlosen Thieren im Arm sah ich hinter den schwarzen Fenstern schlafen. Das kleine Christkind aber sah mich aus dem Dämmerlichte mit der Ahnung seiner grundlosen Liebe und den schmerzlich süssen Augen der Kindheit so tief beweglich an, dass ich die Gedanken meines frivolen Bluts vergass, und still hinabstieg, und, Marias gedenkend, wie eines jungen Engels, mich zu Bett legte[2].

On the whole however Laube was more inclined to quarrel with the asceticism of Christianity than to sing its beauties, obeying here the dictates of his own more hardy nature; but even here he speaks with the tongue of Heine, when he does not actually borrow his similes:

Die Glocken sind die richtigste Erfindung des Christenthums, lebensfeindliche, erdenhassende, todeslechzende Instrumente—ich habe sie von Jugend auf gehasst. Ihr Gesumm ist die persönliche Christenthums-Melancholie[3].

Wherever in fact Laube speaks of Christianity and Catholicism, and it is a constantly recurring topic, the emotional chord of personal suffering, sympathy or hatred, of which I

[1] *Reisenovellen*, I, pp. 366–367.   [2] *Ibid.* I, pp. 370–371.
[3] *Ibid.* II, pp. 444–445.

have just given examples, is touched and made to vibrate. It is not done unskilfully, but it is done with a purpose; and here lies another difference between Heine and Laube. Heine really suffered in himself under the Christian ideal, and part of his complicated nature hated it, whilst another part sympathised with it; the artistic expression he gave to these feelings rings true. Laube understood these emotions and shared them intellectually; he set out to represent them in himself, but they were no true part of his own make up, and he was forced to copy Heine closely here in order to convince his readers.

We find him embroidering Heine's themes again and again in the *Reisenovellen*. The description of the Gothic cathedral is an extreme case, but there are many others. There is a picture of the Catholic priest, the embodiment of the unholy concordat between God and the devil, which had been painted in greater detail in the *Reisebilder*[1]; there is a report of a sermon overheard in a Catholic church on heaven and hell, and here again Heine had led the way[2]; there is a rather more elaborate version of that half blasphemous attitude towards the Madonna at which Heine had hinted in the *Reisebilder*, the earthly love for the Mother of Heaven[3]; there is even the same praise of the coolness and comfort of Catholic churches[4]. Finally Laube symbolised in Hortensia the dread power of religion to overwhelm the soul with remorse for the natural desires of the flesh, as Heine had done in Franscheska.

In order to capture the personal tone of sorrow and doubt, Laube penetrated to such an extent into the spirit of his master that almost his nature 'is subdued to what it works in'; almost we think to hear Heine speaking. There are some passages which might puzzle experts out of their context, for the mood is so often nearly caught. And this is so, I think, because Laube loved Heine and appreciated him. But the truth of these moods is relative only; they are faithful reproductions of Heine's, but they are not the true moods of the writer; they represent his

---

[1] Cf. *Reisenovellen*, I, p. 374 with Elster, III, pp. 386, 390.
[2] Cf. *ibid.* II, pp. 314–316 with Elster, III, p. 403.
[3] Cf. *ibid.* II, p. 174 with Elster, III, p. 244.
[4] Cf. *ibid.* II, pp. 418–419 with Elster, III, pp. 243–244.

intellectual convictions, but they are fused by the fire which had consumed another.

The negative side of Saint-Simonism therefore, the criticism of the Christian dualism and asceticism, Laube had learnt to clothe in the imagery of Heine and to colour with his moods, but he could not attain to the poetry of Heine's conception. He was more competent to speak in his own language of the positive side of the doctrine, the 'rehabilitation of the flesh,' since it appealed directly to his nature. Nevertheless here also Heine's style and Heine's manner were not without effect:

...wacht auf, reklamirt die unbeschönigten olympischen Freuden, die ihr als Sünden stehlt...emancipirt nicht blos die Juden, sondern die natürliche Kraft, vertilgt die Furcht und ihre Tochter, die Heurath, von der Erde....Ich will dich küssen, Mädchen, dass deine Seele jauchzt in Beethovenschen Melodien, und dein Auge untergeht in Seligkeit, dass dein Herz reicher wird und klüger als aller Professoren Weisheitsmund...und wir wollen auf dem Dreikreuzberge ein neues Liebesreich stiften, in welchem die Furcht unbekannt sei, und in welchem die gestorbenen Worte: 'Freuet Euch unter Furcht und Zittern' umgewandelt werden in die lebendigen: 'Freuet Euch unter Jauchzen und Küssen und mit Kourage.'[1]

It is impossible to read this rhapsody on free love and not to be reminded of the prophecy in the *Reisebilder* written on the battlefield of Marengo[2], and of the rapturous description of Apennine nights[3].

There is however another passage on the same subject, sketching the Young German programme as it appeared later in the *Elegante Welt*, and in which the manner of delivery is entirely Laube's:

Ihr habt alle zu wenig Muth, Ihr Poeten einer neuen Zeit....Ihr wagt es nur zu vermuthen, was Ihr vermögt. Ihr stehlt Eure Freuden, und lasst die Welt glauben, Eure unchristlichen Dinge seien kleine, frivole Unarten. Ihr wagt es nicht zu bekennen, dass diese Unarten Euer System sind. Ihr wollt ein christliches Heidenthum, und wagt es nicht zu gestehen, Ihr wollt das Fleisch, die Sünde emancipiren, und schämt Euch vor der Sünde, kokettirt mit der alten verdorrten Tugend, weil Ihr Autoritätsmenschen seid[4].

Laube's manner differs from Heine's here in being more definite and more practical. Heine indeed treated this doctrine

---

[1] *Reisenovellen*, I, pp. 367–368.   [2] Elster, III, p. 281.
[3] Elster, III, p. 318.   [4] *Reisenovellen*, II, p. 470.

purely as a poetical theme, and was hardly, if at all, concerned
in the *Romantische Schule* and *De l'Allemagne* with the practical
difficulties with which it might have to contend. The Saint-
Simonians themselves, however, had had the courage to examine the question of constancy, love and marriage by the
light of this doctrine, and to evolve a code of morality to meet
its peculiar demands. On to this ground, from which Heine held
aloof, Laube had followed them eagerly, and had written a
novel, as I believe, with the intention of working out these
theories in practice. To the questions which they had thus
raised he recurred again in the *Reisenovellen*, although on the
whole in a semi-humorous way. Once more we hear him inveighing against marriage: early marriages break the spirit of
youth[1], marriage is a poorer thing than love[2]; a spell, a formula
of excommunication, used only by people who do not wish to
be free[3]; a clever but boring idea[4]; it debases love to a trade
when it should be a free art[5]; he, Laube, will have none of such
limited constancy:

> 'Lieben Sie treu?'
> Nein, aber oft[6].

And although in a mood which he himself would doubtless have
dignified by the title of *Weltschmerz*, but which could more
truly be called *Katzenjammer*, he may sentimentalise for a while
over the quiet and modest joys of the home to which one true
heart will welcome the wandering sea-farer[7], yet if Laube is to
be judged by his actions, this passing mood was rare indeed in
the *Reisenovellen*.

There is another element in this book, for which it would be
unfair to blame Heine, who was then singing the beauty of the
flesh with all the richness of imagery and poetical thought at
his command, but which may nevertheless be attributable to
him. Heine sang of this beauty in the abstract, Laube attempted
to paint it in the concrete, with unpleasing results. He had
already in *Die Poeten* shown a rather marked tendency to dwell
on the physical charms of the heroines. Such portraits are now

---

[1] *Reisenovellen*, i, p. 256.   [2] *Ibid.* i, p. 275.   [3] *Ibid.* i, p. 366.
[4] *Ibid.* i, p. 425.   [5] *Ibid.* ii, p. 306.   [6] *Ibid.* i, p. 138.
[7] *Ibid.* ii, pp. 7–9.

embellished with descriptions which, if not actually offensive, are certainly in deplorable taste; and in which phrases such as 'voller Fuss,' 'blühendes Fleisch,' 'feister Nacken,' constantly recur. Laube, in his turn, was hymning the beauties of the flesh[1].

He had gained something from the study of Heine's conception of Christianity and mediaeval art; he had gained little from the adoption of the poet's moods, and less still from his rendering of the divine beauties of the flesh; and he had lost something which had been his in *Die Poeten*: he had lost for the moment at least the power of portraying love.

For the stories which Laube told in the *Reisenovellen* are pitiable indeed, and I say this without prejudice to the theories which he held at that time, for I do not believe that the latter were to blame. However little one may sympathise with the views which Laube advocated here and elsewhere, there can be no doubt that the love-scenes in *Die Poeten* were written by a competent hand. It is not the highest conception of love, and these scenes will not stand the test of poetry; but Laube understood passion well enough to make of certain pages in *Die Poeten* exceedingly convincing reading. These pages are written with intensity and fervour, they are downright and frank. This feeling for reality is lost in the *Reisenovellen*. There is a great and inglorious descent from the loves of Valerius and Clara, Hippolyt and Constantie to the banal and frivolous loves of Laube on his travels. There is no love in this book at all, nothing but wearisome and irritating amorous intrigues[2].

There are two tendencies at war in the *Reisenovellen*. In the first place Laube set out to describe a Greek and pagan ideal, the sensuous beauty of a gay and gallant love, untroubled by the sadness of Christian asceticism. He failed utterly and completely. It would be unfair to confront this modern German

---

[1] Cf. *Reisenovellen*, i, pp. 52, 112; ii, p. 454.

[2] 'Liebesabenteuer rechts und links, im Postwagen, in der Passagierstube, im Bade, in der Kirche, auf der Strasse, in Winkeln, überall Liebe; Liebe mit den Fingerspitzen, Liebe mit den Knien, Liebe im Schlafe, Liebe in Haarwickeln, Liebe in Schlesien, Dessau, Braunschweig, Leipzig, Karlsbad, Töplitz, München, Tirol, Italien, Steiermark, Wien, Prag, Liebe überall und mit allen, aber nur—für einen! für H. Laube!' Thus Gutzkow with pardonable exasperation. *Gesammelte Werke*, xii, p. 70.

journalist with the immortal poets of classical antiquity; it
would further be an act against which the most rudimentary
sense of humour must raise a horrified protest. But if we de-
press the standard, and compare, for instance, the story of
Mark Sittich the bishop with the fourth story of the first day
of the *Decamerone* (they are very much alike), we shall see at
once how Laube went clad in the shamefaced rags of irony,
whilst the frank and sunny pagan walked naked and unashamed.

One of the reasons for Laube's failure lay, I think, in the fact
that he was protesting against the Christian laws of morality,
whereas to Boccaccio they were a matter of the supremest unconcern. This protest underlies not only all his sayings about
love, but also all his supposed doings, and lends them the self-
conscious swagger of the law-breaker on principle, the tiresome
conceit of the man who imagines himself ahead of his times and
superior to his fellows.

But the conception of pagan love was distorted by an even
greater fault in the *Reisenovellen*. The only aesthetic and emotional justification of such feelings and desires as he describes
lies in their natural consummation. Possibly in order to placate
the censor, but more likely, I think, owing to another cause,
Laube never brought his stories to their logical conclusion.
This was by no means the fault of the dashing and enterprising
hero-author. It lies in the women, who respond, provoke, incite,
allure, then tease and elude, but never yield themselves abso-
lutely.

And here we come to the second tendency in the book. Laube
was attempting to symbolise the elusive nature of happiness, he
was aiming at an artistic impression:

All' die Gesichter meiner Reisen, die nordische Jerta und Jenny,
die goldne Jugendliebe aus der Sakristei, die blonde Schöne mit dem
blauseidnen Halstüchlein von der Schule, die schöne ach, die schöne
Maria und noch einmal Jenny hüpften über meine Augen und spot-
teten meines armen Herzens, das kein Glück, kein überwältigendes
Glück finden könnte, das an kleinen Gaben verschmachtete[1].

The traveller seeks for joy, and does not find it. He imagines
it close to him, and lo, it has vanished, beckoning him mys-

---

[1] *Reisenovellen*, II, p. 443.

teriously onwards; it is often glimpsed, but never held; he
stretches out longing arms, but, mocking, it slips away. This
theme is a purely romantic one. The blue flower in the fairy
wood may be seen and sung by rare and exquisite twilight
spirits, and their listeners will fall into that mood of dreamy
melancholy, that intimate yet undefinable longing, which no
other strains can induce. Laube emphatically does not belong
to this band, and in unskilful hands such as his, the theme is
heavy with sentimental possibilities. They materialise in the
Reisenovellen in a most unfortunate way [2].

Nor was the author any more successful in his attempt to
surround his Jertas, Jennys and Marias with the glamour of
mystery. For this purpose he borrowed a pseudo-romantic trick
from the *Reisebilder*, where Heine is at much pains to hint that
the Madame of *Das Buch Le Grand* is really 'die kleine Veronika,'
long since dead, and where 'die todte Maria' is to be met with
confessing to Catholic priests in Italy and recognised in a
portrait painted by Giorgone many centuries before her birth.
This trick, the romantic reincarnation it might be called, produces a forced and unpleasant impression in the *Reisebilder*,
but it is carried to ridiculous lengths in the *Reisenovellen*. Laube
is for ever shuffling and reshuffling the personalities of his
heroines, so that no one knows whether the German and English
Jerta are one and the same, whether Jenny is another incarnation of Jerta, and whether Maria is or is not the love of his
school-days. Far from fascinating the reader however these
successive reincarnations prove so wearisome and irritating,
that, if I said just now that no one really knows who these fair
creatures are, I might add with equal truth that no one really
cares.

In the love-affairs of the *Reisenovellen*, therefore, Laube tried
to unite the conceptions of pagan and romantic love, or rather
to present sensual love under a romantic aspect. In this he
failed, as the greatest might fail in attempting such a task, but
he failed ignominiously and all along the line.

His conception of pagan love was marred because he was
looking at it negatively and not positively, as a denial of the

[1] Cf. *Reisenovellen*, II, pp. 340–341.

Christian ideal, rather than as an ideal in itself. This anachronism put his conception out of focus, and it was still further distorted by the unhappy presence of a purpose behind his portrayal of love.

But his greater failure lay in attempting to endow his pursuit of fair women with an element of mystery and romance. Laube was one to whom the world behind magic casements remains for ever unknown. If he was an exile from the sunny slopes of high Olympus, his feet had never trod the fairy realms of romance. Yet Heine beckoned, and he would fain have followed. It was the romantic element in the *Reisebilder*, the predominance of mood, the voice of sentiment, which had such a disastrous effect upon the *Reisenovellen*. It was in fact no good model for anyone. It was a product of those unhappy early days, when Heine, torn between his two natures, gave voice to one after the other, and sometimes to both together. When they laughed in chorus, the result was an often bitter wit, when they cried out together, the result was that troubled and impure sentiment which is called sentimentality. But because his conflict was a real one, the book has an almost painful interest, and because the author was a poet, it is not without great beauties. There is real and poignant sadness, there is sparkling and dancing wit. But it is a nerve-racking experience to read it straight through, and the romantic manner, which corresponded to a part only of Heine's nature, often develops into mannerism. Copy that manner without the genius that underlay it, and a stranger to the conflict that gave it birth, and instead of the *Reisebilder* by Heinrich Heine you will have the *Reisenovellen* by Heinrich Laube, and you will not benefit by the exchange.

(b) *DIE ZEITUNG FÜR DIE ELEGANTE WELT*

If there is any danger of losing sympathy with Laube after a day spent over the *Reisenovellen*, the best antidote to such a state of mind is to be found in the *Zeitung für die elegante Welt*. For here, triumphant and unconquerable, he still lives in all the freshness and vigour of his indomitable youth. Better than the descriptions left to us by contemporary writers, the *Elegante Welt* from January 1833 to July 1834 evokes the figure of Laube

in sharp contours against the stormy background of his day;
a presence so instinct with life that the paper vanishes out of
sight, and the editor himself takes up the tale; bestriding a chair
in one of his favoured Leipzig haunts, he lays down the law on
literature and life, whilst heavy cigar-smoke hangs curling in
the air and waiters hover open-mouthed amidst the marble-
topped tables with their unsightly cardboard mats and foaming
tankards of beer.

In the spirited campaign which Laube conducted with such
happy self-confidence during these eighteen months he sounded
the call to arms of youth and freedom against tyranny and age;
and the triumphant rallying cry was interrupted by shouts of
glad recognition as one after another of the younger writers
was found fighting under the same banner. And the banner
was erected, the call to arms was sounded in the name of the
glorious future which the Saint-Simonians had promised to the
world.

Far more even than *Die Poeten*, where the underlying Saint-
Simonism was largely restricted to the later precepts of Enfantin,
the articles in the *Zeitung für die elegante Welt* reflect the Saint-
Simonian philosophy of life. And although Laube remained outside the magic circle into which Heine was temporarily drawn,
for their mystical premises were beyond his ken, yet he showed
himself enamoured of the system as a satisfactory explanation
of life.

I have given elsewhere the few but important references which
are to be found in this newspaper to a sect now rapidly disinte-
grating into its component parts. The strong belief in the future
triumph of the essential doctrines of Saint-Simonism breathes
through them all, and the same belief is implicit in every line
which Laube wrote for a journal which he had transformed
overnight from hoary age to dashing youth.

Laube adopted as an indisputable truth the Saint-Simonian
conception of the progress manifest in history, moving ever onwards through organic and critical epochs towards ultimate
perfection, and with temperamental optimism he concentrated
on the promise inherent in such times. Thus the stormy age of
transition in which he was living appeared to him as one of

the great critical epochs of the world, heralding the dawn of a future age in which the riddle propounded by the bloodthirsty sphinx of 1830 should be triumphantly solved by the coming generation, and a new era of freedom and happiness (inaugurated, one cannot help supposing, by the editor of the *Elegante Welt*) should blossom for mankind. Indeed he assimilated this doctrine to such an extent that it became the criterion by which he judged the literary phenomena of his day[1].

And if the state of literature seemed to Laube a reflection of the critical epoch of his day, the moral ideas presented him with a similar picture. The general transgression of the accepted code, which he observed in the lives of those around him and in his own life, appeared to him but another aspect of this age of transition[2].

And with youthful optimism he pleaded for new laws to sanction the general custom; he did not see in such transgressions a manifestation of the eternal duel between man and nature, fought according to the laws which at one time and another society lays down, and therefore profoundly modified by society, but fought whether it will or no.

The principle which guided Laube in his attitude towards morality was his worship of life:

Nur das Leben soll herrschen in allen Dingen; die Welt, die Religion und Alles, was gelehrt wird, ist nicht des Todes wegen da; zieht doch nicht einmal der Soldat ins Feld, um zu sterben, sondern um zu siegen[3].

And from this point of view, he thundered against the moral fanatics:

Jene sittlichen Fanatiker, welchen in einem blüthelosen Hirn in dunkler Kammer ihre trocknen Rechnungen zusammenklappern, sind mir noch viel widerwärtiger als ihre Antipoden, die gesetz- und systemlos liederlichen Brüder. Ich halte sie sogar zumeist für lasterhafter als diese, denn Laster ist mir das, was den klaren Zwecken der Natur tyrannisch in den Weg tritt; Leben ist aber das, wodurch die Natur erst für uns da ist, Leben ist ihr Grundelement, und jene Moralisten geben wie Drako lebensfeindliche Gesetze. Sie vernichten durch ihre starren Mauern ganze Generationen, während der Lieder-

---

[1] Cf. *Z. f. d. e. W.* January 10, 1833, lyric poetry; January 24, 1833, drama; March 7, 1833, humour; June 6, 1833, short story.

[2] *Ibid.* December 19, 1833. [3] *Ibid.* September 19, 1833.

liche hier und da ein Individuum ruinirt. Sie sind der Hemmschuh aller Entwickelung, alles Fortschrittes, sie sind die todtenbleiche Kehrseite der lebensrothen Humanität[1].

Nor is it difficult to see why Laube looked on marriage as one of the laws at enmity with life:

Es liegt in der Natur der Ehe, zu der ein Bett und ein Tisch und Essen und Trinken nöthig ist, dass viel sogenannte Liebe verunglücken muss[2].

On the positive side, he once more came back to the teachings of Enfantin, and expounded them at some length in the *Moderne Briefe*:

Und doch ist die Liebe das wichtigste Instrument für die menschheitliche Entwickelung. In ihr hat die Gottheit das Ziel der Civilisation vorgezeichnet, denn sie ist der Tod des Egoismus.... Ich weiss, dass die Baalsdiener unserer Literatur sich gerade Mühe geben, das wegzuentschuldigen, wornach die Fühlhörner der meisten Menschen sich ausstrecken, die weichen schneeweissen Arme und den feuchten verlangenden Blick. Das ist ein alter Rest trüber Christuslehre; ich bin ein Heide, ich lieb' es sehr und glaub' es nicht, dass der Herrgott die Weiber schön gemacht, damit wir's nicht sähen, dem morschen Körper eine reizende Sinnlichkeit gewährt habe, damit wir Gelegenheit hätten, übersinnlich, unkörperlich zu seyn[3].

We seem to hear Valerius speaking in *Die Poeten*, especially when in a later letter faithfulness is defined as 'eine Art liebenswürdiger Philisterei,' and it is stated that 'welthistorische Geister' are strong enough to do without it[4]. Nor is such noble unfaithfulness to be confined to men. Laube uttered a humorous but fervent protest against the conception of 'monoandristische Frauen'[5] which Schiller had made so popular in Germany[6].

This repudiation of the one-sided spiritual conception of love, with the resultant sentimentality, 'Weichwindelei,' and denial of life and happiness is manifest in the criticisms which Laube wrote on contemporary novels, and one of which may serve as an example:

Zwei Leute, die nicht die Courage haben, beschränkten Eltern darzuthun, dass sie beschränkt seyen, opfern ihr Lebensglück der

[1] *Z.f.d.e.W.* July 25, 1833.   [2] *Ibid.* September 12, 1833.
[3] *Ibid.* July 6, 1833.   [4] *Ibid.* September 2, 1833.
[5] *Ibid.* September 12, 1833.   [6] *Ibid.* April 16, 1833.

Dummheit und thun sich sehr viel darauf zu Gute, tugendhaft statt
glücklich zu seyn. Das heisst der Stab der Pflicht, an dem sie zur
Grube wandern. Ganz weiblich, jämmerlich deutsch. Die erste
Tugend ist Gehorsam. Ruhe ist die erste Bürgerpflicht. Eine Nation,
die viel solcher zerbrochenen, in die Knie gesunkenen Geschichten
liest, die wird thatkräftige, starke Söhne erziehen, das werden ge-
waltige, willenskräftige Enkel des Cherusker Hermann werden! Dass
dieser Jammer aus dem wirklichen Leben ist, darauf ist diese Calen-
derheilige...auch noch stolz. Statt solche Kraftlosigkeit zuzudecken,
wird sie vor aller Welt ausgestellt, mit Vergissmeinheit und blassen
Malven besteckt, und das Schneuztüchlein wird darüber geschwenkt,
und die alten Weiber müssen ein Kirchenlied singen[1].

Now as Laube wielded his critical *bâton* in the *Zeitung für die
elegante Welt* and fought for the joys of life, and a literature
strong enough to proclaim these joys and to adopt the new
standard towards life and art, he found that he was not alone,
that others were saying the same things, making the same
demands and fighting for the same ideals. He welcomed them
with enthusiasm and with generous delight, and he greeted
Heine almost with awe. In his reviews of *Französische Zustände,
Zur Geschichte der neueren schönen Literatur in Deutschland* and
Salon I, Laube saluted the poet as his master; the lyrical pages
with which these books inspired him prove how much akin he
felt himself to that elusive spirit, but more distinctly still they
show the wonder and exquisite surprise with which he recognised
his own views translated into poetry, and how breathless he
stood before so stirring a coincidence: 'Es existirt ein mag-
netischer Rapport zwischen literaturhistorischen Ideen'; so
with stammering, eager voice he began his criticism on the first
instalment of the *Romantische Schule,* and he ended by doing
obeisance to the author:

...dieser König aus dem Morgenlande, Heinrich Heine, mit seinen
gold- und purpurstrahlenden Gewändern...vor dem der Stern ein-
herzieht, dem der Jupiter am Himmelszelte selbst den Weg zeigt,
der die Götter besticht um die Wissenschaft, verführerisch Geschichte
zu schreiben[2].

Nor did his enthusiasm confine itself to reviews. He drank deep
of these books, they became a part of his very being, and when
he touched on the romantic movement, it became as clear as

[1] *Z.f. d. e. W.* May 30, 1833.   [2] Cf. *ibid.* April 18 and 25, 1833.

noonday that he had completely assimilated Heine's train of thought[1].

From now onwards too the name of Börne was heard more rarely on Laube's lips, and the tribute which he paid him on the appearance of the third and fourth volumes of the *Briefe aus Paris* reads to-day almost like a requiem on a dead enthusiasm:

> Ich liebe Börne. Nicht weil er unser bester Humorist und Satyriker ist, nicht weil er gegen die alte Zeit und ihre vielfachen Gebrechen wie ein Herakles loskeult, nicht weil ich in vielen Dingen denke wie er—sondern weil er das beste Herz hat. Es hat seit Jahrhunderten Niemand so schonungslos gesprochen wie Börne, und doch hat Niemand mein Gerechtigkeitsgefühl mehr gebildet als er, weil ich selbst in den tollsten Uebertreibungen, im wildesten Zorne sein vor Gerechtigkeit blutendes Herz sah[2].

But if, in greeting Heine, Laube made the reverence due from a subject to a king, it was the hand of a good comrade and a good friend which he extended to those young writers whom he found fighting shoulder to shoulder with himself. And it is with a feeling that might almost be called retrospective presentiment, since we know what the future held in store for them, that we find Gutzkow, Mundt and Wienbarg singled out from amongst the band for special praise and more enthusiastic notice.

Gutzkow's *Briefe eines Narren an eine Närrin* had already been reviewed very appreciatively by Laube in the *Blätter für literarische Unterhaltung*[3], but not content with this, he returned to it in his own paper and compared it with the *Französische Zustände*:

> Ich verweise hier auf meine vorhergehende Recension der Heine'schen französ. Zustände—wie sie einander ansehen, da sie sich auf schmalem Wege plötzlich begegnen. So bildet sich die neue Gesellschaft, so finden sich die Geister, und Jeder hat seinen Kreis, und jeder Kreis hat Berührungspuncte mit einem andern, und so wird eine neue Welt, auch eine der Wissenschaft[4].

This recognition of a kindred spirit in Gutzkow was shortly to lead to the journey together through Italy, during which both

---

[1] *Z.f.d.e.W.* August 15, 1833. [2] *Ibid.* February 7, 1833.
[3] *Bl. f. lit. Unt.* December 3, 1832.
[4] *Z.f.d.e.W.* February 28, 1833.

were to find more points of difference than of sympathy, and which did not end in a real friendship.

Mundt, whose novels Laube praised, because they were written in the service of the new ideas[1], was watched with a good deal of interest, encouraged not to be too sensible and doctrinaire[2], praised for the progress of his style towards warmth and colour[3], blamed again for the dryness and confusion of *Kritische Wälder*[4], and on the whole accepted rather as an exponent of the new ideas than as a likable personality or a good writer. But the watchful interest is in itself important and significant.

It was with much more enthusiasm and with no *arrière pensée* that Laube welcomed the appearance of Wienbarg. He reviewed with much appreciation the book on Holland[5], and almost the last words he wrote for his *Literaturblatt* were words of warm praise for the *Aesthetische Feldzüge*, whose author was soon to be on the staff of the *Elegante Welt*. And here for the first time Laube definitely outlined a Young German programme, which must have occasioned him cold shivers if he remembered this article during his months in prison:

Es sind viele Leute, und sie sind nicht die schlechtesten, welche mit Unwillen, Zorn oder Bedauern auf die junge Generation von Schriftstellern blicken, die jetzt ihr Wesen treibt mit Frivolität, Lüderlichkeit, unsittlichem Wesen, dreistem, frechem Worte. Sie bedauern das Talent, das nicht wegzuläugnen ist, sie behandeln diese jeune Allemagne, wie man die ungezogenen aber hübschen Kinder behandelt,—sie halten die moderne Richtung der Schriftstellerei für eine Entartung. Geschichte zu erkennen ist nicht so leicht, als es scheint; wir haben bereits eine ganz neue Literatur, oder doch die Anfänge dazu, weil wir eine Jugend haben, welche Welt, Leben, Schönheit, Moral anders, ganz anders ansieht. Erschrecken Sie, meine Herren, aber lesen Sie weiter: jene Ungezogenheiten, Frivolitäten et caetera sind System, sie gehen aus einer völlig andern Lebensanschauung, aus völlig andern ethischen und ästhetischen Principien natürlich hervor. Sie sind nur auffallend für diejenigen, welche mit alten Augen daran gehen. In der jungen Literatur ruht wenig Christenthum, viel griechisches nacktes Wesen, unverhüllte Schönheitsform, Witz und Humor, Producte jener grellen Contraste der neuen Zustände[6].

[1] *Z.f.d.e.W.* May 23, 1833.   [2] *Ibid.* May 30, 1833.
[3] *Ibid.* July 4, 1833.   [4] *Ibid.* January 9, 1834.
[5] *Ibid.* March 21, 1833.   [6] *Ibid.* May 1, 1834.

Nothing could well be clearer. The system, which Laube defines here with all the mischievousness of a boy bent on shocking his elders, is built up on the Saint-Simonian philosophy of life, although he refrains from saying so. Indeed in the *Elegante Welt* he never in so many words acknowledged the origin of these theories, even when reviewing Heine's book on the romantic school. Yet Heine, Gutzkow, Mundt and Wienbarg, all in their different ways, had been writing books built up on this system. It is almost the only characteristic they all had in common, and on the face of it, there can be little doubt that, consciously or unconsciously, this is what drew Laube towards them all, and especially to Heine. His paper was indeed the organ for Young German literature and for Saint-Simonian ideas; he was the magnet which attracted these young men to a common centre. Further, he established personal contact with Heine by letter, with Gutzkow and Wienbarg in the flesh.

If Heine is the chief glory of the school, if Gutzkow was its leader at a later hour, Laube, it may truly be said, is responsible for the discovery that there was such a school. He shouted this discovery with glad triumph in the article from which I have just quoted, but even as he proclaimed it, 'erect and sublime for one moment of time,' his fate overtook him; he never finished the sentence. Like the baker in that immortal story he 'softly and silently vanished away,' and although we are to hear of him again, it is to listen with saddened ears to this once so gallant adventurer denying not only his comrades, but also denying the quest.

CHAPTER XIII

SHADES OF THE PRISON-HOUSE

(a) FEAR

Ah Fear! ah frantic Fear!
I see, I see thee near.
I know thy hurried step, thy haggard eye,
Like thee I start, like thee disordered fly.

Of all the mysteries which life offers, the secret of personal identity is one of the strangest and most alluring. For we do not know completely what we are; there lies beneath the surface that hidden self, whose essential nature the greatest poet cannot communicate to his fellow-men, whose actions the subtlest psychologist may trace but cannot fathom. And this sphinx within us holds the riddle of our separate personality, and will not let it go. Yet all we surely know of this secret self is its intense desire to persist as a separate entity. Where our mental or physical balance is threatened, its personal survival is threatened also, and it adopts what means it can command to readjust that balance. It fights therefore for health and sanity, incessantly, unscrupulously, and, whilst we live, on the whole triumphantly; and it fights most often with the weapon of fear. The causes which spell danger to its personal survival may differ slightly with each different self, but fundamentally they are the same, and the greatest danger that has to be faced is death, which means annihilation.

Let the brave man face death without a tremor, let the suicide seek it, let the strong man die fighting for life with his latest breath, they all in varying degrees of intensity know that bitter protest of our inmost being, whose aims are not always our aims, and sometimes seem less worthy than our own. The Claudio whom his sister knew and loved accepted without a moment's hesitation the sacrifice of his life for her honour, but the hidden Claudio sprang up in wild alarm, girt with the sword of imaginative fear, and Isabella saw her brother waver and refuse. The secret self had gained a signal victory.

But there are also certain supreme manifestations of life, which threaten the integrity of our personalities, and here also the fight will be fierce before we are allowed to surrender ourselves to them. The agony which preceded the rapture of the Dionysian reveller as he felt his individuality melt and merge into the spirit of universal nature, is a symbol of the nameless terror which must always be overcome when we wish to adventure beyond ourselves into the uncharted seas of the unknown; whilst the struggle which some natures undergo before the final surrender to love is well known to proceed from a half-felt dread of losing themselves in the individuality of another.

This point of view may help to explain the various retractions of which Laube was guilty during the persecutions of the Young Germans. He was fighting, and fighting consciously against the horrors of another imprisonment; but something within him was fighting, I think, even more furiously against the disintegration of personality which had threatened him before; and it now forced him into treachery rather than allow him to expose himself to a situation, which had already once nearly extended his consciousness to embrace the consciousness of a spirit outside himself. His secret self did not wish to become so fundamentally different as a spiritual revelation would make it. It guarded its continuity, all that it could comprehend of sanity, and in this desperate effort it threw overboard as so much unnecessary ballast all those ideas, principles and enthusiasms which had once been so near to the heart of Laube.

It is not the actual denial that he belonged to the Young Germans, a denial repeated publicly three times[1], that the most rigid moralist could fairly call treachery. Denial is not necessarily treachery. Peter denied Christ, but Judas betrayed him. Nor did Laube as a matter of fact belong to the Young Germans at that date. He had altered much in prison, his ideals were no longer theirs. Nor was he depriving these young men of any very valuable support. In fact his presence among them,

---

[1] In the *Allgemeine Zeitung*, December 25, 1835, in the *Erklärung* in the *Mitternachtzeitung*, January 1, 1836, and in the *Prospektus* in the same paper and under the same date.

suspect as he was, probably added to the severity with which they were treated. Nevertheless he did in fact commit a treacherous action towards them, for not content with negative denial, he embodied in these various recantations a positive attack.

In the *Allgemeine Zeitung* this attack was half-hearted and vague. He spoke non-committally of:

...etwaige Tendenzen des sogenannten 'jungen Deutschland,' welche die bestehende Civilisation angreifen, oder gar stören und bedrohen könnten.... [1]

But in the *Erklärung* for the *Mitternachtzeitung* he spoke more clearly:

Eine junge Schriftstellerwelt, die '*junges Deutschland*' genannt wird, spielt eine Rolle: wer gehört dazu, wer nicht?...Ein für allemal sei es denn hiermit gesagt, dass unser Journal nicht dazu gehört, die Bestrebungen desselben werden von keiner Opposition eingegeben, die Institute unsrer Gesellschaft werden von demselben respektiert. Invektiven gegen diese Institute, wie sie in neuerer Zeit vom '*jungen Deutschland*' ausgegangen sind, werden bekämpft[2].

And in the *Prospektus* he went further still:

Aber auch mit den angegriffen Leuten, mit diesem sogenannten '*jungen Deutschland*' können wir nicht gehen, wie sehr uns Jugend und einzelne gemeinschaftliche Sympathieen befreundet hielten. Nicht im dreisten Auflösen geachteter Pietätsstoffe, nicht in kecken Schlägen, in spöttischen Stössen auf bestehende Gesellschaftsbande soll die Wirksamkeit gesucht werden, das Geschichtliche ist nicht von vornherein zu negiren, sondern eine Auktorität, vor welcher man selbst erst den Degen salutirend senken muss; man wirkt immer nachtheilig auf eine Nation wenn man Institute und Interessen, die ihr heilig sind, verspottet[3].

Now this is treachery indeed. How could Laube attack a tendency, and moreover in this self-righteous tone, which he had inaugurated himself? Neither Gutzkow, Mundt nor Wienbarg had written their contributions to the common cause when Laube had already published *Die Poeten*, and was encouraging and inciting them for all he was worth in the *Elegante Welt*. Was his memory really so short, had he forgotten the article on

[1] *A.Z.* December 25, 1835.
[2] *Mitternachtzeitung*, 1836, preceding the number for January 1, and printed in very large type.
[3] *Ibid.* January 1, 1836.

the new school of writers which he had written to welcome the *Aesthetische Feldzüge*? He probably remembered well enough, but Laube, as I see it, was hardly responsible. Not only was he determined, if by any means it could be done, to obtain the editorship of the *Mitternachtzeitung*, he was also in a panic, a panic created by his unconscious self for its own ends; that tough and stubborn self was determined to survive; it proved fit and did survive, but something else died first.

Yet painful as these denials may be, they pale beside the recantation which Laube made in an essay entitled *Die junge Literatur*, destined for the *Mitternachtzeitung*, and sent to the minister of the interior on December 11, 1835. Although already printed, it was never published until Geiger disinterred it from the Prussian archives, but this suppression in no way exculpates Laube.

This essay is of the utmost importance here. One by one Laube condemned those theories on marriage, love, constancy and Christianity which he had adopted under the inspiration of Saint-Simonism. He did not mention their origin, but reviewed them as part of the Young German programme and rejected them, rejected them moreover with a cynical disregard for anything but his own safety, which makes of these few pages the most unpleasant reading.

More particularly he was at pains to throw *Wally* to the lions. For *Wally*, or so it seemed, was the cause of all the uproar, and Laube made haste to join the ranks of the deeply shocked, he who had written certain scenes in *Die Poeten* beside which Gutzkow's innocent attempt at a symbolical representation of the purity of passion shows pale indeed:

> Stillgeschwiegen zu haben und gepeitscht zu werden für ein loses Maul, das neben mir sich aufgethan, das hat eine ganze Handvoll Lächerliches, und unsere äussere Kultur ist bekannter Weise sehr empfindlich.... Es war nöthig, dass ein Zeugniss abgelegt werde, wie ich, ein Freund Gutzkow's, jene 'Wally' für eine dämonische Ausgeburt halte und mich von den dämonischen Konsequenzen der Schule lossage, wie ich die bar auflösenden Ansichten über Liebe, Religion und Ehe gar nicht theile.... [1]

[1] L. Geiger, *Das junge Deutschland und die preussische Censur*, Berlin, 1901, pp. 164–165.

It is harder to forgive Laube for that 'loses Maul' than for any other word he ever wrote. His sufferings and his fear had brought him low indeed. There was nothing loose or immoral in the whole of Gutzkow's rigid nature, and Laube knew that well enough, and must have known too, in a *genre* where he was so competent to judge, that Gutzkow approached the problem in *Wally* in a purely intellectual, one might almost say, in an academic way.

Laube was not content with generalisations. He had the hardihood to run through the whole list of his former ideals, denying them as he went. He should not be blamed unduly for appearing as the champion of Christianity in this essay. He had never actually attacked the fundamental basis of this religion, and although he may have joined the Saint-Simonians and Heine in condemning its gloominess and asceticism, he had both explicitly and implicitly blamed the priests for this.

But his other concessions can less readily be explained away. When we hear from Laube the following definition of the family: 'die schönste Erfindung der Civilisation...Dieser Mittelpunkt aller christlichen Kultur und Poesie, dieser Mittelpunkt Hegel'scher Socialität,'[1] we are witnessing a complete *volte-face*, which is still more apparent when marriage itself, 'das traurige Einmal Eins' of earlier days, is reverently praised as 'eines vom Innersten, Edelsten der Menschen geweihten Zusammenlebens.'[2]

When Laube came to the question of constancy, he owned with much regret that he might be partly responsible in *Das junge Europa* for the inimical attitude displayed towards this virtue by the Young Germans, but he attested the nobility of his intentions, and saved himself by a casuistical distinction between true constancy and false:

Die lügenhafte Treue habe ich vor Augen gehabt, welche Gefühle heuchelt, welche ihr längst abgestorben sind, welche Gott im Menschen betrügt. Aber eigentliche innere Treue, dies Verdienst des edlen Herzens, das in gleichmässigen Schritten einer sich selbstverleugnenden Bildung hergeht, diese Treue, die Gewähr alles Verhältnisses, aller Gesellschaft, die Heiligung aller Liebe, ist mir stets werth und heilig gewesen, ich werde sie vertheidigen, wie der Ritter das Andenken einer längst begrabenen Liebe vertheidigt, eher den bluter-

[1] L. Geiger, p. 160.   [2] *Ibid.* p. 165.

füllten eigenen Leib treffen lassen, als das leblose Symbol der Herzensregung. Echte Treue ist die Gewährniss civilisirter Zukunft[1].

Laube could not well have hit upon a more unfortunate simile; there must have been a blind spot in his moral nature or he would not have used this comparison from the days of chivalry and knighthood. He cannot be trusted with his own defence.

To some it may seem that in deserting the Saint-Simonian morality for a code which has been slowly evolved by a great civilisation and a great ideal, he was joining the armies of light against the powers of darkness. To others it may appear that he was leaving the steep and difficult path of progress for the stifling valley of convention; but all will unite in condemning his treachery towards his former friends and towards his own past. But he was a victim before he was a traitor; and let it be remembered that he was afraid, and what made him afraid; that an unfulfilled sentence still hung above his head, and indeed was shortly to fall; and let it not be forgotten that the guilt really lay coiled in the heart of a minister of state.

(b) THE LOOSE ENDS

The nature of my task in the present chapter is considerably simplified by the article on *Die junge Literatur*. Saint-Simonism was no longer an influence in Laube's mind; he stood under the shadow of fear, and the dreams of his youth had vanished like smoke. This timorousness is apparent in the *Mitternachtzeitung*, in which he perpetrated many a small treachery towards his one-time comrades, combined with many a vicious little dig at Menzel. *Liebesbriefe*, *Die Schauspielerin* and *Das Glück* may be neglected. The flotsam and jetsam of old thoughts meet us here occasionally, but the conception underlying all these short stories is a denial of his former beliefs; indeed Köchy is to be forgiven for supposing that *Liebesbriefe* was intended as a parody on the ideals of the Young Germans[2].

But things are never quite so simple as they seem, for duty pointed inexorably to the loose ends which were left untied in 1834, and which Laube proceeded to tie neatly and skilfully in

---

[1] L. Geiger, pp. 161–162.   [2] *Mitternachtzeitung*, July 27, 1835.

1835. He had been interrupted in full swing: the editorship of the *Zeitung für die elegante Welt* had been wound up in a hurry. *Das neue Jahrhundert, Das junge Europa*, the *Reisenovellen*, these series were all uncompleted. Here were tasks to be performed and opportunities of exculpation and reconciliation to be grasped. Laube set to work with energy and determination.

He first set about preparing for the press a selection of his articles from the *Zeitung für die elegante Welt*, some of which he altered considerably, besides adding new ones, and he sent the book thus composed into the world in November 1835, with a fine preface breathing peace and good-will, and an interesting general review of the state of contemporary literature as an introduction to the second volume. He included none of the articles on the Young Germans or on Heine, which formed so conspicuous a feature of the literary section of his paper, nor indeed any of those passages which more particularly proclaimed his interest in Saint-Simonism. Recurring to his former adherence of organic and critical epochs, he now asserted that the critical period in German literature was passed and that the organic period had already begun[1]. *Moderne Charakteristiken* is a well written book and it is well worth reading, but it cannot be compared for directness, freshness, enthusiasm, and vigour, with the one which I hope may one day make its appearance, the simple reprint of the literary leaders in the *Zeitung für die elegante Welt*. It is edited by a surer hand and a more calculating eye. It is wary and much more mature; the unexceptionable purpose which dictated it, the desire to reconcile opposing parties, and to concentrate on the beauties of literature instead of on the interests of factions, was inspired, we know it alas, by a less unexceptionable motive. But it was edited and rewritten before the Young German crisis, and there is nothing unworthy of the author in these pages.

He next turned his attention to the uncompleted series. *Das neue Jahrhundert* was allowed to lapse; indeed Laube could not continue it. The third volume was to have dealt with Saint-Simonism, a subject no longer to his taste. The *Reisenovellen* however were rather drearily resumed and the third and

---

[1] XLIX, p. 227.

fourth volumes published in 1836. They passed the censor and they may pass us too, the ghosts of their former selves, written in a mood which darkened steadily as Laube came to review that part of his life when he fled from Berlin to Gräfenberg and back to Berlin with Prussia at his heels. The *Neue Reisenovellen*, published in 1837, are even less lively in tone, a certain hypochondriacal element is distinctly noticeable, and the story of Nell, who is brought up to do whatever she likes, and is then suspected of being mad, is an obvious allegory, which ends with the discouraging pronouncement that he who would attack the spirit of his times is a lost man[1].

The last of the series to be published was *Das junge Europa*, *Die Krieger* and *Die Bürger*, in the autumn of 1837. These volumes did not pass the censor, and a curious and interesting reason was given for the prohibition. The censor condemned them 'because they seemed likely to produce gloomy thoughts in the reader and to give colour to the already wide-spread belief that the social conditions of the day are in contradiction with high thoughts and ideals, with all that is noble and good.'[2]

(c) DIE KRIEGER

When Laube first conceived the scheme of *Das junge Europa* it was in a spirit of youthful optimism, and even at the end of *Die Poeten*, as we have seen, the social revolution was not so much abandoned as postponed. If we are to judge by Laube's letter to Heine of December 6, 1833, the second instalment was to show the revolution in action, and *Die Bürger* was to clinch the theories underlying it:

Ich schicke Ihnen anbei die erste Abtheilung meiner Novelle; es ist mir lieb, wenn Sie selbige lesen und mir was darüber sagen, es ist die Exposition, die zweite Abtheilung wird die eigentliche Handlung, das fleischige Leben der Novelle und die dritte resumirt unsre Confessionen und mordet und räumt auf[3].

The first intimation of a change of conception is to be found in the autobiography which Laube dictated in the 'Hausvogtei'

---

[1] *Neue Reisenovellen*, Mannheim, 1837, II, p. 282.
[2] I, p. vi.   [3] *Deutsche Rundschau*, CXXXIII, p. 229.

on September 11, 1834, in which he characterises *Die Poeten* in these words:

Ich lasse darin die Matadore bestimmter gesellschaftlicher Ansichten auftreten und wegen einseitigen Verfolgens ihrer Bestrebungen und Disharmonie mit dem Herkömmlichen untergehen.

This is true enough as far as it goes, and if Laube did not draw attention to the note of hope at the end of the book, no one can blame him, but an uneasy memory caused him to add carefully:

Dieser Theil schliesst ohne die Tendenz des Verfassers zweifellos auszusprechen. In dem zweiten Theile beabsichtige ich die Leute durch allerlei Inconvenienzen zu führen und zu erläutern, dass die Bildung nach allgemeinen Principien selten zu einer ruhigen körperlichen Existenz leite und dass es wichtiger sei, aus dem Einzelnen herauszubilden, das Nächste zu beachten und statt der Allgemeinheit das Individuum ins Auge zu fassen[1].

Laube had already written a large part of *Die Krieger* when he appeared before Dambach and made this statement, which is completely borne out by the conception of the second and third parts of *Das junge Europa*. He had capitulated to hard facts, and the difficulties in the way of the 'social revolution' which had become clear to him in *Die Poeten* probably accounted for the promptitude of the capitulation. He was obeying not only outward necessity but also inward promptings. Nor did he, in these books, turn traitor to his former ideals; it is rather that the mood has changed. In *Die Poeten* these ideals were considered hopefully, in *Die Krieger* doubtingly, in *Die Bürger* with resigned pessimism.

In *Die Krieger* Laube abandoned the letter-form and told the story of the Polish Revolution, the war of liberation against Russia, and the final downfall of Poland. Valerius, who has enlisted in the Polish army, is the hero of this book, whose main thesis is outside the scope of this study. William, who has recovered himself, and become once more a respectable member of society, although he still pursues Constantie with his attentions, makes his appearance as a rigid and unsympathetic reactionary. Leopold is discovered in Warsaw doctoring the

[1] XLI, p. 453.

cholera on poetic principles, as airy a will o' the wisp as here-
tofore. Constantie finally plays heroine to Valer's hero in a
love-story which differs little from similar adventures in *Die
Poeten*, and which culminates in a *liaison* of great intensity but
of short duration.

Valerius is depicted throughout in a painful state of transition
and development. 'In all seinen Ueberzeugungen war er jetzt
so schwankend geworden,'[1] this is the angle from which he is
contemplated in *Die Krieger*; his balance has been disturbed,
he no longer has any claims to be considered 'calm' and all the
impressive attributes which were borrowed from Enfantin have
melted like snow, leaving the perplexed figure of Laube face to
face with real life. Indeed it is obvious that the author had
experienced a considerable reaction against the Valerius of *Die
Poeten*, and that he now regarded him as a solemn prig[2].
Valerius 'the calm' has disappeared, and the whole elaborate
mechanism of the constant and the inconstant has disappeared
with him, but something remains of the Saint-Simonian attitude
towards love. Valerius still believes in the divine beauty of the
senses[3], and indeed the only happy moments which he knows
in *Die Krieger* are those in which he abandons himself to his
passion for Constantie, and during one of those moments he
formulates a pantheistic confession of faith, which differs from
the Saint-Simonian formula only in being more elaborate, and
from Heine's well-known verse-rendering only in missing his
impudent gaiety[4].

The problem of faithfulness and unfaithfulness is once more
considered by Valerius in *Die Krieger*, and although in the end
he abandons the struggle to be true to the absent Camilla, and
feels that in doing so he has gained a victory and been healed
from an illness[5], yet his whole attitude towards this problem is
now coloured by that doubt which assails him from all sides, and
is moreover little more than a reproduction of the position
adopted by Laube in the essay on the young literature[6].

If Valerius abandons Camilla for Constantie, it is because

---

[1] II, p. 109.
[2] Cf. II, pp. 42, 82, 90, 98, 245.
[3] Cf. II, p. 87.
[4] II, pp. 153–154; cf. Elster, I, p. 228.
[5] II, pp. 124–125.
[6] II, pp. 109–110.

Laube is still the same in one respect at least; he cannot do without women. Constantin had exclaimed in *Die Poeten*: '...was ist doch die Weltgeschichte trocken ohne den Odem der Weiber,'[1] Laube himself had owned in the *Reisenovellen*: 'Mein Herz braucht Mädchenaugen, wie mein Kopf Bücher,'[2] and now Valerius sighs in *Die Krieger*: 'Ohne Weiber ist das Leben arm, arm, sehr arm.'[3]

But his temperament no longer enjoyed the complete approval of his principles, and although Valerius blames himself for leaving Constantie at the call of a conventional honour which forces him on to the battle ground, still he is no longer strong enough to defy the conventions:

Die Ehre mag ein zufälliges Uebereinkommen sein, aber unsere ganze Gesellschaft ist ein solches; wenn wir in ihr bestehen wollen, müssen wir uns in die wesentlichen Pflichten gegen dieselbe fügen[4].

The proud Constantie did not forgive him for his neglect, and their relationship came to a disastrous close during the last terrible days in Warsaw, when he witnessed the ruin of the cause for which he had been fighting. He narrowly escaped being hanged for a spy, and took to the woods in the company of the unfortunate Joel, an embodiment of the tragedy of the Polish Jew, leaving wreckage and death behind him, disillusioned in the nation he had come to help, more than sceptical of revolutionary methods and seeing freedom once again chained to the conquering chariot of despotism. If the social revolution of *Die Poeten* ended on a gallant note of desperate hope, the political revolution of *Die Krieger* ends on a mournful note of hopeless despair:

Lasset singen: 'Jetzt ist Polen doch verloren!'[5]

(d) DIE BÜRGER

For all its sad ending, *Die Krieger* is an interesting and a stimulating book. It is a piece of real history shown in action, an admirable pendant to *Die Poeten*, which is theory put into practice. But the only part of *Die Bürger* which lives to-day is the autobiographical fragment, in which Laube, under the

[1] I, p. 172. [2] *Reisenovellen*, I, p. 113.
[3] II, p. 110. [4] II, p. 174. [5] II, p. 294.

transparent disguise of Valer, detailed his unhappy experiences in the 'Stadtvogtei' and the 'Hausvogtei.' For the rest it is quite obvious that he had lost interest in the other characters, who have become so pale or so distorted, that we only peruse their fantastic adventures (once more retailed in letter-form) for the sake of old times.

Leopold drifts to Brussels, where he has one unconvincing love-affair after another; he then reappears in Paris, writes a book on the harmony of soul and senses in music, and is imprisoned for debt at 'Sainte-Pélagie.' Here he meets a Saint-Simonian, and he and a scatter-brained little wife he has acquired in his light-hearted way join this sect and proceed to influence the world through the medium of the stage[1]. So we leave him playing the harlequin and making proselytes for Saint-Simonism. The lightest character of them all, a purely negligible buffoon, is fittingly allowed to become a member of a society which Laube had once hoped to join himself. He could not well have proclaimed his change of heart with greater thoroughness.

William makes his last appearance in a spiteful letter to Constantie, with whom he is now on an intimate footing, warning her against Valerius, who has been set free from prison only to fall under suspicion of having murdered Julia and Constantie. Constantin is dramatically introduced in *Die Bürger* as the 'Herr Oberrichter' who is personally responsible for Valerius' captivity, and who comes to cross-examine him in prison. His heart is dead; he and Julia are unhappy in their married life; she has loved only Hippolyt all her life. Now remorse comes to add itself to the burden of his miseries. He resolves to put an end to his life; Julia, who shares his despair, joins him in death, and two more characters are out of the way.

Hippolyt meanwhile has been going rapidly from bad to worse. After a series of unpleasant intrigues, the scene of which is laid in Brussels, Paris and England, and in which he plays an ever less conquering and a steadily less fastidious part, he flies at length to America, pursued by Margarita, the spectre of revengeful love. To the credit of Laube's heart be it said that

[1] III, pp. 114–115.

he was obviously distressed when it came to parting with Hippolyt, who by now has become a caricature of his former magnificent self. It is significant that Hippolyt alone in this last volume is heard praising the beauties of the flesh[1], and inveighing against the poor-spiritedness of Christianity[2]. But Hippolyt must go; there was no room in the world as Laube now saw it for such as he; nevertheless as he sent him to his fate he realised well enough that he was saying good-bye to his own youth[3].

Valerius was allowed to survive, and even to find a recognised place in the social life he had once wished to shake to its foundations, but only by means of the same compromise to which Laube himself had been forced to submit. On his release from prison, Valerius adopted the *rôle* of a humble farmer, but it is difficult to feel that the one-time social reformer had found his true vocation in tilling with gentle patience the peaceful land, or in turning his restless energy from the welfare of mankind to the well-being of cattle; the note of a Faustian reconciliation is not entirely convincing.

But if Laube in the person of Valerius resigned himself with a fairly good grace to the inevitable and allowed the world to look after itself henceforward, there remained one problem which he must make some attempt to solve, the problem of marriage. Now before Laube put the finishing touches to *Die Bürger* he had solved this problem practically for himself by marrying a very charming lady, a step which, ironically enough, he seems never to have regretted during the long life they shared together[4]. It is not surprising therefore that he set himself resolutely to overcome Valerius' hatred of marriage. It was a position which he could not be allowed to maintain, but which on the other hand he must not abandon without putting up some sort of a fight. Laube therefore engineered the long-delayed free union between Valerius and Camilla, who conveniently reappears for this purpose, with the result that our

[1] III, pp. 26 and 108. [2] III, p. 144.
[3] Cf. III, pp. 146–148.
[4] She was a widow with one son, a Frau Iduna Hänel, whom all her contemporaries united to praise, and who found a great admirer in Heine; he repeatedly comments on her charm.

hero finds that he cannot bear the gossip, the slander and the insults to which Camilla is subjected. She, having fulfilled her mission, conveniently disappears again without leaving any embarrassing traces, and Valerius begins rather drearily to open serious relations with a young girl in his valley. His final position is stated in these words:

Haltet die Ehe offen, wie der Herr des Himmels seine Hand offen erhält für den wahrhaft nothwendigen Wechsel der irdischen Welt, den Wechsel von Tag zu Nacht, von Schnee zu Blumen; schüttelt die Personen, welche durch Lüge mit dem Institute Frevel treiben, schütztet diejenigen, welche von der Unwahrheit einer Verbindung gefesselt und zertrümmert werden, kämpft gegen und für die Verehelichten, haltet die Thür der Erfindung offen, doch vermengt damit nicht die Ehe selbst[1].

He had once been the disciple of Enfantin, behold him now the apostle of Rodrigues.

But in spite of the patched-up ending, the mournful note on which *Die Bürger* concludes shows that Laube was still in 1837 unable to contemplate the loss of his youthful ideals as serenely as he could have wished:

...Alles neben dem ich geworden, ist zerplündert, verwüstet: Constantin erstarrte und schied, William, der uns nie mit Wärme nah' getreten war, ist im kalten Hochmuthe ein einseitiger, unbedeutender Herr geworden, in welchem gar keine Welt sich entwickelt hat, Leopold blieb, was er war, ward, was er werden musste, ein Narr, sein Ende wird im Spitale sein... die Weiber sind gestorben, verdorben, zerknickt, Du[2] kämpfest den letzten Verzweiflungskampf mit Leben und Tod—ich allein habe mich in ein grünes, stilles Thal gerettet; aber ich bin auch verarmt... ich kann nicht mehr lieben!... Warme Thränen fliessen mir seit langer Zeit auf das Papier, ich weine sie unserem Genie, das sich aufgebröckelt hat an einer feindlichen Welt[3].

This lament might almost as fittingly have been sung in 1837 on the Young Germans themselves as on the heroes of this trilogy, which begins with laughter and love in a romantic castle, continues amongst the thunder and smoke of battlefields, and nearly ends in a gloomy prison-house. The doors are opened at last, but the hero steps out into an altered world. The days of spring are over, and drear November covers earth and sky.

[1] III, p. 132.   [2] Valerius is writing to Hippolyt.
[3] III, pp. 146–147.

(e) THE DEBT OWED TO ENFANTIN

Börne, Enfantin, Heine; these were the influences which swayed Laube during his youth. Three of the most remarkable men of the age approached him and modified his ways of thinking. Börne taught him to love liberty, Enfantin showed him a picture of free love, and Heine gave him his friendship.

The debt which Laube owed to Börne was an ethical one, and although it found a literary expression in *Das neue Jahrhundert*, it was, aesthetically speaking, sterile and doomed to be short-lived.

To Heine he owed an emotional debt, which he paid generously by loyal friendship and service during his friend's life-time; but his admiration during these early years had a bad effect on his writings. In imitating the impressionism of Heine, he did violence to his style and to his powers of composition; worse still, he did violence to his nature. In the *Reisenovellen* the manner of the master is grafted on to the temperament of the disciple with a not very happy result.

But what of the debt which he owed to Enfantin? It was a psychological debt; for the theory of the 'emancipation of the flesh' appealed to the secret needs of his temperament, and impelled him to write a book which is not without emotional truth. A debt of some magnitude it must be owned; but it was only a temporary loan.

For Saint-Simonism did not modify the whole trend of Laube's inner life. It did not colour the dreams of a life-time as it coloured Heine's dreams. His interest in Saint-Simonism was an altogether lighter affair. It did not alter him much; he was ripe for just such an influence as this. It gave him a sanction for his own unruly thoughts and intemperate desires, for it brought them into harmony with the doctrine of progress and freedom to which he was already a convert; it taught his intelligence to understand the beauty of the sensuous world which his senses had already taught him to feel. It was not a revelation, but an interpretation. It transformed his vague longings into a plan of campaign, and for a short time it filled him with enthusiasm.

The general influence of that part of Saint-Simonism which

he accepted, the doctrine of the law of progress in history and religion, and the essential beauty of the material world, can be traced in the writings of the later Laube, but intermittently and on the whole superficially. The special influence of the theories on love and marriage affected him profoundly during his early years, but was not destined to last. His preoccupation with love and women was an outcome of his nature and remained with him through life; his dream of free love was inspired by Enfantin and did not endure.

For Laube's dream of free love cannot be dignified by the name of vision. Not for him the unearthly promise of *Epipsychidion*; it was a mirage suggested to his mind by his natural cravings. He was not really the passionate lover of freedom which he seemed in 1833. Like most of us he desired more intensely than anything else his own personal happiness. He found it in marriage; he grasped it robustly, tamed it, and the blue bird became a household pet. Laube was not, as he had once thought, one of those rare unhappy spirits whom to hold is to kill; for to such the happiness he found is incomprehensible and unattainable. But Laube was made of sterner stuff; he threw off with but little regret the romantic cloak of the wandering lover and donned the prosaic frock-coat of the bridegroom. The cloak was lined with the true blue of Saint-Simonism, but what matter? It was only a lining and the cloak was old. Eagerly adopted, worn with a certain swaggering grace, abandoned with a facile sigh; it was relegated to the lumber room and never worn again.

It was of an extravagant cut, but it had suited him well, reflecting the colour of those handsome eyes, which saw clear and saw straight, but did not see very far.

HEINRICH LAUBE

PART V
GUTZKOW AND SAINT-SIMONISM

CHAPTER XIV

GUTZKOW'S CRITICISMS OF SAINT-SIMONISM

(a) KARL GUTZKOW

It is a tragic thought that Gutzkow, whose life was spent in creative effort which earned him a much-disputed reputation in his own age, should have failed so signally to survive for posterity. *Zopf und Schwert* in the school-room, *Uriel Acosta* and *Das Urbild des Tartüffe* for students of the drama, and blank looks in well-read circles, this is the tale that is told of Gutzkow fifty years after his death. And if all such failures are tragic in a general sense, there is a special tragedy here. For it seems on closing the book of Gutzkow's life that as he was to be denied the last gift, the fates were too hard on him when he was alive. There is a certain grand justice apparent when the unrecognised genius triumphs after death. But that a man should undergo all the worst tortures of the unknown great; that he should imagine himself one of them, know their dark despairs and their spiritual isolation; that he should be their blood-brother in sorrow, yet not their fellow in joy; and akin to them by temperament should not rank with them by achievement, this is a refinement of cruelty against which one's sense of justice rebels. And this was Gutzkow's fate. His unhappy life, the misunderstandings he encountered, the persecutions he endured, the bitterness of mind, the fierce despair; it reads like a prosaic version of *Chatterton* or *Moïse*, the poet at war with the world, the genius in his terrible solitude. But the hero of this tragedy was neither a poet nor a genius, nor yet by virtue of his character can he claim to rank among the great.

There were elements of greatness in Gutzkow. He might even be called an intellectual giant when measured by the stature of his Young German compeers; for with the exception of Heine, he dominated them all. And the word giant is not an ill-chosen one here. From Polyphemus to the ogre in *Jack and the Beanstalk* these gloomy and surly figures, half-frightening and half-ludicrous, have all laboured under some more or less monstrous physical deformity as an offset to their height and strength. Karl Gutzkow, with his giant intellect and his dwarfed affections, gives the same impression of broken harmony and shattered proportions. He arouses uneasy feelings: pity which is not quite sympathy; impatience which struggles with compassion; a discomfort which is three parts distaste, a painful bewilderment, a half-unwilling respect. And if the majority of his contemporaries found him difficult to like, posterity, if it read him, would find him depressing in the extreme.

The environment into which Gutzkow was born and the adventures which befell him during his youth and early manhood were gloomily prophetic of his subsequent career, which moved in an ever-recurring cycle of struggles, sorrow and strife; darkened in his maturity by madness, ending in an unlovely death. And indeed by shaping his character in a certain way, and by giving him certain habits of mind, the early years may have been largely responsible for the colour of his later life.

His father was a groom attached to the royal court in Berlin, and his childhood was spent in extremely penurious surroundings. The parents and three children lived and slept in one room and shared a kitchen with their neighbours, the family of the 'handsome Lorenz.' The fathers had been fellow-soldiers in the Napoleonic wars, and were almost as brothers; but the mothers were such bitter enemies that the kitchen was rigidly divided into two parts, and it was woe to the unwary trespasser caught on the wrong side of the boundary. But Lorenz' little daughter died and the two women forgot their quarrel when the coffin was placed in the kitchen for want of room. Karl Gutzkow remembered and described this scene, remembered too the terrible sequel of Lorenz' suicide, which set his nerves vibrating with a terror only known to imaginative children, an impression never completely obliterated, a dread and a fascination never quite overcome.

In such surroundings, the clever little boy grew up and in due time was dragged off to school by an elder sister. He went protesting, and crying as if his heart would break that he knew nothing and could not go to school and would not go to school until he had learnt something. He was persuaded at last against his better judgment; and this anecdote of his babyhood is not insignificant, for it shows that the acute sensitiveness to criticism, which was one of his outstanding characteristics in later years, was a plant of early growth. We must leave him here ploughing his way through the alphabet and rejoin him many years later on his departure from Berlin. His school and university years are behind him and he knows something now; pale, studious, with bespectacled blue eyes, he has become a very walking encyclopaedia of knowledge, particularly in the theological and philosophical departments; an omnivorous reader, he has been won by the July Revolution to liberal principles and the opinions of Börne; and Gutzkow, editor of the *Forum der Journalliteratur* for the last nine months, is now, in November 1831, not yet one and twenty, on his way to Stuttgart to join forces with the redoubtable Menzel of the *Literaturblatt zum Morgenblatt*.

He has struggled out of the environment which might so easily have engulfed him, but at a certain price. The long hours, early and late; the pupils taken whilst he was still at school; the gradual estrangement from his own people have left their mark on this young man and have robbed him of his birthright of youth. His enthusiasm will be earnest but never spontaneous; his intellectual zeal will be vigorous rather than fresh, and he will express himself best by means of an ironical humour which will never know the frank geniality of happier spirits. He will be a hard fighter, but not a good-tempered one; ambitious, honest and industrious, he will never be welcomed as a boon companion; and in the more delicate side of his nature, the shrinking sensitiveness and longing for sympathy, there lies a great danger, for no real liking of his fellows is there to counterbalance it.

So Gutzkow left Berlin, his susceptible heart already a captive. He had escaped from a dreary entanglement with one Leopoldine Spohn, whose sister Bertha had been the object of his youthful affections, and he was now the prospective husband of Rosalie Scheidemantel, a gentle and affectionate creature not yet out of her teens and deplorably under her mother's thumb. And the mother disapproved of Gutzkow, for he was going to Stuttgart to become a free-lance journalist, instead of entering some solid profession, either theological or scholastic as was his bounden duty. He had no claims to be considered a promising son-in-law, and she regarded him with dislike.

(b) THE CONSCIOUS ATTITUDE

Gutzkow declared in 1839 that his knowledge of Saint-Simonism was vague and slight[1]; nor is this difficult to credit. His only certain German source was Carové[2], and although he probably read the German newspaper articles, almost certainly those in the *Allgemeine Zeitung* and the *Morgenblatt*, and Menzel's contribution to the *Literaturblatt*; whilst he must have been acquainted with Börne's views as expressed in the *Letters from Paris*, still this does not argue a profound or detailed knowledge. He referred twice to the *Enseignements d'Enfantin*[3], but not in a way to suggest that he had read them; indeed his contention that he had learnt the term 'rehabilitation of the flesh' from Mundt would seem to prove that he cannot have done so, although Gutzkow was probably in error here[4]. The term does not occur in his early writings, which contain some allusions to Saint-Simonism, reproducing the conscious attitude towards the sect which Gutzkow adopted before the world.

The first reference to Saint-Simonism which I have been able to find occurs in the *Literaturblatt* of June 1, 1832:

Das Ewige bleibt das Bedürfniss, in der Gemeinschaft zu leben, und nur diese Sehnsucht kann einst das höhere Band der Einheit seyn. Sie wird von einer tieferen Spekulation zu einem bestimmten, der Wissenschaft genügenden Gedanken verklärt werden, und das Mittel ihrer allmählichen Befriedigung kann kein andres seyn als ein

---

[1] *A.W.* XII, pp. 85–86. Wherever possible I use Gutzkow's *Gesammelte Werke*, Jena, 1872–1876, for reference under the abbreviation *G.W.*, supplementing it by Houben's edition of Gutzkow's *Ausgewählte Werke*, Leipzig, under the abbreviation *A.W.*, or by the first editions, which in each case have been consulted; the original spelling has been retained throughout.

[2] *Briefe eines Narren an eine Närrin*, Hamburg, 1832, pp. 38–39.

[3] *A.W. loc. cit.*; and in a letter to Börne of October 2, 1835; cf. Houben, *Jungdeutscher Sturm und Drang*, p. 111, where he also mentions the *Globe*.

[4] For he also maintains that he only recognised this system in *Madonna* after others had pointed it out. As three chapters in this book are entitled 'Wiedereinsetzung des Fleisches,' this is not very likely to have been the case. In 1875 Gutzkow attributed his knowledge to Heine; cf. *A.W.* XI, pp. 155 ff.

politisches. Der Simonismus ist nur die Anregung der Frage. Ueberhaupt ist hier nicht die Rede von Morgen, oder vom nächsten Jahre, sondern von Jahrhunderten.

There is no clash of trumpets here, and no roll of drums. A more muted note could not well have been struck, a vaguer reference could hardly have been made, and of the two further mentions of Saint-Simonism in the same paper, the first is distinctly ironical in tone, the second shows at most that Gutzkow knew something of their theories of property:

> Während wir alle Lust bezeugen, dem St Simonismus seine Widersinnigkeiten zu nehmen, und den lezten Anstrengungen der Väter vom Merilmontant [sic] mit der ganzen Energie unsrer Begeisterung zu Hülfe zu kommen, fangen die Franzosen an, auf unsre mystischen Zustände zu lauschen....[1]
>
> Es ist wahr, die Lebensversicherungsanstalten machen dem Erbrechte ein Ende, wie die Jakobiner und die St Simonisten; und es wundert mich, dass die Advokaten und die Regierungen noch nicht gegen sie aufgestanden sind[2].

Meanwhile the *Briefe eines Narren an eine Närrin* had been published anonymously in the autumn of 1832, and contained several references to a theme which, for all his aloof airs, was beginning to preoccupy Gutzkow and to intrude on his lines of thought:

> An der Lehre der St Simonisten ist dies das Wahre, dass sie das Bedürfniss einer Coalition unseres geistigen und materiellen Lebens aussprechen. Sie ist ein Symptom des Zeitgeistes und hat daher nur ein vorübergehendes Interesse. Ihre Lehren selbst befriedigen jenes Bedürfniss nicht, sie müssten dazu weniger die Resultate eines speculirenden Kopfes sein, aber sie haben im Schematismus der mannigfachen unsre Zeit durchkreuzenden Tendenzen eine so mathematisch richtige Stellung, wie keine andere neuere Erscheinung im Gebiete der geistigen Cultur. Herr Carové, Licencié en droit, findet zwar in dieser Bedeutung der Simonisten *Jakobinisches, Sitten-* und *Staatsgefährliches*...aber das zeichnet eben ihre Lehre mehr aus, als ein selbstverstandener Satz von la Mennais, Cousin oder wohl gar Hegel[3].

---

[1] *Literaturblatt*, January 18, 1833; reprinted in *Beiträge zur Geschichte der neuesten Literatur*, Stuttgart, 1836, II, p. 17, where it reads: '...und den lezten Anstrengungen der Väter vom Menilmontane [sic] *mit unsern eigenen Thorheiten* zu Hilfe zu kommen....' The italics are mine.

[2] *Ibid.* June 21, 1833.

[3] *Briefe eines Narren an eine Närrin*, pp. 38–39.

There is further a misleading, but possibly ironically meant statement, to the effect that the Prussians had long been Saint-Simonians[1]; but the most interesting passage in this book is the supposed similarity which Gutzkow discovered between Plato's *Republic* and the Saint-Simonian theories on feminism[2], for however much astray Gutzkow may show himself here about the Saint-Simonian attitude towards women, and however much he may attempt to disguise his interest by irony, the interest, not entirely benevolent, but still awakened, is there. In spite of his dry and pedantic nature, Gutzkow's temperament stood peculiarly in need of the sympathy and affection of women. He was just as deeply interested in any question that concerned them as Laube was, although from quite different motives. Moreover like Laube's it was an enduring interest; in later years he abandoned general problems for particular ones; in these early days he was chiefly concerned with theories; and the Saint-Simonian theories were undoubtedly occupying his mind at this time, for there is another allusion to them in *Maha Guru, Geschichte eines Gottes*, published in the summer of 1833, showing the same half-ironical attitude, the same incomplete knowledge, or possibly the same wilful misunderstanding:

Tibet ist das Land der Frauen-Emancipation. Hat der berühmte Orientalist St Martin die Religion dieses Volkes als eine überraschende Annäherung an den Katholicismus empfohlen, so wundert es mich, dass die St Simonisten diesen Staat noch nicht citirt haben, um einige ihrer, die Weiber betreffenden, Lehren zu erläutern[3].

It is strange to find that, for all his wide knowledge and general intelligence, Gutzkow was completely unmoved by the great project of piercing the Suez Canal, although he referred to this scheme in an article on 'Mehemet Ali von Aegypten':

Auch hat sich ein grosser Theil des europäischen revolutionairen Geschwürs nach Aegypten hin zertheilt, von den Exerziermeistern und Renegaten an bis auf Vater Enfantin, welcher nicht glauben kan, dass es die Mission des St Simonismus sey, blos die Landenge von Suez zu durchstechen[4].

---

[1] *Briefe eines Narren an eine Närrin*, p. 119.   [2] *Ibid.* p. 93.
[3] *G.W.* VI, p. 167.
[4] *A.Z.* October 29, 1834; reprinted in the *Oeffentliche Charaktere*, Hamburg, 1835, p. 109; the reference to Enfantin is omitted in *G.W.* IX, p. 72.

There is a not unfavourable notice of Saint-Simonism in the *Literaturblatt zum Phönix* on June 13, 1835, elaborated at greater length in *Wally, die Zweiflerin*, where Gutzkow resumed and emphasised the position he had adopted in the *Narren-briefe* towards the religion as a whole. At the end of the section entitled *Geständnisse über Religion und Christenthum* he charac-terised the spirit of the age as political but not irreligious. It is however unchristian, for Christianity seems to wish to oppose political emancipation wherever it is to be met. Hence those curious phenomena, half-political, half-religious, which have arisen in France, Saint-Simonism and the *Paroles d'un Croyant*:

In diese beiden Bekenntnisse ist zuerst die Anerkennung der poli-tischen Tendenz des Jahrhunderts niedergelegt. Man hat hier die Unverschämtheit vermieden, welche die hungernden Arbeiter auf das himmlische Brod des ewigen Lebens anweist. Die Religion der Ent-sagung mag für Jahre passen, wo die Ernte nicht gerathen ist; aber wo Fülle und Verschwendung rings ihre Feste feiern, da murrt die Menschheit über eine Religion, welche immerfort an das Sichschicken, an die Demuth, an den Rathschluss Gottes appellirt. Von dieser Seite des Christenthums überhaupt, die sich dem Zeitgeiste entgegen-stellt, kann nicht mehr die Rede sein. Der Unterschied zwischen den beiden Bekenntnissen ist der, dass der St Simonismus das Chris-tenthum antiquirt und durch einige materielle Philosopheme, nebst kirchlichen freilich dem alten Glauben entnommenen Institutionen zu ersetzen sucht, die Worte eines Gläubigen dagegen auf den demo-kratischen Ursprung des Christenthums zurückgehen und unverhohlen eine republikanische Tendenz desselben aussprechen. Der St Simon-ismus will den Staat von der Kirche, die Worte eines Gläubigen wollen die Kirche vom Staate befreien. Jener weist auf die Zukunft, diese auf die Vergangenheit. Beide aber kränkeln an ähnlichen Gebrechen: Der St Simonismus an der Philosophasterei: La Mennais am Katho-licismus. Wie soll man in der Kürze über beide Tendenzen urtheilen? Beide sind keine Revolutionen, aber sie sind Symptome. Der St Simonismus verrät ein Bedürfniss der Menschheit: die Worte eines Gläubigen suchen es zu befriedigen, aber sie befriedigen es nur zur Hälfte[1].

In advocating the material prosperity for all, which was one of the aims of Saint-Simonism, at the expense of the resignation and the other-worldliness of Christianity, Gutzkow speaks almost as Heine had done in a letter to Laube[2], but it is the only

[1] *Wally, die Zweiflerin*, Mannheim, 1835, pp. 301–303.
[2] Hirth, II, pp. 36–37, dated from Paris, July 10, 1833.

positive praise he accords to the sect and there is a grave error apparent in this passage. Far from freeing the state from the church, the Saint-Simonian ideal consisted in regarding the church as the state. Here again therefore Gutzkow's knowledge was at fault. Further, he repeats the conviction expressed in the *Narrenbriefe* that Saint-Simonism is only a symptom of the spirit of the age. At the last moment before his downfall therefore he accorded no very great importance to this movement and judged it with all the indifference of the impartial onlooker.

Shortly after the publication of *Wally* the storm broke in the *Literaturblatt*, and Gutzkow was deluged with the attacks, protests and incriminations which poured in on him from all sides, nor did he disdain to protest against the charge of Saint-Simonism in the pamphlet entitled *Appellation an den gesunden Menschenverstand*:

Um die Methode anschaulich zu machen, will ich eine Frage beantworten, wo der soziellen Partei eine der gehässigsten Beschuldigungen gemacht zu werden pflegt. Ich spreche von der St Simonistischen Gemeinschaft der Güter. Wer wird uns den Wahnsinn zutrauen, das Vermögen der Nationen addiren und durch die Millionen Bewohner eines Landes dividiren zu wollen[1]?

In this first definite allusion to the socialist theories of the Saint-Simonians, Gutzkow once more shows himself but ill-informed on the subject. For him Bazard and Enfantin had protested in vain against the charge of community of property when it was made in the Chamber of Deputies several years earlier[2]. It was a charge which cut at the very root of the originality reflected in the phrase 'à chacun selon sa capacité, à chaque capacité selon ses œuvres'; and Gutzkow was in fact distorting the Saint-Simonian theories just as gravely in this passage as his detractors were distorting the theories of the Young Germans, but he was in no mood for the scrupulous examination of a doctrine which at heart he despised.

The extreme restiveness under the supposition that he was preaching the gospel of Saint-Simon is apparent in a long letter written to Börne on October 2, 1835, giving him the history of

[1] *Appellation an den gesunden Menschenverstand*, Frankfurt am Main, 1835, pp. 14–15; cf. *G.W.* IV, p. 373.
[2] Cf. *Œuvres de Saint-Simon et d'Enfantin*, IV, pp. 119 ff., October 1, 1830.

the Young German *fracas* and protesting against his inclusion amongst this fraternity in rather curious terms:

> Ich komme dazu, etwas vertreten zu müssen, was mir eher unter-geschoben wird. Man schleudert mich in eine Aehnlichkeit mit französischen Tendenzen hinein (Sand: St Simon: Fourier), die ich mir niemals gestanden habe[1].

Considering that in later years Gutzkow openly acknowledged the debt which *Wally* owed to *Lélia*[2], this half-and-half repudiation of tendencies 'which I have never confessed to myself' reads almost as if for a moment a conscious attitude and a half-conscious influence had met and saluted; whilst the further disclaimer which follows is not entirely free of traces of a guilty conscience:

> Jezt soll das junge Deutschland eine Mischung aus republikanischen, st. simonistischen und in der Form göthisirenden Tendenzen seyn: ich werde sein Haupt genannt. Das geschah alles hinter meinem Rücken: denn im Grunde bin ich höchstens etwas von einem Poeten und ne-benbey gedankenlos[3].

Moreover in an attempt to translate the German situation into French terms, Gutzkow dubs Menzel's party 'Tierspartei' and his own:

> jene halb aus dem National, halb aus dem Globe und dem Enseigne-ment der Simonisten sich entwickelnde Partei des Reformateur, die es in Deutschland versucht, wenigstens die Kunst unter ihre Herr-schaft zu bringen, solange es mit den Völkern selbst nicht geht[4].

By identifying his party with the *Reformateur*—a paper of republican colouring of which Börne was part-editor—and to which he contributed several articles written in French in 1835, Gutzkow was obviously attempting to enlist the sympathies of his correspondent. The confession of the Saint-Simonian origin of the theories held by his party is illuminating taken in conjunction with the personal disclaimers which precede it, but the mention of the *Enseignement der Simonisten* is ambiguous. If

---

[1] Houben, *op. cit.* p. 110.

[2] Cf. *G.W.* IV, pp. 241–242, *Vorrede zur zweiten Auflage der Wally*, 1851.

[3] Houben, *op. cit.* p. 111.

[4] *Ibid. loc. cit.* Cf. *Literaturblatt zum Phönix*, April 30, 1835, *Wolfgang Menzel und der deutsche Tiersparti*, in which article the Young Germans are identified with the *National* but without any reference to the *Reformateur*, the *Globe* or Saint-Simonism.

Gutzkow meant the *Enseignements d'Enfantin*, we may be fairly certain that he had not read this book, or he would have known better than to have suggested any connection with the *Reformateur*.

In this letter therefore Gutzkow acknowledged the Saint-Simonian leanings of the Young Germans whilst denying his own adherence to these views. It is a position to which he recurred in later life, and the tone of these exculpations, uneasy and restive, is that of one who protests too much. This state of mind is symbolised in the temperamental outburst to be found in the *Gedanken im Kerker*:

Saint-Simonismus, Wiederherstellung des Fleisches, junges Deutschland; kenne von dem allen nichts, kenne mein Herz nur, mein Leben, meine Todten.... [1]

It is a small but ironical comment on the first part of the above denial that in the *Deutsche Blätter*, an abortive attempt to replace the *Deutsche Revue*, an article by Gutzkow entitled 'Traum des Saturn' contained another reference to the Saint-Simonian ideas on women, reprinted later in *Philosophie der Geschichte* in 1836[2]. Mock as he might, deny as he would, the relative frequence of these special references proves that Gutzkow's indifference was feigned.

On his release from prison Gutzkow showed a certain grimness towards the subject of Saint-Simonism, which had hitherto been absent, but otherwise there is not very much change in the attitude he had consciously adopted from the outset. In the *Beiträge zur Geschichte der neuen Literatur*, published in 1836, he reprinted the scornful remark about the German interest in Saint-Simonism from the *Literaturblatt zum Morgenblatt* of January 18, 1833, emphasising it slightly by the alteration of a phrase, and he tried to clear Heine of the charge of supporting by his activities[3] the 'Ungereimtheiten des Vater Enfantin'; whilst in *Philosophie der Geschichte* he poured out the vials of his

[1] *A.W.* XII, p. 96. Written in 1836 and included in the essay entitled 'Vergangenheit und Gegenwart' in the *Jahrbuch der Literatur*, Hamburg, 1839.

[2] Cf. *G.W.* XII, p. 119, *Philosophie der That und des Ereignisses*.

[3] *Beiträge zur Geschichte der neuen Literatur*, I, p. 88.

scorn over Enfantin's feminist ideals, using a much more violent
tone than in the *Narrenbriefe*, for anger had taken the place of
irony, and interest had been swamped by irritation:

> Die Emanzipation der Frauen ist die albernste Idee, welche unser
> Zeitalter ausgeheckt hat, und schon desshalb, als wenn es Wunder
> ein Glück wäre, in der Maschinerie der Staaten als ein kleiner Stift
> gebraucht zu werden!...Die St Simonisten waren verrückt[1].

In the novel *Seraphine*, published in 1837, when the Jewish spy,
whose prototype was probably Joel Jacoby, is denouncing the
party of progress to the minister, he compares: '...diese moderne Destruction aller Verhältnisse mit einigen über der politischen und moralischen Versumpfung Frankreichs aufgeschos-
senen Wasserblumen sogenannter socialer Theorieen, mit St
Simon, Fourier, Enfantin'[2]; an interesting passage since it
shows that Gutzkow had not forgotten that Saint-Simonism
had played its part in the unpopularity of the Young Germans.
Indeed it would have been difficult to forget, for it was now an
often repeated reproach, and Gutzkow had roused himself to
a further protest in the *Telegraph für Deutschland* directed
against Karl Hase, who had touched on the Saint-Simonian
system underlying the Young German theories[3]:

> Auch Herr Hase nimmt ein neues Evangelium an, das das junge
> Deutschland von dem verödeten Berge Menilmontant habe über den
> Rhein bringen wollen....Weil der St Simonismus in Frankreich auf-
> getaucht war, so musste man ihn nun auch mit Gewalt in Deutschland
> haben. Hatte man doch so gründliche Kritiken, so salbungsvolle
> Reden gegen ihn bereits vorbereitet![4]

It is not surprising therefore that Gutzkow now felt it imperative
to place on record his opinion of a sect to which he was erron-
eously supposed to belong, and this considered opinion is to be
found in the pseudonymous book *Die Zeitgenossen, ihre Schick-
sale, ihre Tendenzen, ihre grossen Charaktere. Aus dem Englischen
des E. L. Bulwer*, Stuttgart, 1837[5].

He opens with the statement that in spite of great imper-

---

[1] *Philosophie der Geschichte*, Hamburg, 1836, pp. 149–150.
[2] *G.W.* II, p. 426; in first edition: 'mit St Simon, mit Fourier.'
[3] Karl Hase, *Das junge Deutschland, Ein theologisches Votum in einer
academischen Rede*, Parchim und Ludwigslust, 1837, p. 26.
[4] *Telegraph für Deutschland*, Frankfurt am Main, August, 1837, No. 24.
[5] Cf. *G.W.* VIII, *Säkularbilder*, pp. 141–147, for the whole of this passage.

fections the political and industrial theories of the Saint-Simonians are of the utmost importance, and that their religion differs from Christianity only in wishing to give to this world some of the rights which the Christians have reserved for their all-too-privileged heaven. Their goal was the harmony between the demands of the spiritual and physical aspects of human existence, one of the great problems of the day, and although one may doubt that they achieved this goal, yet by their desire to emancipate the working classes they have stated the terms of a future task and have shown it to be justified. But the spirit of the hierarchy which possessed them proved their undoing, for the idea behind the Saint-Simonian priesthood was a hidden and destructive egoism. Saint-Simonism therefore did not prevail and Fourierism and communism stepped forward to replace and develop it.

What were the special reasons for this failure? Gutzkow is at no loss to account for them, and Enfantin was once more forced into the *rôle* of whipping-boy:

Das Lächerliche und Unverschämte am St Simonismus kommt zum grossen Theil auf Rechnung Enfantin's, eines verschmitzten Cagliostro, der nur durch Zufall nicht die Wahl gehabt zu haben scheint, lieber als katholischer oder als ketzerischer Heiliger selig gesprochen werden zu wollen. Enfantin hat durch seine Thorheit und Uebereilung das Gebäude der Lehre St Simon's untergraben. Enfantin wollte Papst sein, ehe noch eine Kirche da war. Er allein erfand die Simonistische Tracht, das Dogma vom freien Weibe, von der Intervention des Priesterthums bei der Ehe, die zweideutige Lehre von der Wiedereinsetzung des Fleisches, Behauptungen, die weder von St Simon aufgestellt waren, noch von allen Genossen Enfantin's gebilligt wurden, und die mit dazu beigetragen haben, die neue Religion in einen Strassenspectakel, in einen Concursprocess zu verwandeln[1].

With one impatient gesture Gutzkow swept all Enfantin's particular contributions to one side, coming further to the original but unjust conclusion that if the Saint-Simonians had emigrated to America and not to the East, to America where one must work to live, 'graben, dämmen, bauen, handeln, hobeln, zimmern, sägen,' then they would have shown that they were in earnest:

[1] *G. W.* VIII, p. 142.

So aber, nach dem trägen und sinnlichen Orient auswandernd, hat er (der St Simonismus) gezeigt, dass nur schlaffe, blasirte Empfindungen ihm seine gesellschaftliche Theorie eingegeben haben, und dass er, gerade wie der Jesuitismus, das Product einer entzündlichen, fast wollüstigen, jedenfalls faulen Phantasie ist. Hierüber herrscht kein Zweifel mehr[1].

This last statement contains perhaps the unfairest stricture ever passed on the Saint-Simonians. Not only does it leave out of count the work of first-rate magnitude which they had hoped to accomplish, but it ignores the great hardships gallantly accepted under most difficult conditions in engineering the damming of the Nile. It was in Egypt if anywhere that the Saint-Simonians showed their grit and demonstrated practically the power of their ideals. Possibly Gutzkow regarded Michel Chevalier with such peculiar benevolence[2] because he did in fact visit America; but his one-time companions, decimated by the plague, poorly fed and unsuitably clad, deserved all the praise which Gutzkow gratuitously bestowed on Western emigrants at their expense.

In the same book, Gutzkow broke a lance for marriage in despite of the 'free woman' and of *Lélia*[3], and asserted the subjection of matter to mind in opposition of the Saint-Simonian system[4], so that in 1837 at least he could prove himself innocent of the great offence of holding those Saint-Simonian views which are more particularly connected with the Young Germans, whilst his further references do little more than illuminate a position which by now he was doggedly determined should be his.

Thus the humorously ironical ending of the very unsatisfactory Blasedow family in Egypt[5], a group of ne'er-do-weels whose absurd education has been their ruin, forms a fitting counterpart to Leopold's final conversion to Saint-Simonism in *Die Bürger*; for in both cases the refuge is implicitly understood to be adapted to the morally, mentally or temperamentally unfit; and that Gutzkow had the Saint-Simonians in his mind is proved by the adieu:

Nimm Dein Tuch und wehe ihnen noch einmal Deinen Abschied

---

[1] *G.W.* viii, p. 146.   [2] *Ibid.* viii, p. 142.
[3] *Ibid.* viii, p. 326.   [4] *Ibid.* viii, p. 465.
[5] *Blasedow und seine Söhne*, Stuttgart, 1838.

zu! Grüsset die Kuppeln des Minarets von Stambul, grüsset die Ruinen Trojas, grüsset den heiligen Nil und den Vater Enfantin[1].

In *Die Rothe Mütze und die Kapuze*, written in 1838, Görres earned a sneer for forgetting to include the blasphemies of new fancy religions *à la* Saint-Simon among the revolutionary horrors which obsessed him[2], and Heine received a pin-prick in *Götter, Helden, Don Quixote* for accepting a Saint-Simonian bonnet from Egypt[3], obviously an allusion to Enfantin's letter, which had been circulated in Germany. Later, when Gutzkow and Heine were at war over the *Schwabenspiegel*, Gutzkow scornfully called him 'unser Père Enfantin.'[4] And there is further to be considered an angry repudiation of the identification of Young Germany with Saint-Simonism and the theory of the 'rehabilitation of the flesh' as understood by Steffens in his novel *Die Revolution*:

Wir suchen den *freien Mann*—nicht das *freie Weib*,—wir suchen die *Wiedereinsetzung des Geistes*—nicht die *Wiedereinsetzung des Fleisches*; —wir suchen Gott—nicht weil wir ihn verloren haben—sondern weil in ihm nur der wahrhaft selig ist, der ihn *selber* gefunden hat![5]

And since on second thoughts, this defence could not apply to the year 1835 by the greatest possible stretch of imagination, Gutzkow set himself in his essay 'Vergangenheit und Gegenwart,' in which he gave a literary review of the years 1830–1838, to saddle Mundt with the greater part of the blame for these theories which he owned played some part in the Young German movement[6].

And here we may leave Gutzkow's references to Saint-Simonism, for from now onwards until his death they are so rare, so slight and so unimportant as to be hardly worth considering[7]. Whether his complete correspondence, when it comes at last to be published, will bring forward other allusions, and

---

[1] *G.W.* VI, p. 140.   [2] *Ibid.* X, p. 105.
[3] *Götter, Helden, Don Quixote*, Hamburg, 1838, pp. 204–205, reprinted from the *Telegraph*, August 1837, No. 20.
[4] *Telegraph*, May 1839, No. 75.
[5] *Götter, Helden, Don Quixote*, p. 451.   [6] *A.W.* XII, pp. 85–90.
[7] Cf. *Telegraph*, 1837, October, No. 10, 1838, June, No. 90; *A.W.* XI, p. 251, *Literarische Elfen*, 1838; *G.W.* XII, p. 383, *Börne's Leben*, 1840; VII, pp. 95 and 286, *Briefe aus Paris*, 1842; IV, p. 234, *Vorrede zu Wally*, 1851.

throw any light on this question, must remain for the years to show. I should be surprised myself if Saint-Simonism were found to figure to any great extent in Gutzkow's letters; among his manifold interests, schemes, quarrels and feuds it played on the surface of his mind a modest and minor part. The scattered letters published here and there in newspapers, journals and books, bear out this theory. The references to this subject in the letter to Börne from which I have quoted are the only ones of their kind.

The attempt to analyse Gutzkow's pronouncements on Saint-Simonism yields a distinctly negative result, a result which dwindles almost to nothingness when these meagre gleanings are compared with the thousand of pages of printed matter from which they have been obtained. No sketch of Enfantin appeared in the *Oeffentliche Charaktere*, where one might reasonably expect one; the description of Paris in 1834 has the slightest of references[1]; the *Letters from Paris* in 1842, whilst giving a long account of Michel Chevalier's life, hardly touch on the Saint-Simonian period; the banquet in honour of Fourier, which Gutzkow attended, awakened no memories of a closely related reformer; finally in the *Rückblicke auf mein Leben* Saint-Simonism was completely ignored.

Moreover the tone in which Gutzkow spoke of this system, when he did speak, reflected no ardent enthusiasm, no deep interest, no reckless desire to embrace a new cause. From the very outset his allusions showed at the best a modified and wary appreciation tinged with irony and often distorted by ignorance; they became less benevolent in tone after 1835 when they were often interspersed with hot denials. Throughout he would seem to have rejected the feminism and the hierarchical system, whilst reserving a certain approbation for the socialist theories. The Saint-Simonian conception of marriage and the doctrine of the 'rehabilitation of the flesh' were not openly canvassed by Gutzkow until after 1835, when he actively condemned them. Yet I believe that these theories interested him and influenced him in his early years, although he would not acknowledge the influence and repressed the interest. And the reason for this

[1] *G.W.* VII, p. 29.

lay perhaps in the attitude adopted by his masters Börne and Menzel who certainly had given no sanction to such leanings[1].

For Gutzkow the disciple faithfully copied the attitude of Börne and Menzel in this matter until 1835. He had no difficulty in attacking the hierarchical system and in praising the socialist theories, curling his lip the while over the feminist doctrines; but although he did not directly refer to the proposed abolition of marriage and the 'rehabilitation of the flesh,' signs are not wanting in his early works that he felt the attraction of this forbidden fruit; and we can take his later denials with a grain of salt, since by then these views had become dangerous ones to hold. The question of his attitude towards the feminist doctrines is a more complicated one and must be held over for the moment. We have noted however the presence of a more active interest than his own statements allow. It must be remembered that in all these references we have been face to face with a conscious attitude adopted before the world. There remains to be estimated the influence that was secretly at work within him before 1835.

[1] Cf. Ludwig Börne, *Gesammelte Schriften*, VIII, p. 60; x, pp. 112–120; and Menzel in the *Literaturblatt zum Morgenblatt*, August 1, 1832; neither mentions the 'emancipation of the flesh'; and both of them refute the theories on women and marriage.

CHAPTER XV

THE HALF-CONSCIOUS INTEREST

(a) UNDER MENZEL'S BANNER

On his arrival in Stuttgart Gutzkow settled down to his work
as a regular correspondent to the *Literaturblatt* and a fairly
frequent contributor to the *Morgenblatt*; a promising beginning,
for the *Literaturblatt* exercised an undoubted authority over
literary Germany, whilst the *Morgenblatt* had the widest circulation of any magazine in the country. He had fallen under
Menzel's sway in his university days, and had written his articles
in the *Forum der Journalliteratur* to the glory of the master and
the confusion of his enemies. Menzel responded by summoning
him to his side. Thus began a partnership which was to end, like
some chemical experiments, in deafening noise and an overwhelming stench.

Gutzkow's contributions to the *Literaturblatt* show but slight
signs that the Saint-Simonian religion was at work in his mind.
His quarrel with the pietists[1], for example, had a personal
origin. He had been sickened of them in his own home; for his
father had embraced religion after the death of Lorenz, and had
sunk the good-fellowship of the gay campaigner in the gloomy
and unenlightened piety of an emotional convert. Gutzkow, like
Laube, had been destined for a theological career; he had been
the round of all the churches in Berlin, and had even preached
himself in the *Dreifaltigkeitskirche*. Temperamentally he was a
deep and earnest thinker in religious matters; and although a
sceptical habit of mind had by now made itself apparent, and
was soon to become confirmed, it was the kind of scepticism
which often attacks the more earnest type of youth and almost
as often ends in deep-seated and unshakable faith. Meanwhile
he girded at the pietists whenever an opportunity arose.

It is in vain also to search among the articles on political
economy for any trace of the Saint-Simonian theories on property and on the state; whilst his theories on women and on

[1] *Literaturblatt zum Morgenblatt*, Stuttgart, June 6, 1832.

marriage were in direct opposition to those of Enfantin. Gutzkow was entirely at one with Menzel in the warfare which that mighty critic waged against the 'contemptible little army' of women authors; and in particular he took it upon himself to condemn in a high moral tone the embittered attitude towards marriage of one Therese Huber[1].

With angry impatience he stigmatised such views as 'lügenhaft' and glorified 'den Zauber des bräutlichen und den wahrhaften Werth des ehelichen Standes.' There is a rather ugly tone in this review, a tone which puts one in mind of an over-used and ugly word: sex-warfare. The definition of marriage as a 'curious institution for which women alone seem to be intended' gives the key to Gutzkow's anger. He was not really satisfied with marriage himself, but he considered it quite good enough for women, and was outraged that they should dare to protest against it. And Therese Huber, now a good deal more dead than Queen Anne, seems to have provoked Gutzkow past bearing by her ill-advised and unconcealed hatred of the sex to which he belonged. So the picture flashes past: an angry and disappointed woman, a sneering and unchivalrous young man; it illustrates an irritable spot in Gutzkow's nature.

He returned to the charge on the occasion of another novel by a different authoress, and here he made the disillusioned pronouncement that nothing is more usual than marital infidelities on both sides, but he demanded that one should be open with oneself on such occasions, acknowledging one's faults in private, or confessing them to a priest, instead of blaming the institution against which they have transgressed. This is no very lofty moral or intellectual position; but in truth Gutzkow was in a cleft stick, since he was aware of the unsatisfactoriness of the marriage laws, yet could not overcome his prejudice against the same dissatisfaction apparent in the stories of these female novelists.

Meanwhile in the *Briefe des jüngsten Anacharsis*, which appeared in the *Morgenblatt* in the month of May 1832, Gutzkow

---

[1] *Literaturblatt zum Morgenblatt*, Stuttgart, February 13, 1833, reprinted with slight alterations in *Beiträge zur Geschichte der neuesten Literatur*, I, pp. 229–230.

took an opportunity to air his views on feminism. This topic is
made the subject of a dispute between two women and Jean
Paul. The supposed Jean Paul judges between the extreme
feminist on one side and her adversary on the other in language
which vaguely recalls the tones of Enfantin[1], for in accepting
the perfectibility of women, in recognising their different degrees
of development, and in the use of the terms material and spiritual,
Gutzkow, although he does not commit himself to any definite
programme, speaks like a Saint-Simonian in the making; and
this suggests the conclusion that where his anger was not
aroused, or his personal feelings involved, he had vague and
undefined feminist leanings. They do not amount to very much,
but in this passage he has already shown signs of a certain
inconsistency; for it is in the nature of a surprise to hear this
benevolent judgment proceeding from the same mouth that
read Therese Huber so sharp and so intolerant a lecture.

(b) BRIEFE EINES NARREN AN EINE NÄRRIN

It is not my intention to thrust on the reader a detailed
analysis of a book which has once been seriously rendered into
English as *Letters from a Male to a Female Fool.* This chance
and ignorant translation may give a better idea of the impression produced than pages of descriptive writing; but *Narr*
stands here for madman as is clear from the *macabre* preface in
which Jonathan Kennedy, grave-digger at Bedlam, claims to
have discovered the letters in a skull which he found coquetting
with another skull in the church-yard, a piece of ironical humour
not without its distasteful side. In order to deceive the censor
Gutzkow attempted to keep up the farce of madness here and
there throughout the book, and furthermore began and ended
each letter in a vein of extravagant love-making. He succeeded
in this ruse, for the book was published, although shortly afterwards forbidden in Prussia, and he was therefore justified in the
attempt; but the reiterated insistence on madness is not to the
author's advantage, whilst the introduction of the love-story
only adds to the general confusion which is all that the book
can show in the way of composition.

[1] *G.W.* xi, p. 22.

The *Briefe eines Narren an eine Närrin* appeared in the summer of 1832, dominated by the ideas of Börne, and written in a laboured imitation of the manner of Jean Paul. There is however quite perceptibly a Saint-Simonian influence at work, an influence which is a good deal stronger than the tone of the references to the subject would lead one to suppose. The reason for this positive result may be found perhaps in the fact that the book was published anonymously, for a certain feeling of irresponsibility which this anonymity entailed probably set free the unconscious influence which he was consciously denying, and which here and there succeeded in mastering his pen.

He identified himself with the programme of the Saint-Simonians in his demands for the material prosperity of the poorer classes, the lack of which no amount of spiritual sustenance can supply[1], and he was equally at one with them in their condemnation of the other-worldliness of Christianity, although he saw the origin of this evil not in Christianity itself but in the mythology of the Germanic peoples[2]. Gutzkow therefore suggested an earlier origin for the Christian dualism, enriching the Saint-Simonian conception by his knowledge of northern mythology, yet he agreed with them in condemning it; and he did not attempt to free Christianity from a large part of the blame.

Two aspects of the Saint-Simonian doctrine therefore, the religious and the socialistic, were working in Gutzkow's mind and occupying his thoughts rather more seriously than would seem to be the case in his allusions. But the difference here is one of degree only and not of kind. The references are slighter and more careless, but they tally on the whole, and what is more important, they entirely conform with his final position in 1837. It is generally thought that Gutzkow's interest was mainly reserved for the socialist doctrines of the Saint Simonians; but if this is so, it must also be granted that the interest was slight, much overlaid by other doctrines of the same kind, and of a more republican nature than theirs[3]. The most that can be said

---

[1] *Briefe eines Narren an eine Narrin*, pp. 69–70.

[2] *Ibid.* pp. 99–100.

[3] Cf. *Briefe eines Narren an eine Närrin*, pp. 105 ff., where he argues that the only hope of eternal peace lies in the republican form of government.

here is that he approved of their theories without according them any great importance. As for the religious question, whilst echoing their opinion of the Christian dualism, he was to tread a path which the Saint-Simonians could only have viewed with horror unless it were to lead him finally to their fold, the path of downright scepticism in religious matters; and here his master was neither Saint-Simon nor Enfantin, but Strauss; and he was far from adopting their pantheistic conception of the universe, as is shown in the passage where he mocks at the 'Weltgeist' as none other than 'der liebe Herrgott selbst.'[1]

He gave a very garbled version of the Saint-Simonian theories of feminism in this book, but whether this was a deliberate attempt to be unfair to them or the result of ignorance, it is certain at least that they had given him furiously to think and the outcome of these musings is to be found in the following passage:

Ein Frauenzimmer muss gar keine Ideen haben, am allerwenigsten liberale. Die Politik der Frauen soll nicht einmal die ihrer Männer sein. Wenn es eine Zeit gab, wo die Mädchen Lorbeerkränze von Eichenlaub für die aus dem Felde zurückkehrenden Sieger wanden, und dabei recht martialische Kriegslieder anstimmten, so verzeiht man solche Tollheiten, weil man weiss, dass sie nur so zu Männern kommen wollten. Jetzt aber wären viele Deiner Schwestern im Stande, und liessen Flugschriften drucken über Vertretung am Bundestage, da sie höchstens solche Begriffe nur mit Gold auf Fahnen sticken sollten, um heimkehrende Deputirte damit zu ehren[2].

Allowing for the extravagant tone in which these letters are written, and the ironical exaggeration which is one of Gutzkow's mannerisms, there still remains a fairly definite statement here that the sphere of the woman is the home. And if women were not to be allowed to escape into the political world, Gutzkow watched with some grimness the place they were attempting to conquer in the world of letters[3].

But, lest it should be thought that he could not see two sides of a question, he turned round and argued the case for the women:

Jedes Bankett fangt Ihr mit dem constitutionellen Königthum an, und zum Schluss ruft Ihr die Republik aus. Was uns Weibern zuträg-

---

[1] *Briefe eines Narren an eine Närrin*, p. 183.
[2] *Ibid.* p. 52.   [3] *Ibid.* pp. 169–170.

licher scheint, darnach fragt Niemand. Vergessen wird die Bedeutung des Weibes, wie sie durch das Christenthum in die Welt
eingeführt worden ist.... So wie Ihr überhaupt gewohnt seid, Alles
nur in seiner nächsten Aeusserung zu erfassen, so habt Ihr auch die
Tiefe des weiblichen Charakters immer verkannt[1].

A faint and far-away reminiscence of Saint-Simonism is apparent here, but when Gutzkow goes on to plead the necessity
for a woman's paper, he becomes unpleasantly ironical; nevertheless, whether he is speaking for or against this subject the
feverish interest is manifest in his inability to leave the question
alone.

The theories on love and on marriage however fell on more
promising ground. The dissatisfaction with marriage which he
had registered in the *Litcraturblatt* now led to a half-fantastic
proposal for the creation of a republic of love; and here, although
he expressed himself with the vagueness of the romantic school,
there is an undercurrent of seriousness and hope which makes
this passage a fit companion for Heine's very similar prophecy
in the *Reisebilder*:

Einstweilen aber, Du geliebtes Bild, constituiren wir uns Beide zu
der Republik der Liebe. Wir wollen das Beispiel aufstellen, dass es
auch in dieser Staatsform Treue, Hingebung, Aufopferung geben
könne. Sei auch der erste Sprössling dieser Ehe ein Napoleon, der
zweite die Restauration und der letzte ein Thron, umgeben mit re-
publicanischen Institutionen; unsere Enkel werden dennoch die
Früchte unserer Anstrengungen zu schätzen und zu veredeln wissen.
Das sind Hoffnungen, aber keine Träume. Gewiss, wir werden die
goldnen Früchte brechen; denn unser Arm kann sie erreichen[2].

Is this a dream of free love or a vision of a free country? It is
difficult to say, and possibly Gutzkow wished to remain ambiguous. His conscience, in the keeping of Börne and Menzel,
may have pricked him as he wrote. But when desires are active,
they generally find some means of satisfying the conscience.
Gutzkow applied to his own the soothing salve of putting the
following words into the mouth of Byron. Nevertheless they
show clearly whither the author himself was tending in matters
of love and religion:

Die Liebe soll die Zauberformel sein, die uns die Hölle in den
Himmel verwandelt. Liebe! Liebe ist die Frucht der Eitelkeit.

[1] *Briefe eines Narren an eine Närrin*, pp. 177–178.   [2] *Ibid.* p. 109.

Hört sie nicht auf, Liebe zu sein, wenn sie Treue wird? Ehe! sie ist ein Institut des Staates, das Gefühl der Hinfälligkeit, künftigen Schwäche und Verlassenheit ihre Grundlage. Religion! es gibt einen Gränzstein, wo sie Lüge wird, wo ist der? Auf welcher Station bin ich noch im Gebiete Gottes, auf welcher schon im Gebiet des Teufels?[1]

Take away the pessimism of this diatribe on love and marriage and there remains the doctrine of free love, unshackled by constancy, one of the theories of Enfantin. But there is nothing of him or his followers to be found in the mournful and doubting tone in which Gutzkow speaks of religion. The *Briefe eines Narren an eine Närrin* have shown him politely interested, but no more, in the socialist theories; at one with the Saint-Simonians in the negative aspect of their religious doctrine, but far from embracing their positive creed; contemptuous and yet not indifferent towards their feminist ideals; almost a convert finally to their views on love and marriage. Both Börne and Menzel, if they had read this book more carefully than they did, might have found reasons to be dissatisfied with the writer, but Börne was too much delighted with the republican sentiments it expressed to examine it very closely, and Menzel, having skipped through it in his usual style, proceeded to pat the author on the head and to give the customary extracts[2].

[1] *Briefe eines Narren an eine Närrin*, p. 229.
[2] Cf. Ludwig Börne, *Gesammelte Schriften*, xi, pp. 67–70 and *Lit. Bl.* January 16, 1833.

CHAPTER XVI

THE INTEREST WAXES

(a) MAHA GURU

During the spring and early summer of 1833 Gutzkow was in Munich reading for the law, a final effort to consolidate his position with Rosalie's mother; but he was also and less intermittently writing his novel *Maha Guru, Geschichte eines Gottes,* which was published in the autumn of the same year. Whilst he was here, he became acquainted with August Lewald who had just returned from Paris and from intercourse with Heinrich Heine. Lewald was interested in the Saint-Simonians and in Heine's connection with them, so that now for the first time, as far as we know, Gutzkow was in a position to hear about them at first hand. Also the first book of the *Romantische Schule* was published in March 1833, and this brilliant piece of pleading for the rights of the flesh has left its traces on Gutzkow's novel.

It is characteristic of the author that he should have laid the scene of this story in Tibet, and should have taken the figure of a Dalai Lama as his principal character. It reflects his learning and his ignorance at the same time. The elaborate scenery, the detailed descriptions of the manners and customs of the Tibetans and the Chinese form an academic exercise of merit but of no real value, for it is all book-learning and at second hand. Further in dealing with the ancient and mysterious religion of Lamaism, he betrays an unfortunate tendency towards irony, the humorous air of one who knows better than that. It is a clever book, but it is the product of an arid imagination.

It is the story of a Grand Lama of Tibet whom the priest had sought in vain for so many years that when they discovered him he was already a beautiful and virtuous youth; he was hastily removed from his associates, but the mischief was already done, Maha Guru had fallen in love. The tale begins at the moment when he was proclaimed Dalai Lama of Tibet, and Gylluspa, the heroine of the story, was still in ignorance of the cause of his disappearance. She refused to resign herself and

marry his elder brother (who was passionately pressing his suit)
until Maha Guru should reappear; then, according to the Tibetan
system of polyandry, she would belong in turn to all the brothers
of the family. But the Grand Lama is vowed to celibacy, and
his brother, a Shaman, who knew what had become of Maha
Guru, found himself facing an insoluble problem. Meanwhile
Gylluspa's father, Hali Jong, the head of a great factory for the
production of idols, had been accused of heresy and summoned
to Lhasa to await his trial at the hands of the black Gylongs, the
powerful and rigidly orthodox priests of the monastery in that
capital. His crime consisted in an alteration of the distance
between the nose and the mouth of his idols to a more pleasing
proportion, thus flouting tradition in the interests of art, an
action for which he might have to pay with his life. In this
predicament the Shaman appealed for assistance to his all-
powerful brother; whilst an unexpected meeting between the
god and Gylluspa, at the conclusion of which she learnt his
destiny and fainted in his arms, served even more strongly than
his brother's eloquence to rouse him to come to the rescue.

But he was powerless in the hands of the priests; after a
stormy and dramatic trial Hali Jong met his death, and Gylluspa,
as she bewailed his fate, could not avoid the deduction that
the god whom it was blasphemy to love must be human
after all.

This well-deserved scepticism was shared by the Shaman, and
he proceeded to act upon it. Unable to persuade his brother to
abdicate of his own free will, he betrayed him to the Chinese,
who were plotting to dethrone Maha Guru and to set up in his
stead the Lama of Teschu-Lumbo. The revolution was successful, the palace was stormed and the god discovered in the
innocent pastime of feeding his doves. The Shaman succeeded
in carrying off his brother and they fled from the city together,
Maha Guru rescuing Gylluspa from the burning monastery on
his way. The long-delayed marriage then took place and a period
of idyllic happiness followed. It was of short duration for the
Shaman who died after one year; but Gylluspa lived many years
longer; when she at last followed him to the grave, Maha Guru
turned his thoughts once more towards heaven, and embarked

upon the last fight between flesh and spirit in the attitude of
the holy Buddhist seeking Nirwana.

(b) THE MANTLE OF ENFANTIN

Let no one hope to discover in Maha Guru a portrait of
Enfantin; let no one expect to recognise the theory of the
constant, the inconstant and the 'calm' in the system of polyandry which plays so important a part in the book. Maha Guru
is not Enfantin; nor can his teachings be recognised in the
curious arrangement practised in Tibet, by which one woman
is the wife of all the brothers in a family, whilst fatherhood is
determined in the first instance by seniority and thereafter by
the most impeccable nursery fairness of turn by turn. And yet
in spite of this discouraging conclusion, I am strongly convinced that *Maha Guru* owed its inception less to those English
novels and books of travel which Gutzkow acknowledged as his
sources[1], than to speculations upon the personality of Enfantin
and the questions which he had raised. Since Gutzkow's mind
was an original one, not easily swayed entirely by any one set
of ideas, the story of Maha Guru led him away from Enfantin
and the Saint-Simonians to the investigation of different hypo-
theses and amidst quite other surroundings, but his preoccupation with the problems in this book was a direct result of his
unacknowledged preoccupation with Saint-Simonism.

In his preface to the second edition of *Maha Guru*, Gutzkow
acknowledged that he had set himself the task of discovering
whether a man, claiming to be God, is more likely to be a rogue
or a madman, to be deceiving others or himself. It was a question which all Europe was considering anew in connection with
the divine pretensions of the supreme priest of the Saint-
Simonian religion, and which Gutzkow dismissed summarily in
1837 by dubbing Enfantin a cunning Cagliostro. His attitude
towards Maha Guru is far from being such a simple one. This
youth, who has been caught and taught by the priests and who
can talk like a book, is serenely and sincerely convinced of his

[1] Morier, Cooper, Irving. The *Morgenblatt* and the *Ausland* of this date
also gave exhaustive reviews of Platen, *China und die Mantschurei*,
Klaproth, *Description du Thibet*, etc.

godhead, nor does he show any signs of madness. He is a simple, gentle, passive creature, unacquainted with the ways of the world, with no deep knowledge of himself and unaware, it would seem, that the flowery language with which he regaled his brothers shortly after his accession was nothing but high-flown nonsense. This is not the stuff of which charlatans are made, nor on the other hand is there any sign of that lack of balance which is a symptom of madness. He is a mere cipher, a tool in the hands of the priests. Nothing could well be more unlike Enfantin, that dominant and magnetic personality who was too much given to fashioning tools for himself to become the tool of others, and whose complete incapacity to play, even for a time, a passive part, was responsible for his disasters. But if by nature they are entirely dissimilar, they often talk much the same language, as the following passage will show:

> Es ist eine alte lügenhafte Fabel, dass die Welt aus Liebe und Hass entstanden sei. Widerspruch ist niemals der Anfang der Dinge gewesen....Es giebt nichts Böses auf der Welt sondern nur Verwirrung im Guten....Lasst den Glauben an ein böses Princip und fürchtet nicht, dass ein uralter Erbfeind auf meine Schultern steigen könne....[1]

Moreover the pantheistic disquisitions of Maha Guru are strongly reminiscent of Saint-Simonism, since they postulate a god whose spirit penetrates all his works, but is not to be confused with them[2]. But there is one important difference in the theories of Enfantin and Maha Guru. Whilst he was still convinced of his godhead, Maha Guru not only renounced all earthly passions, but he was also inclined to glance somewhat hesitatingly at the manifestations of sensual love[3].

This is a half-and-half position which Enfantin would have emphatically rejected, and although in the early days he had dreamt of a mystical union with the high priestess, in which the senses were to play no part, he had soon abandoned this idea, for to him the senses were as holy as the spirit; further the more modest claims which he made to a share only of the spirit of God allowed him to contemplate an earthly union with

[1] *G.W.* VI, pp. 229–230. [2] *Ibid.* VI, p. 224.
[3] *Ibid.* VI, pp. 229–230.

an equanimity not to be expected from the lord of heaven and earth. Nevertheless the solution of Maha Guru's problem has a distinctly Saint-Simonian colouring. For when he was conquered by force and unable to maintain his official position as a god, he might still have believed in his own divinity and lived a life of holy abstinence. But matters took a different course; without a shattering conflict, untroubled by doubts or despair, easily and naturally, Maha Guru learnt that he was a man and learnt it with rapture[1].

The theory of the 'rehabilitation of the flesh' is clearly vindicated here in the person of the one-time god. It is better to lead the life of the senses and be a man than to follow the path of lifeless renunciation which is the lot of gods or saints; a completely Saint-Simonian conclusion, during the course of which Maha Guru and Enfantin melt into one and smile at us from the same pair of eyes; whilst Gutzkow seems to be observing benevolently that if you discount Enfantin's absurd pretensions to divinity you will find that he is talking excellent sense.

It is not the end of the story however. Maha Guru as a very old man resolves, after the death of Gylluspa, to concentrate his thoughts on heaven and enter the presence of the gods, his flesh wholly subdued by his spirit, and the description of Maha Guru seeking Nirwana[2] forms an ironical contrast to the picture of the god who learnt the joy of being a man. 'Look here, upon this picture and on this!' Gutzkow had made his choice. Indeed the whole of this concluding chapter, written by a modern and restless European, although objectively and respectfully, is little more than a *reductio ad absurdum* of the conquest of the spirit over the flesh:

Soll der Tugendhafte dem Leben entsagen? Soll er die Freude an glücklichen Unternehmungen, siegreichen Anstrengungen wie Farbenstaub von seinem Dasein streifen? Nein, in Europa ist die Resignation nie eine echte Tugend gewesen[3].

In spite of his undoubted originality, Gutzkow was at heart at one with his Young German *confrères* in this question; like them he regarded Enfantin with distrust, but he accepted the

[1] *G.W.* vi, pp. 404–405.   [2] *Ibid.* vi, p. 411.
[3] *Ibid.* vi, p. 409.

doctrine of the rights of the flesh. He was less enthusiastic, less easily swayed than they were, and much more underground in his methods; but *Maha Guru* is a favourable comment on this point of the Saint-Simonian teachings, and this is the most positive part of the book. It is also a significant fact that it is left to the narrow-minded and hypocritical priests of Lhasa to praise the soul at the expense of the body[1]; and that Hali Jong, who saw the divine nature of beauty and would not betray it to the fanatical worship of tradition, although he fell a victim to his persecutors undoubtedly won a moral victory at his trial; there is also an interesting analysis of the symbolism in religious art, which is put into the mouth of one of his accusers, and which may well have been inspired by the *Romantische Schule*[2]. Local colour and foreign customs notwithstanding, the main influence at work in *Maha Guru* was the influence of the Saint-Simonian gospel.

In dealing with the social question Gutzkow showed himself much more open-minded on the subject of marriage than when he had set out to snub Therese Huber; for although he treated the system of polyandry with a certain amount of irony[3], still it is never shown to produce disaster or unhappiness; on the contrary, he exclaimed more than once at its peaceful and harmonious results, declaring emphatically the while that custom and faith sanctify the affection that one woman may feel at the same time for four men[4]. Enfantin, it may be remembered, although admitting the desirability of successive passions, held that a woman should love only two men at a time, the high priest and one other. Here therefore Gutzkow would seem to go further than Enfantin and as far as Fourier, but it is not necessary to take him seriously; however idyllic he may declare such arrangements to be, comparing them favourably with the disasters brought about by the jealousy which accompanies monoandry in Europe, one suspects him of writing with his tongue in his cheek, although his strictures on European society read sincerely enough:

---

[1] *G.W.* vi, p. 282.   [2] Cf. *G.W.* vi, pp. 277–293 for this trial.
[3] There is in particular one rather unpleasant passage vaguely reminiscent of Sterne in the first edition (p. 172) which is omitted in *G.W.*
[4] *G.W.* vi, p. 154.

Tibet ist das Land der Frauen-Emancipation....In Tibet hört die
Bevormundung auf, welche die Männer fast überall über die Frauen
ausüben. Die prüde Sittenrichterei über den Wandel einer Unverehe-
lichten ist hier unbekannt; man gewährt sich unter einander Frei-
heiten, die man sich selbst nimmt, und verlangt vom Weibe erst dann
Enthaltsamkeit und Beschränkung, wenn sie in eine Familie als Gattin
eingeführt ist—eine Ceremonie, die übrigens in den einfachsten facti-
schen Formalitäten, ohne alle Herbeiziehung priesterlicher Symbolik,
besteht.... Sollten denn die Frauen aufhören, warm und zärtlich zu
lieben, wenn ihnen die Wahl unter den Männern erleichtert wird?
Sollten sie gegen die Treue gleichgültig werden, wenn sich an die
Untreue keine Strafen, nicht einmal mehr die Verachtung knüpfen?[1]

If this rather startling passage is to be taken seriously, and
it is seriously written, it would seem that Gutzkow desired the
emancipation of women from the marriage laws, whilst denying
them, unconditionally, all entrance to the political world, and
ready to expel them, had it been in his power, from the world
of letters. It is a most unusual position for an anti-feminist to
adopt, yet it could only be adopted by an anti-feminist. No
feminist would accept the first kind of freedom unaccompanied
by the second, and most feminists reject the first, whilst they
are all agreed in demanding the second. But bearing in mind
his earlier opinion of marriage as an institution solely adapted
to meet the needs of women, one may well wonder whether
this remarkable change of front was due to the influence of
Enfantin. One thing however is clear throughout the story;
the preoccupation with women, love and marriage had by no
means been laid aside, whilst the doctrine of the 'rehabilitation
of the flesh' had been added to the list of Gutzkow's secret
sympathies. Maha Guru is not Enfantin, but the mantle of
Enfantin fell on Maha Guru when he stepped from his lofty
pedestal and, entering the world of men, as a man learnt the
beauty of love.

[1] *G.W.* vi, p. 167.

CHAPTER XVII

SAINT-SIMONISM PREVAILS

(a) TEMPER

Soon after the completion of *Maha Guru*, Gutzkow established contact with his literary contemporaries. Laube, who had greeted the *Narrenbriefe* with enthusiasm, had opened a correspondence with the author, and on the third of August, 1833, he joined him in Munich in company with Axenfeld, a Leipzig merchant, for a tour through Northern Italy. By temperament these two young men were wholly dissimilar, and each must often have felt the other to be an uncongenial travelling companion; Gutzkow was chiefly anxious to improve his mind, Laube to add to his personal adventures; Gutzkow with his future still uncertain and travelling on borrowed money, Laube a successful editor, his pockets lined with the proceeds of *Die Poeten*. Gutzkow, who was reading *Die Poeten* on the journey, without much enthusiasm to be sure, and horrified by the unscholarly spelling of 'Hyppolit,' nevertheless owned in later years that, as he read, he felt his relation to Menzel becoming slacker. He did not fail to recognise the Saint-Simonian elements in this book, as a later reference proves[1], and one cannot but suppose that the author of *Maha Guru* and the creator of Valerius will have discussed the subject together. Laube had not much to learn from Gutzkow here, although in all other subjects the younger man was the superior in knowledge; and the fearless prophet of freedom in love, practising in his own person the precepts of Valerius, inspired Gutzkow with a half-envious admiration. For Laube, now nearly twenty-seven, giving himself the airs of a man of the world coupled with the elegance of a man about town, was just the kind of phenomenon to impress the shy and learned young man who, for all his pedantry, would much have liked to have shone in a similar part. But what was of greater importance, the open and enthusiastic support which Laube gave to Saint-Simonism in *Die Poeten*, and probably also

[1] *Telegraph*, October 1837, No. 10.

in conversation, may have done something to remove that un-conscious repression which Gutzkow had been practising hitherto. Given a further impetus, his half-and-half adherence to this doctrine might become a whole-hearted one, and the impetus was supplied.

At the end of the Italian journey, in the autumn of 1833, Gutzkow paid a visit to Berlin during which his affection for Rosalie could not blind him to the narrow and uncongenial sphere into which he was shortly to marry and from which it would be difficult to transplant his wife owing to the mother's fierce affection for her daughter, an affection which manifested itself chiefly in a violent dislike for her future son-in-law. In the early days of 1834, Gutzkow was in Leipzig frequenting Laube and Schlesier, rather annoyed but also deeply impressed by the latter's condemnation of *Maha Guru* as an academic exercise, and grimly determined to show enough of his 'heart's blood' in his next venture to satisfy the desires of the most insatiable literary vampire. Meanwhile the intellectual emanci-pation from Menzel was continuing apace, and the ill-advised young man actually dared, in the preface to a collection of short stories which appeared in the spring of 1834, to make a jesting reference to Menzel's habit of writing with one eye on the great rationalist Paulus of Heidelberg[1]. It was a harmless enough joke, and Pückler-Muskau, Heine, Mundt and Laube came off considerably worse in the same passage, to say nothing of Theodor Hell, Rumohr and Clauren; but Menzel who was already both piqued and uneasy at Gutzkow's connection with the *Elegante Zeitung*, read him such a furious lecture on this piece of impertinence, that literary relations were broken off, and friendly relations never thereafter whole-heartedly resumed. One ship was burned behind him, one powerful enemy already made.

But worse was to come. On the death of Schleiermacher on February 12, 1834, Gutzkow, already an occasional contributor to the *Allgemeine Zeitung*, published in this paper on February 23, 1834, a 'Nekrolog' on the famous preacher which set all Berlin by the ears. For by emphasising Schleiermacher's spiritual

---

[1] *Novellen*, Hamburg, 1834, pp. ix–x.

independence and the weakness and resignation three parts
pessimism, which characterised him during his later period, and
which led to his acceptance of the 'Union,'[1] Gutzkow succeeded
in infuriating all those orthodox evangelical and Lutheran
thinkers, strong in their faith and their narrow piety and firm
upholders of the 'Union,' who claimed Schleiermacher as their
own. He had also signed the death-warrant to his hopes of
happiness with Rosalie. She had gone a long way with him,
developing her mind as she followed the developments of his,
overcoming many a prejudice and conquering many a distaste;
but this was too much. To her this article appeared almost a
blasphemy, for Schleiermacher was her chosen preacher, deeply
reverenced and respected. She hardly needed the frantic per-
suasions of her unbalanced and unintelligent mother to break
off her engagement with the author. Gutzkow had burnt another
boat; the enemies he made on this occasion were legion, and he
had lost a tender and devoted friend.

It was the first great trial which he had to face, and the way
he faced it has some unusual features. A not unnatural bitterness with the world, and a very natural sorrow is apparent in
the story which he wrote whilst still smarting from the experience, and which was published in the summer of 1834 under
the title of *Der Sadducäer von Amsterdam*. The tragedy of the
free-thinking Jew, which later formed the theme of his masterpiece *Uriel Acosta*, was the tragedy of Gutzkow himself. Twice
banned by the synagogue for his atheistical doctrines, he twice
recants, on each occasion at the instigation of Judith, the weak
but loving woman who finally betrays him and is shot by Uriel
in mistake for the bridegroom on her wedding-day[2]. But if
Judith is shown to be weak and vacillating and, in spite of her
utmost efforts, unfit to be the intellectual and spiritual companion of Uriel Acosta, the hero of the story himself is por-
trayed as almost equally weak: unable to renounce Judith or to
face his spiritual isolation, he twice turns traitor to his own

---

[1] A union of the Lutheran and reformed churches enforced, in the teeth
of opposition, by Friedrich Wilhelm III, which Schleiermacher had com-
bated at first, but had accepted in his old age for the sake of peace.

[2] Rosalie herself, though she lived to be an old woman, died unmarried.

convictions and plays a coward's part. So that in blaming Rosalie, Gutzkow blamed her gently and did not spare himself[1].

His first reaction to the blow which had fallen upon him was therefore a not unworthy one. The indignation against hypocrisy and fanaticism is pardonable enough and not unduly exaggerated; the treatment meted out to Judith is marked by compassionate tolerance, and if an element of gentle and half-resigned contempt occasionally intrudes, one cannot quarrel with such an attitude at such a time, nor exclaim overmuch at the general conclusion, natural enough in the circumstances, that no woman has sufficient strength of mind to defy the world and face the resulting isolation[2].

Having now written this story and given his sufferings the relief which expression affords, his spirit should have been freed at least from all bitterness and released from the burden which those whose lot it is to bear injustice in silence find so intolerable and so crushing a weight. But Gutzkow's temperament played him here a most unfortunate trick. He was ever slow to overcome a sorrow, or to forgive an injury. He was apt to brood over his wrongs till they assumed enormous proportions. His second thoughts were often more gloomy and more embittered than his first, and his second thoughts about Rosalie Scheidemantel and her defection proved to be no exception to this rule. Condemned by many for his article on Schleiermacher, embroiled with those in authority beyond the hope of a reconciliation, deserted by Rosalie at this unhappy juncture, he forgot, as all his life he was fated to forget, that he himself was in any way to blame; he could see no further than the injury that had been done to him, and not for the last time in his life he was possessed by the desire for revenge. He had not long to wait. A collected edition of Schleiermacher's works was being prepared for the press by that same evangelical party which had taken exception to Gutzkow's 'Nekrolog,' conspicuous among them being the publisher Georg Reimer; moreover it became known that an early indiscretion of the author, the *Vertraute Briefe über die Lucinde*, was to be omitted from the collection. Here was a subject ready to hand. Not only was

---

[1] *G.W.* IV, p. 45.   [2] *Ibid.* IV, pp. 39–40.

Lucinde itself a notorious treatise on free love, but there also were Schleiermacher's letters showing clearly by what a deep chasm he had formerly at least been separated from the rigid moralists who were now uniting to honour him. What an opportunity for an angry young man; to publish the letters and prove himself in the right, thus unmasking the hypocritical priests; to write a flaming preface warranted to shock anyone capable of being shocked; and, most important of all, to hurt the faithless heart of Rosalie by showing what manner of man was the preacher she worshipped, and of what stern and uncompromising stuff the man she had rejected. And now as with the roaring of waters pouring from a lock, there burst into his conscious mind those Saint-Simonian theories on women, marriage and love, which had been pressing against the floodgates for so long. In a sudden ecstasy of relief and in a very passion of temper he proceeded to place on record his adherence to Saint-Simonian views.

(b) *LUCINDE*

Der Pedantismus bat die Phantasie
Um einen Kuss, sie wies ihn an die Sünde;
Frech, ohne Kraft, umarmt er die,
Und sie genass von einem todten Kinde,
Genannt Lucinde.

The result of much reading of the Young Germans is a seasoned tolerance of errors of taste and of tact. But when it comes to Friedrich Schlegel's *Lucinde* this tolerance breaks down. It is the only downright unpleasant book which occurs during the course of this study, and it was a legacy from the romantic school. The ways of the spirit are strange, and it is not in that exquisite movement, which culminated in *Heinrich von Ofterdingen* and died weirdly grimacing in Hoffmann's *Tales* that one would look to find so dreary and so prosaic an achievement. Yet it would be difficult to find anything to place beside it for unrelieved boredom, chaotic composition and cold sensuality in the literature of any country. The story which begins half-way through the book is barren of interest and devoid of characterisation, being the enumeration of Julius' successive *liaisons*, each one less pleasing than the last. His union with

Lucinde finally closes this amorous career, and the hero breaks forth into rhapsodies on the subject of her approaching motherhood, delivered in tortured and metaphysical language, which cannot disguise the extreme lack of originality in the choice and handling of the theme. Thus the finest critic of his day, one of the great critics of all time, complacently perpetrated a blood-curdling aesthetic crime. There was ever a gulf fixed between the theory and the practice of the romantic school, and here it yawns at its widest and most unbridgeable. And if from the aesthetic point of view *Lucinde* deserves nothing but condemnation, ethically considered it also leaves a very bad taste in the mouth. Yet the theory behind the novel is not in itself one to alarm or disgust an unprejudiced mind. It is neither very new, nor very original, nor in any true sense immoral. Starting from the general unsatisfactoriness of the average marriage, Schlegel sets out to prove that a true union is the result of the free choice of two independent and experienced human beings who, having passed through the earlier phases of love and passion, are capable of understanding each other and making each other happy. But the ugly side of this theory is glaringly apparent in the career of Julius, who without a pang of remorse deserts one woman after another, until at last he is wise in the ways of love; and his attitude as he progresses egotistically towards Lucinde is, to say the least, an unedifying one.

Schlegel forestalled the Saint-Simonians in emphasising the harmony that should exist between the sensual and spiritual aspects of love; declaring loudly that true innocence lies in honouring and respecting the senses, nature, womanhood and manhood; whereas those who have lost this innocence will buy every pleasure they enjoy at the price of remorse, until they arrive at a bitter indifference towards the disapproval of their conscience[1]. This theory, inoffensive in itself, is developed by Schlegel in a most objectionable way; for he proceeds to what is in some sort a practical analysis of passion, allowing Julius to record his feelings in the very act of embracing Lucinde, so

---

[1] Cf. F. Schlegel, *Lucinde*. Zweite, unveränderte Ausgabe, Stuttgart, 1835, p. 33.

that it becomes apparent that a cold and calculating sensuality, in which reason and wit play the part of the spirit, is all that he can offer in the name of this much vaunted harmony[1]. His treatise on the ingredients of passion proves indeed with pitiless clearness that he was incapable of feeling what he attempted to describe.

Lucinde was published in 1799 and failed even to obtain the *succès de scandale* which might have awaited it, since it is all too apparent that Julius was Friedrich and Lucinde Dorothea Veit. But even this was powerless to save the 'still-born child'; and the book was either condemned or ignored. It would probably be completely forgotten to-day, had not Schleiermacher rushed forward to commend it in his *Vertraute Briefe über die Lucinde*. He was not of those who are defiled by touching pitch, as one realises with admiration on reading his enthusiastic apology for this inexcusable book. There is no need to wonder overmuch that he found little to criticise from the aesthetic point of view; for this otherwise independent thinker had no confidence in his artistic judgment and was entirely under the influence of the romantic theory. And as he looked at *Lucinde* through the innocent eyes of the idealist, it is perhaps not difficult to understand why he saw beauty in those theories which Schlegel had besmirched, and which in themselves were not ugly ones.

For he too was convinced that harmony between senses and spirit is the basis of true love[2]; whilst the contempt of prudishness and false shame, which was partly responsible for his defence of *Lucinde* and which forms the background of these letters, is also no unworthy feeling and one which most of his readers will share.

In fact, were it read in ignorance of *Lucinde*, this book would seem merely a lofty disquisition on love, of a markedly unpractical nature. But the trail of *Lucinde* is over these letters. It cannot be denied that the uncritical enthusiasm for such a worthless production has at times an irritating effect. 'The still

---

[1] Cf. *Lucinde*, p. 3.
[2] F. Schleiermacher, *Vertraute Briefe über die Lucinde. Mit einer Vorrede von Karl Gutzkow*, Hamburg, 1835. Cf. pp. 14, 33, 41, 71, 95, 97–98.

small voice that whispers fiddlesticks!' will intrude upon one's thoughts, and point to the ridiculous side of the situation. The eternal recurrence of the theme of the greatness and glory of *Lucinde* is responsible finally for an impatient shrug, and one closes the *Vertraute Briefe* with a feeling of thankfulness that the ecstatic and emphatic voice with its sonorous and exaggerated cadences has at last ceased to sound in one's ears.

(c) THE PREFACE

When Gutzkow conceived the Preface he was in a pitiable state of mind; and indeed had he not been blinded by temper it is unlikely that this clever young critic, who knew his way about and was not in the habit of making literary howlers, should have fallen into the gross error of calling *Lucinde* a masterly production. Heine, whose sensitive taste was offended by its indecent tone, remarked with his customary good sense that the Mother of God might pardon the author for having written the book, but that the Muses would never forgive him[1]. But Gutzkow's taste, ever an erratic quality, had left him completely in the lurch. His sneers at the clergy, however unpleasantly they read, will not cause much indignation to-day; for he was tilting against a body of men so well able to defend themselves against him, that his attacks might almost be called quixotic. But it is difficult to pardon his treatment of Rosalie, who is twice explicitly addressed by name, and each time with a cynicism which must have wounded her cruelly in her pride and her affections.

But there was method in Gutzkow's madness; however destructive his mood might be, he had a constructive aim; and this was to graft a social system on to the theories of Schlegel and Schleiermacher, a positive contribution which in its result was almost indistinguishable from Saint-Simonism. And he went straight to the root of the matter: 'Dies meisterhafte Buch,' he said of *Lucinde*, 'wollte das Fleisch mit dem Geiste in der Liebe versöhnen.'[2] This had undoubtedly been Schlegel's aim; but

---

[1] Elster, v, p. 269.
[2] F. Schleiermacher, *Vertraute Briefe über die Lucinde. Mit einer Vorrede von Karl Gutzkow*, p. xxii.

the form in which Gutzkow stated the problem was borrowed from the Saint-Simonian formula $AMOUR = esprit + chair$. And when Gutzkow went on to add that this question was a social one for him, whereas there was no social result to be expected from *Lucinde*, which suffered from its romanticism, he defined with admirable clearness the great and important difference which separated the romantic theories from the Saint-Simonian theories and later from those of the Young Germans. The romantics were individualists first and foremost, whilst the Saint-Simonians were socialists; otherwise the more one seeks, the more apparent it becomes that the theories they held were almost identical. In stressing the social side of the problem, Gutzkow approached it as a Saint-Simonian. In the same spirit he blamed Schleiermacher for having produced in the *Vertraute Briefe* little more than a dialectical tangle whose only positive result lay in the demand that social intercourse should recognise the fact of two sexes, that prudishness should be banished, and tolerance shown towards that delightful form of wit which must always be repressed in the presence of Englishwomen[1].

The positive programme which Gutzkow advocated in the Preface begins with the demand for a wide, positive and luxurious life, which should at length be worthy of our spirit, an echo of the Saint-Simonian demand for the material prosperity which was to ring in the golden age[2]. And Gutzkow also agreed with Enfantin in seeing in the love between men and women a pledge that this hope was no illusion. Meanwhile the reformation of love was one of the articles of his creed; for modern society has forgotten how to love, the torch of Hymen has degenerated into a domestic stove; Cupid is no longer blind, he is merely weak-sighted[3]. And the reason for all this is to be sought for in the women of the period who have lagged so sadly behind the men. Gutzkow painted a depressing picture of the young girls of his day; frivolous and empty-headed, they were no fit mates for the liberal-minded young men who took life with such deep seriousness and earnestness[4]. These unflattering

[1] Schleiermacher, *op. cit.* p. xxix. The terms Englishwoman and prudishness were practically synonymous for Schleiermacher.

[2] *Ibid.* pp. xiv–xv.   [3] *Ibid.* pp. xvi–xvii.

[4] Cf. *ibid.* pp. xix and xxv.

descriptions were probably aimed at Rosalie; but, like Enfantin, Gutzkow did not blame the women so much as the position they have been given in society[1]; so that if Gutzkow's personal grievance led him to write the Preface, the lesson he had learnt from this experience was a lesson of a feminist kind:

Nur gleiche Stellungen können sich lieben. Wenn auch nicht im Umfange der Ideen, doch in ihrer dynamischen, allem Seelischen angebornen Kraft sollten uns die Frauen gleichstehen: sie können unsre Liebe nur tragen, wenn sie sie fassen[2].

In spite of the reservation, Gutzkow, in demanding that women should become the spiritual and intellectual equals of men, is speaking as a Saint-Simonian, and speaking very differently indeed from the impatient young man who declared in the *Narrenbriefe* that women should have no ideas at all. I do not think that even at this moment Gutzkow was advocating a political equality, for a little later he remarks with angry contempt that women are to be found putting their oar in everywhere nowadays[3]. Nevertheless, in wishing to raise the social and intellectual position of women, he had joined the army of feminists under the leadership of Enfantin. There follows the fantastic proposal that, if women are to understand men, they should dress like men. Gutzkow was probably thinking here of George Sand, and the passage is not in itself of any importance except that, addressing Rosalie by name, he appeals to her to tell him if she has not understood his love better since she has worn spurs, breeches[4] and a carbonaro, and has followed him about the world as his young and dearly-loved brother. There is a tastelessness and cruelty in this burlesque question which throws no very pleasant light on the quality of Gutzkow's temper.

The first step, therefore, in the reformation of love was to be the education of women; the second step, the emancipation from the binding effect of first attachments which Gutzkow, following here in the footsteps of Schleiermacher and also in those of Laube, considered to be responsible for '...alle jene schon im Brautstande verkümmerten Ehen, jene Wassersuppen-

[1] Schleiermacher, *op. cit.* p. xx.   [2] *Ibid.* p. xxi.   [3] *Ibid.* p. xxxiii.
[4] 'Eine neue Art Inexpressibles.'

hochzeiten und die ganze Misère ordinärer Kindererzeugung und schimmelichter Broderwerbung.'[1] Men must overcome the egoism and vanity of always wishing to be first in the field; this will enable women to overcome the prudishness, which has been a result of such egoism and which cripples their faculties of loving. There is no need to go as far as Schlegel here, everything must depend on circumstances; but the third step in the reformation of love is freedom: freedom from the state, freedom from the church and freedom from the ugly god of habit:

Der Aufruf ist der: Schämt Euch der Leidenschaft nicht und nehmt das Sittliche nicht wie eine Institution des Staates! Vor allen Dingen aber denkt über die Methodik der Liebe nach und heiligt Euern Willen dadurch, dass Ihr ihn freimacht zur freien Wahl! Der einzige Priester, der die Herzen traue, sey ein entzückender Augenblick, nicht die Kirche mit ihrer Ceremonie und ihren gescheitelten Dienern! Die Sittlichkeit im Verkehr der Geschlechter, wenn ihn die Liebe heiligt, hängt am schlechtesten mit der Gewohnheit zusammen, welche auch immer das Gewöhnliche ist[2].

The holiness of passion, the freedom of choice and the freedom to change, these positions and the language in which they are couched clearly reveal their romantic origin and sound like an echo of the *Reisebilder*; but the fact that Gutzkow was making an appeal to society at large gives to this passage a marked Saint-Simonian colouring; whilst his personal hatred of the clergy is responsible for the tone of vigorous protest which is peculiarly his own. A final thrust at the clergy, one more backhand blow at Rosalie, and he has done:

Die Vikare des Himmels aber...mögen mir ihre Kirchenthüren verschliessen, die ich nicht suche, und Sakramente entziehen, deren Symbole ich im Herzen trage! Auch zur Ehe bedarf ich Eurer nicht: nicht wahr, Rosalie?

Wo ist Franz?

Komm, Du holder Junge, den sie mir heimlich getauft haben! Sprich: Wer ist Gott?

Du weisst es nicht: unschuldiger Atheist! philosophisches Kind!

Ach! hätte auch die Welt nie von Gott gewusst, sie würde glücklicher seyn![3]

---

[1] Schleiermacher, *op. cit.* pp. xxxi–xxxii. Cf. Laube, *Gesammelte Werke*, I, p. 163.

[2] Schleiermacher, *op. cit.* p. xxxv.

[3] *Ibid.* pp. xxxvii–xxxviii. This cynical question to Rosalie entirely distorts their personal relations; they were never lovers in this sense.

No less surely than Laube in *Die Poeten*, Gutzkow proclaimed in the Preface to Schleiermacher's letters a social revolution, demanding more material prosperity for all classes, spiritual and intellectual equality between men and women, progressive unions and complete freedom in love. All these positions were borrowed from the Saint-Simonians, but he differed from them in giving no place to the priests in his society. Enfantin had been unfrocked in *Die Poeten*, he was banished altogether from the Preface and his place was taken by the 'entzückender Augenblick,' the divine right of passion which he himself had proclaimed.

Thus Gutzkow sent out into the world in February 1835 a manifesto written in anger, but also with the fierce joy of one who burns his boats behind him. He had learnt a lesson perhaps from Laube's reckless courage, but it was in the last resort his personal wrongs that made him fling wide the doors to those Saint-Simonian ideas which had hitherto crept up the back stairs. They crowded forward and in their midst was the white and bloodless ghost Lucinde, a literary *revenant*, enjoying a second span of unreal life in the vigorous mind of Gutzkow, for though she had lived for a while in Schleiermacher's enthusiastic letters, this 'still-born child' had never known a life of her own.

Born in a stormy and catastrophic year, this Preface, a mis-shapen child of the unnatural union between anger and love, brought sorrow on the head of his father and an enduring shame. A good man with a great name stood godfather at the font, but the wicked fairy Lucinde accompanied him and brought her baleful gift. Yet the child who screamed so lustily was no weakling and Saint-Simonism smiled on his birth.

CHAPTER XVIII

THE INTEREST WANES

(a) *WALLY, DIE ZWEIFLERIN*

Gutzkow dated the Preface to Schleiermacher's *Vertraute Briefe* from Frankfurt-am-Main. He had obtained the editorship of the *Literaturblatt zum Phönix, Frühlingszeitung für Deutschland*, a literary occupation which assured him at least temporarily an independent existence; and now he assumed openly, by virtue of his intellectual superiority, the position of leader and dictator of the Young Germans which Laube had been forced to resign. There was no longer any shyness or diffidence about Gutzkow; his hardly-won independence from Menzel had cured him of this. He stood firmly on his own feet at last prepared to challenge the world. Nor was he altogether unhappy during this period. The inspiriting feeling that he had a mission to perform upheld him. He found friends and supporters in Frankfurt-am-Main and elsewhere; the tone of his letters to Schlesier is a hopeful one and shows not only that Gutzkow was facing his enemies like a man, prepared for attack as well as for defence, but also that the heart which Rosalie had rejected was not unwilling to be caught on the rebound[1]. The Preface had done what the *Sadducäer von Amsterdam* had failed to do; his outburst of temper had relieved his feelings, but he was still too much excited to feel ashamed and in the general ferment of ideas which was going on all around him he felt as much at home as a fish in water.

Nevertheless if his mood was not uniformly dark it was on the whole defiant and challenging. His literary leaders in the *Phönix* contain a series of slashing criticisms which gave rise to cries of anger all over Germany. He knew no friend in these articles, he spared no foe. Börne, Heine, Mundt, Laube and Kühne, no less than Menzel, Tieck, the Swabian school, and the Pomeranian school, they all fell under his displeasure, and were mishandled in cutting reviews. Georg Büchner, *Lélia* and

[1] Cf. Houben, *Jungdeutscher Sturm und Drang*, p. 37.

Wienbarg alone were accepted with unqualified enthusiasm;
and when at the end of August his reign in the *Phönix* came to
a close, literary Germany sighed loudly in relief, and Kühne
gave public thanks in the *Elegante Welt* that this 'tasteless
terrorism' was over at last.

Although Gutzkow continually proclaimed the aims and ideals
of the new literature, it was with grandiloquent vagueness; and
there is no trace of a Saint-Simonian influence in these articles,
except the *dictum* in the first number that the critical period in
literature was passed and gone, a statement which his own
exaggeratedly critical attitude did nothing to uphold.

Besides these arresting articles, often exceedingly witty, sometimes fulminating with anger, at other times crushing with scorn,
Gutzkow produced in 1835 the chaotic tragedy *Nero* and the
ill-starred story *Wally, die Zweiflerin*. The first impetus to write
the latter was given by the news of Charlotte's death. He was
profoundly moved by this catastrophe[1], and for a moment
entertained the idea of writing the story of Charlotte's life and
death. But Mundt was already engaged in this task, and a
chance glimpse into the mind of another woman, perplexed and
terrified by religious doubts, was responsible for the fact that
the motive for Wally's suicide was shown to be the result of
despair induced by scepticism. Gutzkow then saw a chance to
make use of a book which had just been returned to him by
Campe in Hamburg. Deeply impressed by Strauss' *Leben Jesu*,
published in the early spring of 1835, he had sought for a means
to come to the author's aid in the ensuing theological battle.
To this end he had collected some extracts from the *Fragmente
des Wolfenbüttelschen Ungenannten*, provided them with another
challenging preface, and prepared to launch these free-thinking
utterances, heavy with the weight of Lessing's approval, on a
horrified and startled world. But Campe not unnaturally refused to be a party to this second bomb-throwing expedition,
and the book was returned to the would-be editor. Here was
an opportunity of smuggling a part of it through the press; the
Geständnisse über Religion und Christenthum, which occupy a

---

[1] Cf. *Phönix*, Frankfurt-am-Main, February 25, 1835: 'Cypressen für
Karoline [*sic*] Stieglitz.'

large part of the third book of *Wally*, are almost entirely based
on the *dicta* of that intrepid thinker Reimarus.

Another influence is discernible in this novel. Gutzkow had
reviewed A. Braun's translation of *Lélia* in the *Phönix*[1] and this
turgid but eloquent story, with its superhuman heroine, its
mysterious, wild, fatal and exaggerated heroes, its improbable
and romantic setting, also dealt at great length with the titanic
struggle against unbelief in Lélia's soul, ending in a despairing
but lofty pessimism, calculated to make the orthodox believer
feel exceedingly small. Gutzkow owned in later years that the
sceptic Wally was nothing more than the French witch Lélia in
German costume[2], and this influence is interesting, for George
Sand's novel is so well steeped in Saint-Simonism, that at times
we almost think we hear the sonorous periods of Enfantin.

There are other influences apparent in *Wally*. *Rahel, ein Buch
des Andenkens für ihre Freunde*, undoubtedly contributed something towards his analysis of feminine scepticism; whilst the
jerky and aphoristic style of the novel and its loose composition
reflect the unhappy after-effects of his preoccupation with
Lucinde. But the tale of Gutzkow's borrowings is still incomplete; in an evil hour he remembered a certain charming scene
in *Der jüngere Titurel* and incorporated it in his novel, taking
thus one long step forward towards an unseen doom.

Gutzkow confided to Schlesier that he would choose a subject
for his new novel 'in den ich meine Seele hineinschreibe,'[3] and
although *Wally* leaves the reader a good deal colder than the
Sadducäer von Amsterdam, nevertheless it was just as faithful
a record of personal experience. In telling the story of Uriel
Acosta, Gutzkow had shown the tragedy of the sceptic in conflict with the world; in *Wally, die Zweiflerin* he wished to evoke
the tragedy of the sceptic in conflict with his own soul; and
though the victim is a frivolous and superficially-educated
woman, there is no doubt that Gutzkow had shared the torments
he described. There is much of Gutzkow in his heroine, although

[1] July 25, 1835.
[2] *G.W.* IV, p. 242.
[3] Houben, *op. cit.* p. 26; letter dated from Frankfurt-am-Main, January 7,
1835.

he embodied the positive result of his reflections in his hero
Cäsar, who is also in some ways a portrait of himself.

And now perhaps it is necessary to give a sketch of this novel
which has been often described and commented. It is little
read to-day; and the articles, reviews and pamphlets, the
endless tail of this disastrous comet, have almost faded from
sight; the historical record of its brief and inglorious passage
remains, but the literary firmament knows it no more.

(b) AN 'INNOCENT CRIME'

Wally, a beautiful and frivolous coquette, meets and enrap-
tures Cäsar, a cynical and sceptical young man. She winces
sometimes at his blasphemies, but the understanding between
them grows apace, and the benevolent reader of 1835 probably
foresaw a happy ending. But Cäsar was not a marrying man,
and even Wally, now deeply in love with him, seemed neither
to expect nor to hope for this conclusion to their friendship.
Suddenly and lightly, for no stated motive, with no apparent
heart-searchings or regret, she announced her decision to marry
the 'Sardinian ambassador' and summoned Cäsar to her side
for a confidential conversation. Far from taking umbrage or
overwhelming her with reproaches, Cäsar played a nonchalant
part in the intimate scene which ensued; and Wally on her side
was so amiably yielding that he was emboldened to make a
remarkable request. He begged her to appear naked before
him, as Sigune had done before her parting with Tschionatulander. Wally was startled and ran away, leaving him furiously
angry, not because she had refused what he asked, but because
she had failed to appreciate the beauty of his idea. She herself
soon came to see her crime in the same light, and took the
only means in her power of reinstating herself in Cäsar's eyes.
On the evening of her wedding-day she played Sigune to his
Tschionatulander, and the newly married pair then departed
for Paris, the husband in complete ignorance of what had passed,
although he had received Wally into his arms before Cäsar's
eyes.

Nevertheless it is soon made apparent that Wally's husband
is no husband at all. She had married him on the strict under-

standing that they should lead their separate lives, and declared at the end of the book that she was still 'untouched.' It is no easy matter to decide why she married Luigi in these circumstances. Had there been talk of a bankrupt father, or of an ailing mother, or of a defaulting brother, the reader of 1835 would have known where he was[1], but Gutzkow disdained all such explanations and went on with his tale. Let no one however waste any sympathy on the Sardinian ambassador, for he was a very monster; miserly, cunning and cruel, he fostered the passion which Wally inspired in his brother Jeronimo in order to appropriate his inheritance, and Wally had the pleasure of seeing from her bedroom window this unfortunate youth blow out his brains one cold winter's night. This proved to be the last straw. Cäsar had followed Wally to Paris and had resumed his former relations with her, doing his best, but without avail, to arouse in her some sense of the position in which her husband's intrigues had placed her. He was now commanded to assist her in her flight from Paris and they returned to Germany together.

For a time all went well. Wally wrote in her journal that Cäsar's love made her inexpressibly happy; but he soon deserted her for a beautiful Jewess called Delphine, with whom he contracted a civil union. The despair which this desertion caused the heroine was intensified by the religious doubts from which she had long been suffering. These doubts were finally confirmed and all hope destroyed when, at her own request, Cäsar sent her his *Geständnisse über Religion und Christenthum*. Unable to contemplate a life without love and without hope, she stabbed herself to the heart and died in desolation. Such was the story which raised that ear-splitting chorus in which the words blasphemy and immorality were pitched higher than the rest.

Gutzkow had gleefully announced to Schlesier whilst he was writing *Wally* that he saw his mission to lie in working for the

---

[1] Georg Neumann in *Betty die Gläubige*, Nuremberg, 1836 (an absurd and pious story written in answer to *Wally, die Zweiflerin*, in which the heroine meets the same fates as Wally but reacts to them in a most moral manner), made use of both the bankrupt father and the ailing mother in order to precipitate his noble heroine into a loveless match.

overthrow of the church and as a side-issue the dissolution of the state[1]. There is no doubt that the *Geständnisse über Religion und Christenthum* contain a very definite denial of Christianity and an attack against the church. But there is no hint of a Saint-Simonian influence in this part of the book. Broadly speaking it might be argued that in attacking Christianity Gutzkow was adopting the negative aspect of this religion, but he neither spoke the same language nor followed the main current of thought. He may hope to see the 'blood-red dawn' of a new world in the heavens, ushered in by the stormy genius of the age[2], but that Saint-Simonism was anything more than a symptom of the spirit of the times he strenuously denied[3]. It was not indeed very likely that an ironical sceptic like Gutzkow, who rejected the Christian faith with all the dryness of philosophical logic, should have been able to accept that absurd mythology which began with God the Father and the Mother and continued with Enfantin and the elusive 'mère suprême.' The anti-Christian arguments in this book were borrowed from Strauss and Reimarus; the position they defined had been reached by Gutzkow independently; from the religious point of view Saint-Simonism had always left him cold.

The charge of immorality was chiefly aimed at the 'Sigunen-scene' which it is necessary to consider in detail, since it is the only Saint-Simonian element in the book, and is moreover Gutzkow's swan-song to the glory and the beauty of the flesh. He prepared the way for it with some care. When Wally and Cäsar first declare their love, there is a moving aside of the author's, directed against the barriers of reserve between men and women, and preaching with no lack of eloquence the gospel of universal love and the essential humanity underlying the difference between the sexes[4].

The melancholy note on which this entreaty closes is peculiarly Gutzkow's, but the vindication of the rights and the beauty of sensual love came from the Saint-Simonians, strengthened possibly by the eloquent pleading of George Sand, and

---

[1] Houben, *op. cit.* p. 34, dated from Mannheim, May 18, 1835.
[2] *Wally, die Zweiflerin*, Mannheim, 1835, p. 294.   [3] *Ibid.* p. 302.
[4] *Ibid.* pp. 75–76.

made more appealing by a downright youthful sincerity which
it is quite impossible, one would think, to misinterpret. And
something of the same characteristic, something also that is
very nearly poetry, is apparent in the manner of Cäsar's absurd
request to Wally:

> 'Da gibt es ein reizendes Gedicht des deutschen Mittelalters, der
> Titurel, in welchem eine bezaubernde Sage erzählt wird. Tschionatu-
> lander und Sigune beten sich an. Sie sind fast noch Kinder: ihre
> Liebe besitzt die ganze Naivetät ihrer jugendlichen Thorheit....Nur
> jener Zug ist so meisterhaft schön, wo Tschionatulander, als er in
> die Welt hinaus muss und sein treues Windspiel klug zu den beiden
> Liebenden hinaufsieht, Sigunen anfleht, um eine Gunst—'
> Cäsar stockte und sprach dann leise, mit fast verhaltenem Athem:
> 'dass Sigune, um durch ihre Schönheit ihn gleichsam fest zu machen,
> wie der magische Ausdruck der alten Zeit ist, um ihm einen Anblick
> zu hinterlassen, der Wunder wirkte in seiner Tapferkeit und Aus-
> dauer,—dass Sigune—in vollkommener Nacktheit zum vielleicht—
> ewigen Abschiede sich ihm zeigen möge.'[1]

When it came to the actual scene Gutzkow made the most
valiant attempt to keep to the realm of poetry, and if the result
is rather asthmatic, we must remember that he was not accustomed to breathing the air of these high altitudes:

> Zur Rechten des Bilds aber im Schatten steht Tschionatulander....
> Der Mantel gleitet von des jungen Helden Schulter, seine Locken
> wallen üppig wie von einem Westhauche gehoben. Das Auge staunt;
> ein Entzücken lähmt die Zunge. Zur Linken aber schwillt aus den
> Sonnennebeln heraus ein Bild von bezaubernder Schönheit: Sigune,
> die schamhafter, ihren nackten Leib enthüllt, als ihn die Venus der
> Medicis zu bedecken sucht. Sie steht da, hülflos, geblendet von der
> Thorheit der Liebe, die sie um dies Geschenk bat, nicht mehr Willen,
> sondern zerflossen in Schaam, Unschuld und Hingebung. Sie steht
> ganz nackt, die hehre Gestalt mit jungfräulich schwellenden Hüften,
> mit allen zarten Beugungen und Linien, welche von der Brust bis zur
> Zehe hinuntergleiten. Und zum Zeichen, das eine fromme Weihe die
> ganze Ueppigkeit dieser Situation heilige, blühen nirgends Rosen,
> sondern eine hohe Lilie sprosst dicht an dem Leibe Sigunens hervor
> und deckt symbolisch, als Blume der Keuschheit an ihr die noch
> verschlossene Knospe ihrer Weiblichkeit....Das Ganze ist ein Frevel;
> aber ein Frevel der Unschuld[2].

Now regarded as an academic exercise, a paraphrase of a very
charming scene in a mediaeval poem, there is not much fault to

---

[1] *Wally, die Zweiflerin*, pp. 119–120.   [2] *Ibid.* pp. 129–131.

be found with this description, except that it is rather too
elaborate, and that the emphasis given to such words as 'Schaam,
Unschuld, Keuschheit,' with the conclusion 'Das Ganze ist ein
Frevel; aber ein Frevel der Unschuld,' robs the picture of the
charm of unthinking innocence which it possesses in the original.
Regarded as a symbolical representation of the beauty of the
flesh, and this was Gutzkow's aim, it must also be allowed that,
taken out of its context, it is inoffensive, and more delicate and
poetical than anything that Laube or Mundt produced in the
same line; and although taken in its context there is a certain
tastelessness in the conception, it was meant to be a tribute to
the innocence of natural beauty.

There is therefore a Saint-Simonian element in *Wally*, but it
is not the most important part in the book, nor in any way to
be compared for strength and completeness with the influence
which was apparent in the Preface. Unfortunately for himself
Gutzkow recurred to the theme of the 'rehabilitation of the flesh';
he also continued to express dissatisfaction with the marriage
laws[1], but without laying much stress on positive reforms; and
the adherence to feminist views had become perceptibly weaker.
Although Wally's tragedy is shown to be due in part to the
superficial education she had received, the feminist value of
such a criticism is neutralised by strictures on the fundamental
nature of women peculiarly anti-feminist in tone. Women have
no heart for the sorrows of their sisters[2]; they can only develop
their affections through love of a man, for they are capable of
tearing each other limb from limb and are cold to the miseries
of humanity[3]; they have nothing but scorn and contempt for
the sins of other women[4]; they cannot think philosophically,
and are therefore condemned to anthropomorphic conceptions
of the universe[5]. The future spiritual and intellectual equality
between men and women begins to look like an idiot's dream.

Thus the last book which Gutzkow wrote before his tongue
was tied shows the Saint Simonian influence on the wane, overshadowed by other and stronger interests, and by no means
either the inspiration or the main theme of the book. And this

---

[1] *Wally, die Zweiflerin*, pp. 113–116, 214.   [2] *Ibid*. p. 58.
[3] *Ibid*. p. 72.   [4] *Ibid*. p. 90.   [5] *Ibid*. p. 233.

I think is accounted for by a very natural cause. Saint-Simonism would probably never have played much part in his life, if he had not at the outset suppressed the interest and followed too slavishly his leaders Börne and Menzel. His ironical mind, his sceptical intellect, his unenthusiastic temperament, all make it extremely unlikely that Saint-Simonism as a whole would have had for him a very strong attraction. But the half-unwilling interest, choked back by the attitude he saw fit to adopt, fermented in his mind, attacked him where he was weakest and won a precarious victory in a moment of great mental turmoil. The turmoil was dying down when he wrote *Wally, die Zweiflerin*, and the interest in Saint-Simonism had reached the plane of secondary importance in Gutzkow's mind which it was always destined to occupy. Unlike Heine, unlike Laube, Gutzkow had no message to proclaim now that his temper had cooled. The mood of deep discouragement which pervades this book is proof enough that he was no Saint-Simonian. We have seen the gladness this gospel brought to Heine and to what a pitch it stimulated Laube's love of life. But Gutzkow remained untouched and the gloom his circumstances had engendered was not dispelled. Incurably sceptical, he could not even believe whole-heartedly in the 'emancipation of the flesh,' and sighing over his effort at portraying it, he called it an innocent crime.

It hardly needs the knowledge that Gutzkow was only twenty-four and not very well versed in the ways of love, to contemplate this crude and argumentative novel with indulgent eyes. A disappointed young man, airing his disgruntled views on marriage and God, may plead extenuating circumstances, the more so as these views were expressed in a way that could only endanger the author. It is certain at least that no one who reads *Wally* to-day will reproach Gutzkow with sensuality. It is all so immature that one cannot but find a dramatic irony in the epithet he bestowed on the 'Sigunenscene.' For even granted the immorality of this notorious novel it will be allowed I think by those who read it in good faith that the blundering young novelist who shocked his contemporaries so deeply and who paid so dearly for this privilege was guilty at the very utmost of an innocent crime.

CHAPTER XIX

THE INTEREST DENIED

(a) CONFESSIONS AND DENIALS

It must seem well-nigh incredible to the modern reader, who is used to quite other fare, that Menzel was able to arouse such a storm of indignant horror against *Wally, die Zweiflerin*. But although he had his own axe to grind, and was possibly not acting in complete good faith, a great many honest and disinterested critics were really profoundly shocked and disgusted; and it is a strange fact too that although Gutzkow found supporters as well as detractors, no one seemed capable of treating this fundamentally harmless novel with the lightness of spirit which it certainly induces to-day. Let no one suppose that German literature was in 1830 of so innocuous and irreproachable a character as to make of *Wally, die Zweiflerin* a graceless exception to an immaculate rule. Had Goethe not written *Wilhelm Meister* and *Die Wahlverwandtschaften*? Was Clauren not deluging the lending libraries with his sweet and sticky stories breathing an almost stifling sensuality? Was Saphir never known to make an indecent joke? Why this sudden squeamishness in a nation which was devouring translations of Paul de Kock and the Memoirs of Casanova, and which had in the past digested Wieland, *William Lovell*, Thümmel's works and Heinse's novels without any ill effect? The answer to this question is to be found I think in the fact that not one of these writers with the possible exception of Goethe in *Die Wahlverwandtschaften* had any ulterior social purpose in their descriptions of physical beauty, emotional scenes, lawless passions or illicit relations. And Gutzkow had a serious social purpose which he was too inexpert to present in a pleasing form. The same contention applies with modifications to all the Young Germans; and their various books were banned one after another, but the beauty and wit in Heine's contributions, the unfeigned passion in Laube's *Poeten*, the aesthetic purpose of Wienbarg's manifesto, and the religious inspiration underlying Mundt's *Madonna*, made of these various programmes something more tolerable to contemplate than Gutzkow's cold and awkwardly written story, which was in sober fact so much less dangerous, because so much less alluring, than the works of his associates. Nevertheless it was the serious purpose behind these books which proved their undoing.

And Gutzkow in writing *Wally, die Zweiflerin* fell between two stools; he ruined his novel aesthetically by the presence of a social purpose, and he covered himself with social obloquy by the aesthetic presentment he gave to his problem. The novel had the features of a serious tract; and the tract in its turn masqueraded as a frivolous novel. It was published on August 12, 1835, and on September 11 Gutzkow awoke and found himself infamous—infamous, and notorious as well. He was for the space of a few weeks the best read author in all Germany.

He was not slow in responding to the attacks made in the *Literaturblatt*. He published altogether four defences against Menzel, two in the *Allgemeine Zeitung* on September 19, 1835, and October 20, 1835, and two in pamphlet form: *Vertheidigung gegen Menzel und Berichtigung einiger Urtheile im Publikum*, Mannheim, October 1835; and *Appellation an den gesunden Menschenverstand, letztes Wort in einer literarischen Streitfrage*, Frankfurt-am-Main, December 1835. In these various counter-attacks Gutzkow at first defended the positions he had adopted in the *Vorrede* and in *Wally* as being his own, and allowed at most that he had gone too far[1]. He also attempted the very difficult task of protesting against Menzel's ugly misinterpretations; for the difference that lies between what Gutzkow really said and what Menzel constructed from his utterances is the difference between theory and practice, between ideas and their realisation, between the world of speculation and every-day life[2]. Later however when he was actually being cross-examined on

---

[1] *A.Z.* September 19, 1835.
[2] *Appellation an den gesunden Menschenverstand*, pp. 8–9.

the charge of preaching blasphemy and immorality in *Wally, die Zweiflerin* he fell back on the technical defence, that the opinions put into Cäsar's mouth could not fairly be said to be his own, and this is the first sign that he was beginning to waver[1]. There followed the weary two-and-a-half-months' imprisonment, during which he washed his hands of Saint-Simonism and Young Germany, and on his release on February 10, 1836, this dangerous critic of the marriage laws had nothing more urgently on his mind than to enter into matrimony with Amalie Klönne, step-daughter of the Swedish consul Freinsheim. He had been engaged to her since October, 1835, for Gutzkow needed the affection and sympathy of a woman to an extent which made his theories pale before the practical prospect of obtaining this desire; and it will be remembered that these theories were only held with real conviction during the period when he had been smarting under Rosalie's defection. The marriage with Amalie which took place on July 18, 1836, signalised the victory of his emotional temperament over his intellectual convictions, and was at the same time a practical denial of Saint-Simonian beliefs. It was not a very happy marriage; entered into too hurriedly, darkened by material poverty, burdened by the demands of Gutzkow's difficult nature, threatened by his *liaison* with Therese von Bacheracht, it dragged rather mournfully on its way until the death of Amalie in 1848. At the end of his life he still spoke of this marriage with disillusionment and bitterness[2]. But it seems likely that for the moment at least it did something to lighten the load of care and loneliness which weighed on this young man's shoulders and to raise his depressed spirits[3]; it probably encouraged him in his literary productions and spurred him on in a very difficult undertaking, an attempt to enlist the sympathies of his official persecutors.

There are three letters to be considered here; Gutzkow wrote

---

[1] Houben, *op. cit.* pp. 507–508; R. Fester, *Eine vergessene Geschichts-philosophie*, Hamburg, 1890, pp. 31–33.

[2] Cf. *Briefe an eine Freundin*, in the University Library at Berlin, cut out from some periodical not specified. Letter dated December 6, 1870; pp. 324–325.

[3] Mundt was horrified by the change in Gutzkow, when he saw him again in 1837; cf. E. Pierson, *Gustav Kühne*, 1889, pp. 52–53.

to Tzschoppe[1], to Rochus von Rochow[2], and to Münch-Belling-hausen[3] deploring his former errors, begging for their indulgence in the matter of his two new books *Philosophie der Geschichte* and *Ueber Goethe im Wendepunkt zweier Jahrhunderte*, and pro-mising although in manly and independent tones to make amends for his early indiscretions. There is no mention of Saint-Simonism in these letters, but they contain interesting confessions of Gutzkow's state of mind when he wrote the *Vorrede* and *Wally*, which tally completely with the reasons I have given for his reckless adoption of Saint-Simonian views; he characterised these two works as 'Explosionen eines Ge-müthes, das seine vergangene Bildungs-Periode hasste,' and owned that they were attempts to revenge himself for the coldness he had met with in Berlin. Meanwhile in the *Telegraph für Deutschland* he protested formally against the supposed Saint-Simonism to be found in the Preface:

Die excentrischen Bemerkungen in der Vorrede zu den Lucinde-Briefen, welche nur Ueberdruss an gewissen theologischen Rich-tungen hervorrief und die vielleicht durch persönliche Verhältnisse erklärt werden müssen, tragen bei ihm (Karl Hase) sogleich ein langes Schleppkleid von St Simonismus[4].

This protest was uttered again on a different occasion. Gutzkow, who wished to obtain permission from the authorities in Berlin to edit and publish the *Telegraph* in that city, sent in as an earnest of good faith his article on Steffens' novel *Die Revolution*, which contained an attack on the Young Germans and their Saint-Simonian theories. The greater part of this article was republished in *Götter, Helden, Don Quixote*; but in a passage, which was not reprinted, he openly confessed the malicious in-tention of the Preface, and protested against the unfairness of treating this angry outburst as a serious attempt to erect a Saint-Simonian system[5]. Gutzkow was telling the truth, when he declared that he was no Saint-Simonian, and he was right

[1] Otto Draeger, *Theodor Mundt und seine Beziehungen zum jungen Deutschland*, Marburg, 1909, pp. 164 ff., dated from Frankfurt-am-Main, March 15, 1836.

[2] Geiger, L., *Das junge Deutschland und die preussische Censur*, pp. 190 ff., dated April 3, 1836.

[3] Houben, *op. cit.* pp. 531 ff., dated from Frankfurt-am-Main, April 25, 1836; cf. also *ibid.* p. 536, and *A.W.* XII, p. 69 for similar confessions.

[4] *Telegraph*, August 1837, No. 24.   [5] *Ibid.*, September 1837, No. 45.

to repudiate the whole system as seen through Steffens' prejudiced eyes. There is no doubt that he now looked back on the *Vorrede* with shame; it was never reprinted, and he must often have thought of it later with discomfort on account of the inexcusable use of Rosalie's name. This discomfort naturally spread to the subject-matter; and as he had always been half-ashamed of his interest in Saint-Simonism, it is not surprising that he showed a peculiar restiveness under the charge of advocating it. This restiveness manifested itself in the contemptuous anger with which in the ensuing years he spoke of those social and feminist theories which for a short and disastrous period he had allowed to hold sway in his mind.

(b) RECANTATIONS

We have already seen that during the years 1836–1839 Gutzkow more than once denied the validity of the Saint-Simonian social and feminist principles, implicitly and explicitly disowning his own former adherence to such theories and also to the doctrine of the 'rehabilitation of the flesh.' The references to women, marriage and religion, which are to be found in the books written during this period, illustrate his attitude more clearly and must be briefly considered.

In the section entitled 'Mann und Weib' in *Philosophie der Geschichte*, 1836, Gutzkow, whilst attributing to women the unenviable social function of calming the stormy passions of men, and maintaining that the ultimate end of history will be the victory of the feminine principle[1], denied that they should have any place in the making of history and dissociated himself in coarse and violent language from the Saint-Simonian feminism:

Wie ich denn in der jüngsten Zeit in Deutschland ein System bekommen habe, ohne zu wissen wie? soll ich auch das Apostelamt der femme libre übernommen habe. Der Ausdruck: *Emanzipation der Liebe* findet sich in meinen Schriften und gern fass' ich mit diesem zusammen, was ich in juristischer Hinsicht über die Ehe an verschiedenen Orten ausgesprochen habe. Aber ich sollte verlangen, dass des Aristophanes Ekklesiazusen auf Eure Rathhäuser stürmten, und dass schwangere Weibspersonen als Polizeibeamte die Pässe der wandernden Handwerksbursche visirten?[2]

[1] Cf. also *G.W.* VIII, p. 314 and *A.W.* XI, pp. 255–256.
[2] *Philosophie der Geschichte*, Hamburg, 1836, p. 149.

From this position he never thereafter retreated, and there are many horrified outbursts against the modern women of his day, which show with amusing clearness that he must always have been an anti-feminist at heart[1]. They have understanding but no reason[2], and since they are incapable of creating, their highest development must consist in an incredible degree of receptivity[3]. It will be gathered from these random examples that Gutzkow had reverted to his earlier beliefs. He was never really a feminist. It had proved a good stick with which to belabour Rosalie's back, but it had served its purpose and he looked upon this instrument of torture with a very natural distaste.

In dealing with the social question however Gutzkow showed himself less reactionary and much more progressive. He still clung to his opinion that the first love is an unsatisfactory basis for marriage[4]; and as a result of this conviction he demanded greater indulgence towards illegitimate birth. The foundation of orphanages for such children would be an economic advantage, since it would in his view lower the birth-rate; the parents of a prospective child should no longer be morally and legally bound to marry and thus encouraged to propagate their species without love[5]. But though he wished to free illegitimate birth from the burden of police regulations, he was not desirous of attacking the institution of marriage:

Die Ehe bleibt und ist ein Hebel der Cultur, und kann weder von dem freien Weibe *St Simon's* noch von *Lelia's* spitzfindig sinnlichen Grübeleien untergraben werden[6].

This is a very definite recantation of an opinion he had once openly held and clearly expressed, and there is therefore real hypocrisy to be found in the conclusion:

...allein dass sie desshalb in der Ehe logische und metaphysische Widersprüche zu entdecken glauben, das ist eine Verblendung, von welcher es mir früher leid that, sie von einer so geistvollen Schriftstellerin, wie die Verfasserin der Lelia ist, getheilt zu sehen[7].

---

[1] Cf. *G.W.* ii, p. 444 and viii, p. 39.   [2] *Ibid.* viii, p. 443.
[3] *Ibid.* ix, p. 217, 1839, appeared first in the *Jahrbuch der Literatur*.
[4] *Ibid.* viii, p. 38, 1837.   [5] *Ibid.* viii, pp. 126–127.
[6] *Ibid.* viii, p. 326.   [7] *Ibid.* viii, p. 327.

With regard to the doctrine of the 'emancipation of the flesh' Gutzkow also ranged himself with the antagonists of Saint-Simonism and accepted the Christian attitude towards the dualist principle in *Philosophie der Geschichte*:

Geschichte ist jener tausendjährige blutige Kampf zwischen Recht und Unrecht, zwischen Natur und Geist, sie ist eine Abwechslung von Sonnenschein und Ungewitter[1].

Whilst he spoke more clearly and more emphatically to the same purpose in the *Zeitgenossen*:

Wenn man innerhalb der schottischen und französischen Philosophie und z. B. in den Schematismen, wie sie der Saint Simonismus aufgestellt hat, mit Recht erstaunt über die Weitläufigkeit und Schwierigkeit, welche diesen Methoden die Materie darbietet, so hat die deutsche Philosophie sich vom Fetischdienst der Materie, vom Aberglauben der blossen Erscheinung getrennt. Und mit Recht. Denn mögen wir auch das unmittelbare Gefühl des Dualismus haben und im nächsten Bewusstsein Geist und Materie wol unterscheiden können, so lebt in uns doch nicht weniger die thatsächliche Ueberzeugung, dass die Materie in den Fesseln des Geistes liegt, dass sie Staub ist, war und sein wird, dass sie ihre Bestimmung darin finden wird, einst im leeren Nichts zu verwehen[2].

But however convinced Gutzkow might be in 1837 that matter was the slave of mind he could not but remember with a certain uneasiness that he had once held a different opinion and given expression to it in *Maha Guru* and in *Wally, die Zweiflerin*. He attempted not unjustifiably to smooth the matter over in his essay on Heinrik Steffens' novel *Die Revolution* in *Götter, Helden, Don Quixote*, and if in doing so he was rather unfair to a doctrine he had once acclaimed, this is all of a piece with his determination to shake himself free of a suspicion which had so nearly ruined his career:

Steffens erwähnt die Religion nicht, wol aber die Sitte. Er stellt ein confuses System von St Simonismus auf, um dem 'jungen Deutschland' einen fettigen Spiegel vorzuhalten. Das Unsinnigste, was über Emanzipation u. dgl. vom Vater Enfantin nur debütirt ist, wird den vermeintlichen Jüngern desselben zugerechnet....So weiss auch Steffens viel von der Emanzipation des Fleisches zu erzählen und kümmert sich wenig darum, dass die vermeintlichen Apostel derselben sich längst die schändlichen Ideen, die derselben zu Grunde

---

[1] *G.W.* XII, p. 115, 1836.   [2] *Ibid.* VIII, p. 465.

liegen sollen, verbeten haben. Ueber den Unsinn der Frauenemanzi-
pation verweis' ich z. B. auf meinen Versuch *Zur Philosophie der
Geschichte*[1].

A year later he tried, less justifiably, to lay the whole blame of
preaching this doctrine on to the shoulders of Mundt; whilst in
an angry review of Kühne's *Klosternovellen* he protested against
the use of the term as applied to the Young Germans and wished
to substitute 'Studium der Antike.'[2] But when he wrote the
preface to the second edition of *Wally* in the freer Germany of
1851 he spoke more boldly and more sincerely:

> Wie lange hat der Autor gebraucht, Voreingenommenen zu be-
> weisen, dass 'Emancipation des Fleisches' nur ein albernes Wort für
> einen ganz unschuldigen Begriff ist![3]

It hardly needs the contrast of 'schändliche Ideen' with 'un-
schuldige Begriff' to convince us that his denials of this doctrine did not represent his real convictions. Towards the end
of his life Gutzkow declared that as far as he was concerned the
'rehabilitation of the flesh' had stood for the rehabilitation of
the natural[4]. But there is no need to split hairs with Gutzkow
about the term. He had been a half-hearted and short-lived
feminist; incurably dependent on women, he had felt at one
moment the desire to lean upon something at least as strong
as himself; but the desire had passed and his feminism had
swung back to its opposite extreme. He had been an upholder
of the Saint-Simonian doctrine of freedom in love, but his need
of a wife had cured him of those leanings, though they left a
certain tolerance behind them strengthened by his inborn dissatisfaction with the married state. But more clearly than all
this, he had certainly accepted the gospel of the beauty of the
flesh, although circumstances forced him later to dissociate
himself from these views.

He had ever been a disloyal Saint-Simonian, disguising his
interest by mockery as he played with these edged tools. But
in a moment of irritation he used them as a weapon and very
nearly killed himself as a result.

---

[1] *Götter, Helden, Don Quixote*, pp. 442–444.
[2] *Telegraph*, June 1838, No. 103.   [3] *G.W.* IV, p. 243.
[4] *A.W.* XI, pp. 155–156; *Rückblicke auf mein Leben*, 1875.

(c) THE 'EVIL EYE'

We have been studying Gutzkow's interest in Saint-Simonism through a microscope; it is time to look at it with the naked eye, and it appears almost vanishingly small, when we step back and review his life and the whole body of his writings. We have considered in detail only the years 1831–1835, and even here many of his works have been of necessity omitted, since they show no slightest trace of this interest. The *Forum der Journalliteratur*, the main body of his contributions to the *Literaturblatt*, the *Morgenblatt*, the *Allgemeine Zeitung*, the *Phönix*, the *Novellen*, 1834, the *Soireen, Oeffentliche Charaktere, Nero, Hamlet in Wittenberg*, the *Deutsche Revue*, 1835, to name only some of his writings during this period, have all been consulted and found innocent of Saint-Simonian leanings; whilst the long list of his works between 1836 and 1842 have yielded only meagre and negative traces of an influence which already belonged to the past. There followed from 1842 to 1849 the period of intense preoccupation with the stage, covering also Gutzkow's activities as 'Dramaturg' at the 'Hoftheater' in Dresden; and the plays which made his name, and which often supply interesting evidence of personal experience and of the unreliability of his moral taste[1], are also guiltless of preaching any form of Saint-Simonian doctrine. Then the reign of his lengthy novels was rung in by the *Ritter vom Geiste* and here also in the general welter of democratic ideals built up on freemasonry, Saint-Simonism played no distinguishable part; indeed the very name of this novel is a denial of the fundamental tenets of that system. We need seek no more, Saint-Simonism has vanished into space. It certainly has no part in that most respectable paper, *Unterhaltungen am häuslichen Herd*, a forerunner of the innocuous *Gartenlaube*, which Gutzkow edited from 1852 to 1861; the interest was not even resuscitated in *Rückblicke auf mein Leben* in 1875.

It had never been far-reaching or profound, but it was

---

[1] Cf. especially *Werner, oder Herz und Welt*, 1842. Gustav Freytag in *Dramaturgie des Schauspiels* has given an admirable analysis of Gutzkow's plays, and a very fine and interesting appreciation of his unhappy character.

curiously interwoven in the threads of his life and helped to alter the course of his future career. It was an important element in the quarrel with Menzel which accustomed him full early to that atmosphere of violent polemics in which ever after he moved and breathed, resulting in one feud after another and typified in the libellous lampoon against Hebbel written in the year of his death:

...der Weheschrei eines rasenden Aias der Literatur, eines Dichters, der, in tiefster Seele verwundet, seinen Schmerz in alle vier Winde austoben lässt....Es ist wie das Geheul eines sich verblutenden Kämpfers, der am ganzen Leibe geschunden, zerstochen, zerfleischt, sterbend seine Verwünschungen über die Häupter seiner höhnenden Feinde hinweg schleudert[1].

It played a by no means negligible part in a persecution which may have sown in his mind the seeds of that future insanity which darkened his subsequent years. It helped to awaken the demon of cruelty dormant in his nature. This demon turned and rent Rosalie, and learnt its dreadful power. The women who loved Gutzkow could tell some distressing tales. Amalie suffered before she died; Therese von Bacheracht was cruelly deserted when she should have been made his wife; his second wife Bertha Meidingen lay on no bed of roses. And yet in the end it was probably Gutzkow who suffered most. He has been aptly described as a poet whose muse was born with the evil eye[2]. But it was rather Gutzkow himself who laboured under this terrible curse; and it is symbolical of his relentless fate that his connection with a religion which promised such fair things to its adherents, and which brought to the other Young Germans moments at least of happiness and release, should have had no better gifts for Gutzkow than sorrow and shame.

[1] F. Wehl, *Zeit und Menschen*, Altona, 1889, i, p. 275.
[2] *Ibid.* i, p. 277.

PART VI

MUNDT AND SAINT-SIMONISM

CHAPTER XX

UNPROMISING BEGINNINGS

(a) THEODOR MUNDT

There is nothing to be gained by attempting to disguise or to soften the fact that in Theodor Mundt we are face to face with a perfectly mediocre mind and but a moderate intelligence; a fact which moreover is not counterbalanced by any distinctive gift of temperament. Gutzkow, Laube and Wienbarg, when summoned from the pale land of shades, prove to be men of some distinction and authors of books perhaps unjustly neglected to-day. It is not so with Mundt. The oblivion and obscurity which surround his name become him on the whole so well, that it may seem an ill-considered act to pull aside these veils and to allow the sun of the twentieth century to shine for a moment on the unimpressive and rather foolish figure of a writer whose reputation has so deservedly perished.

And yet apart from the fact that Mundt is inextricably entangled in the history of this movement and therefore could not in any case be omitted, I will not deny that I have found him an entertaining companion and an interesting study. He has some characteristic qualities which save him from being a nonentity, and we shall find that his heart was bigger than his head; but his chief value lies in the very fact of his rather commonplace nature. For if any movement in life, history and literature is to be understood, the voice of the normal man of his time cannot wisely be disregarded. The great reach beyond their epochs, they speak the tongue of the human race; the small are imprisoned in time and space and speak the language of their period. In studying Mundt we hear the voice of the normal man; and although his place is certainly in the large class of mediocre talents, yet there is a certain contradiction between the adjective and the substantive which we are free to interpret in his favour.

It will not be necessary, as it was in the case of Heine, Laube and Gutzkow, to consider the development and change of

Saint-Simonian ideas in the works of Theodor Mundt. He never altered in his attitude towards Saint-Simonism. As he spoke in 1835, so he was to speak in 1856, and between these two dates he spoke again and again, in language almost identical, and from a point of view exactly similar; a fact from which, as we follow the history of his literary output, some important deductions can be made. Neither need we seek for any real discrepancies between his judgments of this movement, and its influence on his writings, for the works in question are the simple expression of his opinions, and indeed were written to illustrate them. The history of Mundt's literary career is in the main the story of his interest in Saint-Simonism; a perfectly straightforward tale, but with some amusing and unusual features.

Gottlieb Theodor Mundt was born in Potsdam in 1808, a posthumous child of undistinguished parentage, and he lived for the greater part of his childhood and youth in Berlin in modest and respectable circumstances. He attended the 'Joachimsthal Gymnasium' and later the university of Berlin, entering in 1825 as a student of law, but changing over almost immediately to the philosophical faculty; he attended among others Hegel's lectures on metaphysics, logic, aesthetics, history of philosophy, natural philosophy and religion, and was much influenced by his master. He left the university in 1828, and took his doctor's degree two years later in Erlangen, with a view to a university career.

Already in 1826, before his eighteenth birthday, he had begun to write, a habit which grew on him till it became an obsession which only death could cure. He was as determined to write as he was determined to lecture, and he did both with a persistence which was certainly worthy of better causes. For Mundt began writing many years before he had anything to say, and continued to write many years after his message, such as it was, had been delivered, and after his stories, such as they were, had all been told. He had two strong intellectual desires all his life: the desire to tell tales and the desire to teach; he never attempted to gainsay either; indeed they took a more and more irresistible hold on him as he grew older, until the

weary reader, dazed by ever more interminable stories and
stunned by ever weightier tomes, looks back on his unpromising
but slighter beginnings with an almost affectionate regret[1].

(b) EARLY STORIES

The student who turns over the pages of the *Berliner Schnellpost* in search of stories by Mundt is in much the same situation
as those children in *Peter Pan* who with resigned but ill-con-
cealed impatience gathered round the figure of Slightly and
listened while he intoned the fatuous tale beginning: 'One—
two—three—four—five—*six*—said the clock'; for they knew
that it was going to be a tiresome story, and so does the student
of Mundt. But there are some interesting symptoms here
and the reader who has stayed the course will not be sent
quite empty away.

In all these tales it is quite obvious that the young author
had his roots in romantic soil, and was obediently following the
tradition of his day. But there was nothing romantic in Mundt's
nature, whose best and most positive side is a frank healthiness
of outlook, an unsimulated love of life and a great enjoyment
of pleasant things. He was a solid denizen of the real world,
and possessed the rather rare faculty of understanding the men
and women around him, a faculty which was happily to become
apparent in his maturer work. When he began to write, however,
the already waning fashion was to ignore real life in favour of
the dream-world of the romantic poets or, more often still in
1826, for the fantastic fourth-dimensional space created by
Hoffmann. Into this world Mundt blundered in all the crudity
of his unimaginative youth, and it is a half-amusing, half-dis-
tressing experience to watch him trying to obey its laws and
submit to its conventions. The result of this experiment is the
unadulterated nonsense to be found in the *Berliner Schnellpost*.

---

[1] Between 1826 and 1834 this dual tendency is observable in the stories
which Mundt published in the *Berliner Schnellpost* (1826–1828) and also
in book-form; and in the literary criticisms in the *Berliner Conversations-
blatt*, the *Blätter für literarische Unterhaltung*, the *Preussische Staatszeitung*,
the *Magazin für die Literatur des Auslands* and the *Jahrbücher für wissenschaftliche Kritik*.

A sinister hunchback, a girl whose love has turned her brain and who is cured by the double of her poisoned lover; wicked fathers, changeling children, ghostly visitants, suicides, violent murders, terrible but unnecessary accidents, these are some of the ingredients from which Mundt prepared his tales, giving them such crude and unpleasant endings as to remind one of the unconscious brutality of an insensitive child. And if the characters are stereotype and conventional, the situations well-worn and preposterous and the stories told without art, there is further cause for dissatisfaction in the youthful author's style. It is impossible to say a word in its praise, insipid, colourless and trivial; these are the kindest epithets which occur to one's mind. For in reality I think it deserves a sterner condemnation, and seems to reflect a vulgarity of thought which might well cause one to abandon all hope of the author. This characteristic is chiefly apparent when Mundt is speaking of women and of love. Here again he was following the prevailing fashion which Clauren had set and was using familiar words, words not peculiar to himself, but tastelessly accepted as expressive of feminine charm and happiness in love. Real life, we can only hope, may teach him better words than these.

A slight progress is to be found in the stories for which Mundt was fortunate enough to find a publisher in 1831 and onwards; they met with strangely indulgent criticisms in contemporary reviews, and the fact that Menzel showed a benevolent interest in Mundt and Laube a certain warmth of appreciation is indicative of the parlous state of German letters in 1830. In *Das Duett*, published in 1831, the characters, although by no means alive, are certainly more life-like than the grotesque figures which people the *Berliner Schnellpost*; and the story itself, save for one episode describing a ludicrous although fatal duel, is devoid of those imaginative gymnastics which marred his earlier tales. It is adequately constructed, and might even come within sight of being a readable book, were it not overweighted with reflections on music and painting, and further enriched with philosophical extracts from the diary of a professor. It was to be one of Mundt's most fatal errors, this desire to combine amusement with instruction, he was an incurable *raison-*

neur, and he was already forming the habit at the early age of twenty-three.

In 1832 Mundt followed up the mild success which *Das Duett* had procured him with a rather more ambitious and interesting book, *Madelon oder die Romantiker in Paris*. The main thesis underlying this book, the contrast between the romantic and classical aspects of life and art, a contrast made in favour of romanticism, forms a logical part of the story into which the arguments are quite naturally introduced. There is something real behind the action, which takes place partly in Paris and partly in Germany; Mundt had found at least a local habitation and a name for his still rather childish flights of fancy. The fact that the July Revolution was barely mentioned and that art in the French capital interested the author to the exclusion of politics serves to underline the difference between Mundt's beginnings and those of his Young German colleagues. And it is vain to look for any sign that he was aware that not romanticism only but Saint-Simonism also was abroad in Paris at that date. The story itself which begins fairly well ends in absurdities and violence; and there are some monstrous purple patches of a most disastrous kind:

> Madelon aber athmete noch laut und stark wie ein sterbender Schwan, dem die entfliehende Melodie des Lebens aus der zuckenden Brust sich heraufwindet, und aus der Wunde des schneeweissen Busens, in dessen Heiligthum der mörderische Dolch gedrungen, rieselte still und zögernd der Tod in langsamen Purpurtropfen des theuersten Blutes hervor[1].

The faint hope held out by *Das Duett* of an improvement in Mundt's style becomes faint indeed.

Mundt was by now thoroughly launched on his career. In 1833 yet another story saw the light of day, *Der Basilisk oder Gesichterstudien*, and here the reader's sadly strained patience begins to give way; for when he finds the author solemnly delivering a lecture on the untrustworthiness of the science of physiognomy the most long-suffering will feel that he has the right to protest. The ludicrous story written round this sterile theme need not detain us long. A handsome but in-

---

[1] *Madelon oder die Romantiker in Paris*, Leipzig, 1832, p. 242.

credibly wicked count, a wronged and suffering wife, a noble
father, a heartless courtesan, an amorous and unscrupulous
prince, an innocent pair of boy and girl lovers, a precocious child
of four, a tame and affectionate lion, such are the principal
characters in the book, united in the end in a common massacre
from which the child and the mother alone escape. The father
puts out his eyes with his sword that they may no longer behold
the face of the 'Basilisk,' his beautiful and ruthless son-in-law;
and we begin to feel that if we were doomed to make no better
use of our own eyesight than to read such tales as this, we
might be tempted to follow his example.

Nor is the critical faculty thus savagely aroused likely to be
laid to rest again by *Der Bibeldieb* which appeared in the
Morgenblatt in the same year; and yet it is perhaps, with the
exception of the catastrophe, a slightly more sensible and readable story. Wilhelmine, a pious and serious-minded young girl,
breaks off her engagement with Richard, a 'new-fashioned
humorist,' on their wedding-day, and the ensuing discussion
leads to an interesting attack from the latter on the prudishness
prevalent in literature and life and reflected in grammar and
style. After this spirited tirade, which represents the author's
own convictions, and comes pouring out of the mouth of the
hero with refreshing vivacity, the composition of the story
breaks down. Mundt's sympathies began to waver towards the
heroine, and the hero goes wavering the same way. There is
nothing therefore to prevent a happy ending, except Mundt's
curious love of violent deaths. Wilhelmine is sent to wander
in the woods, and the now repentant Richard goes down to a
pool to bathe; he crosses her path by accident all naked from
the plunge and remains rooted to the spot in horror. Her feelings
are so much outraged by what she takes to be a wanton and
heartless insult that she incontinently drowns herself in the
same pool from which he had just emerged. If there is something
unnatural in the false modesty which ended in Virginia's death
in the waves, there is no word unnatural enough to characterise
a suicide consummated for such a preposterous reason.

There are some signs in those early stories that the mind
which produced them might be peculiarly open to suggestions

from the Saint-Simonian creed. The following affirmation of life, for example, shows that the author's senses were by no means closed to the beauty and riches of this world:

Aber bald regte sich auch jetzt eine muthige Sehnsucht in die Menschlichkeit und nach einer hellfarbigen Gestaltenwelt, und ihre Wünsche flogen kühn hinaus in das Zukünftige und erstrebten sich, einen reichen, klangvollen, glanzvollen, mit Formen und Bildern begabten Tageslauf. Denn da der Mensch auf's Leben gewiesen ist, muss er auch im Leben und am Leben etwas haben, das ihn freut und selig daran festhält[1].

There is further an increasing interest in women, and a dawning sympathy with their point of view to be found in these stories. This becomes noticeable first in *Das Duett*, in which Adelheid is the principal figure; whilst Madelon is undoubtedly the hero of the story which bears her name. It is also to be seen in *Der Basilisk*, where Mundt is at some pains to give a psychological study of the temperament of the courtesan, and where he pays what is meant to be a handsome compliment to the power of judgment and intuition in women:

Das Urtheil der Frauen hat Schmetterlingsfühlhörner, die sie tändelnd ansetzen an die Gegenstände, die sie begreifen wollen, aber sie schmecken Alles mit einer scharfen Zunge. Das Ahnungsvermögen, das in den Kindern so stark ist, wird in den Frauen zu einer fast wunderbaren Weissagekraft. Diese Kraft hat die Natur dem schwachen Geschlecht zu seinem Schutz gegeben, weil die Waffen der Gewalt nicht für die Frauen sind[2].

Furthermore in *Der Bibeldieb* Mundt abandoned his hero, although he was voicing his own sentiments, in favour of the gentle and pious heroine, because she was a woman and attracted him more. And although the psychology in all these tales is deplorably weak, the women are slightly more natural, slightly better drawn and therefore slightly more interesting than the men. Finally the following passage from *Das Duett*, a definition of the theme embroidered by this book, shows not only an unconventional attitude towards marriage, but also a conception of love which has a faint Saint-Simonian colouring:

Wie aber die Liebe die wahre Tonart des Lebens, so scheint mir die Ehe das wahre Duett aus F dur.... O Leib- und Seelen-Duett

[1] *Abentheuerliches Leben, Berliner Schnellpost*, June 12, 1826.
[2] *Der Basilisk oder Gesichterstudien*, Leipzig, 1833, pp. 52–53.

aus F dur! Und doch, wie schlechte Musikanten sind die meisten
Menschen in diesem Duett, ich meine in der Ehe!...Aber muss man
denn gerade heirathen, um es zu einem Duett in F dur zu bringen?
Du wirst vielleicht *ja* sagen, und hast gewiss ebensosehr Recht, als
ich, wenn ich *nein* dazu sage[1].

'O Leib- und Seelen-Duett aus F dur!' this is not perhaps a
very original definition of marriage, but from Enfantin's point
of view Mundt's heart was in the right place.

(c) EARLY CRITICAL EFFORTS

To turn from Mundt's early stories to his first critical essays
is to leave the society of a rather frivolous person for another
preternaturally grave; and whereas just now we found ourselves
bogged in the quagmire of his imagination, the arid plain of his
intellectual judgment may at first seem even less to our taste.
It is luckily unnecessary to repeat here the wearisome experiment of ploughing laboriously through all the articles which
Mundt produced from 1827 onwards, as the cream from this
rather poor milk was skimmed for *Kritische Wälder* in 1833.

Kritische Wälder is not an entirely negligible book. It contains
some good articles and is indicative throughout of conscientious
methods, a certain learning and no lack of sense. Many of the
pages of this book make but dry reading, and the articles which
were not republished make drier reading still; nevertheless there
is a solidity about the whole performance which does something
to modify the opinion of Mundt which has been forming itself
in our minds. The author of these soberly written criticisms
was not deficient in intelligence and was beginning to show some
glimmerings of taste. The modern reader will find himself in
agreement with the critique of *Wilhelm Meisters Wanderjahre*
and will see nothing to condemn in its style; whilst the article
on Hippel gives proof not only of psychological insight and of
the power of interpretation, but also of a real originality of mind
in the choice and appreciation of an author so well worthy of
study and so much neglected in his day. Mundt was the first
to recognise the value of Hippel, and even to-day he remains
one of his best critics; the sketch of his life and the delineation

---

[1] *Das Duett*, Berlin, 1831, pp. 101–102.

of his character have not yet been superseded; no small subject for praise when we consider the secretive nature of the man, his misleading statements, his complicated motives and his rather mysterious life.

In *Kritische Wälder* therefore is seen at last the promise which has been sought for in vain amongst the absurd and feeble stories of the same date; nor is this promise confined to the critical faculty alone. It would be an error to deduce from this book that if Mundt is to become eminent in the world of letters he must seek his laurels in the field of criticism. The most outstanding gift apparent in this volume of essays is not purely critical, if it is not entirely creative. It is the gift of interpretation, of re-creation, inspired by sympathy and accompanied by penetration and understanding; a gift rare enough to be distinctive, and which under favourable conditions might even assume the proportions of a real creative power.

It is not only because it contains the first hint of promise that *Kritische Wälder* is an interesting book to the student of Mundt. There is an essay in this collection which has an autobiographical value and is tantamount almost to a confession; it is entitled 'Kampf eines Hegelianers mit den Grazien.' The unhappy influence of Hegel on Mundt's style, heavy, balanced and obscure, is all too apparent in those articles here and elsewhere which I have indulgently suppressed. The influence of Hegel's philosophy on his mind during his student years had probably been intense rather than profound, for it is difficult to believe that he ever completely grasped the great idealist system, which Hegel was patiently building up in his Berlin lectures. Nevertheless both Mundt and Kühne, inseparable in this as in everything else, had been for a time convinced Hegelians. Mundt was the first to break away[1]; and the sketch in which he declared his emancipation appeared first in the *Blätter für literarische Unterhaltung* in 1831. Dr Fürsich, the dry-as-dust Hegelian, cuts a sorry figure on that beautiful summer evening, teased by the graces who have no place in his system and mocked at by Mundt, who appears as the champion of nature,

---

[1] Cf. E. Pierson, *Gustav Kühne, sein Lebensbild und Briefwechsel mit Zeitgenossen*, p. 11.

thereby defining the reason for his quarrel with the Hegelian school.

It is conceivable that in denying Hegel's interpretation of the universe Mundt felt the emptiness of mind which is the companion of all doubters, and that he would therefore welcome another philosophy more compatible with his temperament. Nor did the current conception of Christianity satisfy him completely, as is clear from his definition of 'mere religious *feeling*':

...jenes Gefühls, welches wie ein gebrochener Sonnenstral, der durch bemalte Fensterscheiben auf die bangeinsamen Heiligenbilder einer gothischen Kirche fällt, die Nacht des Menschengeistes nur in flüchtig verzitternden Streiflichtern erhellen kann....[1]

He abandoned Hegel because he exalted the spirit at the expense of nature, and he turned uneasily from the gloomy Christianity of the pietists; on the other hand we find him bestowing warm praise on the positive spirit of the Reformation[2]; it seems probable there that the Saint-Simonian synthesis would find favour in Mundt's eyes.

There is an interesting passage in *Kritische Wälder* concerning Hippel's unusually vigorous ideas on the subject of women. This very convinced and determined feminist demanded the political and intellectual enfranchisement of women and complete equality between the sexes in the schools and universities, in the professions and in the state. Indeed the Saint-Simonians themselves were no more thorough-going and no more eloquent on this subject than their German precursor. Mundt took these suggestions calmly and discussed them dispassionately, with no sign of Gutzkow's anger, but with little enthusiasm and with modified approval. They seemed to him curious ideas, and on the whole he condemned them for a characteristic reason: their adoption would mean the destruction of one of life's greatest pleasures[3].

There remains to be considered as an outcome of these early years the political pamphlet entitled *Die Einheit Deutschlands*

[1] *Kritische Wälder. Blätter zur Beurtheilung der Literatur, Kunst und Wissenschaft unserer Zeit*, Leipzig, 1833, p. 9; first printed in the *Bl. f. lit. Unt.* October 10, 1831.

[2] *Bl. f. lit. Unt.* October 27, 1830.

[3] *Kritische Wälder*, p. 245; first printed in *Bl. f. lit. Unt.* November 20, 1830.

in politischer und ideeller Entwickelung, which appeared first in the *Blätter für literarische Unterhaltung* and then separately in 1832. Mundt showed himself to be only moderately liberal in this essay, although he dreamt of a republic in the future. He made unkind fun of the high hopes which led to the Hambach festival, giving it as his opinion that the political union of Germany was an academic proposition, outside the sphere of practical politics, and that the spiritual union was the only aim worth working for. In a letter to Menzel enclosing a copy of this pamphlet he further defined the means by which this union might be attained:

Mein Losungswort ist für jetzt: ein *literarisches Deutschland*! Ein *politisches Deutschland* im wahren und ganzen Sinne des Wortes werden wir Alle, so jung wir auch noch sein mögen, wohl schwerlich mehr erleben[1].

It seems clear from this confident announcement that Mundt considered himself an important, nay a leading figure of the literary Germany of 1832. He was then twenty-four years of age and if quantity were a merit in itself he might have some cause for his pretensions; but the quality of his writings will not bear the test of criticism. An industrious but negligible scribbler, with nothing new or interesting to say, possessed of two most unfortunate manners: pseudo-romantic in one vein, dry and pedantic in the other; there is nothing remarkable about him, except his remarkable conceit. This would be the judgment of an impartial critic. The faint promise latent in *Kritische Wälder* may even be placed to his credit, but it will not loom very large. But there is a plea to be advanced in his favour. Nothing of import had so far happened to Mundt. His talent, if he had one, had lacked the stimulus of contact with interesting minds; his uneventful life had been spent in study and at the writing-desk; he had experienced the pleasures of friendship certainly but he knew nothing as yet of the emotion of love. And although his bent was literary it would seem that he had not yet come within the radius of one of those revealing books which may suddenly arouse within the dullest a more vital and interesting self.

[1] *Briefe an Wolfgang Menzel, Literaturarchivgesellschaft,* Berlin, 1908, p. 208, dated December 8, 1832.

CHAPTER XXI

THE INFLUENCE OF TWO WOMEN

(a) CHARLOTTE STIEGLITZ

Kritische Wälder appeared in the summer of 1833 with a dedication to Charlotte Stieglitz whose friendship with Theodor Mundt was the great adventure of his life[1].

Mundt had sent Heinrich Stieglitz a copy of *Das Duett* in 1831; an unpromising enough beginning towards a literary friendship one might think; but in reality these two young writers, lesser novelist and minor poet, with their slight talent, their overweening ambition and their lively interest in the literature of the day, had much to recommend them to each other. They were soon sworn to mutual admiration, possibly with mental reservations, whilst Charlotte's impressionable temperament led her to overestimate them both; she imagined her husband to be a genius, and she also saw in Mundt a powerful creative talent which is very far to seek.

But if she idealised the writer, the high esteem in which she held the man was justified in a difficult and delicate relationship, that of a man and his wife and a *tertium quid*. It is to the honour of all three that the triangular friendship remained intact until Charlotte's death, but chiefly to the honour of Mundt, since there can be little doubt I think that he was soon deeply in love with Charlotte. It was probably not until Heinrich and Charlotte left Berlin for a visit to St Petersburg in May 1833 that Mundt clearly realised the nature of his feelings for his friend's wife. The tone of the letter which he wrote to Stieglitz during their absence, dated August 14, 1833, contains nothing more revealing certainly than an almost formal message to Charlotte; but the tone of the letters to Esperance in *Moderne Lebenswirren*, dated significantly enough from May 1, 1833 onwards, seems to put the matter beyond all doubt.

[1] Charlotte's letters to Mundt are to be found in *Charlotte Stieglitz, ein Denkmal*; his letters to her have been published by Houben in *Jungdeutscher Sturm und Drang*, with an interesting commentary and valuable additions to the *Denkmal* in the shape of passages and letters which Mundt had suppressed.

It has always been clear to the Young German critics that
Esperance is none other than Charlotte, but the revelation of
Mundt's feelings contained in this book has been passed over in
a dignified silence. Yet it is a startling enough confession from
a friend to a married woman, although the conventions were
respected to the extent of not making the external parallel too
close; Esperance was unmarried and the head of a school for
little girls. Nevertheless the emotional truth of these outpourings, voicing a love more spiritual than passionate perhaps,
but certainly not Platonic, and represented as hopeless, is sufficiently striking. Mundt showed a certain uneasiness before the
publication of *Moderne Lebenswirren,* and Charlotte was not
allowed to see it in manuscript. 'Das verborgene schwermüthige
Herz tiefinwendig'[1] may have seemed to him to have spoken a
language which needed the camouflage of cold print. He conquered this uneasiness however and sent it to her on its publication with an open, affectionate and respectful letter which
gives a very favourable impression of the man who could beautify
a relation too often trivial or ugly by such resolute idealism[2].

But under the guise of fiction he was able to give a freer rein
to the more natural and more human side of those feelings which
must have been more often a torment than a delight:

Ich habe Niemanden in der weiten zertheilten Welt, an den ich
denken mag, als Dich, o Freundin! Schien ich in Deiner Nähe immer
kalt und nichtssagend zu sein, so hast Du mir wohl das selbst nie so
recht geglaubt....Jetzt aber, seitdem ich von Dir entfernt bin, steigt
Dein Gesicht leuchtend aus meiner tiefsten Seele heraus, und alle
Nacht ist es bei mir...und sieht mich an mit den unvergesslichen
Blicken, und ich spreche mit ihm. Der freundliche Eros dieser
Gedankenliebe erhellt dann mein kleines Gemach, ich empfinde Dich
bis zum Küssen nahe, und stammele Dir tausend Worte, die ich Dir
nie zu sagen gewagt. Meine Gedanken alle, wie sie Dir gehören,
tauschen sich alle unaufhörlich gegen Dich aus, ich vertraue Dir Jedes,
und mit dem Kleinsten und Grössten bin ich Dein, und Dein
Antlitz lächelt verstehend, und ich denke, Du bist mein! Verzeih!
Verzeih![3]

---

[1] H. H. Houben, *Jungdeutscher Sturm und Drang,* p. 419, written in
May 1834.
[2] *Ibid.* p. 428, dated June 20, 1834.
[3] *Moderne Lebenswirren. Briefe und Zeitabenteuer eines Salzschreibers,*
Leipzig, 1834, pp. 15–16; cf. also p. 4.

CHARLOTTE STIEGLITZ

If on the whole the love expressed in these pages is well described by Mundt as a 'Gedankenliebe,' it will be granted I think that the passionate element, 'dies bescheiden verborgene Sinnblümchen,'[1] was not entirely absent. There are signs that Mundt had suffered under Charlotte's coldness[2]; whilst the following passage shows in a moving way the blending of exalted idealism and natural longing which Charlotte had awakened in his heart:

Ich möchte mein schönstes Buch schreiben, und es Dir für einen *Kuss* hingeben. Mit diesem Kuss, wenn ich ihn gewiss erhielte, wollte ich alle meine Poesie Dir als Gruss in die Seele hauchen, und nach diesem einen, göttlichen unbeschreiblichen Kuss dann nichts mehr dichten. Einmal muss ich doch einen Kuss von Dir haben, und sollten auch Himmel und Erde darüber zu Grunde gehen, denn einmal werde ich doch mein schönstes Buch schreiben![3]

As one reads these words to-day a shudder of pity for the unconscious author plays along one's nerves. He was to write his 'schönstes Buch,' a greeting to Charlotte Stieglitz spoken as a poet might speak it and as he was never to speak again. But he wrote it when the reward was unattainable and when Charlotte's lips were cold.

The elegiac note which one would expect in a love, which however ideally conceived was humanly speaking hopeless, grows more insistent as the book proceeds. 'Meine einzige Freundin ist nicht meine Frau'[4]; this bald statement has the ring of real despair, which is heard again in the following lament:

Warum müssen wir getrennt leben, und warum flicht kein ewiger Bund unser Beider Dasein zusammen, zu einer starken Einheit? Doch die Einheit liegt fern auseinander, ich werde Dich nie besitzen, und der Wunsch, dass ich das zerrissene Tonstück meines Lebens an Deiner Harmonie wieder herstellen könne, Dieser Wunsch ist nur ein kranker Thor[5].

Mundt conquered his depression at the end of the book, and provided it with a rather curious 'happy ending,' by which the author of the letters becomes a master in the school so admirably conducted by Esperance. But there is no hint of a possible marriage, the natural outcome to the friendship between the

---

[1] *Moderne Lebenswirren*, p. 42. [2] *Ibid.* p. 5.
[3] *Ibid.* p. 161. [4] *Ibid.* p. 195. [5] *Ibid.* p. 230.

two correspondents; when it came to the point he could not
force himself to this.

Mundt's love for Charlotte as expressed in *Moderne Lebens-*
wirren had its roots in sympathy and was strongly idealised; in
no way lawless, it was however human enough to cause him the
suffering which attends the frustration of our natural desires;
the correspondence which lies before us shows that he bore this
suffering manfully and well. His love and admiration, openly
expressed and gracefully offered, form a no more pleasant
subject for contemplation than the disinterested friendship
which he tendered to Heinrich Stieglitz. Indeed these letters
are so frank and warm-hearted, that were it not for occasional
moments of high tension producing an acute sensibility which
betrays him, we might blush for having fallen into the vulgar
error of mistaking friendship for love. But the constant small
misunderstandings which occurred between Mundt and Charlotte, partaking of the nature of lovers' quarrels, wrung from
him accents of sorrow which can bear but one interpretation[1].

Charlotte's answers during such moments of crisis are so
exalted in tone and expressive of such anguish of spirit that
one comes almost unwillingly to the conclusion that her feelings
for him were no less strong than his own. But if they were no
less strong they were I believe entirely different; and if she ever
did love Mundt as he loved her, that day at least had not yet
dawned. She had married the man of her choice, but already
their life together was darkened by his depression and melancholy which were to lead to the tragedy of her death; she was
therefore from the moment this correspondence opens in an
acutely sensitive state of mind, often very unhappy and nearly
always anxious, so that her delicate balance was easily upset.
It must be remembered as well that the fashion of the day
tolerated an extreme sensibility of language, notably in the
expression of affection, which often sounds oddly in modern
ears[2].

Otherwise Charlotte's notes reflect the unembarrassed friend-

[1] Cf. Houben, *op. cit.* p. 409, dated January 13, 1834; pp. 411–412,
dated January 15, 1834.
[2] Cf. *ibid.* pp. 410–411, dated January 15, 1834. This letter was entirely
suppressed by Mundt.

ship which she normally felt for Mundt, whilst he would respond in a manner betraying no deeper feelings than happy intimacy[1].

The first letter which Mundt wrote to the husband and wife before a summer journey through Bohemia, which was to mark an epoch in his life and in their friendship, was dated from Jena and brimming over with the interest and excitement of his new surroundings, but full as ever of affection and love. Indeed the wistful manner in which he accepted Stieglitz' proposal that they should now drop the formal 'Sie' shows clearly enough that his heart was still in Berlin:

Nur wünsche ich dabei mit besonders starkem Gefühl, dass nun meinem dagegen abstechenden Gespräch mit *Charlotten* nicht ein *fremderes* Element, als sonst beigemischt oder angehaucht werden möchte[2].

A lost letter written from Vienna in August was however the cause of a further misunderstanding; it was the last that Mundt wrote to either of them before he returned to Berlin. No doubt he was angry with Charlotte and therefore kept silence; but in addition to this the journey, the first of any length he had made in his life, was providing him with new associations and absorbing interests, and even involved him I believe in an unfinished romance.

For it seems almost certain that the woman whom he was to call Madonna was not the creation of his imagination but a real woman whom he met on his travels and who told him the story of her life. During the course of these confidences the love scene he describes as having taken place in the garden by moonlight was probably enacted between them, a scene that might naturally occur at such a moment. I do not imagine that Mundt's love for Charlotte was either diminished or fundamentally altered by what was after all a passing affair; but he had been worshipping the unattainable long enough for such an episode to make an unusually strong impression. He returned to Berlin not only refreshed by his journey and stimulated by his ad-

---

[1] Cf. Houben, *op. cit.* p. 419, written in May 1834.
[2] *Ibid.* p. 431, dated July 12, 1834.

ventures, but also more self-confident, more robust, in an indefinable way less vulnerable.

He was still the old Mundt however. He hurried over his
homeward journey because it was bringing him to his friends,
devoured the letters awaiting him in his rooms, and learnt to
his dismay that Heinrich and Charlotte were still at Kissingen,
where Heinrich was undergoing a cure, and had neglected to
summon him thither. The letter he wrote to Stieglitz on his
return to Berlin, tendering the most energetic advice and giving
the most bracing encouragement, full of sympathy and friendly
concern, cannot compensate for the loss of the letter he enclosed to Charlotte which ended the estrangement. For Charlotte
seems to have complained that he had become an entirely
different person on his journey, and the question naturally arises
whether he had hinted at his experience in the garden, or
whether perhaps she had read it between the lines. There is
something a little impatient in the way Mundt canvassed the
subject of her coldness to him in this letter to Stieglitz, a possibly
significant fact. He was longing for a reconciliation however
and blamed himself for taking the matter too seriously: 'Aber
mit den Leuten, die Einem so sehr am Herzen liegen, nimmt
man es oft gar erstaunlich ernsthaft.'[1] Charlotte, who had forgiven him even before this letter arrived, wrote a long and
friendly answer, telling her adventures and retailing the gossip
of Kissingen almost as one woman might write to another. She
concluded by asking him to send his next letter through a
certain Schott, and added that she herself had only been able
to write Schott a few lines, and would not care for him to know
how long a letter she had written to Mundt as he was easily
offended. Oddly enough Mundt took this to mean that Schott
was to be kept in ignorance of their correspondence, and protested against such a course in a manner which illustrates the
change in his attitude of mind, noticeable since his return to
Berlin:

...und dann hätte der närrische Kauz (Schott) wohl nicht einmal
wissen sollen, dass ich an *Sie* schriebe? Weiss es doch Stieglitz, der
es aus grossartigem Gesichtspunkt anzusehen versteht! Nein, nein,

[1] Houben, *op. cit.* p. 434, dated September 4, 1834.

ich will kein abgestohlnes Glück, ich bin zu stolz dazu! Ich bin aus tiefstem Herzen Ihr Freund und das hat eine unvergängliche und weitgreifende Bedeutung für mein Leben und mein Dichten gewonnen! Was soll ich mich dabei noch gegen einen närrischen Kauz genieren? Gott sei Dank, dass ich die Welt jetzt mit freieren und keckeren Blicken betrachte, als jemals! ich glaube, Freundin, man darf nicht zu viele Rücksichten nehmen, alle unsere Verhältnisse wären sonst am Ende matt, fahl und aschgrau darüber und verlieren ihre blühenden Farbenunterschiede....Wir Drei, o Theuerste, verdienen etwas Besseres, ich nehme mir die Freiheit, es mir vom Schicksal geradewegs auszubitten. Ihr herrlicher Geist ist der Welt gegenüber zu sehr auf Adel und Grossartigkeit angelegt und begründet, als dass Sie auch nur ein einziges Ihrer Verhältnisse vor derselben zu verstecken nöthig hätten. Fangen Sie doch einmal an, ganz Ihrer freien göttlichen Laune zu folgen, und weniger der Reflexion![1]

This remarkable outburst, magnifying a tactful hint into an appeal for secrecy, was completely lacking in good taste if he really imagined that Charlotte did not wish the fact of their correspondence to be public property; it shows Mundt in the incongruous attitude of lecturing his muse for her own good and giving a rather absurd rendering of the strong man. Charlotte would have been in the right if she had shown serious displeasure at this letter, but strangely enough it does not seem to have been taken amiss. Two days later Mundt wrote to Stieglitz giving a long account of an interview he had had with the minister Schulze on Heinrich's behalf and bubbling over with his own successes and future plans. Indeed he seems now so full of his personal affairs that one learns with something like relief for Charlotte's sake that she still had the power to touch his heart:

Lottchen wieder gesehen zu haben, hat auf mich den heilsamsten Eindruck gemacht. Sage ihr dies recht ausführlich! Gleich heut' habe ich in den letzten Bogen meiner 'Madonna' mehrere Veränderungen gemacht, auf die ich bloss durch die Stimmung ihrer befreundeten Nähe gekommen bin. Da diese Nähe auch auf Dich oft gewiss so gewirkt hat, so ist kein Zweifel, dass sie einmal in der Literaturgeschichte genannt werden muss! Sie ist mein schönerer Genius! Ich kann nichts sagen als: Dank! Dank![2]

[1] Houben, *op. cit.* pp. 437–438, dated October 26, 1834.
[2] *Ibid.* pp. 452–453, dated November 24, 1834.

But the curious mood of robustness and virility had seized upon Mundt in an unhappy hour for Charlotte Stieglitz. She was beginning to sicken at heart and to give up hope as she watched her husband sink back into apathy and melancholy, and realised that the cure at Kissingen had failed outright as other cures had failed before. A desperate resolve was born in her heart and day by day she moved nearer to its execution. In this frame of mind she wrote a piteous letter to Mundt, trying to allay his suspicions before they arose, and lifting by this very action a corner of the veil which shrouded her terrible purpose:

Ziehen Sie aber aus *meinen* Stimmungen ja keine Schlüsse! Alte längst vernarbte Wunden stechen wieder, wenn das Wetter umschlägt; auch in meinem Nervenleben ist seit einiger Zeit wechselndes Wetter und die alten niedergerungen Dämonen erstehen wieder, mich mit glühenden Feueraugen doch nur zur tiefsten Ruhe zu verlocken! Sonderbarer Widerspruch in der Natur, dass man so glühend nach Ruhe verlangen kann! Die Luft wird sich wieder reinigen, es wird wieder klarer Tag werden, und was mir die Hauptsache ist: ich werde wieder gleichmässig tapfer allen Stürmen trotzen können! Und muss ich es nicht? bin ich nicht denn am Ende doch tief glücklich?[1]

It is easy to be wise after the event, and Mundt cannot be blamed for failing to understand these words as we understand them to-day; but it is difficult to forgive this once so sensitive friend for missing the danger-signal in this distracted appeal. His answer may be compared to a bucket of ice-cold water thrown headlong over a patient in raging delirium. Cold water has cured fits of hysteria in its time, but it is a dangerous remedy; for a heart already labouring under too great a pressure may cease to labour at all on receiving a shock like this.

Mundt's reply opened with the cold-blooded assurance that he was the last man in the world to draw conclusions from passing moods, and continued with a philosophical disquisition on the unimportance of happiness or unhappiness. He then warned Charlotte against the dangers of introspection and complacently recounted how he was curing his toothache by abstracting his mind from the pain. And what do our moods

---

[1] *Denkmal*, p. 283, dated December 13, 1834.

really signify? he concluded. It will all be the same a hundred years hence. Read the newspapers, follow the amazing happenings all over the world, forget your personal sorrow; work, work, this is the panacea for all ills. This sensible and useless advice tendered to a woman who was fighting bravely day after day for her husband's sanity was received by Charlotte with gentle irony and thanks, which do not disguise the pain it had given her. She obviously realised that sympathy and help were no longer to be expected from Mundt; she must look to herself alone.

The extract from her diary which she enclosed in this letter affords the painful certainty that her marriage had not made her completely happy; and this was not only due to the nature of her husband's malady. It would seem that she had learnt to suppress her feelings, and that she knew the sense of frustration of love thrown back on itself:

*Zu grosse Fülle übersinnlicher Liebe ist es, welche die engenden Banden dann und wann sprengen möchte! Ich wusste es nie, und weiss es noch nicht, wo ich mit meiner Liebe hin soll; die Welt braucht sie nicht, kein Mensch bedarf sie in dem Maasse, als ich sie zu geben habe....
Ich bin müde zuweilen des ewigen Zurückdrängens meines Heiligsten; der Verstand soll hier herrschen, die Klugheit regieren, und die Liebe darf nicht Liebe sein! Der Mensch muss seine Krone niederlegen und muss zum Bettler werden, sein Heiligstes muss er zu Grabe läuten und Sparpfennige weiser Erziehung mit sich herumschleppen, die er auch noch haushälterisch auszugeben gelernt. Die Münze versteht jeder, sie klappert und klimpert von Hand zu Hand, giebt man etwas Anderes aus, so ist man ein Narr!*[1]

This confession was probably wrung from Charlotte by the desolation and loneliness which were the final outcome of her marriage with Heinrich; but it also expresses perhaps her sense of Mundt's failure in sympathy and love. It may even bear a more startling interpretation; sent to him at this juncture it takes on something of the nature of a declaration of unrequited affection. But it is ill work probing into the depths of this troubled spirit; Mundt's untimely coldness was certainly an additional element in her despair.

His answer, the last letter he was to write to them before the

---

[1] *Denkmal*, p. 285, dated December 15, 1834.

catastrophe, was addressed to Stieglitz, and for all its continued blindness to the dangerous state of Charlotte's mind, for all its fatuous certainty that the clouds would soon blow over, still shows that the mood which was swaying him so disastrously was only a mood and that his heart was unchanged:

Viele und herzliche Grüsse an Dein Lottchen....Aber meinen betreffenden Brief hat sie entsetzlich missverstanden, und jede Zeile darin wie unter einem dicken Nebel gesehen. Nun, dadrum keine Feindschaft nicht!...Das Leben ist lang und gross, und wir werden uns noch Alle eben so oft verstehen, als wir uns missverstehen. Also Hoffnung und Geduld! Sage ihr, dass ich ein ihr unveränderlich ergebenes Herz habe! Ich habe es doch nun einmal![1]

In the night of December 18, 1834, the luckless Stieglitz had that curious dream of Charlotte's death and its liberating effect on his mind, which he communicated to her the following day, an enormity at which one can only stand aghast. To Charlotte in her exalted and abnormal mood it seemed as if an oracle had answered the question she had been asking herself; the sacrifice was approved, the victim had only to act. She wrote two more notes to Mundt before she died. In the first she asked him to tear up any letters of that summer which reflected an unhappy state of mind; with the second she sent him a Christmas present, a small embroidered bag:

...thun Sie Ihre Uhr, wenn Sie sie ablegen, hinein, und so fehlt auch die *Zeitbewegung* nicht darin. Wie Vieles ist Moment im Leben, und wie gut, dass sich durch alle die Momente ein rother Faden hindurchzieht! Vergessen Sie meine Momente und halten Sie sich an den Grundfaden![2]

So ended the last letter she wrote.

If we are to believe Mundt's story in the *Denkmal*, his blindness did not continue up to the end; his last visits and the last good-bye caused him great and painful uneasiness, and the news of her suicide overwhelmed him with the bitterest sorrow:

Ich habe an ihr so viel verloren, dass ich es nicht sagen kann! Ich habe an ihr so viel besessen, als Du nie ahnen konntest! Das Verhältniss zu ihr, das schönste, herrlichste, edelste, erhielt mich aufrecht und heiter! Jetzt ist eine ganze Blüthenstelle in meinem

---

[1] Houben, *op. cit.* p. 458, December 16 or 17, 1834.
[2] *Denkmal*, p. 288, dated December 26, 1834.

Menschen für immer verödet! Sie war die herrlichste Seele, die gelebt hat!...*Ich habe sie geliebt!*[1]

Did he ever blame himself for his lack of sympathy during those last weeks? It is impossible to say, but certainly the following confession to Kühne suggests a less admirable attitude:

Denn mit dem 'Opfertod,' den der unselige und gottverlassene Stieglitz bereits zu einer *Phrase* gemacht hat, habe ich im Innersten meiner Gedanken nie einverstanden sein können, und *ich* konnte es am allerwenigsten. Mein Verhältniss zu ihr kann und darf ich nicht darstellen, und doch spielt es nur zu bedeutsam auch in ihren—Tod hinein[2].

It has generally been considered that Mundt's vanity led him to make the mistake of supposing that Charlotte was in love with him. It was certainly his vanity that betrayed the secret, if secret there were, to a third person. But Mundt had some reason to believe this statement to be true, for the extract from her diary sent to him on December 15 certainly suggests such an idea. It was probably the only hint he ever had, but it was enough. Instead of cursing himself for failing her when she needed him most, he was able to enjoy the melancholy consolation that her love for him had helped to send her to her death. It was suggested at the beginning of this study that Mundt's heart was bigger than his head, and his conduct during his friendship with Charlotte has helped to bear out that contention; but in a moment of irritated vanity the small man came back into his own. He later denied this assertion to the same correspondent, but ambiguously and without conviction, ending however with a description of his own feeling for Charlotte which brings once more before us the essential beauty of a relationship latterly rather dimmed:

Ich kenne keine gcheimeren Motive von Charlottens Tod, ich wage keine zu kennen. Sie starb an ihrem Mann und an ihrem Herzen und an der Welt....Dass *ich* sie geliebt habe? Ich verweise auf das Buch. ...Ich gestehe, sie war mir eine Heilige, und ich habe niemals einen unreinen Gedanken zu ihr gefasst, aber an Keckheit dessen, was ich ihr von meinen Gefühlen *sagen* und *bekennen* durfte, hat es vielleicht niemals ein grossartigeres und geistigeres Verhältniss gegeben.... Ein Verhältniss der reinsten Sympathie, das der Humanität unseres Geschlechts nur zur Ehre gereichen könnte![3]

[1] E. Pierson, *Gustav Kühne*, pp. 22–23, December 30, 1834.
[2] *Ibid.* p. 23. Spring of 1835.   [3] *Ibid.* pp. 25–26–28; ? 1835.

But if Mundt played no very heroic part in the catastrophe, the *rôle* assigned to poor Heinrich was piteous indeed, and it is perhaps not surprising that the friendship between Stieglitz and Mundt did not survive the publication of the *Denkmal*. For although the figure of the unhappy husband was gently treated, and the central situation analysed with reticence and delicacy of feeling, nevertheless the book was a terrible indictment against the unfortunate man who was responsible for Charlotte's death. He dragged with him through life the chain of the contemptuous pity with which he was henceforward regarded by his fellow-men:

Gleichwohl verkenne ich keinesweges, dass unter den Mitlebenden keiner, auch die erbittersten Feinde nicht meinem erscheinenden Menschen eine so tiefe Wunde geschlagen, als dieser wahrlich mich aufrichtig liebender Freund[1].

Not only in this letter, but also in his autobiography and *Memories of Charlotte*, Heinrich Stieglitz made no complaint against Mundt, beyond what may be implicit in a reproachful sigh. He even attempted to renew relations with him in 1848; but this attempt was doomed to failure, and would never have been made by a man with delicate feelings; the friendship between them might have been dragged out of Charlotte's grave; exhumed, but not resuscitated, it would have had all the *macabre* associations of a disintegrated corpse.

(b) RAHEL VARNHAGEN VON ENSE

In spite of the fact that the Young Germans were by no means the united body their enemies supposed them to be, they yet often give the impression of concerted action; and it is curious to watch how one after another gravitated towards the figure of Varnhagen von Ense as if by a common consent. Heine, Laube, Gutzkow, Mundt and the renegade Schlesier; some personal friends, some literary *protégés*, some hardly more than correspondents of the diplomat and writer; they all turned towards him in their troubles, asked for his advice, begged for

---

[1] K. von Holtei, *Dreihundert Briefe aus zwei Jahrhunderten*, Hanover, III, p. 172; letter from Stieglitz to Dr G. Regis, dated from Vienna, September 11, 1839.

his co-operation in their journals, looked upon him as their protector and addressed him as their master. Mundt was not the man to make an exception to this kind of rule. On June 17, 1833, he wrote an introductory letter enclosing a copy of *Kritische Wälder*; and Varnhagen who already knew something of his young colleague on the staff of the *Jahrbücher für wissenschaftliche Kritik*, and who was always on the look-out for rising talent, sent a kind reply together with a copy of the first edition of *Rahel, ein Buch des Andenkens für ihre Freunde*, printed in March 1833 for private circulation only. It was therefore no common favour which he showed this young man, and it could not well have been shown to a more appreciative human being.

This makes one reconsider in a manner favourable to Mundt the impression of his fundamental mediocrity of mind which only the article on Hippel has hitherto done something to dispel. For his first essay on Rahel which appeared in the *Jahrbücher* in October 1833 is a piece of work of some distinction. The understanding with which he penetrated into her complex and difficult personality amounted indeed almost to divination; the psychological problems presented by her unfathomable nature, far from finding Mundt helpless, inspired him with phrases and words which are still classical to-day. He has said, if not the last word about Rahel, then certainly the most revealing words:

Sie war, in der Weise ihrer lebhaften Natur, immer wie eine Thyrsusschwingerin der Zeitgedanken; sie wälzte, wie eine Prophetin, Vergangenheit und Zukunft in ahnender Seele, und sagte daraus für das Werden und Entwickeln der Dinge tiefe, lakonische Weissagungen vorher....Indem sie nur rein die Gedanken aus sich abschreibt, und nach der unmittelbaren geistigen Empfängniss hastig auf das Papier schleudert, wird sie in unruhiger Bewegung die grossartigste Wortbildnerin, und mitten in dem Gefühl der Darstellungsunfähigkeit, das sie beschleichen will, erschafft sie Ausdrücke und Bezeichnungen, die wie eine fertige Minerva mit Helm und Schild aus ihrem Haupt hervorgegangen scheinen...und es herrscht eine so drängende, wogende, oft gewaltsame Gedankengährung in ihrer Schreibart, dass man, so oft sie sich äussert, eine Pythia im Schweiss der Begeisterung zu sehen glaubt[1].

Now what, we may ask here in no little astonishment, has taught this young man to write such admirable prose? For if

[1] *Jahrbücher für wissenschaftliche Kritik*, October 1833, No. 72.

we have already had a glimpse of the gift of divination of character in the article on Hippel, there has been nothing to prepare
us for this sudden achievement in expression. Indeed Mundt's
style has so far been one of his worst points. The answer to this
question is to be found in the nature of the impression made on
him by *Das Buch Rahel*. It was I think his first intellectual
revelation, the first book he had read with all the powers of his
mind awake. Such a moment, when it comes for the first time
relatively late in life, may operate surprising changes, and
changes of the kind moreover which are readily reflected in
style. Mundt was so much swayed by the spirit of Rahel that
he abandoned his ready-made phrases and sought for words
and images which stood in a definite relation to the thoughts
she made him think. And because her thoughts were in the
highest degree original, Mundt's ideas in this essay show something of the same quality, and are reflected in a style which is
dignified throughout by his contact with her striking personality.

(c) *MODERNE LEBENSWIRREN*

Although *Moderne Lebenswirren* was not published until the
summer of 1834, it is mainly the product of 1833 and in many
ways typical of Mundt's state of mind during that year. There
is no very startling progress to be found in this book, which is
not on the level of the essay on Rahel; but it is a distinct advance on Mundt's earlier works and compares favourably with
Laube's *Politische Briefe* and Gutzkow's *Briefe eines Narren an
eine Närrin*, for it is more readable, more interesting and much
better composed. There are many puerilities of style in *Moderne
Lebenswirren*, many solemnly uttered platitudes delivered with
an air of intellectual arrogance which does nothing to improve
them, but the main thesis is an interesting one, and not unskilfully worked out. Seeliger, the hero of the story and author of
the letters to Esperance, is clerk to the salt-works in 'Klein-
weltwinkel,' and meets with his adventures in this sleepy and
backward little town whose inhabitants he heartily despises. By
the eloquence of a mysterious stranger, Herr von Zodiacus,
none other than Mephistopheles in the guise of the 'Zeitgeist,'
Seeliger is won over first to liberalism, then to absolutism and

finally to the 'juste-milieu.' All these political confessions in fact
are tried and found wanting, and Seeliger is left at the end of
the book with nothing more constructive for a political programme than the watch-words: Progress, Freedom, Future;
whilst after an impassioned rejection of the system of Hegel,
whom he christens 'the last philosopher,' he adopts the no more
satisfactory trinity: Love, Music, Time for the basis of a new
philosophy. The whole trend of the book, which Mundt acknowledged to be barren of results in the preface, is therefore
indicative of a mind swept and garnished. The political and
the philosophical demons which had peopled it were turned
away. It was ready for future visitants.

There are Saint-Simonian elements in the book, but it is not
easy to determine where these came from; they may or may
not have been due to an acquaintance with the teachings of
Enfantin; but they show at least that Mundt was in a receptive
state of mind towards certain aspects of this doctrine. During
his period of absolutism he embarks on a panegyric of Don Juan
and speaks of 'das schöne poetisch-duftige Wort Sinnlichkeit,'[1]
but there is nothing surprising in this when we consider how
early he had fallen under the sway of Casanova, and with what
enthusiasm he reviewed the works of Thümmel[2]. There is however an interesting passage exalting poetry above philosophy,
which has a very definite Saint-Simonian colouring:

> Für den Poeten soll es keine Seele ohne Stoff, und keinen Stoff
> ohne Seele geben....Die Philosophie ist noch der Geist, der über
> dem Chaos schwebt; die Philosophie hat die Welt wieder in ihre
> Urmassen aufgelöst, Geist und Leib geschieden...,Die Poesie will
> und sieht nur Gestalt, und sie erst ist die grosse Versöhnung der
> Metaphysik mit der Schöpfung. Aus dem uralten Weltschmerz, in
> dem Form und Geist sich zerrissen und unruhig einander gegenüber
> finden, blickt die Poesie lächelnd empor, und sie befreit den Geist
> von der mystischen Unruhe, und die Form von des Stoffes Wildheit,
> indem sie beide friedengebend zu einem Gedicht verschmilzt[3].

The harmony between the spiritual and material worlds which
Mundt finds in poetry is no way different from the same har-

---

[1] *Moderne Lebenswirren*, p. 129. It may be remembered that Enfantin
exalted Don Juan as a symbol of the inconstant lover.

[2] *Jahrb. f. wiss. Kritik*, May 1833, Nos. 86–87.

[3] *Moderne Lebenswirren*, pp. 144–145.

mony which Enfantin had postulated in love and which may have inspired this passage; and indeed it would seem that Mundt also accepted the Saint-Simonian vision of a future made beautiful by freedom wedded to love[1].

Already in *Der Bibeldieb* Mundt had shown himself inimical towards the prudishness prevalent in his day; it seemed to him a grave denial of life; and here again is found another angry outburst which reflects his dissatisfaction with the social conditions of the time[2]; it is not difficult to see that a social theory which let a little fresh air into the virtuous atmosphere which was stifling him would have a peculiar fascination for Mundt.

There are feminist ideas expressed in this book, but they come from the pen of Esperance, with the exception of the half-ironical suggestion that only women should be kings. We cannot therefore take them to be the expression of Mundt's opinions, and although they undoubtedly tally with Enfantin's views, the manner of their expression is borrowed from Hippel, and they were probably inspired by him[3]. There is a refreshing absence of the overstatement of mockery in such passages, which shows that Mundt, although not speaking in the first person, was capable of seeing the question straight and of stating it fairly.

Before the end of 1833 Mundt had come to years of discretion. His personal and literary experiences had been enriched; he knew what it was to suffer, and he had come into contact with a mind which had stimulated his own to the extent of causing him to produce a remarkable essay. He had further written a book, which, although not a very distinguished achievement, yet lifted him out of the rut of a mere scribbler. He had shown himself furthermore to be in a state of receptivity at least towards those new ideas which were quickening the minds of his contemporaries. But in one important characteristic he had not changed. He was still a writer with nothing particular to say. The negative conception of *Moderne Lebenswirren* is significant of this lack. Now the urge to write was strong in Mundt, and the desire to teach no less so. Hitherto he had been content

---

[1] *Moderne Lebenswirren*, p. 42.   [2] *Ibid*. p. 198.
[3] *Ibid*. p. 87; cf. also p. 260.

to write about nothing and to lay down the law upon any subject ready to hand. But he had developed during the last year, and the elegiac note which runs through *Moderne Lebenswirren* was not due only to his feelings for Charlotte; it was expressive also of an intellectual discontent. He had condemned the systems which explained life to him, and had nothing to put in their place; and if such a state of mind is always uncomfortable, it must have been peculiarly irritating to one so anxious to teach. A prophet *sans* message is without honour, and cannot even prophesy to himself.

CHAPTER XXII

MUNDT DISCOVERS SAINT-SIMONISM

(a) THE DISCOVERY

This unsatisfactory state of affairs came to an end in the year 1834, which brought to Mundt further experiences, foreign travel and the discovery of the Saint-Simonian doctrine of the 'rehabilitation of the flesh.' It was a tardy discovery, and Gutzkow was not far wrong when he complained to Schlesier that Mundt was nothing but a straggler in the march of progress[1].

Mundt was two years younger than Laube, but he was three years older than Gutzkow, and it is certainly rather remarkable that he should have lagged so far behind them all in his interest in Saint-Simonism. Heine was wide awake to the importance of the new religion in February 1831; Laube's references on this subject followed each other thick and fast from March 1832 onwards, and Gutzkow's began only a few months later. In the year 1833 all three published books which owed their conception to one aspect or another of this doctrine; whilst Wienbarg was delivering his form of the message to the students of Kiel by word of mouth. In 1835 Laube was already in the clutches of reaction; Gutzkow in a fit of temper shot his last bolt and began to retire; and although Heine still dreamt of a Saint-Simonian future, *Salon II* was his second great contribution to the cause. And in this year for the first time Mundt raised his voice and began to shout aloud his discovery and interpretation of a message which the others had discovered and interpreted some years earlier.

I have found no mention of Saint-Simonism before 1835 from the pen of this author; and although there may have been allusions in letters now destroyed or inaccessible, and references in articles I have not been able to trace, nevertheless such proofs of previous knowledge would in no way alter my contention

---

[1] Houben, *op. cit.* p. 27, dated January 16, 1835; a letter voicing great dissatisfaction with *Moderne Lebenswirren*.

that Saint-Simonism meant nothing to Mundt before the year 1834. For even in the absence of these proofs it is difficult to believe that he was in ignorance of a doctrine which was causing so much excitement in France and receiving so much attention in Germany. Like everyone else at the time he was a daily reader of the *Allgemeine Zeitung*[1]; he seems further to have had rather more than a bowing acquaintance with the *Evangelische Kirchenzeitung*[2]; he was a contributor to the *Blätter für literarische Unterhaltung*; most important of all he was on the staff of the *Magazin für die Literatur des Auslands* in 1832, the same year in which Veit published in this paper those articles which were to form the major part of his book. And Mundt and Veit were personal friends, so that this subject must surely have been discussed between them. Mundt criticised the book rather unfavourably on its appearance, but it may well be that he owed a large part of his knowledge to the author. It is said that knowledge is power; but it is often a passive force until some spark of intimate interest sets a light to the train of gunpowder hitherto undisturbed. And this I think was the situation with Mundt in 1834. Veit's book appeared at the end of 1833[3], so that even if Mundt had read no other word on the subject until then, he had here all the knowledge that he needed; it remains to determine the influence which aroused his dormant interest and revealed to him in a sudden flash all that he might find in the doctrine of the 'rehabilitation of the flesh.'

Aesthetische Feldzüge may have been such a revelation to Mundt; but if it were to come to him through the channel of literature, it is strange that Rahel's confessions and Heine's book on the Romantic School should have had no noticeable effect. But Wienbarg's eloquence may have touched him more than Rahel's visions and Heine's dreams; and since he registered a warm enthusiasm for *Aesthetische Feldzüge*, published in the spring of 1834, it must be granted at least that this book came at an opportune moment.

It is unlikely that Charlotte quickened his intellectual interest

[1] Cf. *Madonna oder Unterhaltungen mit einer Heiligen*, Leipzig, 1835, pp. 64–65.
[2] Cf. *Moderne Lebenswirren*, p. 23.
[3] It has the date 1834 on the title-page however.

here; if this had been the case there would have been some mention of the subject in their correspondence, which reflects the enthusiasms they had in common. Mundt never suggested later that Charlotte had any Saint-Simonian leanings; indeed there is a passage in the *Denkmal* which serves to support Stieglitz' statement that she did not care for the doctrine:

'Denn was kann eine Frau *thun*?' rief Charlotte selbst einmal aus; 'sie kann höchstens vor Kränkung *sterben*!' Und was der St Simonismus, dieser Wunderdoctor der kranken Weltinstitutionen, hier angeboten hat, um der socialen Verhältnisse Emancipation zu vollbringen, möchte am allerwenigsten von den Frauen selbst annehmbar gefunden sein[1].

Charlotte's influence was probably exerted here on the negative side, and may be recognisable later in the critical attitude adopted by Mundt towards the feminist ideas and the rejection of Christianity. His natural predisposition towards other aspects of the new religion may even have been held in check for a time by Charlotte's dislike; and this may help to account for his silence until the year 1834. And yet his admiration for Charlotte held feminist elements in it; whilst his friendship with her undoubtedly exposed him to the lure implicit in the theory of the 'emancipation of the flesh.'

For in this unnatural relationship Mundt was perpetually denying his healthy and normal desires; transmuting them into spiritual aspirations and courageously accepting the ideal for the real, a process which dignified his character, whilst it remorselessly bruised his heart. But until his journey in 1834 he was unaware I think of all that this sacrifice meant. Until then he had loved Charlotte only, and if he had known adventures of a lighter kind, they had left his heart untouched[2]. He knew spiritual love on the one side; he may have known sensual love on the other; poles apart, these two extremes in his nature had so far never met. But the experience which he relates in *Madonna* altered all this; for the young girl whom he describes with so much enthusiasm touched his heart, even if only for a moment, and the scene in the garden was the first of its kind in Mundt's life; the real and ideal melted into one and spirit

---

[1] *Denkmal*, p. 67.   [2] Cf. E. Pierson, *op. cit.* p. 18.

and senses met. Henceforward there was no voice louder than Mundt's in the chorus uplifted in Germany to sing the beauties of the flesh. It was this initiation I believe which led to the robust and bracing tone he now saw fit to adopt towards Charlotte; for he saw clearly at last what he wanted, and he knew he could never have it from her; being a man of honour he attempted to put such thoughts aside and was more chary than he had been in his expressions of devotion and love; for love meant to him now a completer consummation than the single kiss he had dreamt of once.

Another woman played her part in Mundt's interest in Saint-Simonism, Rahel Varnhagen. He had paid no attention to her views on this subject when they appeared in the first edition of *Das Buch Rahel*, for at that time they did not interest him. In the summer of 1834 however the enlarged edition appeared, and the long review which Mundt published in the *Jahrbücher für wissenschaftliche Kritik* in June 1835 was almost entirely devoted to an analysis of Rahel's Saint-Simonian ideas as shown, not only in her judgments on the new religion, but also in other passages occurring throughout the book. In fact it is obvious to one who has followed in his footsteps, that he read the three volumes now before him with the Saint-Simonians uppermost in his mind. And he found her prophesying much that they were about to preach, welcoming their advent with generous delight and acclaiming them as the heralds of a new and happier era. But Rahel's eyes were not blinded to their faults; she winnowed the chaff from the grain of Saint-Simonism, and she would have nothing to say to it as a religion, a position Mundt was also to adopt. In her confessions therefore he received a very high sanction for his own enthusiasm, and the intellectual stimulus of an enlightened point of view.

The force which drew Mundt into the vortex of Saint-Simonism was mainly his own private history, but he owed many debts by the way. Veit coordinated his knowledge for him if he did not actually supply it; under Wienbarg's hands the knowledge came to life; Charlotte was responsible for the ache of an intolerable desire which made Enfantin's message peculiarly irresistible; Maria, if that was her name, revealed the beauty of the passionate conception of love; whilst Rahel read him the riddle of Saint-Simonism and interpreted his dream.

(b) *MADONNA*

The first and most complete expression which Mundt gave to his new philosophy of life is to be found in a book of which the title alone survives in the minds of men to-day, but which played an important part in the history of the Young Germans and in its author's life. Although not published until April 1835 it was probably finished before Charlotte's death and belongs by its conception to the summer and autumn of 1834. Written in the manner of Heine's *Reisebilder* and Laube's *Reisenovellen* it has no pretensions to artistic unity; it is a collection of reflections on life, literature, philosophy, religion and art, written round one central theme, the story of Madonna. Nor are we spared the obvious descriptions of towns, churches, monasteries and pictures so fashionable at that time. But the most grave objection to *Madonna* is that it is overweighted by reflections. The 'Posthorn-Symphonie' might pass as a long introduction if Mundt had then settled down and kept to the story. But this was not his aim; he had joined the ranks of the 'Tendenzdichter' and now applied himself with much vigour to his task, for at last he had a story worth telling, and at last he had a message to proclaim.

Mundt christened this book 'Ein Buch der Bewegung' and justified its chaotic composition in this name, which symbolised for him the great principle guiding the history of the human race. It is only another term for the law of progress, and indeed Mundt's conception of history was borrowed from the Saint-Simonians, for he saw it in terms of the struggle between spirit and flesh:

In der ganzen Welt lag von Uranfang her eine unendliche Zer-rissenheit ausgesäet, seufzte ich!...Und durch jede Brust ging nun das ewige Ziehen und Bewegen nach der Einheit, sie war der Uni-versalschmerz des gesammten Geschlechts....Ein ohnmächtiger Groll seufzte durch die ganze Existenz, und die düstre Melancholie des im Fleisch versunkenen Aegyptens und die in Verzweiflung endigende Heiterkeit des an der Kunstverschönung des Fleisches bildenden Griechenlands mischten als die beiden Hauptelemente die Weltgeschichte. Und es war, als hätte Gott im Himmel nicht länger Ruhe, so sehr erbarmte ihn der Welt....Er kam in die Welt....Da schaue ich umher und schaue zurück, und finde Welt und Gott nur feindlicher getrennt sich gegenüber, als früher, wo die griechische Kunstansicht sie wenigstens zu einer äusseren Lebensplastik verschmolzen, und den Fluch des Fleisches durch seelige Formen beschwichtigt hatte[1].

It will be granted I think that Mundt was presenting here a poetical version of the *Doctrine de Saint-Simon*, and like the Saint-Simonians he looked for an end to this struggle in the reconciliation between the body and the soul:

Und ich trachte nach der Einheit von Leib und Geist, darum bete ich auch an die Schönheit, und ein heiliger Anblick ist sie mir[2].

Like the Saint-Simonians too Mundt held that the harmony between spirit and flesh must be accomplished by dignifying and sanctifying the latter, which had been vilified and anathematised in the past; nor did he shrink from using the term they had coined to drive his meaning home:

Es muss anders mit uns werden. Die Welt und das Fleisch müssen wieder eingesetzt werden in ihre Rechte....Wenn Geist und Welt sich ganz versöhnt und durchdrungen haben, dann bricht die Ordnung des neuen Lebens an, für das wir jungen Geschlechter, ich und Der und Jener, zu kämpfen und zu schaffen geboren sind[3].

Later, 'um der Schwachen willen,' he proposed to use the word 'Bild' for 'Fleisch,'[4] but this adoption of a less startling term in no way altered or weakened the point of view expressed in the passage I have just given, and which is the Saint-Simonian point of view. There are many such passages throughout the book. The demand for a worldly religion[5], the panegyric on Casanova[6], the definition of a coquette[7], the constant recurrence to the theme of the beauty of this world, above all the name he gave to Maria, 'Weltheilige,' show him completely banned in the magic circle which the Saint-Simonians had traced.

It may come as a surprise perhaps when I say in conclusion that Mundt, far from wishing to preach Saint-Simonism in *Madonna*, had no more startling purpose than to convince his

[1] *Madonna. Unterhaltungen mit einer Heiligen*, pp. 386–389.
[2] *Ibid.* p. 392; cf. also pp. 394–395.
[3] *Ibid.* p. 274.   [4] *Ibid.* pp. 406–407.   [5] *Ibid.* pp. 141–142.
[6] *Ibid.* pp. 74 ff.   [7] *Ibid.* pp. 163 ff.

readers that Christianity was the religion to which humanity must look for the establishment of a new era. The asceticism which he deplored quite as strongly as Enfantin and with something of the personal sorrow of Heine was not, he considered, the true interpretation of the teaching of Christ:

Falsche Propheten seid ihr gewesen, ihr St Simonisten! sage ich. Denn wenn ihr predigt, Gott sei Geist *und* Fleisch, so betet den menschgewordenen Gott in Christus an! Eure mit unreinen Schlacken gemischte Lehre ist im Christenthum längst und ursprünglich als etwas Reines und in eine grosse Zukunft Hineindeutendes enthalten. Ich meine, dass ich an eine Perfectibilität des Christenthums glaube, ja dass ich sie weiss an mir selbst[1].

In undertaking the task of reconciling Christianity with the 'emancipation of the flesh,' Mundt stood half-way between Saint-Simon and his followers; for whilst he accepted the theory of the perfectibility of Christianity from Saint-Simon, he did not go as far as the Saint-Simonians, who rejected Christianity altogether. There is no doubt that the gloominess and asceticism which darkened the Middle Ages and later Puritan England were a distortion of a religion which has a place for joy as well as for sorrow; and that the strongest argument against the supposition that the anathema against the flesh is an inherent part of the Christian dogma is the one used by Mundt, by Veit, and by other writers of the time; that God became flesh in the person of Christ, and by doing this sanctified the material side of our nature. Nevertheless if the scourging of the flesh is not implicit in Christianity, neither is a glorification of the senses any true part of that doctrine. Christ was no light-hearted pagan god wandering among the children of men and offering his love to their daughters; he was 'a man of sorrows and acquainted with grief' and he lived a celibate life. The Saint-Simonians were logical enough to perceive that a religion based on the equal divinity of body and soul could not be called Christianity. Mundt, however, no very straight thinker at any time, imagined that it was possible to make the best of both worlds and combine the two conceptions. Yet in spite of the fact that he rejected Saint-Simonism and accepted Christianity

---

[1] *Madonna*, pp. 397–398; cf. pp. 380–417 for the whole of this passage.

he was more truly a Saint-Simonian than a Christian. He identified himself with Bazard's interpretation of history; he dreamt like Enfantin of the 'rehabilitation of the flesh'; he also demanded imperatively a full measure of worldly pleasures, pressed down and running over; and if he called himself a Christian, this was an error in thought.

Mundt extended his adverse judgment of the Saint-Simonians to their feminist ideas. In the chapter called 'Bohemiconympomachia' he gave an amusingly written version of the 'Mägdekrieg' in which he treated this early attempt to emancipate women with genial irony, and showed the final result to have been disastrous. During the course of the story one of the amazons embarks on a prophecy on the future of women, and sees a vision of the *salle* Taitbout:

Dort ist ein Saal, in dem Männer mit langen Bärten versammelt sind, die eine besondere Weisheit unter sich verabredet haben, die heisst der Saint-Simonismus. Sie tragen eine weisse, hinten zugeknöpfte Weste, weisse Beinkleider, eine blaue Jacke, und Kopf und Busen sind ihnen ganz entblösst. Sie sehen närrisch aus, und sprechen über die Weiber. In ihrer Mitte sitzt Einer mit Namen Enfantin, der sich den obersten Vater der Simonisten nennt, und neben ihm steht ein leerer Stuhl, auf dem *das freie Weib* noch erwartet wird, damit sie, sobald sie erscheine in der Welt, sich gleich setzen könne. Alle Anstalten zu ihrem Empfange sind gemacht, und ihre Unabhängigkeit vom Manne ist ausgesprochen. Was Libussa gedacht, was Hippel geschrieben, wollen die Simonisten endlich ausführen. L'élévation de l'épouse au niveau de l'époux! so hallt es wieder aus dem Munde des obersten Vaters, der das freie Weib sucht. Es giebt eine gesellschaftliche Person, das ist nicht mehr der Mann allein, sondern Mann *und* Frau, und alle Geschäfte des Lebens werden daher paarweise verrichtet. Dieses Paaren ist die Ehe, und in ihr nimmt die Frau Antheil an den Geschäften des Mannes....Der kühne Vater Enfantin aber hebt die Freiheit des Weibes noch über die Ehe hinaus, und erklärt die Ehe nicht für geschlossen. Ein so freies Weib aber will sich gar nicht finden lassen, und darum sehe ich hier und dort Simonisten hinauswandern in den Orient, um das freie Weib da zu suchen[1].

This very interesting account of the Saint-Simonians and the 'free woman' shows the mixture of sympathy and amusement with which Mundt contemplated their feminist ideals. He did not deny that they contained much that was true, but he con-

[1] *Madonna*, pp. 319–321.

sidered them on the whole rather absurd, and was not at one
with Enfantin's views on marriage.

The story round which these various reflections were written
was the first and last of its kind from Mundt's pen, and shows
a startling enough progress when compared with *Der Bibeldieb*.
I believe that it was a true story in its essentials and gave him
an opportunity to use his peculiar gifts. He was incapable of
creating life-like characters, and his imagination was always
marred by childish and incongruous features which spoil his
original work. But he had enough insight to explore some
unusual temperaments, and enough of the creative spirit to give
to such interpretations the breath of real life. So that when
we find in *Madonna* a psychological study which bears the stamp
of truth, we are probably right in deducing that a real woman
sat for this portrait, and that with the exception of some improbable details, the story which he claims that she told him
was really the story of her life.

The author writes in the first person (we need have no hesitation in calling him Mundt, in spite of the attempt at mystifi-
cation in the 'Nachwort')[1], and the autobiographical element in
the book deals with the meeting between Maria and Mundt, and
their conversation in a moonlit garden. The narrow and gloomy
life, devoid of pleasure and romance, which she led with her
father, a surly old schoolmaster, was in the nature of a tragedy,
and she confessed to Mundt that she was deeply unhappy; by
temperament a child of this world, loving its pleasures and open
to all its delights, she was forced into the circle of a narrow and
uncongenial piety, for which a tragic experience in the past
made her peculiarly unsuited. Mundt's share in the conversation was painfully dogmatic; he delivered a long and not very
interesting disquisition on the virginity of the Mother of God,
followed by interminable reflections on Catholic paintings, music
and sculpture to which she is described as listening with passionate attention, and which are illuminating from our point of
view because they show so plainly the influence of Heine[2].

---

[1] *Madonna*, p. 435.
[2] Cf. *ibid.* pp. 124 ff. for painting; pp. 131 ff. for music; pp. 139 ff. for
sculpture; and pp. 347 ff. for the Gothic cathedrals.

The peculiar lack of humour with which he complacently unburdened himself of his views on philosophy and art at such a
moment shows how incapable he was of dissociating the budding
lecturer from the writer of tales; we can only hope for Maria's
sake that his practice was better than his theory and that he
did not really improve a romantic occasion by using it for
educational purposes. The lecture drew at length to a long-
deferred close on a more promising note, and ended in an
exalted farewell[1]. Incurably dogmatic, Mundt thenceforward
wrote Maria long letters on the lines of the lecture he had
delivered to her in the garden, and she sent him the 'Bekenntnisse einer weltlichen Seele' which forms the kernel of
this book.

When quite a little girl she had left the village in which she
was born and her strict and unloving parents to be educated
and brought up by an aunt who lived in Dresden. This aunt
was not only worldly and irreligious, but proved to be immoral
and corrupt. Maria's expensive education, her luxurious surroundings, her beautiful clothes, all these were supplied, as she
gradually came to realise, by an aristocratic voluptuary, who
intended to make her his mistress. From her childhood she had
always disliked him and suffered his caresses with disgust, and
when the actual moment arrived, she proved strong enough to
resist temptation and to make good her escape. For the situation held elements of temptation for her. Her education and
her temperament made her peculiarly susceptible to the appeal
of the senses, and there was a moment when she was nearly won[2].
The moment passed, she was able to overcome him and to fly
from the room down into the court-yard. In this desperate
situation she sought refuge with her former teacher, a young
theological scholar called Mellenberg, who had also given her
instruction in the Protestant religion unknown to her aunt, and
whom she had long half-consciously loved. This young man,
sunk in deep poverty and far from handsome, was considered a
sufficiently negligible figure to be allowed to continue his resi-
dence in this ambiguous house after his lessons with Maria had

---

[1] Cf. *Madonna*, pp. 141–149.
[2] *Ibid.* pp. 227–228.

ceased. She now rushed into his room for protection with the
almost inevitable result. He had loved her too for many years,
and she came to him in a state of mind which led to mutual
avowals made in a moment of high emotional tension. Next
morning Maria awoke happier than she had ever been in her life,
and poured out a prayer of thanksgiving to God. But her
happiness was shortlived. Mellenberg, overcome with remorse,
committed suicide; Maria fled from Dresden and found her way
home. Her mother was dead, her father very old and ill; she
took up her joyless existence with him, an obedient daughter
and a self-sacrificing nurse. At the end of the book she wrote
to Mundt that her father had died, and that she had found a
home with relatives in Munich, that she was happy at last, and
had been baptised into the Protestant church.

There are many details in this story which show Mundt's
curious imagination at work. Whilst analysing the central
psychological problem with great insight, he gave the outline
of the story a grotesque and fanciful shape. Had the house
Maria escaped from so easily been really the kind of house he
suggests, she would not have found the doors open to her flight;
nor would Mellenberg at any time have been allowed to darken
its doors. Maria's aunt was probably nothing more sinister than
a worldly and unscrupulous woman, ready to force her niece
into a marriage of convenience or even something worse; and
the count may well have used the means to overcome her resistance which are so vividly described. But it is difficult to
believe in the elaborate pains he took to educate Maria from the
age of eight in order to fit her to become his mistress, and that
these plans should have been already laid before he had seen
the child in question. Wealthy and aristocratic wrongdoers
know shorter cuts than these to the gratification of their desires.
I am inclined to think also that Mellenberg's suicide was another
invention of Mundt's and that Maria met with a more subtle
form of betrayal, the horror of a rigid moralist who has performed a deed which his conscience condemns. The solution of
Maria's problem finally, her conversion to the Protestant faith,
seems rather too apt an illustration of the theories in this book
to be accepted without scepticism. Psychologically it is an anti-

climax, and although life is full of these, this particular one seems extremely unreal.

But if we except the unhappy effects of Mundt's unaided imagination, the story of Maria's relations with the count and with Mellenberg reads like a real confession and is most interestingly told. The scene in the bare little study, following on the events in the luxurious room below, is a scene from real life, and Maria's feelings when she awoke next morning were not invented I feel sure by this clumsy inventor, but faithfully transcribed[1].

In telling the story of Maria, Mundt was in fact using this tale as an allegory for the epic of the 'rehabilitation of the flesh.' Maria, a worldly saint, has to fight against the asceticism of Catholicism symbolised by her parents on the one hand, and against sensualism on the other in the person of the count. Unnatural spiritualism and unpurified flesh fight, as it were, for her soul. In the union with Mellenberg we are shown the triumph of the flesh united with the spirit in complete harmony, and for a moment the battle seems to be won. But spiritualism claims Mellenberg for a victim[2], and the issue hangs in the balance once more. Maria, deeply unhappy, still fights for the freedom of her soul, oppressed by the one-sided spiritual teaching of the Catholic church. Mundt then comes into her life, continuing Mellenberg's instructions in enlightened Protestantism, and the conflict is finally solved by Maria's conversion to a religion which, according to Mundt, preached the harmonious union between body and soul; the 'rehabilitation of the flesh' was complete. Maria, as a worldly saint, betrays no conventional remorse in telling the story of her past; and Mundt, who plays the part of worldly priest, interprets it entirely to her glory[3]. It was this unusual attitude towards a 'fallen woman' which gave his enemies so powerful a handle against him, and which estranged the Protestant party who might otherwise have defended the book. For Mundt's position was not consistent with Christianity, however enlightened its followers. The famous

---

[1] Cf. *Madonna*, pp. 240–242.
[2] Mundt was aiming here at the pietists among the Protestants.
[3] *Madonna*, p. 187.

story in the gospel ended with forgiveness and an injunction to sin no more. But from Mundt's point of view there was nothing to forgive, since no sin had been committed; on the contrary there was much to applaud. In spite of his condemnation of Enfantin's theory of marriage, he held the same view of freedom in love; and the story of *Madonna* shows clearly that he was more truly a Saint-Simonian than he knew.

CHAPTER XXIII

THE SUMMIT OF HIS CAREER

(a) *LITERARISCHER ZODIACUS*

The year 1834 was certainly a year big with consequences for Mundt; it opened his mind to the promise in Saint-Simonism and introduced him suddenly into the presence of others who were also thinking the same thoughts. As far as one can tell, Mundt had troubled his head not at all with the Young German writers until the publication of *Aesthetische Feldzüge*; henceforward however he was on the alert, as is shown in *Schriften in bunter Reihe*[1] and particularly in the *Literarischer Zodiacus. Journal für Zeit und Leben, Wissenschaft und Kunst* which came into being under his editorship in January 1835. Mundt's personal contributions to this paper proclaim the same message he had already delivered in *Madonna*, the necessity for the 'emancipation of the flesh.' In January 1835 he boldly announced this programme in the article entitled 'Ueber Bewegungsparteien in der Literatur.' The theory of movement or progress in history which he had adopted from the Saint-Simonians was now applied to literature. Goethe and the romantic school belonged to the past according to Mundt. Heine was the first poet of the new movement, and as such of the utmost importance, for he gave voice to the despair of the times; but he was frivolous at heart, and his day was now over; as a poet he was dead, and his history of German literature had made him ridiculous in the eyes of Germany. We can leave him to the oblivion which is already overtaking him. Börne was treated rather more respectfully and with more affection, but it is obvious that Mundt relegated him also to the past, although with regret:

Wir sind es müde geworden, uns mit Heine, Börne und ihren Anhängern in dem blossen *Nichts* herumzuwälzen, und wir sind noch zu jung und zu stark, wir haben zu viel gelernt und gelebt, um uns mit dieser Verzweiflung an allem Inhalt des Daseins abfinden zu lassen....Für uns sind Börne und Heine bereits wie todt, diese Propheten haben wir überstanden[2].

[1] Cf. *Schriften in bunter Reihe*, October 1834, pp. 4 and 141.
[2] *Literarischer Zodiacus*, Leipzig, January 1835.

Either Mundt was really dull enough to fail to understand
the positive message in Heine's last book, a rather unlikely
supposition, since he had drawn largely on it in *Madonna* for
his theories of art, or else he was playing here a rather perfidious
part; and the second volume of the *Salon* which was to appear
at the end of this month, ten weeks before *Madonna*, was a
well-merited retribution. For the task which Mundt now declared to be facing the younger generation, and which he
announced with all the air of making a profoundly original discovery, was nothing but the 'rehabilitation of the flesh' in the
realm of art:

Die Aufgabe der Productivität in unserer Zeit ist keine geringere,
als die zu irgend einer anderen Epoche, ja vielleicht die grossartigste,
an der das Geschlecht, auf diesem heutigen Gipfelpunkt seiner Cultur,
zu arbeiten berufen worden....Es ist—wenn wir, ohne missverstanden
zu werden, so sagen dürfen—es ist eine *Wiedereinsetzung des Fleisches*
im Reiche des Geistes, eine Wiedereinsetzung, von der schon die St
Simonisten theils als falsche Propheten gesprochen, theils nach
einigen Seiten hin das Rechte angedeutet haben[1].

In the same number Mundt printed under the title 'Unterhaltungen in Prag' the story of the Bohemian amazons, with an
interpolation on Veit's book on Saint-Simonism, which serves
to emphasise a tendency more clearly discernible in Mundt's
attitude towards Heine, the desire to establish a monopoly in
the right interpretation of this doctrine.

The month of February brought nothing from Mundt but the
'Posthorn-Symphonie,' the opening chapter of *Madonna*, with
the rather absurd refrain 'Trarara! Trara! Trara!' about which
Gutzkow made cruel fun both in a letter to Schlesier and in the
Phönix[2].

Nor did the article called 'Windrosen' in the March number
add anything positive to the programme already outlined. But
by now *Salon II* was in his hands, and Mundt probably sustained
something of a shock. For Heine, it appeared, was also proclaiming the 'rehabilitation of the flesh'; Heine, whom he had
so summarily dismissed as bereft of all positive ideas; but then
he was proclaiming it with a difference. The unprejudiced will

---

[1] *Literarischer Zodiacus*, Leipzig, January 1835.
[2] *Literaturblatt zum Phönix*, April 1, 1835.

construe this difference to Heine's advantage, but the author of *Madonna* was convinced that his own views were infinitely more lofty and spiritual than Heine's; and he set himself the task to point out the mote in his brother's eye. The review which he wrote of *Salon II* in April is quite on a par with the general outcry which this much condemned book aroused in the contemporary press. Mundt began with an appearance of moderation, but he proceeded to pulverise the philosophical ideas, laughing at Heine's ignorance and deploring his frivolity; then when the victim was sufficiently discredited, he came to grips with him on the religious question:

Der Verfasser hat hier nämlich die *Rehabilitation der Materie* im Sinne, bei der er jedoch nicht über die flache und im eigensten Sinne *geisttödtende* Bedeutung der St Simonisten hinauskommt....*Rehabilitation der Materie* heisst allerdings das grosse Wort, welches zu lösen und zu verarbeiten die heutige Menschheitsepoche vor allen berufen ist....[1] Diese Versöhnung liegt in der positiven Offenbarung des Christenthums selbst, es bedarf dazu nicht erst des St Simonismus.... Wir bedürfen keiner *neuen Religion*, weder vom H. Heine, noch vom St Simon....[2]

In June 1835 Mundt's second article on Rahel appeared in the *Jahrbücher für wissenschaftliche Kritik*, and was devoted for the most part to the examination of her Saint-Simonian views. And here Mundt was able to quote an ally, and a very strong ally, in his attack on Saint-Simonism as a religion:

Aber gleichwohl will sie das, was der weltverbesserungslustige St Simonismus den modernsten Bedürfnissen hierin entgegenzubieten gemeint hat, keineswegs als die sogenannte *neue Religion* gelten wissen, und widerspricht überhaupt, dass dies, welchen Werth sie ihm auch sonst beilegen möchte, irgendwie *Religion* genannt werden könnte[3].

Mundt took this subject exceedingly seriously; he was indeed prepared to defend his position against all comers; and he proceeded to strengthen his defences against Heine by printing an article by Alexander Jung, 'Ausstellungen über Heinrich Heine,' in the August number of the *Literarischer Zodiacus*. This well written essay was composed entirely on the lines of Mundt's

---

[1] A reference to *Madonna* here.
[2] *Literarischer Zodiacus*, April 1835.
[3] *Jahrbücher für wissenschaftliche Kritik*, June 1835, No. 112.

previous review, to the confusion of Heine and the glorification
of Christianity interpreted according to Mundt, and contained
in addition a reference to *Madonna*. Meanwhile in the October
number Mundt reviewed *Wally, die Zweiflerin* in an extremely
critical fashion, and his chief complaint against this novel was
Gutzkow's sceptical attitude towards Christianity:

> Was Rahel in scheuer Metaphysik und halbverhüllten Prophezei-
> ungen nur bange angetönt...was die St Simonisten, die aus der
> Religionslosigkeit doch immer wieder eine neue Religion zu machen
> suchten, am geistigen Leben der Menschheit zur Herstellung einer
> glücklichen materiellen Zukunft niedergerissen; was selbst Heine
> noch mit Salonsanstand und gefallsamen Witzen vorgetragen...das
> nimmt hier ein blonder, verwegener Knabe, Namens Carl Gutzkow,
> wie einen Bagatellprocess leicht auf die Zunge, und speit es, wie die
> Kinder knisterndes Theaterkolofonium, in die Welt hinaus, um sie
> danach brennen zu sehen, und sich dann, ein kleines Nero-Ungethüm,
> vor Freuden die Hände darüber zu reiben[1].

Although Mundt condemned Wally and Cäsar as 'zwei Rechen-
exempel der Gutzkow'schen Absichten, welche aller Blutswärme
entbehren,' he did not waste any time exclaiming over the
'Sigunenscene,' nor did he accuse the author of immorality; he
was concerned alone with the denial of Christianity.

There are one or two half-jesting references to the emancipation of women and the 'free woman' in the *Literarischer Zodiacus*[2] in the same style as the allusions in *Madonna* and the
attitude adopted in the essay on Rahel, where he referred to
the Saint-Simonian feminism as an 'abenteuerliche Theorie'[3];
but an interesting article on Amalie, Duchess of Weimar, shows
that Mundt was in no danger of confusing the cause with its
too-zealous votaries:

> Für die Bedeutung des weiblichen Geschlechts hat in neuester Zeit
> eine glänzende Epoche begonnen....Die Frauen, sonst bloss eine
> Sache, müssen jetzt ihre Individualitäten geltend zu machen an-
> fangen! Und sind nicht wundersame Frauengebilde unter uns aufer-
> standen, die, nach weiblicher Sitte lange im Stillen verborgen, doch
> endlich mit dem Reichthum ihrer grossartigen Bildung der Oeffent-
> lichkeit angeheimgefallen sind, davon zeugend, dass die Organe ihres

---

[1] *Literarischer Zodiacus*, October 1835.
[2] *Ibid.* June, July, December 1835.
[3] *Jahrbücher für wissenschaftliche Kritik*, June 1835, No. 113.

Geschlechts nicht bloss für die Fortpflanzung berechnet! Man staune sie nicht als Ausnahmen an, die nichts Allgemeingültiges hätten![1]

He went on to instance Rahel and Bettina and to ridicule a question which was often raised at that time: Should women be allowed to write and to take part in literature or not?

Was ist denn Literatur? Liegt sie ausser der Welt? Ist sie etwas Unmenschliches? Gehören Beinkleider dazu, um die Blüthe menschlicher Cultur mitzugeniessen?[1]

A man who could write like this might laugh at the 'free woman' and consider the Saint-Simonians absurd, but he had not much to learn from them in the appreciation and admiration of women.

The year 1835 saw Mundt still repeating with great conviction the views expressed and implicit in *Madonna*, that is to say he was still teaching the essentials of the Saint-Simonian doctrine, the 'rehabilitation of the flesh' and the spiritual emancipation of woman. He was a more moderate feminist to be sure, and he called his religion Christianity, but these differences were exceedingly slight. Nevertheless they seemed great to him, and this led him to deny his fellow-thinkers instead of welcoming them. Both Heine and Gutzkow were rejected because they attacked Christianity, Laube was completely ignored, and Wienbarg alone found favour in the eyes of Mundt. And yet both Laube and Heine had much in common with Mundt, and one cannot help supposing in particular that he stood under the influence of Heine for all his scornful airs. Mundt was a solitary figure among the Young Germans, the fifth wheel on that ramshackle coach. Heine and Laube had gravitated naturally together, Gutzkow and Wienbarg were working in partnership; but Mundt, although he was of them was not with them, and yet he was not alone. There is unluckily no special place in this study for Gustav Kühne, who was deeply involved in the Young German movement, and who counted himself amongst its members in 1835; but his importance in Mundt's literary life can hardly be exaggerated. In 1835 he became editor of the *Zeitung für die elegante Welt*, a position which he held until 1842, and which he used to exalt his friend and to attack their

---

[1] *Literarischer Zodiacus*, July 1835.

common enemies with the most bare-faced partiality. Indeed
the portrait of Mundt, shamelessly flattered and much larger
than life-size, meets us on every page of this paper. Mundt was
by no means ploughing a lonely furrow; he had the most loyal
and energetic of assistants; he may seem a small and rather
puny figure when compared with the other four, two of whom
he had so recklessly attacked, but a little behind him, wary
and watchful, there stalked the champion bruiser, Ferdinand
Gustav Kühne.

(b) CHARLOTTE STIEGLITZ, EIN DENKMAL

With Theodor Mundt's *Memoir of Charlotte Stieglitz*, published in the late summer of 1835, we reach the summit of his
literary career. *Moderne Lebenswirren* had marked a step upward from the morass in which Mundt had hitherto had his
being; *Madonna* showed him already many feet above this
dreary level, and in the *Denkmal* he has at last gained the
hill-top and attained to vision. It is perhaps a lowly eminence
when compared with the mountains which others have climbed,
but the road has been steep, and it is not only from the highest
hills that we meet with inspiring views. The book which he
wrote about Charlotte has absolute merits, beauties and subtleties which greater men than he might envy him, and it has, or
should have, a place in literature to-day. His portrait of
Charlotte achieves real beauty and evokes the living woman
before the reader's eyes; the implicit expression of his love per-
vading the pages is touched with the wings of poetry; the
complicated motives which led to her death are analysed with
delicacy and penetration, and the tragic moment itself is
described with true artistic economy:

Sie stellte das Licht auf den Waschtisch und begann sich zu ent-
kleiden. Sie wusch sich erst, that ein reines, weisses Nachtkleid an,
und bedeckte den Kopf mit einem weissen Häubchen. Dann legte
sie sich, wie sonst zum Schlummer, in ihr Bett, und senkte hier, mit
einer furchtbar sicheren Hand, gerade mitten ins Herz hinein den
treffenden Stahl. Den Dolch zog sie wieder heraus aus der Wunde,
und legte ihn neben sich hin im Bett. Die rechte Hand hielt sie über
die Wunde gedeckt, mit der linken zog sie sich das weisse Bettuch
bis an den Hals herauf, und in dieser Lage, in der sie gefunden wurde,

gab sie sich, das Haupt ruhig zurück in die Kissen drückend, leise an ihr Ende hin. Kein Schrei, kein absichtlicher Laut[1].

There are innumerable murders, suicides and death-bed scenes already on the wrong side of Mundt's account. This one at least may be written down to his credit. There are no allusions here to dying swans or broken lilies; no false pathos, no romantic sensibility. His nature, as reflected in his style, had undergone a process of refinement which may be attributed to his association with Charlotte; whilst the terrible experiment designed to save her husband's soul made a man instead of her friend. Fate was ironical enough further to decree that Stieglitz' slight gift should wither beneath the shadow of this awful deed, but that Mundt, whose gift was no less slight, should for a moment be worthy of her act. Had Heinrich and not Theodor met her sacrifice in this way, she might herself have judged perhaps that it was not altogether in vain.

From the point of view of the present study it is interesting to observe that Mundt interpreted the life and death of Charlotte Stieglitz by the light of his Saint-Simonian ideas; not I think in this case in order to propagate them, but because he could not help himself. His own personality and feelings were kept rigorously in the background, but his interpretation of life he could not exclude. Thus we find him deploring the influence of a pietistic teacher on the mind of the sensitive little girl:

Das kleine Mädchen verging in ihrer starken Empfindung, wenn sie an Gott dachte, und ihre Weltanschauung zerriss in jene unheilvolle Trennung zwischen dem Diesseits und Jenseits, aus welcher der Pietismus sein süsses Gift sich saugt.... Und doch war der Gott, der erlösen kann, nicht jenseits geblieben, sondern er war in die *Welt* getreten, und gern und am liebsten hatte er die fröhlichen Kinder zu sich kommen lassen, die schon als Kinder das Himmelreich haben[2].

And he welcomed her later conception of Christianity as a sign of spiritual health[3]; whilst there are many passages which show clearly that in Mundt's view the relationship between Charlotte and Heinrich erred in being too spiritual and that the conflict between flesh and spirit was one which caused them both unusual suffering[4]. Stieglitz' malady was explained by Mundt

---

[1] *Charlotte Stieglitz, ein Denkmal*, pp. 308–309.
[2] *Ibid.* p. 4.   [3] *Ibid.* p. 67.   [4] Cf. *ibid.* pp. 14, 41, 301.

on the supposition of a conflict between body and soul[1], and
Charlotte he considered had moments when she too fell victim
to the same disease:

> Nur nach einer Seite hin trennte sich ihre Lebensanschauung öfter
> in eine Spaltung, die ihr manchen kecken Genuss des Daseins raubte,
> manche fröhliche Lichtseite der Existenz verfinsterte. Dies war die
> aus früheren Jugendrichtungen zuweilen wiederkehrende Stimmung,
> den Körper nur als den *Kerker* der Seele anzusehn, und das frische
> starkerhaltende Gefühl der Einheit von Leib und Geist, worin die
> Lust aller Lebensbewegung ruht, verloren zu geben. Daher in solchen
> Momenten das athemlose Ringen der Seele, die Riegel zu sprengen.
> Dies ist das Leiden, von dem sie selbst spricht in den nach ihrem
> Tode hinterlassenen Worten: 'Wir litten beide *ein* Leiden; Du weisst
> es, wie ich in mir selber litt!'[2]

Mundt therefore attributed some part of Charlotte's unhappiness to the conflict within her of the spirit and the senses, and
in particular to an over-idealistic conception of marriage; this
conflict indeed according to his way of thinking had a share in
leading her to choose death instead of life. He went even further
in his Saint-Simonian interpretation of Charlotte's death and
hinted at least that the subordinate position of women caused
her discomfort and pain which induced at times a feeling not
far removed from despair. She would sometimes express the
wish that she were a man:

> ...theils aus jener in ihr drängenden Freiheit der Gesinnung, die sich
> vor allem über die sociale Begränztheit und Bornirtheit des weib-
> lichen Berufs hinauserheben möchte zu einem kräftigeren und
> gedeihlichen Ergreifen des Daseins. Diese Stimmung, von der wohl
> jede bedeutende Frau, eben weil sie bedeutend, einmal beschlichen
> wird, gehört in die vielverschlungene Kette der Emancipationsfragen.
> ...Und ein Geschlecht, dessen Geschichte jahrhundertelange Miss-
> handlungen und Misskennungen aufzuweisen...wie sollte es nicht
> bei der geringen Selbstständigkeit, die ihm zum Grund und Boden
> seiner eigensten Entwickelung gegönnt wird, leicht in Conflicte mit
> seinen engen hausbürgerlichen Verhältnissen gerathen, wie sollte es
> nicht, je regsamer es das schöne Gewächs seiner Seele ausdehnen
> möchte, in Gefahr kommen, den Topf, in den es gepflanzt ist, zu
> sprengen! 'Denn was kann eine Frau *thun*?' rief Charlotte selbst
> einmal aus; 'sie kann höchstens vor Kränkung *sterben*!'[3]

---

[1] *Charlotte Stieglitz, ein Denkmal*, p. 301.
[2] *Ibid.* p. 313; cf. also pp. 62–64.
[3] *Ibid.* pp. 66–67.

Finally in defining Charlotte's death as 'die ungeheuerste Tragödie, die aus den socialen Verwickelungen der modernen Welt nur hervorgerufen werden kann,'[1] Mundt took yet another step forward and would seem to lay the blame at the doors of society:

Und was sollen *wir* thun? Wird es uns nicht gemahnen, einen tiefen Blick in unser sociales Leben, in unsere verirrten und unnatürlichen Einrichtungen, in die Zustände unserer Ehen, unserer Liebe, unserer Freundschaft zu werfen?[2]

This appeal which comes at the end of the book would be entirely out of place if Mundt had imagined that Charlotte's death had been dictated alone by those strange motives which have been generally assigned to her. It is an appeal for greater freedom of love, which he imagined, with a bitter and resigned melancholy, that no one would understand but himself. He believed, rightly or wrongly, that Charlotte had been in love with him, and that this had been a contributing cause in her death; and for a moment he visualised a society which would have an acknowledged place for such an affection. Her union with Stieglitz being almost entirely spiritual there was in fact no natural reason why she should not have belonged to Mundt, but society would not have tolerated such an arrangement. Mundt therefore hinted that part of the responsibility should be borne by the upholders of social conventions, thinking in this too as a Saint-Simonian.

Asceticism, the position of woman, and the unnatural conditions of social life, these three reasons given for Charlotte's suicide are reasons which Enfantin himself might have adduced. And although Mundt by no means ignored Stieglitz' part in the tragedy, and indeed gave it as the principal cause, accumulating besides other motives, such as Charlotte's lack of health and her nervous condition, nevertheless these reasons, reflecting a completely Saint-Simonian outlook, are no negligible part of the book.

(c) THE CATASTROPHIC YEAR

The year 1835 was a catastrophic year for Mundt. It had been rung in by a funeral march and it was rung out to the sound of a commination service in which his name was amongst

---

[1] *Charlotte Stieglitz, ein Denkmal*, p. 305.   [2] *Ibid.* p. 311.

those accursed. At the beginning of the year he had lost his
hold on happiness, and by the end of the year he saw his career
in ruins and was threatened with the loss of his only means of
subsistence.

The first blow after the publication of *Madonna* was both
prompt and shrewd. In April 1835 Mundt stood on the eve of
fulfilling a long-cherished ambition. He had obtained after some
delay the permission to become a teacher of the University of
Berlin; he had given his trial lecture at a meeting of the philosophical faculty on March 28, and only one formality remained
unobserved, a public Latin lecture to be held on April 29. But
when Mundt arrived with his papers under his arm he found the
door of the lecture-room locked against him by the order of
Steffens, then chancellor of the University. Steffens had received a copy of *Madonna* the day before from a member of the
'Obercensurcollegium' who were even then sitting in horrified
disapproval over this book. One can hardly blame Steffens,
who had only time to read the passages marked as peculiarly
dangerous, for coming to the conclusion that the man who held
such ideas was a very doubtful asset as 'Privatdocent.' It is an
opinion which might well be held to-day and Steffens could not
but feel the heavy responsibility of his position, the more so as
the copy was sent to him by a member of an official body.
He applied to the dean of the faculty who was helpless before
this emergency, and he then acted on his own initiative. It was
a measure hastily adopted in a moment of fluster, but it retarded
Mundt's University career by seven years and his bitterness on
the subject of Steffens is pardonable enough.

Meanwhile the 'Obercensurcollegium' drew up a report on
Madonna, placing Mundt among the Young Germans, whose
gravest crime they asserted to be the proclamation of the 'rehabilitation of the flesh.' It is not unlikely that Mundt himself
helped these amateur critics to form their first constructive
view of a body of men whom they had hitherto attacked singly;
for the main tendency which they condemned with such pious
horror is far clearer in *Madonna* than in any other works produced by the Young Germans, not even excepting *Salon II*.
Mundt's beginnings were obscure and colourless enough, but in

1835 he stepped full into the glare of publicity, holding forth for all to see a brightly illustrated copy of the doctrine of Saint-Simon.

Heine, Laube and Wienbarg had presented the same doctrine under the differing guises which their varying personalities suggested and modified by their temperaments and views; so that it became in each case the gospel according to Heine, or to Laube, or to Wienbarg. But Mundt, who set out to champion Christianity, produced instead so highly coloured a version of Saint-Simonism that the 'Obercensurcollegium' may suddenly have become aware of the bond in common between all four[1]. Be that as it may he was now a marked man, not only in academic circles, and there is a certain irony in the fact that this laggard in the chase had overhauled his comrades before they came to the fatal fence.

Indeed he was soon in the thick of the fray, considered generally to be a member of the school, and receiving a number of hard blows. Menzel made a notable exception here; he wrote to him asking for his support in the conflict with Gutzkow and Wienbarg, and never included him in his animadversions against the Young Germans. Mundt's answer to this letter and his reply to an article of O. L. B. Wolff in the October number of *Minerva*, two definite statements of his attitude towards the school, are the only ones of their kind before the catastrophe and are therefore particularly interesting:

Ich frage nicht viel nach der Kategorie: '*junges Deutschland*' [he wrote in answer to Wolff's article], die uns der Verfasser als einen gemeinsamen und prägnanten Ekelnamen aufzuheften gedenkt.... Eine Schule, eine Coterie unter irgend einem Namen zu bilden, läuft den Richtungen der jungen deutschen Literatur schnurstracks zuwider....Man wird sich zwar freuen, wenn man sich in der Hitze des Schlachtfeldes unwillkürlich Kopf an Kopf findet, aber von den genannten, unter sich höchst verschiedenartigen fünf Schriftstellern möchte schwerlich Einer für den Andern stehen und gänzlich gelten wollen....[2]

This calm and sensible view of the matter was also true as far as Mundt was concerned, and it is to his credit that although

---

[1] Gutzkow's name did not appear in this report.
[2] *Literarischer Zodiacus*, November 1835.

he was rather severe on Wolff's favourite Laube, 'der Dandy der jungen Literatur...ein Damenrevolutionair,' he took up the cudgels for Gutzkow's personal character and did not refer to his own unfavourable review of *Wally*. As a public statement at a difficult time this article, except in its attacks on Wolff, could hardly be bettered and leaves a pleasant impression of dignity and honesty.

The letter to Menzel is perhaps rather less admirable, for one cannot help wishing that he had expressed in it some dissatisfaction at least with the way in which Menzel was conducting his campaign. He certainly refused to be dragged into the quarrel but he was far from right in stating later that this letter was in the nature of a 'zweckdienliches und kräftiges Dazwischentreten.'[1] His one cry throughout was that Menzel should leave him alone. He had never entered into any alliance with Gutzkow and Wienbarg; the name Young Germany was a category nowhere adopted by him; nothing was further from his thoughts than any agreement with Gutzkow's principles; he and Kühne had always been badly treated in the *Phönix*; certainly he was not Menzel's enemy; he only demanded to be left in peace:

Hüten Sie sich wenigstens davor, die Grundsätze in meinen letzten Schriften mit dem, was Ihnen jetzt angreifenswerth scheint, zu vermengen, und die christliche und moralische Basis meiner eigenen Bestrebungen zu übersehn! Wenn es Ihnen unklar ist, wie Sie mit mir daran sind, so lassen Sie mich für jetzt aus dem Spiele!...Nur bei einem kleinen Theil des Publikums kann es mir schaden, dass ich das Unglück habe, zum jungen Deutschland gerechnet zu werden, währenddess ich ruhig fortfahre, meine eigenthümlichen Bestrebungen immer sicherer auszuprägen[2].

One thing at least is clear in this appeal which reads almost like a threat: Mundt was in earnest about his theories and was not going to allow Menzel to interpret them as he was interpreting Gutzkow's if he could help it. The philosophy he had preached in *Madonna* and in the *Literarischer Zodiacus* seemed to him so important that every possible effort must be made to save it.

---

[1] *Freihafen*, Altona, 1840, IV, p. 270.
[2] *Briefe an Menzel*, p. 214, dated November 15, 1835.

And when these efforts proved unavailing he wrote to Kühne in great despair:

Nicht den literarischen Krämer-Vortheil beklage ich ja, sondern den unleugbaren Ruin unserer liebsten Ideen[1].

Mundt applied himself to the task of saving what he could in an article entitled 'Tieck in Dresden und die literarischen und sittlichen Zustände in Deutschland' which appeared in the *Literarischer Zodiacus* on January 1, 1836, and which he enclosed in a letter to Rochus von Rochow begging for permission to continue the publication of this paper, and defining his position among the Young Germans:

Gleichzeitige Bestrebungen anderer Schriftsteller, mit denen ich zusammenrangirt worden bin, ohne jemals gemeinsame Verabredungen mit ihnen gehabt zu haben, sind mir offenbar ebenso schädlich, wenn nicht schädlicher geworden, als meine eigene Jugend und meine eigenen Tendenzen. Ueber die letztern bin ich dermassen mit mir zu Rathe gegangen, dass ich auf Ehre und Gewissen die Versicherung abgeben kann; es sei in mir kein gefährlicher und verderblicher Widerspruch gegen die bestehende Ordnung in der sittlichen, religiösen und politischen Welt vorhanden![2]

There is not much fault to be found with this letter, for Mundt showed only common sense in trying to correct the erroneous and damaging impression that he had been associated with Gutzkow; nor need we criticise adversely the assurance he gave about his political, moral and religious views. Politically he had never done much more than dream of a future republic and tilt at the legitimist party; his religion was, or at least he thought so, nothing more dangerous than a progressive form of Protestantism; and if his moral theories had certainly been in contradiction with the established order, it will be seen later that he was by no means prepared to recant. An uncompromising moralist would no doubt prefer this passage to have remained unwritten, but the struggle for his literary existence wrung the confession from him, and it is at least neither ignoble nor treacherous.

The article he enclosed consists of a spirited attack on Tieck's

---

[1] E. Pierson, *op. cit.* p. 41, dated 1835.
[2] O. Draeger, *Theodor Mundt und seine Beziehungen zum jungen Deutschland*, Marburg, 1909, p. 84, dated December 23, 1835.

novel *Eigensinn und Laune,* which was generally supposed to
be a satire on the social theories of the Young Germans. The
heroine, Emmeline, begins with an aversion towards marriage
and continues by falling in love with a coachman, only to fall
out again when he has been educated to become a fit mate for
her. After many disastrous love-affairs she ends her career as
the proprietor of a brothel; so that if Tieck did in fact intend
to chastise the Young Germans he was using the rod so much
beloved by Menzel:

> Dieser Dichter wollte jedoch zeigen, dass solche St Simonistische
> Tendenzen, wie sie der Gesinnung Emmelinens sich bemächtigt
> hatten, zu keinem andern Ziel hinführen, als zum—Bordell! Guter
> Gott! welche Tendenzen hatten denn Tieck dahingeführt?

So wrote Mundt with pardonable anger; he had, it must be
confessed, an easy victim in Tieck, and although some of
Mundt's insinuations and suggestions are not exactly endearing,
we can but echo the cry he addresses to the author of *William
Lovell:* 'Wie kommt jetzt Saul unter die Propheten?'

> Inmitten mancher schmutzigen Conflicte und widrigen Auswürfe
> unserer Tage muss man doch auftreten, und mit hochemporgeho-
> bener Hand und festem Auge an die allgemeine Sittlichkeit dieser
> Zeit appelliren.... Ich rede von den Frauen, den Engeln und den
> Richtern aller wahren Sittlichkeit, und von der Anerkennung ihrer
> höhern geistigen Natur, die unsere Zeit und gerade die neueste
> Generation unseres Volkes mit eigenthümlicher Liebe ihnen zollt.
> Die unsittliche Stellung, welche die Frauen in den Gesellschafts-
> verhältnissen einnahmen und einnehmen, so lange sie nur als Mittel
> und mechanische Vorrichtungen für die häusliche Existenz und die
> fleischliche Gleichgewichtserhaltung angesehen werden, ist in keiner
> Zeit so lebhaft empfunden worden und verneint, als in einem
> Augenblick, da die menschliche Sittengeschichte durch der Frauen
> geistige Freisprechung ihr Blüthenalter anstrebt.... Die heutige
> Schriftstellergeneration Deutschlands hat bei weitem sittlichere Ten-
> denzen, als die romantische Schule.... Bettinens Liebe, Charlottens
> Tod und Rahels dunkle Weissagungen sind durch unsre Brust
> gefahren[1].

Mundt's idealistic feminism, a legacy to him from Charlotte
Stieglitz, was a flag which he still kept flying above the fortress
temporarily abandoned rather than surrendered. It is the only
part of his former programme which found expression in this

[1] *Literarischer Zodiacus,* January 1836.

essay; the 'rehabilitation of the flesh' was passed over in discreet silence, and the author once more, and this time rather more definitely, dissociated himself from the category Young Germany. The high moral tone taken by Mundt throughout this article may strike the unsympathetic reader as absurd, if no worse, coming as it does from the author of *Madonna*, and his strictures on Tieck reminiscent of a conversation between the pot and the kettle. But although one cannot help smiling a little at his solemnity and grandiloquence, it would be an error of judgment to believe that he had been animated by frivolous motives when he wrote his novel. He wrote it in a cause which he believed to be moral; and if he were mistaken he erred at least in good faith. Tieck, more artist than moralist, had no such purpose in *William Lovell*, which deserves Mundt's strictures if we accept the view of literature as a handbook of politics, morals and religion which was the hidden cause of the whole Young German pother.

Even the sympathetic reader however will observe with regret that the sober and high-minded personage who wrote this essay is a very different Mundt from the excited and jubilant figure who made the hills re-echo to his 'Trarara' and fell down to worship his worldly saint. But what would that reader have? It would have been sheer insanity to persist along a path which led over so dangerous an abyss. Mundt stood still, moralised for a moment by the edge, and then turned aside. He did not by this act deny that he had ever trodden that road; and if he announced rather too often that he had not been in the company of certain suspicious characters found loitering on the same path, he was only telling the truth; he even tried rather uncertainly to suggest that they would probably reform.

The various statements which Mundt made from November 1835 to January 1836 have a common denominator of honesty. He was trying during these years to play for what safety might still be within his reach and yet not to violate the rules of the game. His first duty he conceived to be to himself in these straits, but not entirely at the expense of others. He was only a normal man with decent feelings, and not of that exalted mind which puts the cause first, the comrades next and self last of all. For his comrades, he left them to shift for themselves, and we cannot blame him much when we consider how hardly Gutzkow had treated him in the *Phönix*; he owed him no allegiance, and in his plain statement of the facts he even achieved something that might pass for magnanimity though it could never be mistaken for quixotism. For the cause; well, he lowered his standard in the face of his foes, but he did not deliver it into their hands; he concealed it on his person, and flattered himself that if he should escape it would escape with him. He was not cut out for a hero of romance, but he tried to act honourably and yet sensibly; a very difficult task; and if he did not entirely succeed, neither did he ignominiously fail.

CHAPTER XXIV

SEVEN THIN YEARS

(a) DETERIORATION

Until the year 1842 when Mundt made his peace with the government he dragged out a precarious and hazardous literary existence under the tyranny of a special censorship and with the disquieting knowledge that his movements were watched. It is not surprising in such circumstances that there should have been a great deterioration in the quality of his writings, but there was no corresponding check to the quantity of his literary output, and his articles, almanacks, journals and books form a very considerable volume during these years.

There is little indeed in these many and varied productions that will appeal to the lover of literature, whilst those who have been cherishing some hopes of Mundt on the strength of his performance in 1835 will with some regret see him slipping steadily backwards; for the stories which are to be found in *Dioskuren*, in *Charaktere und Situationen* and in *Der Delphin* show Mundt once again sunk to that uninspiring level from which he had struggled upwards in 1835. *Désirée's Lebensstufen*[1] if it is entirely innocuous is also completely meaningless, and disfigured by an unnecessary suicide. In *Charaktere und Situationen* we meet an old *bête noire*, *Der Bibeldieb*, complacently reprinted from the *Morgenblatt*, and realise with sorrow that Mundt is without the power of retrospective self-criticism. *Antoniens Bussfahrten* is a worthy pendant, and here the self-righteous critic of Tieck made use of the *motif* which had shocked him in *Eigensinn und Laune*, and which he himself had already introduced into *Madonna*. *Lebensmagie, Wirklichkeit und Traum* embroiders an even more questionable theme, and the disastrous influence of Hoffmann on Mundt is nowhere more apparent than in this pathological story of a sleep-walking hero, with its grotesque and ugly consequences of rape, madness and death. *Mutter und Tochter* which appeared in the *Delphin* of 1838 is less

[1] *Dioskuren*, Berlin, 1837.

offensive but not much more credible and scarcely more interesting. The same desperate desire for originality, the same
psychological absurdities, the same lack of sense and taste are
reflected in the play which Mundt published in 1839 under the
title *Komödie der Neigungen*[1] written in what he was pleased to
consider blank verse. This monstrous product of a sterile and
prosaic imagination shows all too clearly that if the epic muse
had never really smiled on Mundt, the dramatic muse had
no greater favour to bestow on him than a sardonic and
jeering grin.

The best book which Mundt produced during this period is
undoubtedly *Spaziergänge und Weltfahrten*, particularly the first
two volumes which recounted his experiences in London and
Paris; these are readably written and not devoid of entertain-
ment for the modern reader. His portraits of the famous men
and women in both capitals are skilfully sketched; his reflections
if rather too frequent and too long are at least in their right
place; whilst the pleasant geniality, the humane and benevolent
attitude of the writer do something to strengthen our weak-
ening sympathy and restore our confidence in the man.

For there is a further deterioration apparent in Mundt during
these years, a regrettable change in the not unworthy position
towards the Young Germans which had been his in 1835.
A decidedly bitter tone now makes itself heard, and vitupera-
tion takes the place of the former impartiality which he had
been at some pains to maintain. The first fault I fear was
Gutzkow's. He had visited Berlin in 1837 and Mundt had met
him in a most friendly spirit. He had even given a dinner-party
in his honour with twenty covers, and had done what he could
to express his sympathy with his fellow-sufferer; this effort resulted for a short time in what might best be described as a
wary concord. But it was not to last; Gutzkow, who never could
realise that the feelings of others might be as sensitive as his
own, published the fantasia *Literarische Elfenschicksale* in the
Telegraph from February to April 1838, in which Mundt and his
Berlin associates were made to play a ridiculous part. Most
hurtful of all probably and showing an uncanny instinct for a

[1] *Delphin*, Altona, 1839.

sore place in Mundt's heart was the manner in which Gutzkow interpreted Charlotte's death:

Man war auf den Tod der Stieglitz gekommen. 'Eine Culturtragödie!' hatte er (Mundt) gesagt.—'Nein, ich bitte Sie,' entgegnete Speculantia, 'machen Sie die Welt nicht confus! Gestorben ist sie aus Mangel an Liebe. Ihr hattet hundert Redensarten für sie und nicht einen einzigen warmen Händedruck, nicht einen Kuss!'[1]

From this moment onwards Kühne redoubled his attacks against Gutzkow in the *Zeitung für die elegante Welt* and Mundt began to pour out the vials of his wrath in the *Freihafen*; Gutzkow was not slow to make venomous reply; Kühne retorted with fury and bitterness; Mundt adopted crushing airs in *Spaziergänge und Weltfahrten*; Gutzkow was stung to make a final annihilating statement in the *Jahrbuch der Literatur* in 1839, which Mundt countered in the *Freihafen* by publicly washing his hands. It was a violent and distressing quarrel, and although the polemics were carried on with a spirit which makes these articles still interesting to-day, the reader feels at times as if he had blundered in between the combatants and were receiving the blows himself.

Mundt adopted a high moral tone in his articles, but with little justification; he and Kühne between them positively persecuted Gutzkow for many years, and one's sympathies are all with that fierce and lonely figure, blindly striking to right and to left. The *Zeitung für die elegante Welt* appeared daily and hardly a day would pass without some sneer, some diatribe or some unfair insinuation directed against the editor of the *Telegraph*. Page after page was devoted to fulsome praise of Mundt; Wienbarg was exalted at Gutzkow's expense; Heine was given a place in its columns for his virulent attack on Gutzkow and Wihl; *Seraphine* and *Blasedow*, infinitely superior after all to anything that Mundt was producing, were relegated to 'das Lazareth'[2]; it cannot be said that this devoted couple were not experiencing all the joys of revenge. Literary polemics are a depressing subject and there is no task less exhilarating or less fruitful than the attempt to determine who should be

1 Cf. *Gutzkows Ausgewählte Werke*, ed. Houben, XI, p. 249.
2 Cf. *Zeitung für die elegante Welt*, October 1 and 2, 1838.

made the recipient of the greater share of the blame. There is no need to follow this violent quarrel in detail, but it is necessary to note the lamentable change in Mundt.

(b) MARKING TIME

Although there are many references to Saint-Simonism during these years when Mundt's chief aim was to keep on the right side of the law, they are on the whole colourless and devoted rather to the industrial and feminist aspects of the doctrine than to the religious side. His most positive contribution is to be found in a long article on 'George Sand und die sociale Speculation' first published in the *Zeitung für die elegante Welt* and reprinted in *Charaktere und Situationen*, a careful review of *Lélia*, *Jacques*, *Indiana* and *Valentine* in the light of the social theories of the Saint-Simonians. This was a congenial task for Mundt, since it meant an analysis of the feminine mind, whilst the social theories of the novelist came within a province where he was very much *au fait*. The ideas which the Saint-Simonians had attempted to organise into a system, thereby hastening their ruin, had now become a part of the general progress of the world and were everywhere at work; this is the angle from which Mundt contemplated those ideas which he had once tried to systematise himself:

Diejenigen Praktiker, die heutzutage den Gedanken einer allgemeinen Völkerassociation durch Eisenbahnnetze ins Werk setzen helfen, würden seltsame Gesichter dazu machen, wenn man ihren Ingenieurfleiss durch den St Simonismus motiviren wollte. Man hat auch nicht nöthig, die Richtungen, welche sich aller Gemüther zu gleicher Zeit bemächtigen, auf eine Secte zurückzuführen, welche das erste Bewusstsein davon gehabt, aber durch den Blitzschlag der Wahrheit, der sie zuerst getroffen, eher wahnsinnig als vernünftig geworden war....Der St Simonismus, kann man sagen, hatte den Pantheismus auch auf die socialen Lebensverhältnisse, auf die Stellung der Geschlechter, und auf die Nationalökonomie anzuwenden gesucht.... [1]

From this point of view therefore Mundt interpreted the novels of George Sand and gave the key to the problem in *Lélia*:

Was will Madame Dudevant mit dieser entsetzlichen Geschichte, die sich wie ein Vampyr an unser Lebensblut ansaugt? Sie hat darin

[1] *Charaktere und Situationen*, Wismar und Leipzig, IV, pp. 200–201.

in schreienden Misslauten das wichtigste Thema der modernen Weltanschauung angeschlagen, die Harmonie von Geist und Körper[1].

There is another reference to the Saint-Simonians and the railways in an article on 'Rückblicke von Eduard Gans' reprinted from the *Jahrbücher für wissenschaftliche Kritik*[2], and elsewhere an allusion to their philosophy of history:

> Die andere, welche mit dem Morgenrothshauch der Zukunft malt, lässt diese ferne Aurora zugleich zur Brandfackel werden, an welcher Alles verlodert, was die Welt von bisher bestehenden Formen und Zuständen, von bisher gekanntem Menschheitsglück, in socialer, ethischer und geistiger Lebensbedeutung, besessen[3].

But the most significant aspect of *Charaktere und Situationen* lies in the fact that there is no new material to be found in it; Mundt was already beginning to repeat himself. This book is a collection of stories, sketches and essays from the *Morgenblatt*, the *Literarischer Zodiacus*, the *Jahrbücher für wissenschaftliche Kritik* and the *Zeitung für die elegante Welt*. Such collections have always been a feature in the lives of most literary men, but Mundt's constant and unblushing repetitions far exceed the usual custom, and the fact that they began thus early points to an imagination which had ceased to be productive. In this book we meet again the essays on Rahel and on Ludwig Tieck; there is nothing new to be learnt from these.

There is a reference to the 'gespensterhafter St Simonismus' in the *Delphin*[4] and several more in *Spaziergänge und Weltfahrten*, most of them the merest allusions[5], but it is interesting to learn that Mundt visited Carnot in Paris and had conversations with him on this subject:

> Herr Carnot beklagte sich öfters gegen mich, dass man in Deutschland eigentlich nur die kranke und chimärenhafte Seite des Saint-Simonismus vorzugsweise aufgefasst und dieses System, denn ein solches sollte es werden, dort nur an den Ausschweifungen abgemessen habe, in denen es sich bei einigen erhitzten Köpfen gezeigt. Ich versicherte ihn indessen, dass es in Deutschland auch sehr vernünftige Ansichten über den Saint-Simonismus gäbe, die alle Thor-

---

[1] *Charaktere und Situationen*, IV, p. 219.   [2] *Ibid.* IV, pp. 308–309.
[3] *Ibid.* IV, p. 353.   [4] *Delphin*, 1838, p. 262.
[5] Cf. *Spaziergänge und Weltfahrten*, Altona, 1838–1839, I, pp. 224, 231, 388; II, p. 88.

heit und Weisheit dieser Doctrin zu würdigen und daraus ein Prognostikon für die Zukunft zu gestalten wüssten[1].

But Mundt called on Heine in Paris, and wrote to Varnhagen von Ense after one of his visits:

Er hat noch einen Brief von Rahel gefunden, worin die grosse Verewigte sich auf eine merkwürdige Weise über den St Simonismus ausspricht und wird Ihnen denselben schicken; er gab ihn mir zu lesen, da es aber in seiner vertrauten Menage in der Rue Cadet war, und er unterdess mit seiner Dame scherzte, war ich sehr zerstreut bei der Lectüre. Er hat seiner Frau vorgeredet, dass Christus früher Archevêque von Paris gewesen und sie glaubt es wirklich[2].

A disappointing conversation, to say the least. Heine had lost in Rahel a dear and intimate friend; Mundt understood her better and admired her more than the common run of men, and all three were united by their interest in Saint-Simonism. A stimulating exchange of ideas or a revealing confession from Heine might have ensued. But the poet was not in the mood for this; perhaps he held in no high esteem the young man with the curly brown hair who had expressed such a light opinion of himself. Nor was he in the humour in 1837 to take Saint-Simonism seriously; it was disappointing him, and he covered his discomfiture with laughter. His wife was conveniently present, and whilst Mundt tried to study the letter of the 'grosse Verewigte,' Heine began to tease Mathilde in his light and frivolous way. And Mundt was easily distracted; he left the dead past to bury its dead and fell to listening instead. With incredible tactlessness he then hastened to describe this scene to Varnhagen, for whom it could certainly contain no element of mirth.

In *Spaziergänge und Weltfahrten* Mundt expressed himself very coldly on the subject of railways, which by annihilating distance destroy romance, and might bring about a stifling conglomeration of the peoples of Europe[3], so that his sympathy with the Saint-Simonians did not extend to this line of progress; whilst his definition of Christianity in connection with *Les paroles*

---

[1] *Spaziergänge und Weltfahrten*, II, p. 213.
[2] Dated May 23, 1837; from Mundt's unpublished letters to Varnhagen; by kind permission of the State Library of Berlin.
[3] *Spaziergänge und Weltfahrten*, I, pp. 108 ff.

d'un croyant is so fundamentally different from the definition in *Madonna* that it reads almost like a recantation:

Es liegt offenbar eine Bevorzugung der Armen im Christenthum, den Armen hat Christus gewissermassen ein Privilegium auf das Himmelreich gegeben, in das zu gelangen für die Reichen sich bei weitem schwieriger stellt. Daraus folgt aber nach dem Christenthum, dass die Armen arm bleiben sollen, weil sie sonst dieses Himmelsegens verlustig gehen würden....Aber was als die hauptsächlichste Lebensstimmung dem Christenthum im Sinne liegt, ist doch die Unterwerfung, die Demuth und das süsse Gefühl, durch das Unterdrücktsein auf Erden erst die rechte Anwartschaft auf den Himmel zu erwerben. Das Erste bei einem wahren Christen, ist es, zu *dulden*.... [1]

There is certainly no possibility of combining the theory of the 'rehabilitation of the flesh' with the other-worldliness, the poverty, the meekness and the love of suffering which are here considered as the most fundamental characteristics of the true Christian. Mundt had taken a long step backwards from his former position towards Christianity, and was expressing himself here in the language of the pietists whom he had once so heartily disliked. This did not mean however that he had abandoned the doctrine of the 'rehabilitation of the flesh'; rather I think he had come to see at last that the two philosophies were mutually incompatible:

Der Reichthum ein Uebel und die Armuth ein Fluch und ein Schimpf, das sind jetzt die beiden Angelpunkte der heutigen Weltansicht, die darin ihren klaffenden Spalt, ihre tiefste Lebenswunde aufzeigt. Hier kann nur Gott wieder helfen, in einem Zwiespalt der Weltanschauung, für den die alte Religion keinen Tropfen Balsam mehr übrig zu haben scheint [2].

But if he abandoned his defence of Protestantism, in his hatred of Catholicism and especially of the Jesuits, Mundt was still the same and was for ever to remain unchanged [3].

In another respect he was also the old Mundt. The position of women in society and the social conditions in which this position was apparent were still among his chiefest interests and were the subject of innumerable reflections throughout this book. The Magdalen Hospital in London, the *grisettes* in Paris,

---

[1] *Spaziergänge und Weltfahrten*, I, pp. 293–294.
[2] *Ibid.* III, p. 343.　　　　　　　　[3] Cf. *ibid.* III, *passim*.

Julie Bondeli in Bern, all these phenomena were considered by him from a feminist point of view, and although he had nothing to offer in the shape of a constructive programme, yet here at least he was certainly holding his ground[1].

Mundt's unhappy habit of vain repetition is nowhere more obvious than in the article entitled 'Heine, Börne und das sogenannte junge Deutschland' published in the *Freihafen* of 1840. It was written on the occasion of Heine's book on Börne and was also in the nature of a retort to Gutzkow's *Vergangenheit und Gegenwart*. With the exception of the story of Steffens and *Madonna*, and Menzel's letters to Mundt this article contains no new material for the student of the Young German movement. There is a long quotation from *Die Einheit Deutschlands*; another from the article in the *Zodiacus* of January 1835 on the subject of Heine and Börne; the articles on *Salon II*, on *Wally*, on Gutzkow and Wienbarg were also reprinted, and although there is a frank confession of the underlying idea in *Madonna* and in the end a positive statement of his literary programme, which tallies more or less with what he said in 1835, it is clear from his works during this period that his theme was now sterile, and from the way he expressed himself here that he had nothing new to say[2].

During the years 1836–1842 Mundt was doing little more than marking time. He still held that the harmony between flesh and spirit was the ultimate object of history[3]; but he was more chary now of attempting to establish this dangerous equilibrium in print. And it was not only fear which barred the way to another Saint-Simonian book from his pen; these ideas had ceased to stimulate his slight creative gift; as a dynamic force they had had their little day in his mind. But as ideas they are so simple and so easily expressed that unless they are to be transmuted by a poetic imagination like Heine's, they can only lose by being stated anew; and indeed they lose considerably in interest, force and freshness as they trickle monotonously through his writings during these seven years.

---

[1] Cf. also *Freihafen*, 1838, iii, pp. 210–211; and 1841, i, pp. 200–203.
[2] *Ibid.* 1840, iv, pp. 273–274.
[3] *Ibid.* 1841, i, p. 203.

(c) THE 'SOCIAL COUPLE'

Saint-Simonism ceased to act as a creative force in Mundt's mind in 1836, and the influence of Charlotte Stieglitz, much weakened by the rival claims of the censor, a god to be placated and propitiated at all costs, was finally overcome in 1839 by a far more formidable opponent, Clara Müller, *alias* Luise Mühlbach, soon to be Clara Mundt. Ironically enough it was Charlotte who brought Mundt and Clara together, for on reading his Memoir, she conceived a violent school-girl passion for the author; she entered into correspondence with him, sent him her first literary efforts, arranged a meeting in the spring of 1838, and married him in 1839. She was then twenty-three years of age, and he was thirty-one. Mundt was more than ripe to be picked by this eager and energetic young hand:

Wie soll man sich aber retten, alter Freund? [he wrote to Kühne in 1836] Man kann, man muss sich retten vor seiner Epoche! Man muss *lieben*! Ja *Liebe* ist mir und Dir die einzige Rettung! Thue Dein Tagewerk redlich, wie Du nicht anders kannst und darfst, aber liebe! Wirf Dich an eines Weibes Brust![1]

He had no need to follow this excellent advice himself, and to seek that female breast which he imagined waiting for such an accolade, he had but to open his arms and to receive the impetuous Clara. She flung herself into them and stayed there; in his own words 'sie hat sich an mein Herz geworfen.'[2] Clara made the first advances and was at the beginning at least much more in love with him than he was with her, a happy illustration of the entirely different experience which awaited Mundt in his second serious love-affair. Clara indeed was so different from Charlotte that they seem to have nothing but their sex in common. The one, all delicate and exquisite sensibility, was gentle by nature, spiritual by temperament, of a high courage and doomed to a tragic end. The other, blooming and robust, vital and vivid, energetic, warm-hearted and passionate, lived a completely happy life and survived her husband by many years. They each made an appropriate appeal to Mundt's heart. If he had sat at the feet of Charlotte, he found himself bene-

---

[1] E. Pierson, *op. cit.* p. 48.　　　[2] *Ibid.* p. 122.

volently stooping towards Clara; if he had languished sighs on his first love, he showered quite other caresses on his wife; if renunciation and self-sacrifice had been his lot in his friendship with one woman, fulfilment and satisfaction crowned his marriage with the other; if Charlotte had had a refining influence on his nature, Clara I fear brought about the opposite effect. It seems at least unlikely that if he had been engaged to Charlotte he would have written about her in the following vein; and yet this passage reads as if Mundt were comparing the two women and giving the palm to Clara Müller:

Die Liebe, welche mir dies herrliche und gluthvolle Geschöpf schenkt, hat den Ichor meines Blutes erfrischt und es liegt mir im Sinne, sie dauernd an mich zu fesseln, weil ich sie von Herzen lieb habe und eines solchen Umgangs für das tägliche Dasein, für Leben wie für Production, bedarf....Das ganze Mädchen ist auch erst 23 Jahre alt. Halb Wildfang, halb Schwärmerin....Sie ist durch und durch gesund, natürlich, kraftvoll und ganz Weib in allen Stücken; keine Spur von Kränklichkeit....Ihre Gestalt, die etwas zu viel Fleisch hat, nimmt sich etwas ungünstig aus, und setzt zum Starkwerden an, welcher Neigung man vielleicht durch die Emancipation des Fleisches einen andern Ausweg geben kann...unter lauter Scherzen bringt man den Tag mit ihr zu. Sie steckt voller Uebermuth wie voll Zärtlichkeit. Noch vor Kurzem hiess sie unter den Ihrigen nur 'die wilde Hummel' und ich liebe diese Art Geschöpfe. Dabei hat sie tiefe Einsicht in das geistige Wesen der Dinge[1].

This full-blooded portrait may not be to everyone's taste, and there may be few to echo Mundt's cry: 'Ich liebe diese Art Geschöpfe'; but it is quite certain that she suited him admirably in spite of the fact that he looked at her with eyes which in no way idealised what he saw. His remark about the 'emancipation of the flesh' in this context shows a regrettable coarseness; it is symbolical of the very great difference between Mundt's reactions to Charlotte and Clara respectively. In spite of the last sentence, added as an unimportant afterthought, it is clear enough that it was his natural man which arose to meet Clara and that the spirit played a very minor part in the affair. In turning from Charlotte to Clara, in choosing for his wife a woman so different from the one who had hitherto inspired his thoughts, he turned from the triumphant spirit to the ever-

[1] Pierson, pp. 121–122, dated 1839.

conquering flesh. In his private life if not in his public writings
he was now living up to the tenets of his creed. Gutzkow and
Laube were untrue to their principles when they married; and
Heine when he fell under the spell of Mathilde abandoned all
hope of the harmonious life he longed to lead; but Mundt, in
embracing his Clara, certainly betrayed no principles. It was
a union which Enfantin would surely have blessed, and which
had probably been consummated in a Saint-Simonian manner,
for Mundt's proposal of marriage certainly reads as if it came
after the event[1].

Another aspect of this marriage remains to be considered.
Mundt had united himself to an authoress, and an authoress
moreover who had taken the Young Germans as her models, in
particular Theodor Mundt. We find his conception of love
rampant in her books, and we meet in *Welt und Bühne* the same
devoted and soft-hearted lion who had already played so preposterous a part in *Der Basilisk*. She wrote with the utmost
rapidity during the whole of her life, achieving two hundred
and seventy-six volumes before death at last put an end to her
production. She had an exuberant imagination and the power
to tell a story, but her novels are almost unbearably sentimental and contain situations of the utmost absurdity; revealing
also much insensitiveness to the finer shades of morality and
the higher aspects of conduct. Crude, strong and sweet, full of
errors in taste, they may be fitly compared to the novels of
Florence Barclay and Ethel Dell, for they show the same vigour
and vitality, the same rank luxuriance of growth, as of a
creative power which has escaped control or been turned into
alien channels. And indeed Clara Mundt lived to produce and
to go on producing, to be doing, no matter what; there is something attractive in contemporary portraits of our authoress[2];
but all the witnesses declare that it was an extremely happy
marriage. The literary critics are inclined to shake their heads
over her deplorable influence on Mundt's writings, and it is
probably true that in marrying Luise Mühlbach he extinguished

[1] Thea Ebersberger, *Erinnerungsblätter aus dem Leben Luise Mühlbachs*,
Leipzig, 1902, p. 287, dated June 1, 1839.
[2] Cf. F. Lewald, *Meine Lebensgeschichte*, Berlin, 1871, III, p. 339; and
M. Ring, *Erinnerungen*, Berlin, 1898, I, p. 240.

for ever the faint hope that he might in the future equal or
surpass his 'schönstes Buch.' But if she dragged him down to
her level, it was no high eminence from which he fell in 1839;
and she certainly cleared the way for his literary production by
bombarding the king and the ministers with piteous letters and
dictating other letters of the same kind to Mundt, until in 1842
the special censorship was abolished and he became a free man
again, obtaining also in the same year the long-deferred lectureship at the University of Berlin. This lectureship he later combined with the curatorship of the University library, and henceforward he was beyond the reach of want. Both husband and
wife sank comfortably ever lower in the scale of literature, but
there is no need to follow them in that fall. 'Beide arbeiten und
haben ein Publikum—und noch dazu ein stets applaudirendes im
Nebenzimmer.'[1]

There is a particularly amusing aspect to this marriage; for
Luise Mühlbach and Theodor Mundt were giving in their union
an admirable illustration of Enfantin's theory of the 'social
couple.' Man and wife performing the same office in the community, playing the part of one social individual; behold this
pair of authors teaching history by the vehicle of novels; helping
each other to their sources, listening to each other's productions;
perhaps, oh muse of comedy, criticising each other's style.

For with the entrance of Clara on the stage, this rather depressing play which had latterly begun to drag, overbalanced
into comedy, and Mundt found his right place at last. He had
strayed into tragedy and been caught up into drama, but now
he was acting under his own colours, the twin hero of an entertaining play. He had written a Saint-Simonian book and had
then been forced into silence; but real life remained to him and
he was a true Saint-Simonian in this. And if a more sympathetic mood intrudes on our laughter and points back to a year
of promise which even held one achievement, we may indulge
that mood by remembering that comedy is not by any means
a book for 'Reading without Tears.'

[1] E. Pierson, *op. cit.* p. 185; Frau von Gr. to Gustav Kühne; dated 1842.

CHAPTER XXV

A DREARY ENDING

(a) VAIN REPETITIONS

Between 1842 and 1861 when Mundt died of a stroke after several years of illness there are three main tendencies in his writings. There is a steady flow of critical, historical and sociological works, in many cases representing the results of his lectures at the university; there is a last faint flicker of unaided imagination; and a combination of the two in a long row of historical novels. In all these kinds there are traces of his Saint-Simonian leanings, and in all three also that plagiarism from his earlier writings which had begun in 1837 and which now became so persistent that it might be called a mania. Many of his works contain repetitions for the third, fourth and even fifth times. In *Geschichte der Literatur der Gegenwart*, 1842, we find the article on George Sand, which stood first in *Die Zeitung für die elegante Welt*, then in *Charaktere und Situationen*, and which is to be met again in abbreviated form in *Allgemeine Literaturgeschichte*, 1846. The same applies to the articles on Rahel, Heine and Tieck, which last appeared in 1846 as it had appeared in the *Literarischer Zodiacus, Charaktere und Situationen*, the *Freihafen* and *Geschichte der Literatur der Gegenwart*. The *Kleines Skizzenbuch*, again, published in 1844 and containing a collection of sketches from the *Literarischer Zodiacus*, the *Delphin*, the *Freihafen* and elsewhere, went much beyond what is legitimate in such collections by reprinting many of these sketches for the second time. Thus 'Ein frommer Tag in Neuwied' had stood first in the *Literarischer Zodiacus* and then in *Charaktere und Situationen*; 'Kunstabenteuer' first in the *Zeitung für die elegante Welt* and again in *Charaktere und Situationen*; and we meet for the third time an old friend 'Kampf eines Hegelianers mit den Grazien' which had been reprinted from the *Blätter für literarische Unterhaltung* in the *Kritische Wälder*[1].

---

[1] Many chapters of *Geschichte der Gesellschaft* also appeared first in the *Freihafen* of 1844.

But this is not all; passages in one book are made to serve their turn in another; thus pp. 397–398 in *Geschichte der Gesellschaft* are identical with pp. 198–199 in *Carmela oder die Wiedertaufe*, whilst pp. 405–406 are a literal repetition of *Spaziergänge und Weltfahrten*, I, pp. 127–128. The worst and most glaring example of this unholy practice is to be found in *Carmela*, his last original effort, where the 'Friday and Steevens' episode is uprooted from *Das Duett* and transplanted bodily into the new novel without so much as a change of names; the absconding partner, his avenging friend, the absurd duel, they are all here looking more foolish than ever; one can hardly believe the testimony of one's eyes, but such indeed is the case.

Now it is peculiarly interesting to observe that if this self-plagiarism is at its worst here, because Mundt's weak imagination had finally given way altogether, it is at its second worst in the multiple repetition of those articles which had reflected his Saint-Simonian views. It may be deduced from this that he was still anxious to air those views, but that they had neither developed nor progressed; they were a positive part of his mental make-up however; one is sometimes tempted to believe the only positive part, and certainly the only interesting one. It was his preoccupation with Saint-Simonism which led him to the subject of his first historical novel, Thomas Müntzer, the anabaptist; and to a restatement of Saint-Simonian ideals in *Carmela oder die Wiedertaufe*, where the modern anabaptists with their respectable theories and their unprincipled practice may even have been intended as a satire on Enfantin and his disciples. Whilst the diary of the hero Sylvius elaborates once more those views on the dualism of Christianity as a false doctrine which Mundt had earlier published in *Madonna*, for the main thesis of the book is quite in the old style:

Das hohe Streben dieser Zeit ist dies, die wahre Wirklichkeit der ewigen Ideenwelt darzustellen, sie zu Form und Gestalt zu bringen, und die himmelweit gerissene Kluft zwischen dem *Geist* und der *Materie* auszufüllen durch das *Glück*, die *Freiheit* und die *Einheit* des Menschengeschlechts[1].

But the story itself, a tissue of unlikely adventures, has no

---

[1] *Carmela oder die Wiedertaufe*, Hanover, 1844, p. 211.

organic connection with this thesis and need not be more closely considered. This completely Saint-Simonian conception of the future of mankind was repeated again in *Geschichte der Gesellschaft* and was indeed the connecting idea behind the composition of this book and probably the reason for writing it:

Diese Natursehnsucht der Neueren...ist das charakterische Streben...ein neues Reich der Versöhnung zwischen Natur und Geist zu begründen, wozu der ursprüngliche Gedanke des Christenthums alle Elemente in sich trägt[1].

This conception, persistent and yet somehow completely sterile, is also stated as the main thesis of his *Aesthetik* in which Mundt makes use of some pages from *Carmela*[2], whilst the whole uninspired volume was probably written to illustrate the theory of the 'Wiedereinsetzung des Bildes' he had adopted in 1835.

But Mundt was no longer writing in the service of an idea; on the contrary the idea which he had once envisaged as a trust was now made to serve his personal ends, to help him in the composition of his books, in the routine of his profession. It was a convenient springing-board from which his tired mind could attempt those daily athletic feats which were necessary for the support of his wife and family. And although this unscrupulous tendering of old lamps for new gives no very favourable impression of Mundt's professional conscience, still something like a fellow-feeling for the author suggests that the husband of Luise Mühlbach did well to practise a wise economy of energy.

But the greatest disappointment which has to be faced here is of a different kind. Mundt gave three sketches of Saint-Simon and Saint-Simonism in his later writings; the first in *Geschichte der Literatur der Gegenwart*; the second in *Geschichte der Gesellschaft* of which an augmented edition appeared in 1856; and the third in *Allgemeine Literaturgeschichte*. He was the only member of the Young Germans to give an historical account of a doctrine which was preached in his own day and of a story which had unfolded itself during his youth. Here therefore one

[1] *Die Geschichte der Gesellschaft in ihren neuen Entwickelungen und Problemen*, Berlin, 1844, p. 50; cf. also p. 33.

[2] Cf. *Carmela*, pp. 211–216 and *Aesthetik. Die Idee der Schönheit und des Kunstwerks im Lichte unserer Zeit*, Berlin, 1845, pp. 11–14.

naturally hopes for a real contribution to the knowledge of the Young Germans and the Saint-Simonians, or at least of Mundt himself; all that first-hand knowledge in fact which only a contemporary can supply. There is nothing of the kind to be found. The very slight sketch in *Geschichte der Literatur der Gegenwart* was repeated almost word for word in *Allgemeine Literaturgeschichte* and has no distinctive features. It is the kind of sketch which is to be met with everywhere in the contemporary press, barren of special interest and devoid of inside information. The much longer history in *Geschichte der Gesellschaft* is almost entirely devoted to Saint-Simon whom Mundt treated with great respect, following in this a custom prevalent at the time, whose most typical German exponents were Moritz Veit and Friedrich Buchholtz. In this portion Mundt referred to Jules Lechevalier, *Religion saint-simonienne, enseignement central*, Paris, 1831, for his sketch of Saint-Simon's life, and also to L. Reybaud, *Études sur les réformateurs contemporains ou socialistes modernes*, Paris, 1840. He further alluded to many of Saint-Simon's works, amongst them the *Nouveau Christianisme*, with an occasional quotation, but there is nothing to prove that he had read these books himself and was not quoting from others.

The portion of space allotted to Saint-Simonism is relatively small; there is no sketch of the history of the school, but the *Doctrine de Saint-Simon* (1828–1830) is mentioned in a way which suggests that Mundt knew both the first and the second parts. The socialist and industrial aspect of the doctrine is adequately analysed; but in the chapter headed 'Die Emancipation der Frau,' which touches on the 'rehabilitation of the flesh' and the theory of the constant and the inconstant, Mundt refers to Moritz Veit as his only source and also copies several passages from his book without the formality of quotation marks[1]. His attitude towards the Saint-Simonians is extremely severe[2], whilst their theories on the emancipation of women were rejected by him with more scorn than he had ever shown before:

---

[1] Cf. *Geschichte der Gesellschaft*, pp. 353–356, and Moritz Veit, *Saint-Simon und der Saintsimonismus*, pp. 195–202.

[2] *Geschichte der Gesellschaft*, p. 283.

Die Emancipation der Frauen, wie sie der Saint-Simonismus zurecht gemacht, hat schon in alter Zeit, namentlich bei den Griechen, die ganze Stufenleiter ihrer Thorheiten und Tollheiten durchlaufen. Dies beweist die schon früher erwähnte Komödie des *Aristophanes*: 'die Ekklesiazusen oder die Weiberherrschaft,' welche noch heut als die erschöpfendste Travestie dieser Richtungen angesehen werden kann[1].

This does not mean however that Mundt had retreated from his own more moderate feminist position. It is to be found again towards the end of his life in *Pariser Kaiserskizzen* and in *Paris und Louis Napoleon*, undeveloped certainly, fixed and unmoving, but not abandoned or denied.

(b) A FOOL'S PARADISE

Mundt died when he was fifty-three, but he had begun to write when he was seventeen, so that his literary career covers the not inconsiderable period of thirty-six years. A dispassionate survey of this career suggests that he found in his conception of the historical novel the most appropriate occupation for his talent, and a task most congenial to his nature. These novels are devoid of literary merit; and in spite of Mundt's careful researches they do not evoke the spirit of the times; the power of summoning the past into the present was a witchery beyond his puny imagination; nor was he sensitive enough to feel his way back into the past. But as history entertainingly written, as readable chronicles of events, these novels might still have a modest place on the upper school-room shelves. His most positive gift, the reading of other men's minds, the faithful portrayal of their mental features, stood him here in excellent stead; whilst the fact that he was teaching history and at the same time unfolding a tale gave a legitimate scope at last for the double desire which had always plagued him. That he did not in these circumstances write better historical novels may be explained partly by the fact that he wrote them too fast, and partly I think by the suggestion that he wrote them too late. Had he discovered his peculiar niche earlier in life, when

---

[1] *Geschichte der Gesellschaft*, p 360. It will perhaps be remembered that Gutzkow referred to the same comedy in this connection.

Charlotte Stieglitz was alive, he might have produced something in this style still worth reading to-day. And yet in the light of the previous investigation it would seem that this influence alone was not strong enough to kindle the sulky fire that smouldered beneath the rubbish in Mundt's mind. She cleared away the rubbish, a very necessary task, but she did not feed the flames. *Moderne Lebenswirren*, written directly under her inspiration, was empty of all true substance. At this point however Saint-Simonism came into his life; it proved most inflammable material, and for a space the fire burned bright and clear. But the refining influence of Charlotte was removed too soon; the rubbish began to accumulate again, whilst the buckets of cold water provided by the government soon got the better of this not very dangerous conflagration. In 1842 the fire was out and Mundt spent the rest of his life in raking the cinders together and presenting a long-suffering public with pieces of dead coal.

From another point of view it seems certain that Saint-Simonism presented Mundt with the only religious, sociological and semi-philosophical ideas that he was ever able to grasp. Mundt, when he discovered Saint-Simonism, knew a moment of real illumination and spoke with an eloquent tongue. Nor did he ever really outgrow the religious doctrine of the Saint-Simonians, unlike the other Young Germans who took it rather like the measles. The emotional experience it brought to him soon faded away, but it remained the point of view from which he examined life, the only philosophy he had.

Now Saint-Simonism is undoubtedly a young man's religion; it is in the nature of a fool's paradise, beautiful only before life unseals our eyes; but we must all be fools if we are ever to be wise, and this is what makes one consider the Young Germans' declaration of Saint-Simonism a sign of promise, a mark of distinction above their fellows; they were looking at beauty though their eyes were shut. But such an occupation cannot detain the intelligent for long. One after another they left the paradise of fools, and refused to be self-deceived. Not so Theodor Mundt. In clinging to the Saint-Simonian synthesis long after the beauty he had glimpsed for a moment had vanished, he gave proof of the kind of foolishness which refuses to see and prefers to walk blindfold through life.

But it would be a grave lack of justice to conclude this study on a negative and critical note. Judged by any fair standard Mundt deserves positive praise. He was a man like thousands more, with a medium-sized intelligence, with no outstanding gifts of temperament and no high qualities of character. These are not the kind from whom one can demand great books and stimulating thoughts. But his heart was not quite so ordinary, and the adventure of his love for Charlotte made of Mundt a bigger man than nature dreamt of when she formed his mind. In one book at least he rose far above the average his kind are destined to produce; and even in the other, *Madonna*, he was on a level which such as he do not often attain. This book, with all its drawbacks, is a better book than *Wally* and almost as good a one as *Die Poeten*; and although it falls considerably below Heine's and Wienbarg's contributions, it is not unworthy to be considered with these. Saint-Simonism came to Mundt through his heart, and it came to the others through their temperaments. He was a normal man, and it came to him differently, in a more normal way; but it raised him to their side. And when we look back on his unpromising beginnings and contemplate his no less dreary end, we are forced to acknowledge that the achievement of 1835, coming from a man of such poor quality, was a great achievement indeed.

PART VII
WIENBARG AND SAINT-SIMONISM

CHAPTER XXVI

THE SAINT-SIMONIAN INFLUENCE

(a) LUDOLF WIENBARG

Ludolf Wienbarg was only a few years younger than Heine and he was converted to Saint-Simonism twelve months before Mundt; chronologically therefore his right place in this study would seem to be after Karl Gutzkow. But I have placed him last, partly in order to emphasise the many differences between him and the others, partly from a wish, familiar to most of us in our nursery days, to save something good for the end. For to turn from Laube, Gutzkow and Mundt to Ludolf Wienbarg is to experience something in the nature of an escape; to climb up beside a noisy, chattering, sometimes roaring waterfall, and to find at the turn of a path a quiet mountain tarn reflecting the hills. The contrast is great, and indeed, although Wienbarg is a man, one might almost say, of one book only, nevertheless the quality of his thought and the beauty of his style place him apart from the rest; just below Heine as an artist in prose; above him perhaps in purity of intention, in an indefinable nobility, which pervades like a perfume the few pages he wrote during the short flowering of a mind doomed to bear no fruit. For the tragic chord which is so insistently recurrent in the story of the Young Germans dominates in the life of Wienbarg to an extent which would be hardly bearable, were it not for the fact that his later life is shrouded in obscurity, so that we may contemplate through the softening mists which becloud it his lamentable and unhappy end.

The external happenings of Wienbarg's life, of which our knowledge is meagre and fragmentary[1], are subordinate in importance to the central secret, the hidden malady of his mind. Although this did not declare itself fully until 1868 under the

[1] Cf. G. Kühne, *Portraits und Silhouetten*, Hanover, 1843, pp. 179 ff., for an autobiography of Wienbarg written in 1838; and Houben's admirable and sympathetic biography in *Jungdeutscher Sturm und Drang*.

guise of acute melancholia with recurrent attacks of persecution mania[1], it was latent probably from his birth and traces of it can be found in his earliest writings: in unfinished sentences and mis-spelt words; whilst the failing of his mental powers is all too sadly apparent after 1835. It is happily no part of the present study to follow the depressing story of Wienbarg's intellectual decline; but perhaps it is necessary to glance a little more closely at the moral bankruptcy which accompanied the author's tragic failure to honour his intellectual cheques dated in 1834. The act of artistic creation produces a state of nervous exhaustion which often leads to the use of stimulants or narcotics according to the nature of the artist. If the creative act is a prolonged one the temptation to use stimulants to assist the flagging nervous energy may prove irresistible, although the stronger the creative power, the less the need for such outside aids. Now Wienbarg was deserted in the heyday of his maturity by a power of which he had just learnt the intoxicating strength; he would sit down to write and find the dead hand of inhibition lying inertly on his spirit. He called this phenomenon 'der Scheu des Wortes,' attempting to deceive himself by a poetic fiction; but it was not the fear of the written word which obsessed him, it was the almost insuperable difficulty of finding words in which to clothe the thoughts which thus escaped him. And yet when the inhibition lifted, beautiful words and revealing images came crowding into his mind. Wine is the sovereign cure for inhibitions and Wienbarg took to drink. Gutzkow complained that as early as 1835 he was continually in the taverns; we may picture him talking to an admiring circle, remembering certainly those other young listeners in Kiel, tasting once more the moment of his supreme glory, wit in his utterance and inspiration on his tongue. Memories of Dick Steele and Charles Lamb will ensure a gentle judgment here. But wine conquers other restraints and does not only free the impulses of the mind. In a private letter to Liesching Gutzkow asserted bitterly enough that Wienbarg frequented brothels, and a spy reported to

---

[1] C. F. van Vleuten in an article entitled *Wienbarg-Pathographie, Die Literatur*, Stuttgart, March 1925, states that Wienbarg was a clear case of dementia praecox.

Metternich that in spite of his well-known strength of character he was notoriously immoral.

He was thus the only one of the Young Germans who at all resembled those ugly sketches of moral degradation which Hengstenberg, Menzel and their consorts fashioned with such gusto. Heine at one time led a light life, but fastidiously; Laube in his youth a gay one; Gutzkow was not altogether faithful to the marriage bond, but his gloomy quest for happiness could not fairly be called immorality; Mundt was completely and contentedly uxorious and most reassuringly respectable. Wienbarg alone sought inspiration from dangerous sources and looked for beauty where it was least likely to be found. And yet his essential nobility of character remained unspoiled; his latent insanity torturing him in the cruel guise of mental sterility led him down dark and slippery ways, but he trod them, we must suppose, with his head in the clouds; for in his rare and rarer utterances we still find beauty, mystical sometimes and not a little strange, but nothing unworthy, nothing to regret. Like water bubbling up in a desert, the stream of his inspiration dwindled gradually away, then was lost in the drifting sands of his mind, but even the last drops were clear.

There is a quality in Wienbarg's writings which results in an immediate contact between him and his readers of the twentieth century. We seem to know him at once and to understand him with no effort, although the material at our disposal is depressingly slight. The persuasive quality of his style is in part responsible for this, but also I think the nature of his thought. He was different from the other Young Germans in many ways; but his fundamental difference lay in the fact that their aim was social and political freedom whilst his aim was beauty. Politically and even socially Europe has changed very much since the days when they wrote in the cause of liberty. Humanity has progressed beyond them and in interpreting them we must use the historical tense. But Wienbarg's ideal of beauty is independent of time and change; it has been shared and will be shared by some minds in all the ages past, present and to come. And this is why the fragmentary writer, who accomplished so little, stands out in bolder relief from the background common to them all.

At the very root of his nature, and part of his inmost being, was a fervent love of his country, which found a practical expression when he fought for Germany against Denmark, and in the pamphlets which this war inspired him to write; whilst Brenning tells us that in the confused welter of papers left behind him when he died, hardly a crumpled leaf among them all but bears witness to the passionate love of a fatherland which had treated this son so ill[1].

An almost mystical counterpart to the love of his country was his love for the sea, and for the stormy North Sea in particular, which symbolised to his mind the soul of the northern peoples, and whose troubled beauty appealed to him more intimately than the blue seas of Greece:

Woher dieser Zauber? Der Süden kennt ihn nicht, der Franzose fühlt ihn nicht, der Grieche ahnte ihn nicht. Ueber seiner ionischen See, seinem Mittelmeer schwebt epische Ruhe—blauer Himmel, blaue Fluth, glückliche Insel, goldene Aepfel, hesperidische Gärten. Die Nordsee ist lyrisch, leidenschaftlich, voll Klippen, Untiefen, Stürme, Strudel, Gefahren, Abentheuer. Im ionischen Meer sieht der Schiffer von Insel zu Insel den wirthlichen Rauch der Hutten aufsteigen, in der Nordsee schweift der Blick über eine unermessliche wüste Fläche, und Land und Menschen ahnen sich nur in weiter Ferne. Im ionischen Meer ziehen die Schiffe wie stille Schwäne durch die Fluth, in der Nordsee kreisen sie wie Möven mit flatternden Flügeln am Horizont.

In beiden lebt die Seele der Menschen und die Seele des Nordens ist, wie ihre See, wetterwendisch, ungestüm, sehnsüchtig, sich verlierend ins Unermessliche. Die Nordsee wird nie zum Mittelmeer und der Nordmensch nie ein Grieche trotz Winckelmann und Goethe.

Ich habe die See in allen ihren Zuständen und Beleuchtungen gesehen, bei Auf- und Untergang der Sonne, bei Mond- und Sternenlicht, im hellen Glanz des Mittags, leise athmend, wie im Traum, brüllend wie in der Wuth, gähnend wie ein nordischer Riese, der Langeweile fühlt, mit Schweiss und Schaum bedeckt, als käme sie aus dem Kampf, himmelhochjauchzend, zu Tode betrübt, immer anders, immer dieselbe[2].

Even in Heine's *Nordsee* there is no passage to equal this wonderful description of the restless and storm-tossed beauty of the wild North Sea.

[1] E. Brenning, *Ludolf Wienbarg's Nachlass, Euphorion*, Bamberg, 1908, xv, p. 536.

[2] *Holland in den Jahren* 1831 *und* 1832, Hamburg, 1833, i, pp. 45–46.

Another of Wienbarg's enthusiasms will have become clear from the passage quoted above; his beauty-loving mind was enchanted by the serene and sunny skies of ancient Greece. But he contemplated this past glory with the eyes of an alien race; the classical ideal, he maintained, could never find a home among the nations of the north; yet however courageously he was prepared to banish it from the future of his country, the following lament on the death of Goethe shows that he did so with regret:

Goethe ist gestorben.... Ausgeleuchtet hat die Sonne seines Jahrhunderts, das schöne griechische Kunst- und Südlicht, das Winckelmann am deutschen Himmel heraufführte; es ist verflogen, wie sein Wiederspiel, das kalte Fouqueische Nordlicht und wie der romantische Mondschein der Schlegelianer und Tieckianer, der, Gott weiss, in welcher alten deutschen Burg- und Klosterruine steckt und verwittert. Wer aber führt uns wie Winckelmann die Sonne des neuen Jahrhunderts am deutschen Himmel herauf, wer ist der Sonnengott des neuen Tages, der, gleich Goethe, im goldenen Sonnenwagen sitzt und die schnaubenden Rosse spielend bändigt? Hähne genug, die den Tag ankrähen, die auf dem faulen Mist des Eigendünkels dem alten Tage und der untergegangenen Sonne spöttisch nachkrähen, Häute genug, die fröstelt und schauert, Nasen genug, die Morgenluft wittern, Spreu genug, die im Morgenwinde, im französischen, umherfliegt[1].

In these few passages are heard the cadences of a voice beside which Laube's is shrill, Gutzkow's harsh and Mundt's monotonous; whilst a deeper seriousness, a more impersonal melancholy, differentiate Wienbarg from Heine, even where they are most alike, in their love of the sea. But not only does he express himself in a different language, he has other things to say. There is no sign of that windy liberalism apparent in the early writings of his colleagues; the well-worn *clichés* are absent, the feverish political interest is to seek. For his main preoccupation was with beauty; he did homage to it in the past, he sought it by the waves of the sea; he worshipped its incarnation in Goethe, as he fired the last salute over the great pagan's grave. Then he turned towards the future, scanning the empty horizon for a sign that beauty should come again. And the sign was granted to him, but it came from the west.

[1] *Holland in den Jahren* 1831 *und* 1832, I, pp. 79–80.

(b) THE APOSTLE OF HEINE

Wienbarg would probably have been both surprised and annoyed had anyone suggested in 1833 that his lectures on aesthetics were in any way inspired by Saint-Simonism. What slight knowledge he had of this doctrine was most likely derived from hearsay and from the newspapers; and his only comment until 1835 took the form of a comparison between the Saint-Simonians and the Anabaptists made in favour of the latter[1]. Wienbarg's prejudice against the French was strong enough to make him suppose that no good thing could come out of Paris[2], and his lack of interest in Enfantin was most assuredly unfeigned. But it was written that not one of the Young German writers should be proof against the spell of the Saint-Simonian gospel; Wienbarg was drawn blindfold into the circle which the others had entered with open eyes. And fate chose Heinrich Heine for her decoy.

They had met in Hamburg in 1830, and Wienbarg had early been a lover of his lyric poems. But although the influence of the *Reisebilder* is clearly apparent in *Holland*, his warmer enthusiasm was not expressed until after the publication of *Zur Geschichte der neueren schönen Literatur in Deutschland*. Not that he greeted this particular work with any immoderate expressions of regard. He reserved his highest praise for the prose of the *Reisebilder*, and treated the book on German literature with a certain coldness which is obviously accounted for by his uncompromising patriotism[3].

Nevertheless this book, which had gone straight to Laube's heart, had for Wienbarg the strength of a twofold appeal; in form and in content it satisfied the desire for beauty which was the dominant impulse of his spiritual nature. The lightness, the grace and the wit with which Heine played on the hitherto formidable instrument of German prose were not lost on the impressionable senses of the younger man. But it was not only and not chiefly the quality of Heine's style which appealed to him in this book, it was also the prophetic spirit dreaming on

---

[1] *Holland in den Jahren 1831 und 1832*, I, pp. 153–154.
[2] Cf. *Wanderungen durch den Thierkreis*, Hamburg, 1835, pp. 106 and 120.
[3] *Aesthetische Feldzüge*, Hamburg, 1834, p. 289.

days to come and revealing the secret of the new form in which beauty should rise again. In the very heart of *Aesthetische Feldzüge* is to be found the 'rehabilitation of the flesh,' and there is no cause to regret this; for Wienbarg as well as for Heine it meant the resurrection of beauty, and for the former in particular it had no other meaning than this.

The task which Wienbarg set himself in *Aesthetische Feldzüge* was to conquer for art its rightful place as a manifestation and expression of national life. The divorce between life and art in this sense, perhaps one of the most salient features of modern times, was to his mind disastrous for both; and he was bold enough to declare that national feeling must precede the feeling for beauty, and that political education was the only true basis of aesthetic appreciation[1]. The historical periods during which such a union had been consummated had received from the Saint-Simonians the clumsy label 'époques organiques'; and although Wienbarg never used this term, there can be little doubt that he owed his conception of history to Bazard, probably at second hand. For he distinguished also two periods in the course of the human race in which life, religion and art had been united by a common spirit, resulting in complete harmony between private beliefs and public institutions, and reflected in undying works of art: pre-Socratic Greece and the Middle Ages[2]. And he also accounted for the decay of these periods in the Saint-Simonian manner; the positive spirit which animated them died leaving a dead body of institutions and dogma behind it; and these were attacked in the first case by Christianity, in the second by Martin Luther[3]. The tragedy of modern times lies in the fact that although the spirit of the Middle Ages is dead, its bodily ruins still cumber the ground, waiting to be swept away, choking the new life and retarding its growth[4]. Not one of the Young Germans with the exception of Heine felt so strongly and yet so hopefully as Wienbarg the

[1] *Aesthetische Feldzüge*, pp. 8–9.
[2] *Ibid.* pp. 22–23. This view is also to be found in embryo in Heine's *Reisebilder*; cf. Elster, III, pp. 92–93, 304.
[3] *Ibid.* pp. 34–37; this is one of the main theses of *Zur Geschichte der neueren schönen Literatur in Deutschland.*
[4] *Ibid.* pp. 20–21.

melancholy character of that age of transition into which they
were born, a present labouring under the curse of a dead past
which would not bury its dead, yet with a new life stirring
beneath its surface[1]. This attitude towards the present is
strongly reminiscent of Bazard's eloquent description of the
modern critical epoch, and is implicit throughout in *Zur
Geschichte der neueren schönen Literatur in Deutschland*; whilst
the following characterisation of the Greek and Christian philosophies of life follows the Saint-Simonian lines exactly and is
to be found again in Heine's book on the romantic school, and
also, it may be remembered, in the *Reisebilder*:

Ueber dem alten Götterhimmel wölbte sich ein neuer Himmel, und
wenn einst der sinnlich glückliche Grieche sich von seinen Göttern
selbst über die irdische Seligkeit beneiden liess, so schlug nun die
Sehnsucht ihren Blick in die Höhe und die himmlische Seligkeit
überstrahlte die irdische, welche keine mehr war, sondern eine Prüfung, ein vergänglicher Wandel, ein Leben im Fleisch, in dem das
Böse wohnt und gekreuzigt werden muss, damit das Leben im Geist
beginne[2].

Further when it came to the characterisation of classical and
romantic art, Wienbarg contented himself with a simple paraphrase of Heine's brilliant analysis of the main difference between them, emphasising the symbolism of the latter compared
with the straightforward presentation of ideas by the classical
artists[3]. All this is enough to show that if Heine had never
written about religion and art, Wienbarg's lectures might have
taken a different course; for even his main idea, the dependence
of art on the prevalent philosophy of life, with its consequent
denial of an absolute standard of beauty, had been expressed
by Heine before him, and illustrated by much the same examples[4].

But Wienbarg's book was no mere academic treatise, written
to illustrate some theories of Heine's, it was an aesthetic battle
fought in the name of the future against the cohorts of the past,
and here his debt to the poet is of almost incalculable importance.
For had it not been for Heine's message in his book on the

---

[1] *Aesthetische Feldzüge*, p. 115.
[2] *Ibid.* p. 110; cf. also p. 124.
[3] *Ibid.* pp. 23–25; cf. Elster, v, p. 224.
[4] *Ibid.* pp. 129–131; cf. Elster, v, pp. 250–251.

romantic school Wienbarg would probably never have delivered his particular challenge. He would have fought for beauty no doubt since it was his nature to do so; but it is questionable at least whether he would have attained unaided to the vision which is the positive part of the book, and which had been revealed to Heine in his turn by another dreamer of dreams.

The banner which Wienbarg unfurled before the eyes of those students who thronged to his lecture-room in Kiel had for its device the progress of humanity foretold by Bazard and Enfantin; and when he cast the horoscope of the future they may well have swayed before his eloquence as reeds before the wind. For the muted and mournful opening was touched with the first faint stirring of a trembling hope, gradually growing more confident, more courageous, more insistent, until the final triumphant affirmation swept all doubts aside; and the young men before him saw a vision of the future well worth striving for, whilst the modern reader becomes enmeshed in the web of the past and feels his pulses stirring to the rhythm of that scene:

Ueber unserer Asche wird sich ein neues europäisches Griechenthum erheben, angemessen dem geistigen Fortschritt, den das Christenthum vorbereitet hat. Nur zweimal hat der Erdball die Erscheinung erlebt, dass Menschen in sinnlich-geistiger Eintracht organische Monaden bildeten und ein Leben der Frische und Gesundheit führten. Von dem Einen berichtet uns die Sage des Paradieses, von dem Andern die Geschichte Griechenlands. Indien vernichtete das Sinnliche, Palästina überhob das Geistige, zwischen beiden blühte Griechenland wie zwischen zwei Abgründen, deren bodenlose Tiefe es ahnungslos mit Rosen und Lorbeeren überstreute. Aber die Menschheit musste hinüber und dem germanischen Stamm war es vorbehalten, in die tiefste Tiefe hinabzuschauen und selig den zu preisen, 'der lebt im rosigen Licht.' Dem germanisirten Europa bleibt die dritte Entwicklungsstufe der Menschheit vorbehalten, in der das Sinnliche durchgeistigter wie bei den Griechen, das Geistige durchsinnlichter wie bei den Christen zur Erscheinung kommt. So gleicht das Menschengeschlecht in seiner geschichtlichen Entwicklung einem wahren Organismus, einer erhabenen Pflanze, die von Zeit zu Zeit in neue Knoten anschliesst, sich zusammenschliesst, um sich desto kräftiger wieder zu entfalten[1].

This dream of a better Greece and a happier Christianity has lost nothing of its force and has gained in beauty by coming to

[1] *Aesthetische Feldzüge*, pp. 125–126.

Wienbarg through Heine instead of coming direct from Enfantin. And he looked to the Germanic peoples of Europe to inaugurate the third epoch in the progress of humanity, a characteristic addition born of that resolute confidence in his race which was his own peculiar gift. Nor does he seem to be aware that the prophecy of which he was the mouthpiece had arisen among a Latin people and been handed on to him by a Jew. Yet in this very lecture he repeated the Saint-Simonian rallying-cry 'emancipate the flesh.' It occurred in a quotation from Heine, and Wienbarg paused neither to comment nor to explain, but passed on as if this startling formula were a self-evident truth. This would seem as if he did not know that it originated from the 'ridiculous Anabaptists'; but it also shows to how great an extent he was imbued with the spirit of Saint-Simonism, for the most hardy proselytes could rarely refrain from some ennobling definition when using this term for the first time[1].

Wienbarg's dream of beauty, inspired by Heine, was therefore in the main the same dream which was even then beguiling many a tedious hour for Enfantin in Sainte-Pélagie; nor did he recoil from the first step towards its realisation, the 'emancipation of the flesh.' And yet there was a fundamental difference between them, which becomes apparent when Wienbarg approaches the subject of the new morality. Following once more in the footsteps of Heine he rejected the idea of an absolute standard of morals, since this has varied and will vary from age to age and from one people to another, and must always be an integral part of whatever religion or philosophy of life dominates at a given time or obtains among a particular race[2]. And since he held like the Saint-Simonians that the Christian religion had played its part in Europe, he was also convinced that the code of morals built up on this religion was now obsolete. Morality should be the art of life, and the Christian morality has no answer to the questions which life propounds in modern times[3].

This doubtfulness on the part of the prevailing code of morals was nowhere more apparent to Wienbarg than in the far from

---

[1] Cf. *Aesthetische Feldzüge*, pp. 123–124, and Elster, v, p. 261; the quotation is not quite accurate.

[2] Cf. *ibid.* pp. 177 ff.   [3] Cf. *ibid.* p. 168.

unanimous opinion excited in Germany by what was for him a
typical 'beautiful deed,' the revolt of the Polish nation. Where
twelve were gathered together, he averred, one would detest
this deed, and ten would applaud it as if they were watching a
play, whilst only one would be found to admire it as it should
be admired, and for whom the living historical truth would
prove an inspiration towards similar deeds[1]. In all this the
angle of approach towards the morality of the future is a different
one from that which is to be found in the works of the Saint-
Simonians and the Young Germans; but there is nothing so far
which actually runs counter to the Saint-Simonian creed; and
when Wienbarg announces that life itself is the true end of life,
and gives the following definition of the purpose of humanity:
'Aufzublühen, ins Leben hineinzublühen, Farben auszustrahlen,
Düfte auszuhauchen, das ist die Bestimmung der Menschen-
blumen,'[2] he is very near indeed to the ideal of Enfantin. And
yet only a few pages further on there is a sketch of life as it
should be lived which is more reminiscent of the age of chivalry
than applicable to the promised era of peace, plenty and harmonious happiness, which would indeed have little use for most
of the virtues detailed below:

...er [der Mensch] soll sich freuen an menschlicher That, sich
hingeben menschlichem Genusse, das Spiel seiner Kräfte entfalten,
für Recht und Wahrheit in die Schranken treten, die Unschuld lieben,
die Tugend ehren, die Lüge hassen, die Bosheit entlarven, den
Frevel rächen, die Gefahr verachten, und wenn's nöthig, sein Leben
für die höchsten Güter, sei's zur Erringung oder Behauptung derselben, für Freiheit und Vaterland in die Schanze zu schlagen[3].

'Sich hingeben menschlichem Genusse' has a Saint-Simonian
flavour, but otherwise there is something noble and yet practical
in this conception of the life of man which he owed to no one
but himself. It is a high ideal but by no means unattainable.
Enfantin's future age is unthinkable; and although Heine makes
no such exorbitant demands on the imagination, this is mainly
because the world of his dreams is never submitted to a close
inspection. But Wienbarg's ideal will stand the light of day.

The difference between them is clearer still in Wienbarg's re-

---

[1] *Aesthetische Feldzüge*, pp. 141–143.
[2] *Ibid.* p. 74.   [3] *Ibid.* p. 78.

jection of Kant's categorical imperative. According to his way
of thinking the victory of duty over passion is the victory of
unnatural sophistry over human nature, and would be entirely
out of place among a strong race of men:

So wird unsere Seele dann vorgestellt als der Kampfplatz aller
möglichen widerstrebenden Kräfte und Neigungen und über dem
Gewühl und Wellen der ruhig ernste kategorische Imperativ, der
quos ego donnert. Eine solche Vorstellung schickt sich in der That
für solche Zeiten, die wir erlebt; aber sie ist Gottlob nicht die natürliche und wahre, sie gehört dem Gebiete an, woraus sie stammt, dem
Gebiet der Schwäche und der Unnatur. Schafft uns ein kräftiges
Geschlecht, sprengt die Bande, die den Krafterguss schöner Neigungen und Triebe sündhaft gefesselt halten, befreit die Welt von
den Sünden der Schwäche, und dann seht, wie viele Rudera eurer
jetzigen Pflichtenlehre sich in der Umgestaltung des Lebens erhalten
werden, und um wie Vieles kürzer und bündiger das Kapitel von den
Kollisionsfällen zwischen Moral und Trieb ausfallen wird. Aber das
ist eben der Haupt- und Grundfehler unserer Moral, nur zu negiren,
nur zu verbieten, nur zu vernichten, dagegen sie sich Mühe gibt, alles
Treibende und Liebende in uns als das Unmoralische, als das zu
Negirende, als das Sündhafte darzustellen[1].

Enfantin would have read this condemnation of the old morality
with its negation of beautiful instincts and the desires of love
with approving smiles; nevertheless the emphasis is on the
beauty of strength and not on the beauty of passion; and here
Wienbarg differs from Enfantin and from Heine and appears
rather as the forerunner of Nietzsche. His hatred of weakness
and his worship of strength form a new and more virile contribution to the doctrine which aimed at the achievement of beauty
by means of the 'emancipation of the flesh.' 'AMOUR, *esprit,
chair*; BEAUTÉ, *force, sagesse*,' chanted the Saint-Simonians;
but Wienbarg called out clearly: 'SCHÖNHEIT *ist* KRAFT.'
The focus is altered and the paths begin to diverge; down one
vista we catch a glimpse of free love, down the other the
shadowy figure of the superman. But the difference went
further than this. A fundamental tenet of the Saint-Simonian
creed was the essential divinity of love under all its aspects,
and Wienbarg also conceived of love as born of the feeling of
beauty and noble by nature. But he made a sharp distinction

[1] *Aesthetische Feldzüge*, pp. 162–163.

between love and passion, which he considered an incalculable element, attending hatred and ugliness as well as beauty and love:

...diese aber verbindet sich bekanntlich eben so oft mit der Liebe, als mit dem Hasse, diese strebt eben so oft das Hässlichste als das Schönste an, diese, wie sie die Erzeugerin alles Grossen in der Weltgeschichte ist, war auch die Mutter aller Gewaltthaten und Gräuel, die nicht vom kalten Blut und der vertrockneten Bosheit diktirt wurden. Nicht allein die Liebe, die auf dem Schönheitsgefühl beruht, hat ihre Leidenschaften, auch die Religion hat die ihrigen und die liebevollste unter allen, die christliche, hat sich mit den furchtbarsten gesellt und ist durch sie in die blindeste Befangenheit trauriger Irrthümer gestürzt[1].

This attitude of distrust towards passion contained the germ of a heresy which neither Enfantin nor Heine would have approved. By denying the inevitable beauty of passionate love, Wienbarg was in fact voicing a blasphemy against one of the manifestations of the Saint-Simonian god and against Heine's dearest belief. For the moment however he went no further than a modest hint, and his implicit acceptance of pantheism held nothing that distinguished it from theirs[2].

In another but a less important matter Wienbarg differed from the Saint-Simonians. He acknowledged no Messiah of the new era; so that if he had heard of Enfantin's claims he hereby disallowed them; whilst the fact that Heine was given no personal prominence as a prophetic writer seems to suggest that Wienbarg was not consciously aware of the direction whence his own inspiration came:

Welche Lippe hat aber das Wort ausgesprochen, worin sich der neue Geist inkarniren will, wo ist der Messias, wo sind die Apostel, wo sind die gemeinsamen Symbole dieses Geistes? Es ist wahr, er weht durch die ganze Welt und wir hören sein Brausen, aber wissen wir auch, woher er kommt, wohin er geht?...Prophetisch ist jede Zeile, die gedruckt, jedes Wort, das gesprochen, jede That, die vollführt wird, aber messianisch keine...vorüber sind die messianischen Zeiten, wo die Offenbarung ausging von einem Einzigen, die Zeit selbst ist forthin der gebenedeite Schooss der Jungfrau, der vom Geist befruchtet wird....[3]

---

[1] *Aesthetische Feldzüge*, pp. 158–159.
[2] *Ibid*. pp. 180–181, 198 ff.   [3] *Ibid*. pp. 118–119.

Wienbarg sought to evoke the future spirit of beauty in *Aesthetische Feldzüge* and it bore a remarkable resemblance to Enfantin's ideal as interpreted by Heine; so close a resemblance indeed that we are justified in saying that this young North German lecturer, who despised the French and ignored the Saint-Simonians, was responsible for spreading the gospel which had been expounded in the *salle* Taitbout. And he taught it by word of mouth, in a manner well calculated to make it extremely popular. For he combined it with an exhortation to the young men who attended his lectures to follow in the footsteps of Martin Luther and to protest; to protest against the tyrannical forces of history and tradition, to sweep away the rubbish of the past and to clear the ground for the future[1]. Youth will not be youth when this cry fails to arouse a response; youth must have been old indeed if in the oppressed, unhappy Germany of 1833 it should have listened unmoved.

Houben has likened *Aesthetische Feldzüge* to a clear trumpet call dominating for a moment the confused babel of voices uplifted in Germany after 1830. The simile is an apt one. Hoary ruins crumble and fall at the sound of this clarion note, whilst blind bats wheel silently away and melancholy owls fly from the rising sun. But if Wienbarg sent forth a rousing summons to pull down the old, he also voiced a gallant challenge to build up anew, to assist in the resurrection of beauty from the sordid grave of his times. Then, before his voice had ceased to echo through the deserted hall, he published these lectures in book-form with a dedication to 'Young Germany' which reads like a call to arms. It is not surprising that all but the temperamentally old should have made a vigorous response; still less that the real 'Young Germans,' now officially baptised, should have flung themselves at the feet of this orator of the golden tongue and the Saint-Simonian dreams.

Laube, then on the eve of his downfall, was inspired to publish a programme of the new literature which transcended in boldness anything he had so far produced; Mundt made haste to make use of Wienbarg's ideas in *Schriften in bunter Reihe*[2];

---

[1] *Aesthetische Feldzüge*, pp. 32–34, 37–38.
[2] Cf. *Schriften in bunter Reihe*, October 1834, pp. 4 and 141.

and if Gutzkow still bided his time this was partly because he had then no organ of his own, partly because he was a more half-hearted Saint-Simonian than the other two; his unqualified enthusiasm was expressed later and in a characteristic connection. Meanwhile those in authority reacted with even greater promptitude. *Aesthetische Feldzüge* was forbidden in Prussia on May 28, 1834; and although the conservative press remained silent for the most part until 1835, one or two unfavourable reviews were duly published[1]; whilst Viktor Amadeus Huber set himself to annihilate Wienbarg in the *Mecklenburgische Blätter* in much the same style which Hengstenberg and Menzel were later to adopt towards Heine and Gutzkow[2]. In spite of these dissentient voices however the author of *Aesthetische Feldzüge*, who had been forced to abandon his lectureship, was much in request; Laube secured him for the staff of the *Zeitung für die elegante Welt*, and hardly had this enterprise been checked by his imprisonment, before Wienbarg was appointed literary editor of the *Literarische und kritische Blätter der Börsenhalle* in Hamburg. It would seem that his fortune was made.

(c) THE FORERUNNER OF NIETZSCHE

In the spring of 1835, exactly a year after the publication of *Aesthetische Feldzüge*, Wienbarg produced a volume of essays entitled *Wanderungen durch den Thierkreis* in which is to be found a further and most interesting development of his Saint-Simonian views. They reflect an originality of thought which might have resulted, had his mental powers remained unimpaired, in the construction of a system at once greater and less complete than Saint-Simonism; not so neatly fitted together, but penetrated by a deeper knowledge of human nature. Unhappily this system was never erected; isolated blocks of rough-hewn stones lie scattered in the *Wanderungen durch den Thierkreis*, but the architect abandoned his plans.

The rehabilitation of industry formed no part of Wienbarg's

---

[1] *Literarische und kritische Blätter der Börsenhalle*, September 1, 1834; *Bl. f. lit. Unt.* October 19, 1834.
[2] *Mecklenburgische Blätter*, 1834, Nos. 2 and 3; 1835, No. 10.

programme; on the contrary he regarded the age of the dominion of gold with the utmost hatred and dislike:

Saubere Frucht, fluchwürdige Civilisation, welche die ehrloseste und verderblichste aller Aristokrasien, die des Reichthums, zu der Aristokrasie der Geburt hinzugefügt und ein halbgeschundenes Emporkriechergesindel zu Herren der Nation gemacht hat.

Dort oben, im Sonnenschein des Glückes, sah ich riesige Giftpflanzen, emporgeschossen aus Sumpf und Moder, Brillenschlangen, die halbe Königreiche zum Frühstück verzehrten, feiste Blutigel, die die ganze Nation ausschröpften.

Und am Fusse dieser hohen und noblen Gesellschaft lagerte sich eine grausige Wolke des Elends, aus deren gelblich schwarzem Qualme mich von Zeit zu Zeit ein hohläugiges Kindergesicht, ein bleifarbiger Maschinenengel anstarrte[1].

The Saint-Simonians might not have quarrelled with this indictment of the unequal distribution of riches, in so far as it stood in no direct relation to the capacities involved, but they would certainly have protested against the theory of the destructive nature of wealth itself, and would not have identified themselves with Wienbarg's view that it was the mission of youth to conduct a campaign against the evil power of gold[2].

But if the rehabilitation of industry had no charms for Wienbarg, the enfranchisement of women was received by him with outspoken approval. Under the sign of the Archer he took up the cudgels for German women against the German men; and although his patriotism was stronger than his feminism ('Der Himmel weiss, was das für wippfüssige und kippherzige Dinger sein mögen, die Französinnen')[3] nevertheless this article, devoted to the glorification of women, was strongly influenced by Saint-Simonism and even contained his only commendation of this doctrine:

Es [das Christenthum] zeigte sich der ächten Frauenliebe mehr ungünstig als günstig.... Die Päpste machten aus einer erhabenen freiwilligen Ausnahme ein Gesetz für Tausende, ein Gesetz, das die Verachtung der heiligen Natur, die finstre Abscheu vor dem weiblichen Geschlechte verhängt zu haben scheint, wüsste man nicht zu bestimmen, dass es der Politik sein Dasein verdankte.... Die Saint-Simonianer, die Christus durch Saint-Simon ablösen wollen, suchen in der weiten Welt umher nach dem Weibe, ihrer *Mutter*. Die armen

---

[1] *Wanderungen durch den Thierkreis*, 1835, p. 41.
[2] *Ibid.* pp. 55–56.   [3] *Ibid.* p. 187.

Leute, die zu Hause in Frankreich keine gefunden. Bei keiner Sekte trug das Lächerliche mehr die Schleppe des Erhabenen. *Nicht der Mann allein, Mann und Weib sind das gesellschaftliche Individuum*, der Satz ist eine der herrlichen Grundsäulen ihres Systems, die sie, wie alle übrigen, oben auf dem Knopfe mit ihrer Schellenkappe behängt haben[1].

It will be seen that he had slightly altered his opinion since the days when Saint-Simonism meant no more to him than an absurd form of the doctrine of the Anabaptists. He had probably come to know these theories rather better, and to realise that in many ways they coincided with his own; for by now he was in communication with the other Young Germans, who will almost certainly have enlightened him on this subject. But his standpoint was different from theirs; Heine, Laube, Gutzkow and Mundt were agreed in rejecting the theory of the 'social couple' and all that it involved as the most ridiculous part of the doctrine. Wienbarg alone reserved his highest praise for this aspect of the new religion, although even here he heard the tinkle of the jester's bells. It is also significant that the only other reference to Saint-Simonism made during these years deals, although lightly, with the same theme:

Diese Mathilde F....ist mir eine reizende Unbegreiflichkeit. Wäre ich der Vater der Saintsimonisten, so würde ich mich versucht fühlen, die endliche Erscheinung *des Weibes* in ihr zu begrüssen und den couple révélateur mit ihr zu stiften[2].

Wienbarg would not be Wienbarg if he had attempted in this article to elaborate a definite plan for the emancipation of women. He rarely descended from the realm of theory and rousing apostrophes to the realm of practice and detailed schemes; but he was sincere enough in his feminism, and his promise to the women of Germany, in spite of its high-sounding vagueness, was made in good faith:

O Weiber, tragt und duldet uns feige Despoten noch eine Weile. Freilich steht's in eurer Macht, uns sammt und sonders aus dem Hause und aus Deutschland zu jagen....Aber lasst Gnade vor Recht ergehen. Wir gedenken, an unserer Besserung zu arbeiten, und werden uns bemühen, nicht allzuschimpflich von euch abzustechen. Und sind wir wieder, was unsere Väter, und haben wieder Muth zum Muthe und Muth zur Freiheit und freie Hand zu schalten und zu

---

[1] *Wanderungen durch den Thierkreis*, pp. 195–201.   [2] *Ibid.* p. 43.

walten, dann wollen wir euer Loos auch bürgerlich verbessern, gleich dem Loose aller Unterdrückten und an Recht und Freiheit Gekränkten[1].

In this volume the first faint sign of Wienbarg's mental deterioration can be detected, but only sporadically. Many of the essays show no lack of intellectual concentration, and in particular under the constellation of the Gemini, he gives proof of constructive poetical thought, which places him high among the thinkers and makes of his subsequent collapse something tragic rather than pitiful. This article entitled 'Wollust und Grausamkeit' contains a confession of religious faith, and the greatness of the conception which gave rise to it is no mere triumph of words. Perhaps no one has ever rejected the God of our fathers, that holy, awful and eternal being, with so much infectious anger and with such refreshing contempt:

Und über dem ungeheuren Schmerze der Schöpfung, die sich selbst zerstört, erhebt sich der einsame Thron eines Wesens, dessen gefühllose Ewigkeit durch keine Welle der Lust und des Schmerzes ausgehöhlt wird. In ächter Tyrannenlaune schuf er die Welt, um sich an dem tragischen Gaukelspiel des ringenden flüchtigen Daseins ironisch zu weiden. Er zündete die Brautfackeln an, lud die Gäste ein und liess die Bluthochzeit beginnen, die niemals aufhört. Er selber lächelt vom hohen sichern Balkon der Unsterblichkeit göttlich ruhig in die weite ewige Bartolomäusnacht hinaus....Ihr Gott ist schrecklich heilig, schrecklich ewig, schrecklich selig. Er ist nicht der meinige[2].

This rejection is followed by a definition of pantheism, although Wienbarg does not use the term, which far transcends in mystical beauty the conception of the Saint-Simonians, adding moreover the austerity of the gospel of strength to their rather emasculate ideal of divine beauty:

Der Gott, an den ich glaube, theilt mit mir die Bürde der Sterblichkeit, indem er zugleich meiner schwachen Brust einen Theil seiner Ewigkeit anvertraut. Er taucht sich in die Schmerzen und Freuden der Welt, er versenkt sich in die Leidenschaften und Triebe, er erniedrigt sich nicht allein zum Menschen, selbst zum Wurm und empfindet den Todesschmerz des unter meinen Füssen zertretenen Geschöpfes....Ja, ich wage es auszusprechen, Gottes ist die Gebrechlichkeit so gut als die Kraft, die flüchtige Lust sowohl als die ewige Seligkeit, der Tod sowohl als das ewige Leben; und nichts

[1] *Wanderungen durch den Thierkreis*, pp. 207–208.
[2] *Ibid.* pp. 93–96.

Ungöttliches gibt es auf der Welt als die absolute Schwäche, die sich
selbst verlässt und daher auch von Gott verlassen wird. Es ist uns
gepredigt worden von einem Gott, der aus seinem Himmel herabstieg
und Fleisch wurde und in Palästina wandelte und auf Golgotha den
Kreuzestod litt. Das ist ein Bild und Gleichniss von dem Gott, der
im Fleisch durch die ganze Welt wandelt und dessen Kreuz sich
erhebt aus dem Abgrund der Wesen und über Sonnen, Sterne und
Milchstrassen hinausragt—dessen Evangelium die Zukunft predigen
wird[1].

This sympathetic interpretation of the life of Christ as a beautiful parable of God immanent in the world, incarnate in the
lowest worm and present in the most transient desire as truly
as in eternal life, whilst his cross reaches beyond the stars and
the suns, is not only a poetical combination of eastern and
western faiths; it contains a new element in the worship of
strength, and Wienbarg must be acknowledged in this respect
as the forgotten forerunner of Friedrich Nietzsche:

O ihr Menschen, wenn denn nichts Ungöttliches an und in euch ist,
als die Schwäche, welche im Gewande der Heuchelei und am Stabe
der Lüge einherzuschwanken pflegt, so bittet Gott vor allen Dingen
um Kraft und Stärke, der Triebe sowol, durch die ihr leidet und
vergänglich seid, als vornämlich der sinnlich schönen Gewalten,
durch deren Hilfe ihr das Vergängliche in aller Lust und in allem
Schmerze männlich besieget, oder wo ihr euch hingebt, mit dem
Schimmer des Unsterblichen anhauchet[2].

In spite of the obscurity of this passage, sadly eloquent of the
clouds which were gathering in his mind, the prayer for strength
at all hazards, combined with the passionate invocation to the
powers of sensuous beauty, shows that Wienbarg, starting from the
same premises as the Saint-Simonians, had arrived at a different
conclusion. Like them he aimed at the ultimate harmony of spirit
and flesh, but he accepted courageously sorrow and pain and
sought to transcend them. In his doctrine the anguish of mortality was faced and vanquished by the immortality of beauty;
the only sin he knew was weakness and the most god-like virtue
strength. They on the other hand had no place in their system
for pain and for sorrow; they resolutely ignored the problem
of death; they denied the possibility of sin, and all qualities to
them were equally divine. Their doctrine seems chimerical and

---

[1] *Wanderungen durch den Thierkreis*, pp. 96–97.   [2] *Ibid.* pp. 99–100.

their optimism childish when compared with his triumphant affirmations and his undaunted hope.

But the difference between them went deeper than this. Enfantin held theoretically, it is true, that all our qualities, instincts and desires are equally god-like; but when it came to his personal predilections, it seems safe to assert that he saw in the passion of love the quintessence of divinity, beauty at its most beautiful, love at its most sublime. And here the other Young Germans ranged themselves enthusiastically on his side. Heine, Laube, Gutzkow and Mundt, whatever else they might criticise, saw nothing to criticise here; the essential divinity of passion was to them the most axiomatic of laws.

Wienbarg's nature was a more passionate one than either Gutzkow's or Mundt's and not so light as Laube's; like Heine he knew the meaning of 'la tristesse du chair'; but whereas for Heine this lay in the eternally irreconcilable struggle between spirit and flesh, Wienbarg explained it in a manner which struck at the very root of the hypothesis that passion is purely divine:

Eine andere Sage und Klage weht von den Palmblättern Indiens herüber. Nach dieser unendlich zarten pflanzten die ersten reinen Menschen sich fort durch Vermischung ihrer stillleuchtenden Liebesblicke. Aber des Mannes Auge verlor allmählig seine schöpferische Kraft und des Weibes Auge wurde unfruchtbar. Mann und Weib drückten sich zitternd die Hand. Und des Mannes Hand gab, und des Weibes Hand empfing das Leben. Allein auch diese Art der Fortpflanzung entsprach nicht lange mehr dem vergröberten Sinn der beiden Geschlechter. Der Kuss, die heissere Vermischung des Athems und der Lippen, trat an die Stelle derselben. Damals, glaube ich, in der Ehe des Kusses, brach die Schwester der Wollust, die Grausamkeit, sichtbarer hervor. Denn als Liebe und Verlangen glühender und vergeblicher wurden und auch der Kuss das Küssen nicht mehr befriedigte und stillte, da brauchten sie Gewalt und der Liebende machte der Geliebten Pein durch Athementziehen, Lippenpressen, Wundküssen und alle jene Grausamkeiten des wollüstigen Kusses, welche die Sprache der Liebe süsse nennt. Und die Menschen sanken noch tiefer und die Liebe, die einst fern und schüchtern die Jungfrau überstrahlte, überschattete sie mit ihren Flügeln. Und ihr einer Flügel ward die Wollust und ihr anderer Flügel die Grausamkeit[1].

In this interpretation of the Indian myth Wienbarg penetrated into the mystery of passion in a way which makes

[1] *Wanderungen durch den Thierkreis*, pp. 91–92.

Enfantin's theory seem shallow and jejune; whilst his description of love overshadowing the trembling virgin with its wings: 'And one wing became passion, and the other cruelty,' is something more than a poetical simile; it is a tragic confession. And a still more startling personal confession is to be found in this book under the sign of the Virgin. The sketch of Eduard's love for Julie is undoubtedly taken from Wienbarg's life. Even the heroine's name is not altered. The daughter of one of the professors at Kiel University, who married the same year his mother died, was also called Julie and probably broke his heart. In this sketch Wienbarg communicated a poem purporting to be written by Eduard, but which was undoubtedly his own. In transcribing the following verses, which are almost frightening in their intensity, it is hardly necessary to comment on the mixture of passion and cruelty which they contain, heightened by the despairing triumph of desire fulfilled and innocence destroyed:

> Du selber schufst in meiner Brust dis Feuer,
> Damit entzünd' ich deine keusche Brust,
> Und Gott und Geist, was heilig dir und theuer,
> Das giess' ich hin in einen Strom der Lust,
> Schau auf, schau rings in der entflammten Welt
> Nur Mann und Weib, das sich umschlungen hält.
>
> Schon wird die rothe jungfräuliche Rose
> An deinem Busen glüh'nder, feuriger.
> Bald taumelt Wollust auf dem grünen Moose
> Von Blatt zu Blatt verschmachtend hin und her,
> Bis jedes Blatt, von Liebe angesteckt,
> Als Flammenzunge eine Flamme leckt.
>
> Und Wollust knistert in den Bettgardinen—
> Einst Engelsfittichen, die Schlaf geweht
> Der Jungfrau, die vom keuschen Mond beschienen,
> Süssträumend lag auf ihrem Ruhebett—
> Sie flattern auf—begib dich nur zur Ruh—
> Ein Flammenmantel deckt die Houri zu.
>
> Dann Mädchen, wenn der Mond, des Himmels Kerzen
> Herniedertaumeln in der Sinne Gluth;
> Wenn des Erlösers Kreuz auf deinem Herzen,
> Auf deinem Herzen nicht mehr sicher ruht—
> Dann bist du mein, mein, sag' ich, schreie nicht!
> Ich riss umsonst dich in die Flammen nicht[1].

[1] *Wanderungen durch den Thierkreis*, p. 143.

Wienbarg's conception of the passion of love is a tragic conception arousing pity and terror rather than happier emotions, and it may seem strange that a man, who could feel and write on this subject as he did, should be found amongst those who were demanding the 'emancipation of the flesh.' But his hatred of weakness allowed him to hold no converse with the monkish virtues of abstinence and denial; and with his eyes fully open to the danger as well as the beauty of passion, he courageously maintained that it was more god-like to sin than to abstain:

Gebt euch nicht dem mönchischen Glauben hin, Gott gefälliger und tugendhafter zu werden durch blosse gewaltsame Schwächung und Unterdrückung eurer Leidenschaften.... Aergert euch nicht an den göttlichen Passionen. Gott in seiner tiefsten Erniedrigung bleibt immer Gott. Was ihr Laster scheltet, ist fast immer göttlicher, als eure Tugend, eure scheinheilige Erhabenheit, eure eunuchische Lasterlosigkeit. Gott ist euch näher im flammenden Busche der Wollust, als im herbstlichen Blättersäuseln der Prüderie[1].

Here therefore, starting from different premises, Wienbarg arrived at the same conclusion as Enfantin; but there is a note of courage in this passage and of undefeated strength prevailing over suffering which lifts it beyond the sphere of day-dreams into the realm of ideals.

(d) THE PARTNER OF GUTZKOW

In a biographical sketch which Gutzkow sent to O. L. B. Wolff in 1837, he declared that he first met Wienbarg in the summer of 1834 in Hamburg, but that their principles were divergent and that he saw very little of him[2]. This statement, which is coloured by his embittered feelings towards the Young Germans at that date, must be taken with a certain amount of scepticism; for it seems as if Gutzkow must have felt himself attracted towards the older man, since he invited him to Frankfurt in the summer of 1835 as co-editor of the *Deutsche Revue*. Wienbarg reciprocated this liking. He brought with him a small collection of essays, the fruit of his labours for the *Literarische und kritische Blätter der Börsenhalle*, including a review of Gutzkow's *Vorrede* which had not succeeded in passing

---

[1] *Wanderungen durch den Thierkreis*, p. 100.
[2] Cf. Houben, *Jungdeutscher Sturm und Drang*, p. 536.

the Hamburg censor, and which now saw the light of day for the first time. This volume was published by Löwenthal under the title *Zur neuesten deutschen Literatur*. With the exception of a sharp criticism of marriage from the feminist point of view[1], hitherto rather implied than expressed in Wienbarg's works, this volume is chiefly interesting here on account of the essay on the Preface. For the other articles have nothing new to add to the portrait of Wienbarg as a Saint-Simonian. His enthusiasm for Goethe, expressed in *Holland in den Jahren 1831 und 1832*, and developed in *Aesthetische Feldzüge*, is to be found here again. His admiration for Heine, which had been the driving force behind his lectures and had not been absent from *Wanderungen durch den Thierkreis*[2], led him to write an appreciative article on *Salon II*; and now a new allegiance was added to these:

Tapfrer Gutzkow, Du hast dem Andenken Schleiermachers und der Liebe, die ach! so schlecht und ordinair geworden ist in deutschen Landen, dass sie kaum mehr diesen heiligen zaubervollen Namen verdient, Du hast ihnen beiden einen wackern Ritterdienst geleistet. Dass Deine Vorrede zugleich ein Kreuzzug gegen das moderne Pfaffenthum werden musste, lag in der Natur der Sache....Sie (die Pfaffen) sind der Liebe und allen schönen und freien Regungen der Menschennatur von jeher Feind gewesen....[3]

It was the application of his own ideals to social life which drew Wienbarg towards Gutzkow, and the influence of the younger man may be traced in the definition of marriage as a crucifixion of poetry in the essay on Goethe. He had advocated a new morality in *Aesthetische Feldzüge*, but in vague and general terms. He now boldly applauded Gutzkow's definite scheme for the emancipation of love. He was the only one among the other Young Germans to do this. Laube, Mundt and Kühne were too much shocked by the passionate tone of the Preface to approve of it, and much too startled by its reckless-

---

[1] *Zur neuesten Literatur*, Hamburg, 1838, second edition, p. 16: 'Leidet denn nicht das deutsche Weib an unsern Erbärmlichkeiten? Habt ihr niemals die leidende Poesie am Kreuz der Ehe erblickt oder hinter den grünen Myrthen ihres Brautkranzes ihre Dornenkrone nicht gesehen?'

[2] Cf. *Wanderungen durch den Thierkreis*, an essay on Heine's poems, under the sign of the Scorpion.

[3] *Zur neuesten Literatur*, pp. 162–163; cf. also pp. 158–159.

ness to welcome Gutzkow as an ally; in fact this violent outburst, if it created many foes, also alienated a number of friends.
Wienbarg's championship therefore came at a moment when
Gutzkow was beginning to feel an almost god-like isolation, and
he hastened to express his thanks in the *Phönix*, combined with
a gentle hint that the enthusiasm for Heine was less admirable
and should be expressed more warily[1].

The partnership thus inaugurated proceeded smoothly enough.
Gutzkow sincerely admired his style and was probably drawn
to him as well by something chivalrous in Wienbarg's nature.
And yet it was in Frankfurt, if we are to believe Gutzkow's
later statements, that Wienbarg's mental and moral deterioration began; thirty sheets of paper were wasted over the opening
sentence of a programme for the new literature; procrastination
and dissipation governed his days and nights; the grim spectre
of inhibition was already playing havoc in his mind. But at
least there was nothing cowardly in his nature; he was to have
been Gutzkow's second in the duel which Menzel so virtuously
refused; he signed his name to the statements published in the
Allgemeine Zeitung, and made no attempt to dissever a connection which was proving disastrous to himself. More than
this, whilst all the unfortunate Young Germans domiciled in
Germany were busy dissociating themselves from each other
and writing to various ministers either retracting, denying,
modifying or at best interpreting their principles, Wienbarg
boldly joined the ranks of those who stepped forward to defend
Gutzkow, and like Börne and Heine launched a pamphlet
against Menzel. And here he gave proof of courage and strength
of character. He was not safe within the walls of that fortress
of freedom whence Börne and Heine fired their annihilating
guns; nor was he in the relatively secure position of a dispassionate observer. On the contrary the most damaging conclusions were already being drawn by Menzel and others from
the fact of his association with Gutzkow. Wienbarg could not
be blamed if he had attempted to clear his literary character
by expressing a modified disapproval of *Wally, die Zweiflerin*;
without actually joining Gutzkow's detractors he could have

---

[1] *Literaturblatt zum Phönix*, August 8, 1835.

hinted by implication that his own views were less alarming, his own point of view more lofty, his own motives less mixed. But such subtle disloyalty was foreign to Wienbarg's nature; rather he set himself to show that the monster of immorality and blasphemy which Menzel had fashioned from *Wally, die Zweiflerin* was a creation of that critic's unsavoury mind:

> Er nahm die 'Wally,' einen kürzlich erschienenen Roman Gutzkows zur Hand, knetete daraus einen alarmirenden Popanz, ein Ungeheuer der Irreligiosität und Sittenlosigkeit, und, nachdem er, der deutsche Mann, eingängig eine persönliche Infamie dem jungen Autor ange-schmitzt hatte, gab er dem ganzen monströsen Gebäck seiner Hände den Namen Gutzkow, ad libitum junges Deutschland. Warf's darauf zur Zermalmung unter die Hufen seiner Rosse[1].

Later when his own fate overtook him in the shape of a decree of banishment from Frankfurt, Wienbarg wrote to the senate of this town asking that the decree might be reconsidered. This solitary expostulation is dignified in tone and contains neither treacherous disavowals nor craven confessions of guilt:

> Ich lebe still für mich, den Wissenschaften und der Literatur, ich habe keine andern Verbindungen, als literärische und buchhänd-lerische, letztere nicht in Frankfurt. Ich bin unbescholten und für meine Person bürgerlich und polizeilich ausser Vorwurf. Sollte mein literärisches Streben nicht überall Billigung finden, so scheint mir dieses kein Motiv zu sein, mich, wo es auch sei in Deutschland, die Luft nicht einathmen zu lassen. Auch bin ich bereit, mich in dieser Hinsicht, vor jedem kompetenten Forum einzufinden[2].

There is one point about this admirable and restrained de-claration which is worthy of note; it is the quiet assurance with which Wienbarg refers to his irreproachable private life. It seems unlikely that he would have made such an assertion, if his conduct was then really as debauched as Gutzkow stated in his letter to Liesching in 1846[3]. For he could not have led this life in the public resorts of Frankfurt without the know-

---

[1] *Menzel und die junge Literatur. Programm zur deutschen Revue*, Mann-heim, 1835, p. 8. I have unfortunately not been able to see the anonymous pamphlet written in answer to this, entitled *Ludolf Wienbarg und die junge Literatur*, Marburg, 1836.

[2] Houben, *Jungdeutscher Sturm und Drang*, p. 196, dated from Frankfurt, November 17, 1835.

[3] Cf. *ibid.* p. 199.

ledge of the authorities; and of what use therefore to protest
his innocence? Moreover although the spies duly reported
Wienbarg's moral collapse later, there is no such accusation at
this time, when it would surely not have been omitted if there
had been a breath of scandal to give rise to it. On the contrary,
Beurmann, then secretly in the pay of Austria, called Wienbarg
'einen Ritter ohne Furcht und Tadel.'[1] It is possible that Gutzkow
used the dark colours of a later period to produce a more
damaging effect, or from a not unlikely confusion of memory.
And if he committed such an anachronism then also, it seems
more than probable that the persecution of 1835 exercised a
peculiarly baneful influence on this unhappy man. And I am
inclined to believe this the more strongly since the year 1835
did not actually belie the promise of the *Aesthetische Feldzüge*.
There is constructive thought in the *Wanderungen durch den
Thierkreis*, whilst the essays in *Zur neuesten Literatur* are finely
written and show no lack of critical power. Granted that he
wrote slowly and with great difficulty, he achieved the kind of
prose that is not likely to come flowing from a facile pen, and
many a great artist has gone through similar struggles; Virgil's
name alone is sufficient proof that such a process does not
necessarily argue mental sterility. And although in the case of
Wienbarg this difficulty proved to be a symptom of latent insanity, still until the flight from Frankfurt it would appear that
the signs were almost negligible and he himself had no doubt
that his creative powers would overcome the resistance which
they found in his mind:

> Weiss ich's doch an mir selbst, wie unflüssig und verstockt noch so
> viele Ideen in mir sind, die zum Strom der jungen Welt gehören,
> glaube ich doch noch gar nichts gethan zu haben und harré der
> Stunde, wo die schöpferische Kraft, die in den Tiefen meines Lebens
> braust, mein ganzes Ich ergreifen und glühend in die harrende Form
> überströmen wird....[2]

We know further both from *Wanderungen durch den Thierkreis*, and from a letter to a publisher communicated by Houben,
that he was maturing the plot of a novel which was to be ready

---

[1] E. Beurmann, *Vertraute Briefe aus Preussens Hauptstadt*, Stuttgart,
1837.

[2] *Wanderungen durch den Thierkreis*, p. viii.

in 1836[1]. This does not look as if his powers were altogether failing him; it is another story in 1836.

We may conclude from these facts that Wienbarg's inclusion among the Young Germans and his connection with Gutzkow were partly responsible at least for an earlier appearance of mental and moral derangement than might otherwise have occurred; and it is further certain that he suffered cruelly in his mind from the persecution to which they were all subjected; he seems to have been a broken man from that time onwards; the others were made of tougher stuff. And yet, looked at from another point of view, he bore the blow better than they did. He never became embroiled in those distressing feuds which raged amongst the others well into the forties. It is a rather remarkable fact that the Young Germans as a whole bore Wienbarg no ill-will; for, by the unfortunate publicity which he gave to the phrase Young Germany, he did them all a disservice and helped to arouse the suspicions of those in authority; nor should it be forgotten that it was Prussia's condemnation of *Wanderungen durch den Thierkreis* at the Federal Diet which gave Austria her opening to propose radical measures for the suppression of the whole school. And yet even Gutzkow spared him publicly until the appearance of *Rückblicke auf mein Leben* in 1875. This may be accounted for partly by the fact that Wienbarg showed no trace in the *Literarische und kritische Blätter der Börsenhalle* of that polemical spirit which gives so much violent life to the other Young German newspapers and journals; but it must also be remembered that from 1836 onwards he became a less and less important figure in German literature and even in the press, so that he was hardly worth their attention; nevertheless this solitary example of peaceable relations must be set down to Wienbarg's credit. To his honour also is the fact that he never condescended to make any appeal against the unjust and cruel laws which fettered all their pens. These laws probably pressed much less hardly on him than his own complete incapacity to produce work requiring a sustained effort. Yet there was pride in the silence he maintained

---

[1] Cf. *Wanderungen durch den Thierkreis*, pp. 257–260, and Houben, *op. cit.* pp. 194–195.

towards the government, even if one can sympathise with Gutzkow's rage at such an explanation being offered for his intellectual decline. The one held in it a quality of dignity and restraint which none of the others possessed; the other was pitiable enough, though only a Gutzkow could have thought it contemptible.

And when in 1842 Laube eagerly, Mundt almost enthusiastically and Gutzkow rather casuistically crept to the cross and swore to offend no more, should the special laws be repealed, Wienbarg was able to publish a statement that no such declaration had ever been made by him; but he did it in so chivalrous a manner that those who read his announcement would almost certainly deduce the extreme improbability that the others had made this concession:

Wenn ich indess, einer der Genannten, und gleich ihnen unfrei-williges Mitglied eines so und so charakterisirten, von Bundestags-Maassregeln betroffenen 'jungen Deutschlands,' die Erklärung abgebe, dass mir niemals Versprechungen irgend einer Art von irgend einer Regierung angemuthet worden, noch dass ich jemals Versprechungen irgend einer Art gegeben, so werde ich das Publicum in den Stand gesetzt haben, über dergleichen allgemeine Verdächtigungen das richtige Urtheil zu fällen[1].

The tone of this denial, embodying a generous attitude towards his sometime fellow-martyrs, is another proof of Wienbarg's essentially noble mind. He had fallen lower than them all, and yet he was incapable of their compromises, of their suspicions, of their bitterness towards each other, of their never-ending strife. Their minds were still alert and vigorous, and his was fast falling into decay, but he thought better thoughts than they did, and he knew of better dreams.

(e) THE MYTH OF WIENBARG

In einer starken und handelnden Zeit würde es mein Ehrgeiz sein, ihr würdige Schöpfungen hervorzubringen, Dichter, Künstler zu sein, dazu habe ich Anlage....Unter Bürgern Bürger würde ich mich überglücklich schätzen, mein Talent in Freiheit auszuüben, und auf den der Kunst geweiheten Altären die Flamme des Schönen zu unterhalten. Dies klingt wie Prahlerei. Ich habe nichts geschaffen, was einem Kunstwerke ähnlich sieht. Ich kann antworten, ihr habt nichts

[1] *Staats- und gelehrte Zeitung des Hamburgischen unpartheiischen Correspondenten*, July 13 1842.

gethan, was eines Dichters und Künstlers würdig. Ja, eure Zustände sind nicht einmal derartig, dass sich eine dichterische Sehnsucht nach dem Schönen und Grossen kund geben kann, ohne für ein Verbrechen zu gelten. Ich spreche aus bitterster Erfahrung. Und seitdem datirt sich meine tiefere Theilnahme an der Politik....Seitdem schätze ich den Liberalismus, trotz seiner Prosa, seiner Einseitigkeit und Beschränktheit....[1]

This statement, made by Wienbarg in 1840, may be considered an inadequate explanation for his failure to produce those works of art with which he dreamt that he might have enriched a freer and stronger age; but it sheds an interesting light on the change of ground apparent in his writings after this date. For whereas he had hitherto been concerned chiefly with literature and art, he became in the forties a liberal, patriotic and historical pamphleteer. And although in 1852 he undertook a half-imaginative, half-scientific investigation into the meaning of words, and resumed an early campaign against the Low German dialect in 1860, whilst his reviews for his paper kept him in touch with literature until 1846; still the centre of interest had changed; his campaigns were henceforward political rather than aesthetic, and his interest in beauty waned. It bade fair at one time to be the main inspiration of his life, but it had ever a strong rival in his enthusiasm for his country, and this proved the stronger in the end.

Now Wienbarg had adopted as his standard of beauty the harmonious balance of matter and mind which was the basis of the Saint-Simonian faith and he had also explicitly accepted two conclusions from this hypothesis, the 'rehabilitation of the flesh' and the emancipation of women. But his passion for beauty became absorbed by a stronger and less intellectual emotion after the shattering experience of his literary proscription, and we find that his patriotism was in part responsible for his final rejection of Saint-Simonism:

Soll ich von Laube als von einem Repräsentanten der Emancipation des Fleisches und der Frauen reden? Was an diesen Ideen sich gröblichster Missdeutung aussetzte, die prahlende Theorie, das grelle Aushängeschild der Namen, der Schein des Societätartigen, als handelte es sich um die Stiftung einer Gesellschaft zur Abschaffung

---

[1] *Vermischte Schriften*, Altona, 1840, pp. vii–viii.

der Sclaverei, dies Alles war undeutsch, und das Wahre daran der allgemeine Gedanke, dass alle Menschennatur mit dem schwindenden historischen Druck sich immer mehr zur Ganzheit und Freiheit seiner besonderen Erscheinung entwickle, in sich völliger und selbstständiger werde und aus Kraft zur Schönheit sich entfalte....[1]

We are accustomed by now to hear the Young Germans denying Saint-Simonism after 1835; and it has generally seemed that the instinct of self-preservation played its part in these recantations. The date of this passage however weakens such a supposition; the more so since certain phrases and passages in the intervening years show that Wienbarg had not feared on occasions to utter Saint-Simonian thoughts[2]. The clue to his present lack of enthusiasm for the 'rehabilitation of the flesh' and the enfranchisement of women is to be sought in the epithet 'un-German' with which he peremptorily dismissed them. And if we penetrate further and seek for the reason why patriotism should have dominated to the exclusion of Saint-Simonism, the answer seems painfully obvious. Saint-Simonism was the basis of a system of life, religion, morality and art which he had sketched in *Aesthetische Feldzüge* and begun to elaborate in *Wanderungen durch den Thierkreis*. But from 1836 onwards his constructive powers began to fail him. He was all too soon in a condition in which the complicated stimulus of a philosophy of life could produce no reaction; still less was he capable of achieving anything in the nature of a coherent system; poetical symbols and rhetorical appeals stood him in lieu henceforward of creative thought. Patriotism on the other hand is a strong and simple feeling with a driving power behind it which demands expression in words or in deeds. An enfeebled mind may still respond to its summons when other ideas have long since lost their force. Patriotism, like wine, unloosed his tongue, and drove him to action during the war against Denmark. In the service of his country he could still write with vigour; and at the call of his nation he could still bear himself like a man. It

---

[1] *Lit. u. krit. Bll. d. B.* December 19, 1840; a review of Laube's *Jagdbrevier*.

[2] Cf. *ibid.* September 21, 1836: an invocation to the priests of the future; and October 10, 1840: the emancipation of women; also *Z. f. d. e. W.* October 19, 1837: an attack on the asceticism of Christian art as unsuitable to the modern non-Christian philosophy of life.

was his inspiration and his strength during those long and wretched years when no other theme could uplift him and when he had no other guide.

The story of Wienbarg's career as a Saint-Simonian is as fragmentary as the story of his life; it does not finish, it breaks off; for the impulse which led him to embark on it became atrophied as his vision of beauty became blurred. But during the short period when he stood under the sign of Saint-Simonism he went further than the other Young Germans who at the most interpreted this doctrine to meet their own needs; he brought into it a new element of profoundly original thought. In his analysis of passion and the nature of God, he penetrated deeply into the mystery of life; and in his doctrine of strength he laid the foundations of a system whose far-reaching influence is still at work to-day. But before he had well begun, his powers forsook him, and we have no choice but to forsake him too with a feeling of deep regret that a mind which promised such great things should have been overclouded so soon.

But a word remains to be said. I am conscious that in this short sketch there is a degree of enthusiasm which may appear ill-judged. I have called Wienbarg noble when he was a drunkard and worse. I have given to what proved an unfulfilled promise the kind of praise generally reserved for achievement. I may fairly be accused of partisanship and a lack of dispassionate thought. But the explanation should be sought for in a strange quality of Wienbarg's rather than in any characteristics of my own. He has that curious power of life which leads to the creation of myths. It is a temptation difficult to resist when one comes within the radius of that strangely attractive spirit still so startlingly alive. And his contemporaries felt it so strongly that they did in fact build up a legend about Wienbarg during his life-time. The first impetus was given by the *Tagebuch von Helgoland* published in 1838. Wienbarg had retired to this island in 1836 to breathe for a time the air of freedom and to bathe his unquiet spirit in the restless sea, and the journal which appeared two years later is full of passages of great beauty, two of which may be quoted here to show how he contributed the outlines of the legendary figure which later bore his name:

Ich suche eine Handweit Erde ausser dem festen und gefesteten Europa, eine Lagerstätte unter den Menschen der fluthenden Wildniss, den Sturm, der allmählig schrillend die trägen Wellen vor sich aufrollt, vor allen Dingen die stürzende Brandung, die mich von dem Athem der Verhassten reinigen wird[1].

In früherer Zeit war die Schweizerreise ein romantisches Bedürfniss. Die Jugend begegnete sich in Tells Bergen, lange Alpenstäbe in der Hand. Die Schweiz hat viel von diesem Magnetismus eingebüsst. Die Poesie und die Freiheit suchen die Inseln und Küsten der Meere.... Von dort kam das Heldenkind, die deutsche Sage, und ihr Flügelschlag peitschte die leuchtenden Wogen. Am Stern der geschnäbelten Schiffe, hoch über den gewappneten Ruderen, stand der Sänger und sang kühne Lieder den Kühnen, die nach Kampf und Abenteuern zogen. Die deutsche Poesie ist auf der See geboren, im Binnenlande vergreiset und kindisch geworden[2].

In an enthusiastic review of the *Tagebuch von Helgoland* Gustav Kühne drew on such passages as these for the creation of a mythical Ludolf Wienbarg who never really existed in the flesh. He endowed him with the appearance and qualities of the hero of some Norse saga, a valiant warrior of olden days, blond of hair, giant-like of stature, akin in spirit to the stormy sea, a mystical kinsman of the island where he had sought refuge from the world[3]. Later, in 1846, when Wienbarg thought of emigrating to America, the legend was amplified: wrapped in a lofty silence, too noble to pander to the petty tyranny of those in authority, he was now seeking the land of freedom where his proud spirit might breathe at ease. We meet this mythical conception reflected in the memoirs of the time. His eyes, said Immermann, were reddened as if by many a tear; Hebbel emphatically rejected the supposition that his silence was due to impotence; Beurmann compared him to Bayard; Zeise likened him to a rock towering in lonely greatness towards the clouds. In vain did Gutzkow rage and scoff and tell a very different tale; the story of a blear-eyed drunkard and a pretentious fool, whose pitiable lectures were cut down to fifteen minutes for lack of subject-matter; who owed his reputation to him, Gutzkow, and had repaid him by the grossest ingratitude[4].

[1] *Tagebuch von Helgoland*, Hamburg, 1838, p. vi.
[2] *Ibid.* pp. 163–164.
[3] G. Kühne, *Portraits und Silhouetten*, Hanover, 1843, II, pp. 172 ff.; appeared first in the *Z. f. d. e. W.* June 23, 1838.
[4] K. Gutzkow, *Ausgewählte Werke*, XI, pp. 32–34.

The legend was stronger than his spite and still survives to-day[1]. And although we may reject it for our part, and smile at Kühne's picture of the wind-blown hair and the encircling sea-gulls; yet in some subtle way we find ourselves compelled to follow his example; to draw a nobler likeness of this writer than the facts may seem to warrant. It is as if he demanded it and insisted upon its truth; for Wienbarg of the clouded mind and the far from blameless life will wrestle with your spirit when he meets it, and you must exalt him before he lets you go.

[1] Cf. W. Schendell's introduction to the reprint of the *Tagebuch von Helgoland*, Hamburg, 1921.

CONCLUSION

It is the fashion to-day to pay some attention to the Young
German movement as a semi-political phenomenon; but it is
generally taken for granted that it produced no works of outstanding artistic merit, and that it was a failure from the literary
point of view. If this judgment is correct, the whole movement
is in a parlous state; for if it is to stand or fall by its political
achievements, then it must certainly fall. Politics played a
certain part in the early and even in the later works of these
men, but the converse is not true; they played no real part in
politics. They wrote in the cause of freedom in their youth,
and continued throughout their lives to give expression to
liberal ideals; but they reflected in this the spirit of their age,
and did not modify it greatly. There were others than they in
the progressive camp, mightier in action and mightier with the
pen. The Young Germans have little enough to show on the
practical side; Laube was a member of the first parliament, but
by that time he was too moderate to be effective. Gutzkow was
obliged to retire from participation in the public events of 1848
owing to the illness and death of his wife; and although Mundt
is rumoured to have fought on the barricades in Berlin, whilst
Wienbarg was a soldier in the war against Denmark, neither of
them attained to leadership or distinction. Their theoretical
contributions were rather more valuable; Heine's life-long campaign for liberty had its effect on his own age and also on
posterity by teaching many of his readers to think bold and
untraditional thoughts; but he was overshadowed by Börne
whose *Letters from Paris* were far more epoch-making than
Französische Zustände, let alone the pale imitations of Laube,
Gutzkow and Mundt.

But the statement that Young Germany was a political movement is not comprehensive enough; it should be amplified to
include the more important religious and social elements which
it contained; and as these elements were Saint-Simonian in their
origin, the only satisfactory definition of the school is to call it

a Saint-Simonian movement; it then becomes possible to determine how much they influenced the march of future events, and what were their positive achievements. At a first glance it would seem that they did not accomplish much, for they attacked both Christianity and the institution of marriage, and Christianity and marriage have survived.

As religious reformers the Young Germans contented themselves for the most part with violent attacks upon Catholicism, praise of the Protestant spirit and the advocacy of a less spiritual religion, which some called Christianity and others did not, prophesying, these latter, not without eloquence and fervour, the advent of a new and happier faith; whilst they were all agreed that great changes were to take place in the immediate future and that they were living in messianic times. These prophecies have not been fulfilled; the old religions pursue their unaltered course and no new Messiah has arisen to change the destinies of the world. But by proclaiming the rights of the sensual nature of man, they heralded that wave of materialism which swept over Europe and especially Germany soon afterwards and was finally engulfed in the recent war; so that, whether they influenced the future or not, they may be regarded as precursors.

Their subversive theories of marriage did not result in a social revolution, nor would they have done so if the governments had not intervened. Society has come unscathed through far worse storms than this; and there seem to be only two ways by which a sudden change in the fundamental social institutions may be permanently effected; the invasion by stronger races, for these have in the past imposed their customs on the conquered, or a great religious upheaval sweeping like a tidal wave over the earth and obliterating familiar landmarks. And even in such cases as these, the submerged society had probably already lost the principle of vitality. For humanity in the long run lives under a majority rule. The disaffected minority, often recruited among the more intellectual and enlightened of a given age, will only in very unusual circumstances be able to accomplish sweeping social changes. But by stating their grievances and by advocating reforms, they make a convert here and there; until many generations later, perhaps, the minority may become the majority, and the changes may take place. This is the modest part which the Young Germans played in social life. The institution of marriage remains, but its aspect has changed; the greater freedom between men and women offers a wider basis for choice, and women, being economically less dependent on marriage, can look before they leap. These three changes have made of the married state something much less rigid and inevitable; there is also considerably less rigidity about the accomplished fact; but marriage itself, being the basis of the family, a fact too little regarded by these headlong young men, persists and shows no signs, a hundred years after they wrote, of approaching dissolution.

As political, religious and social innovators the Young Germans were awkwardly placed, for they were neither statesmen nor priests; they attempted to influence the world through the medium of their writings, but these were too academic to be widely effective; whilst their literary value was undoubtedly diminished by the alien presence of an unaesthetic purpose. In so far as they had a common literary aim, they reacted rather violently against romanticism which they held to be divorced from actual life, imprisoned in the fortress of mediaevalism, entangled in the web of Catholicism and deaf to the call of liberty. By way of protest they set up the standard of 'Tendenzliteratur' and advanced threateningly on their foes. But although they dealt the *coup de grâce* to the already moribund school, their conscious literary aims played no part in this rather strange affair, and indeed those aims were a danger to no one but themselves. Saint-Simonism was responsible for the death of the romantic school, for although this curious religion was romantic in its origins it absorbed other elements as it grew which are incompatible with romance. It became logical, practical, socialistic and dogmatic, where German romanticism had been visionary, philosophical, subjective and poetical. It transplanted the romantic theory blooming in a mysterious wood into a tidy kitchen-garden where it withered away in despair.

For it is one thing to explore the bowels of the earth in search of fairy gold, and another to hasten the advent of a money-grubbing age. It is possible to prophesy a 'Ganzmensch' who shall be man and woman in one, and yet not to welcome a 'social couple' who are rather like Siamese twins. There is a fascination in dreams of a future where love shall be unfettered by laws, a quality conspicuously absent among the constant, the inconstant and the 'calm.' Whilst to experience the harmonious sensation of being one with the sensuous world is not to enter a conspiracy to 'emancipate the flesh.' And one may know religious longings and mystical communion with God, and yet remain aloof from a clamorous sect with a practical programme of reforms.

Such roughly was the kinship between the theories of the German romantic school and those of the Saint-Simonian religion; and it seems as if the younger movement must have been an offshoot from the German tree of romance, although whether by a conscious process of grafting or by unconscious fertilisation it is not easy to say. Nor is it always possible to determine whether the Young Germans went back for their theories to the romantic school or across the Rhine to the Saint-Simonians. But they certainly interpreted them in the Saint-Simonian way, bringing reality and romance into such violent contact that reality became distorted and romance gave up the ghost. Pathological cases have been known in which the patient having slept peacefully for many years awoke at length and incontinently died. The romantic theory was some such dreamer as this, and during her protracted trance she had visions of lifting the veil from truth. But roughly awakened by the Young German cheers, she opened full those dreaming eyes, saw reality for a moment's space, then turned away and slept again.

In the province of literature therefore the Young Germans performed one outstanding destructive action which was probably beneficial to the health of poetry, too long sequestered in the ruined castle of romance, but this was not their only achievement here. Three of these men, and perhaps four, produced works during the period 1830–1835 which have a place in the world of letters. Heine's contributions are in no danger of being forgotten and in no need of an apology, but the fact that they belong to the Young German movement is apt to be overlooked. Wienbarg's *Aesthetische Feldzüge* and Mundt's *Memoir of Charlotte Stieglitz* should be added to these, and possibly Laube's *Poeten*; they are not immortal works of art, but outstanding and typical monuments of an age whose task it was rather to prepare the way for others than to win lasting fame for themselves. For it would be possible to sum up their achievements negatively as a series of reactions against the tyranny, piety, prudishness and romanticism of their day, but these achievements have their positive side. The Young Germans were humble pioneers on the road of progress and they have enriched literature by the way. So much for their relative importance, so much for their status in the world. But no one who has studied them closely will be content to judge them by their success, for this misleading standard does not measure their absolute worth. Not one of these men but is interesting for his own sake, and for the most part they are better worth knowing than their books.

Nor is the story of their ill-starred venture absorbing from the human point of view alone—there were deeper issues involved. The Young Germans were not, as it superficially appears, fortuitously and arbitrarily grouped together by an unenlightened government; they were predestined victims, akin to each other by an unusual sensitiveness to the spirit of their times. They responded almost unanimously to the July Revolution; they caught up and passed on the enthusiasm for Poland; with one accord they re-echoed Enfantin's war-cry 'emancipate the flesh.' And this acclamation proved their undoing; they fell as victims to reaction, for the old ideas were strong. They paid a heavy penalty materially—and spiritually as well. Heine alone preserved the integrity of his inmost self; but he was soon at war with Gutzkow and embroiled in endless feuds. Laube turned traitor to his comrades and his erstwhile dearest beliefs. Gutzkow became suspicious, and more gloomy, more bitter than before; Mundt underwent a mental and moral deterioration, whilst Wienbarg fell into silence and drifted towards a pitiable end.

It was not entirely in the cause of progress that they

suffered this cruel fate. There were many ideas abroad at that date—Saint-Simonism embraced them nearly all—but some only were destined to prevail; the others, which belonged more particularly to that period and endowed it with a quality of its own, have not survived. The Young Germans dissociated themselves from industrialism; they rejected feminism with scornful amusement, they were moderately interested, but no more, in socialism. Yet these phenomena have taken root and flourished; whilst the desire for a new religion which should acknowledge the senses as divine has dwindled to sporadic outbursts in the minds of mystical cranks. And this was the vision which dazzled them all, and to which they raised a paean of praise.

Heine spoke with the inspiration of a poet who had suffered in the spirit and the flesh; Laube as a lover of women with strong and unruly desires; Gutzkow shaking with temper and the sense of an intolerable wrong; Mundt like a youthful pedant who had suddenly learnt to be a man, and Wienbarg with the passionate enthusiasm of one who sees beauty unveiled. They all responded differently; their similarity lay in the response to that strange fantastic vision of a hundred years ago. Like the strings of a harp played upon by the wind, they caught the essential spirit of the times in which they lived and expressed it in ephemeral sound. Such renderings are doomed to be transient; posterity hears them faintly, and may one day hear them no more.

The Young Germans were too much the sons of their age to outlive it for long; but the movement has been saved from oblivion by its association with Heine's name. He lifts the whole school into a prominence which it could not attain alone. It will be remembered by the power of his genius until the world is so much and so sadly changed that men will no longer listen to his music, respond to the appeal of his sorrow and delight in his merciless wit.

INDEX

Aesthetische Feldzüge, 239, 420, 423
  Mundt influenced by, 349
  Saint-Simonian ideals in, 404 ff.,
    427
  shows influence of Heine, 405
Allgemeine Kirchenzeitung, anta-
    gonism to Saint-Simonians, 63
Allgemeine Zeitung, 173, 181, 242,
    261, 317, 349
  attitude to the Saint-Simonians,
    60 ff.
  prints anonymous articles on
    Saint-Simonism, 61, 62
  Heine's articles for, 90
  Donndorf's articles on Saint-
    Simonism in, 97
  Laube attacks Young Germans in,
    243
  Gutzkow's defence of his opinions
    in, 310
  Wienbarg's articles in, 421
Almansor
  criticisms of Christianity in, 131,
    144
  argument of, 132
Année de la Mère, 32
Antoniens Bussfahrten, 377
*Appellation an den gesunden Men-
    schenverstand*, Gutzkow's pro-
    test against charge of Saint-
    Simonism in, 265
Arnim, Bettina von
  and the Young Germans, 80
  publication of correspondence with
    Goethe, 80
  her kinship with the Saint-Simon-
    ians, 81
Aurora, Laube's editorship of, 196
Ausland, prints articles on Saint-
    Simonism, 62

Barrault, Emile, 20, 21, 32
  fined for association with Saint-
    Simonians, 30
  his search for the 'femme Messie,'
    80, 34, 103
Busiliah oder Gesichterstullen, Der,
    324, 325
  argument of, 325
Baud, Henri, 20, 103
Bazard, Amand (see also under
    names of works), 5, 9, 10, 15 ff.,
    96, 97, 102, 103, 131, 137, 174,
    405, 406

early career of, 12, 13
recognises Enfantin as head of
  Saint-Simonian religion, 18
breaks with Enfantin, 19
his protests in the *Globe*, 22
his views, on progress, 37, 38; on
  the law of property, 39; on
  education, 40; on Christianity,
  41 ff.; on the organisation of
  society, 44; on industry, 44
Bazard, works of
  *Doctrine de Saint-Simon. Première
    année*, 37 ff.; *Doctrine de Saint-
    Simon. Deuxième année*, 37,
    42 ff.
Bazard, Claire, 16, 17, 28
*Beiträge zur Geschichte der neuen
    Literatur*, 267
Belgiojoso, Princess Christine, 90,
    157
Béranger, Pierre Jean de, 20, 97
Berliner Schnellpost, stories by
  Mundt in, 322, 323
Bibeldieb, Der, 326, 346, 356
  argument of, 325
Biedenfeld, Ferdinand L. K. von,
    173, 174, 179
Blanc, Louis, his account of meet-
  ings of Saint-Simonians, 18
Blasedow und seine Söhne, 270, 379
Blätter für literarische Unterhaltung,
    181, 190, 349
  Laube's articles in, 179, 200
  Laube's criticism of Christianity
    in, 201
  Mundt attacks Hegelian system
    in, 328
Bocage, Pierre Martinien, 160
Börne, Ludwig, 67, 112, 187, 199,
    223, 265, 272, 273, 279, 421
  his *Briefe aus Paris*, 67, 197, 238
  his attitude to the Saint-Simon-
    ians, 68, 69
  his personality, 69, 187
  influences Laube towards Liberal-
    ism, 176, 178, 196 ff., 255
  his letters to Jeannette Wohl, 199
  Deutsche Postschnecke, his mono-
    graph on, 223
  his influence with Laube wanes,
    238
  influences Gutzkow towards Li-
    beralism, 260
  part-editor of the *Reformateur*, 266

Börne, allusions to, in Mundt's
  articles, 361, 384
Breslauer Zeitung, 173
  Laube's dramatic criticisms in, 196
Bretschneider, Karl Gottlieb, 173
Briefe aus Paris, 67, 197, 238
Briefe eines Narren an eine Närrin,
  264, 276 ff., 280, 297, 344
  reviewed by Laube, 238
  references to Saint-Simonism in,
    262
  Gutzkow's attitude to the woman
    question, 263, 268
  influence of Börne shown in, 277
Briefe über Deutschland, 162, 167
Brisbane, Albert, 71
Brockhaus, Heinrich, 179, 193, 194
Büchner, Georg, 300
Bürger, Die, 248 ff.
  argument of, 252
  pessimism of, 254
Burns, Robert, 12
Byron, George Gordon Noel, Lord, 279

Campe, Valeger Julius
  Heine's correspondence with, 91,
    92, 106, 111, 113, 165
  Heine's financial struggle with, 112
    and Gutzkow, 301
Carmela oder die Wiedertaufe, 390
Carnot, Lazare-Hippolyte, 19, 96, 112,
  116
Caseaux, Euryale, 18, 19
Charlotte Stieglitz, ein Denkmal, 83,
  331, 338 ff.
  literary merit of, 366 ff.
Charton, Edouard, 19
Chasles, Philarète, 107
Chevalier, Michel, 29 ff., 46, 99 ff.,
  121 ff., 272
  editor of the *Globe*, 29
  before the court of assizes, 29, 30,
    32
  imprisonment in Ste Pélagie, 32
  his break with Enfantin, 32, 34,
    102
  his friendship with Heine, 90, 93,
    97, 122, 123, 126
  Gutzkow's opinion of, 270
Christianity
  Saint-Simonism and, 7, 8, 9, 41 ff.,
    219
  Heine and, 131 ff., 139, 143, 144,
    147 ff., 157, 163
  Laube and, 178, 188, 189, 198, 219
  Mundt and, 354, 363, 365, 383
  Wienbarg and, 406, 416
'Compagnons de la femme,' 33

David, Félicien, 113, 152, 192
De l' Allemagne, 108, 155, 229
  dedication to Enfantin, 104
  second edition of, 119 ff.
  Enfantin's reception of, 152
  Saint-Simonian doctrines in, 155,
    157, 162, 168, 169
Depping, G. B., 63
Deutsche Blätter, 267
Deutsche Revue, 267, 317
  Gutzkow and Wienberg joint
    editors of, 419
Doctrine de Saint-Simon, 37 ff., 94,
  129, 144
Donndorf
  his anonymous articles on Saint-
    Simonism, 61, 62
  his acquaintance with the Saint-
    Simonians, 62
Du Camp, Maxime, 193
Duett, Das, 323
Dugied, 19
Duveyrier, Charles, 12, 29 ff.,
  100
  his 'De la femme,' 29
  before the court of assizes, 29
  charges against, 29
  his eloquence at trial, 30, 114
  escapes term of imprisonment,
    32
  letters from Heine to, 90, 107
  his *Lettres Politiques*, 114

Eichthal, Gustave d', 12, 25, 31, 63
Einheit Deutschlands, Die, 329
Elementargeister, 147, 158, 159, 161,
  169
Enfantin, Barthélemy Prosper (see
  also under names of works and
  letters), 10, 13 ff., 67, 73, 97, 99,
  100, 102, 103, 108, 109, 111, 113,
  122, 123, 125, 152, 155, 174, 181,
  194, 195, 265, 269, 354, 356,
  406, 407, 409, 410
  early history of, 12
  opinions on the relations of the
    sexes, 14, 15, 21, 47 ff.
  his quarrel with Bazard, 19
  his ascendancy in Saint-Simonian
    movement, 20
  proceedings against, 21
  his retirement to Ménilmontant,
    23
  his personality, 23 ff.
  trial of, 29, 30, 100
  his influence wanes, 31
  confinement in Ste Pélagie, 32
  second trial and acquittment, 32

Enfantin, abandoned by Chevalier, 32, 34, 102
his plan for the Suez Canal, 35
the teaching of the *Enseignements*, 46 ff.
his relations with Heine, 88, 92, 103 ff., 123
his reception of *De l'Allemagne*, 152
influences plot of *Die Poeten*, 204 ff.
resemblance of *Maha Guru* to, 283 ff.
Enfantin, works of
  Enseignements, 20, 21, 27, 29, 46 ff., 156, 173, 218, 266, 267
  La lettre sur le calme, 25
  Œuvres complètes, 27
Enfantin, letters of
  to his mother, 17
  to Morin, 26
  to Heine, 105
Enseignements d'Enfantin, 20, 21, 27, 29, 46 ff., 156, 173, 218, 266, 267
Erinnerungen, 172, 193
Erziehung des Menschengeschlechts, 12, 101
Evangelische Kirchenzeitung, 349

Fanfernot, Julie, 15
Fichte, Johann Gottlieb, 150
Figaro, 21, 69
Forum der Journalliteratur, 317
  Gutzkow, editor of, 260, 274
Fourier, Charles, 13, 74, 269, 286
  debt of Saint-Simonism to, 50
Fournel, Cécile, 19, 29
  founds *Le livre des actes*, 32
Fournel, Henri, 19
Französische Zustände, 98, 158, 238
  reviewed by Laube, 237
Freihafen, 379, 384

Gedanken im Kerker, 267
Gemäldeausstellung in Paris, 96
Geschichte der Gesellschaft, 390 ff.
Geschichte der Literatur der Gegenwart, 391, 392
Geschichte der neueren schönen Literatur in Deutschland, 100, 119, 403, 405
  references to Saint-Simonism in, 107, 108
  reviewed by Laube, 237
Geschichte der Religion und Philosophie in Deutschland, 100, 119, 159, 161, 162
  Saint-Simonian influence shown in, 108, 142, 147

Geständnisse, 119 162
  French version of, 120
Geständnisse über Religion und Christenthum, 264, 301, 304
Globe, 13, 15, 20, 68, 98, 101, 102, 103, 173
  ceases publication, 22, 23
  references to Heine in, 96
  Heine's interest in, 97, 98
Glück, Das, 246
Goethe, Johann Wolfgang von, 78, 80, 146, 309
Götter, Helden, Don Quixote, 271
Göttin Diana, 158, 161
Guéroult, Adolphe, 48, 49
Gustav Adolph, 196
Gutzkow, Karl (see also under names of works and letters), 79, 83, 85, 112, 183, 238, 348, 423 ff.
  his connection with Laube, 238, 288
  his personality, 258
  early years, 259, 274
  and Rosalie Scheidemantel, 260, 290, 291
  early criticisms of Saint-Simonism, 261 ff., 269, 276
  attitude to feminism, 263, 267, 268, 270, 276, 278, 287, 313
  and the Young Germans, 265 ff., 270, 271, 292, 312, 316
  influenced by Menzel, 272, 273, 274 ff., 288, 300
  influenced by the Saint-Simonians, 277 ff., 281 ff.
  his criticism of his friends, 289, 300
  alienates the Lutherans, 289, 290
  his preface to the *Vertraute Briefe über die Lucinde*, 291, 295 ff.
  the attack on Christianity in *Wally*, 304, 305
  his waning interest in Saint-Simonism, 307, 308
  outcry of public opinion against *Wally*, 307
  his defence against attack, 310
  his marriage, 311
  denial of Saint-Simonian ideals, 312, 313 ff.
  persecuted by Mundt and Kühne, 379
  his condemnation of Wienbarg, 422, 429
Gutzkow, works of
  Appellation an den gesunden Menschenverstand, 265
  Beiträge zur Geschichte der neuen Literatur, 267

Gutzkow, works of
  Briefe eines Narren an eine Närrin,
    238, 262, 263, 264, 268, 280, 297,
    344
  Geständnisse über Religion und
    Christenthum, 264, 301, 304
  Götter, Helden, Don Quixote, 271
  Hamlet in Wittenberg, 317
  Maha Guru, 263, 281, 288, 289, 315
  Nero, 301, 317
  Novellen, 317
  Oeffentliche Charaktere, 317
  Philosophie der Geschichte, 267, 312,
    315
  Ritter vom Geiste, 317
  Rothe Mütze und die Kapuze, Die,
    271
  Rückblicke auf mein Leben, 317, 424
  Sadducäer von Amsterdam, Der,
    290, 302
  Seraphine, 268, 379
  Soireen, 317
  Telegraph für Deutschland, 268
  Ueber Goethe im Wendepunkt
    zweier Jahrhunderte, 312
  Urbild des Tartüffe, Das, 258
  Uriel Acosta, 258, 290
  Vergangenheit und Gegenwart, 271,
    384
  Wally, die Zweiflerin, 79, 244,
    264 ff., 300 ff., 309 ff., 421, 422
  Zeitgenossen, Die, 268
  Zopf und Schwert, 258
Gutzkow, letters of
  to Börne, 265
  to Tzschoppe, 312
  to Rochus von Rochow, 312
  to Münch-Bellinghausen, 312
  to Liesching, 399, 422

Hamlet in Wittenberg, 317
Hebbel, Christian Friedrich, 160, 176,
  429
Hegel, Georg Wilhelm, 137, 152,
  166, 329
  references of Heine to, 166, 167
  emancipation of Mundt from, 328
Heine, Heinrich (see also under
  names of works and letters),
  35, 60 ff., 68, 175, 182, 195, 271,
  348, 361 ff., 382, 403 ff., 421
  influences Donndorf's articles in
    Allgemeine Zeitung, 62, 97
  his friendship with the Varnhagens,
    70
  first allusion to Saint-Simonism, 70
  character and personality of, 88,
    89, 128 ff., 139 ff.

  references to Saint-Simonism in
    works, 89 ff.
  relations with the Saint-Simonians,
    90 ff., 94, 98
  plans for book on Saint-Simonism,
    91
  his lost Memoirs, 92
  present at meetings of Saint-
    Simonians, 102, 103, 109
  conversation with Michel Cheva-
    lier, 102
  friendship with Enfantin, 103,
    109, 110
  denies membership of Saint-Si-
    monian sect, 107, 108
  and Gutzkow, 112
  his duel with Strauss, 112
  his marriage, 112
  financial straits, 118, 123 ff.
  illness, 118, 163
  his 'confessions of faith,' 119, 165
  and Emile Pereire, 123 ff.
  expressions of religious opinions,
    131 ff., 139, 144, 154, 157, 159 ff.
  his political opinions, 135, 136
  his kinship with the Saint-Simon-
    ians, 138 ff.
  his attitude to Romanticism,
    144 ff.
  and the Young Germans, 146, 147,
    153, 157
  his pantheism, 149 ff., 161
  his interpretation of Saint-Si-
    monian doctrine, 152 ff.
  abandons Saint-Simonian ideals,
    157 ff.
  his religious conversion, 163 ff.
  influence of Hegel on, 166 ff.
  his debt to the Saint-Simonians,
    168 ff.
  attacks the Saint-Simonians,
    170 ff.
  his friendship with Laube, 175,
    223 ff.
  a meeting with Laube, 192
Heine, works of
  Almansor, 131
  Atta Troll, 159
  Briefe über Deutschland, 162, 167
  De l'Allemagne, 104, 108, 119,
    120, 152, 156, 157, 162, 168 ff.,
    229
  Elementargeister, 147, 158, 159,
    161, 169
  Faustballet, 158, 161
  Französische Zustände, 158, 237,
    238
  Gemäldeausstellung in Paris, 96

Heine, works of
  Geständnisse, 119, 162
  Götter im Exil, 169
  Göttin Diana, 158, 161
  Heinrich Heine über Ludwig
    Börne, 158, 159, 161
  Lutetia, 114, 116
  Nachwort zum Romancero, 119
  Reisebilder, Die, 106, 107, 135 ff.,
    158,165,166,223 ff.,279,298,403
  Romantik, Die, 145
  Romantische Schule, 142, 144 ff.,
    161, 162, 224, 225, 229, 237,
    280, 281
  Salon I, 153
  Salon II, 165, 167, 348, 362, 363
  Schriftstellernöthen, 112
  Schwäbische Dichterschule, 112
  Stadt Lucca, 133
  Vorrede zu Kahldorf über den Adel,
    96
  Zur Geschichte der neueren schönen
    Literatur in Deutschland, 100,
    107, 108, 119, 237, 403, 405
  Zur Geschichte der Religion und
    Philosophie in Deutschland, 100,
    108, 119, 142, 147, 159, 161, 162
Heine, letters of
  to Cotta, 62
  to Varnhagen von Ense, 70, 95, 99,
    101, 108, 112
  to Michel Chevalier, 90, 121, 123
  to Duveyrier, 90, 107
  to Camille Selden, 91
  to Campe, 91, 92, 106, 111, 113, 165
  to Hartwig Hesse, 94
  to Laube, 113, 153, 264
  to Moser, 157
Hengstenberg, Ernst Wilhelm, 160,
  400
Hesse, Hartwig, 94, 95
Hippel, Theodor Gottlieb von, 343,
  344
  Mundt's criticism of his views on
    women, 329
Hirth, Friedrich, 89, 90, 94
Holland in den Jahren 1831 und 1832,
  420
Huber, Therese, 275, 286
Huber, Viktor Amadeus, 412

Industrie, L', 6
Introduction aux travaux scienti-
  fiques, 7

Jahrbuch der Literatur, 379
Jahrbücher für wissenschaftliche
  Kritik, 343, 381

Mundt's reviews of Das Buch
  Rahel in, 351, 363
Jarcke, Karl Ernst, 197
Jugements de la Doctrine de Saint-
  Simon sur les derniers évène-
  ments, 13
July Revolution, 196, 197, 260, 324
  Saint-Simonians and, 13
Junge Europa, Das, 245, 247, 249
Junge Literatur, Die, 246

Kant, Immanuel, 150, 409
Komet, Der, 196
Krieger, Die, 248 ff.
Kritische Wälder, 239, 327 ff., 330
Kühne, Ferdinand Gustav, 79
  his friendship with Mundt, 365,
    375
  relations with the Young Ger-
    mans, 365
  editor of Zeitung für die elegante
    Welt, 365, 366
  his attack on Gutzkow, 379
  his appreciation of Wienbarg,
    429, 430

Lafayette, Marquis Gilbert de, 13
Lamartine, Alphonse de, 11, 12, 35
Lamennais, Félicité-Robert de, 160
Laube, Heinrich (see also under
  names of works and letters), 69,
  83, 113, 116, 152, 160, 288, 348,
  425
  his Saint-Simonian tendencies,
    172 ff., 189 ff., 193 ff.
  early years, 174, 175, 196
  and the Young Germans, 175, 187,
    189, 191, 192, 239
  his friends, 175, 238
  character and personality, 175,
    176
  his relations with women, 176, 186
  religious opinions, 178, 188, 189,
    219, 226
  editor of Zeitung für die elegante
    Welt, 180, 182
  and Enfantin, 181, 182, 191, 195,
    255, 256
  political views, 183
  banishment, 184
  arrest and imprisonment, 185 ff.
  release from prison, 189
  marriage, 191, 254
  a meeting with Heine, 192
  his literary career begins, 196
  Börne's influence on, 197, 198
  his revolutionary ideas expressed
    in writings, 197, 200 ff.

Laube, Saint-Simonian ideas in his writings, 201, 207 ff.
his attitude to feminism, 202, 213, 220, 221
the argument of *Die Poeten*, 203 ff.
influence of Heine on, 223 ff.
his sensuality, 229 ff.
his connection with Gutzkow, 238, 288
attacks the Young German movement, 243 ff.
denial of Saint-Simonian ideals, 244, 245
Laube, works of
Blätter für literarische Unterhaltung, 181
Bürger, Die, 248, 251 ff.
Erinnerungen, 172, 193
Glück, Das, 246
Gustav Adolph, 196
Junge Europa, Das, 245, 247, 248, 249
Junge Literatur, Die, 244, 246
Krieger, Die, 248 ff.
Liebesbriefe, 246
Moderne Charakteristiken, 173, 247
Nachträge, 172, 173, 193
Neue Jahrhundert, Das, 180, 183, 194, 197, 200, 247, 344
Neue Reisenovellen, 248
Nicolo Zaganini, 196
Poeten, Die, 173, 176, 183, 191, 194, 203 ff., 250, 251, 288
Reisenovellen, 183, 185, 194, 209, 211, 223 ff., 247
Schauspielerin, Die, 246
Laube, letters of
to Pückler-Muskau, 190
to Heine, 193, 248
Laurent, P.-M., 20
Leben Jesu, 301
Lechevalier, Jules, 16, 19, 392
Lélia, 270, 300, 302
Leroux, Pierre, 19, 96, 114 ff., 160
Lesseps, Ferdinand, Vicomte de, 36
Lessing, Gotthold Ephraim, 12, 101
Lettre sur le Calme, La, 25
Lettres d'un habitant de Genève, 7
Lewald, August, 281
Liebesbriefe, 246
Liszt, Franz, 160
Literarische und kritische Blätter der Börsenhalle, Wienbarg literary editor of, 412, 419
Literarischer Zodiacus, 381
Mundt's articles in, 361 ff.
Literaturblatt zum Morgenblatt, 261, 267

Gutzkow's contributions to, 274, 279, 317
attacks on Gutzkow in, 310
Literaturblatt zum Phönix, 300, 376, 421
Gutzkow's literary criticisms in, 300, 317
Gutzkow's review of *Lélia* in, 302
Louis-Philippe, 35
Lucinde, 291
the argument of, 292 ff.
Lutetia, 114, 116
Lytton, Bulwer, 186, 194

Madelon, oder die Romantiker in Paris, 324
Madonna. Unterhaltungen mit einer Heiligen, 79, 335, 352 ff., 361, 362, 370
Saint-Simonian ideas in, 353
Magazin für die Literatur des Auslands, 201
Mundt on the staff of, 349
Maha Guru, Geschichte eines Gottes, 265, 281 ff.
the argument of, 281, 282
Saint-Simonian ideas in, 283 ff.
Mehemet Ali, 35
Ménilmontant, 23 ff., 63, 98, 99, 102, 103, 179, 192
foundation of Saint-Simonian community at, 23
ceremonies at, 28
disbandment of the community at, 32
Menzel, Wolfgang, 85, 260, 261, 280, 330, 371, 372, 421
his attacks on the Young Germans, 85, 153, 371
Gutzkow a disciple of, 273, 274, 279, 308
his influence with Gutzkow slackens, 288
his attack on Gutzkow, 309, 310, 371
his interest in Mundt, 323
and Wienbarg, 421, 422
Michelet, Jules, 160
Mitternachtzeitung, 191, 243, 244
Moderne Charakteristiken, 173, 247
Moderne Lebenswirren, 344 ff.
Saint-Simonian ideas in, 345
Morgenblatt, 274, 381
articles on Saint-Simonism in, 63, 64, 261
Gutzkow's contributions to, 274, 275, 317

Mundt, Theodor (see also under names of works and letters), 70, 79, 238, 239, 271, 316, 425
his personality, 320
early work, 322
encouraged by Menzel, 323, 330
feminist opinions, 326, 329, 346, 350, 355, 364, 365, 374, 383, 393
early Saint-Simonian ideals, 326, 345
his critical essays, 327
his emancipation from Hegel, 328, 329
friendship with Charlotte Stieglitz, 331 ff., 350
interest in Rahel Varnhagen, 342 ff., 351
and the Young Germans, 342, 370, 371, 378
his essay on Rahel, 343
Saint - Simonian influences strengthened, 348 ff.
his religious opinions, 354, 356, 363, 364, 383
his review of Salon II, 363
his memoir of Charlotte Stieglitz, 366 ff.
under the ban of the government, 370 ff.
the accusation of Young German sympathies, 370
later works, 377
his attack on the Young Germans, 378
his quarrel with Gutzkow, 378, 379
later references to Saint-Simonism, 380 ff., 389 ff., 392
his marriage, 385 ff.
republishes earlier works, 389
later years and death, 389 ff.
scope of his work, 393
Mundt, works of
Antoniens Bussfahrten, 377
Basilisk oder Gesichterstudien, 324, 326
Riheldieb, Der, 325, 326, 346, 356
Carmela oder die Wiedertaufe, 390, 391
Charaktere und Situationen, 377, 380
Charlotte Stieglitz, ein Denkmal, 040 ff., 366, 367 ff.
Delphin, Der, 377, 681
Dioskuren, 377
Duett, Das, 323, 324, 326
Einheit Deutschlands in politischer und ideeller Entwickelung, Die, 329, 333

Geschich ie der Gesellschaft, 390 ff.
Geschichte der Literatur der Gegenwart, 391, 392
Komödie der Neigungen, 378
Kritische Wälder, 239, 327 ff., 330
Literarischer Zodiacus, 361, 363 ff.
Madelon, oder die Romantiker in Paris, 324
Madonna. Unterhaltungen mit einer Heiligen, 335, 352 ff., 361, 362 ff., 370
Moderne Lebenswirren, 331 ff., 344
Pariser Kaiserskizzen, 393
Paris und Louis Napoleon, 393
Spaziergänge und Weltfahrten, 378, 379, 382
Mundt, letters of
to Menzel, 330
to Charlotte and Heinrich Stieglitz, 335 ff.
to Kühne, 341
to Varnhagen von Ense, 382
Musset, Alfred de, 12

Nachträge, 172, 173, 193
Nachwort zum Romancero, 119
Naturphilosophie, 149
Nero, 301, 317
Neue Jahrhundert, Das, 180 ff., 194, 196, 197, 199, 200, 247
Saint-Simonian ideas in, 181 ff.
Neue Reisenovellen, 248
Newton, Sir Isaac, 7
Nicolo Zaganini, 196
Notice Historique, 93, 102
Nouveau Christianisme, 8 ff., 15, 144

Oeffentliche Charaktere, 317

Pereire, Emile, 12, 90, 123, 124
Pereire, Isaac, 12
Philosophie der Geschichte, 267, 312, 315
Phönix, Frühlingszeitung für Deutschland, 300
Planet, Der, 196
Poeten, Die, 176, 183, 191, 230, 244, 249 ff., 288
argument of, 203 ff.
influence of Enfantin in, 208 ff.
Polen (see Neue Jahrhundert, Das)
Politische Briefe (see Neue Jahrhundert, Das)
Politisches Wochenblatt, 197
Prospektus to Mitternachtzeitung, 248
Pückler-Muskau, Fürst Hermann von, 76 ff., 175, 185, 198
life and character of, 76, 77

Pückler-Muskau, his introduction to Saint-Simonism, 77, 78

Quinet, Edgar, 160

Rahel, ein Buch des Andenkens für ihre Freunde, 70 ff., 343 ff., 351
Reformateur, 266, 267
Reisebilder, Die, 106, 107, 135 ff., 158, 223 ff., 279, 298, 403
political and religious conflict in, 136, 137
pessimism of, 137, 138
sentimentality of, 139
French edition of, 165
a model for Laube's Reisenovellen, 223, 225 ff.
Reisenovellen, Die, 183, 185, 194, 209, 211, 223 ff., 247
influence of Die Reisebilder on, 223, 225
sensualism of, 231
Réorganisation de la société euro-péenne, 9
Rességuier, Jules, Comte de, 12, 13
Revue de Paris, 107
Revue des deux Mondes, 108, 119
Revue Encyclopédique, 173
Reynaud, Jean, 18 ff., 103
Richter, Jean Paul Friedrich, 276, 277
Ritter vom Geiste, 317
Rodrigues, Eugène
his translation of Erziehung des Menschengeschlechts, 12, 101
letters, to Burns, 12; to Rességuier, 12
Rodrigues, Olinde, 7, 10, 18, 20, 29, 30, 32, 41, 49, 93
and the Comte de Saint-Simon, 12
his Note on marriage and divorce, 17, 21, 49
Romantik, Die, 145
Romantische Schule, Die, 142 ff., 161, 162, 224, 225, 229, 280, 281
Heine's attitude to Romanticism in, 145
Laube's criticism of, 237
Rothe Mütze und die Kapuze, Die, 271
Rückblicke auf mein Leben, 317, 424

Sadducäer von Amsterdam, Der, 290, 302
Sainte-Hilaire, Aglaé, 29
Saint-Simon, Claude Henri de Rouvroy, Comte de (see also under names of works), 4 ff.
his early life, 4
theories of social progress, 5, 6
his religious opinions, 6 ff.
the position of women in his scheme, 7
poverty and attempted suicide, 8
Christianity and sensualism reconciled, 10
Saint-Simon, works of
Industrie, L', 6
Introduction aux travaux scienti-fiques, 7
Lettres d'un habitant de Genève, 7
Nouveau Christianisme, 8, 9 ff., 12, 15, 392
Réorganisation de la société euro-péenne, 9
Saint-Simon und der Saintsimon-ismus, 392
Saint-Simonians, the (see also under Heine, Laube, Gutzkow, Mundt, Wienbarg, Börne, Kühne, etc.)
early days, 11 ff.
schisms, 14 ff.
search for high priestess, 14, 15, 33
theories on marriage and divorce, 15 ff.
proceedings against, 21, 28, 97, 100
financial difficulties, 22
community life at Ménilmontant, 23, 24, 27
the Society disbanded, 30
Saint-Simonism
and Christianity, 7, 8, 9, 41 ff., 219
the doctrine of Bazard and Enfan-tin, 37 ff.
its connection with the Young German movement, 50, 70, 72 ff., 79, 81, 83, 268
reports of, in German press, 52 ff.
knowledge of, in Germany, 61
attitude of German public opinion to, 63, 64
influence of, on Heine, 142 ff.
influence of, on Laube, 172 ff., 189 ff., 193 ff., 208 ff., 225
Gutzkow's criticisms of, 261 ff.
Gutzkow influenced by, 274 ff., 283 ff., 295 ff.
Mundt influenced by, 348 ff.
Mundt attacks its tenets, 363
Wienbarg influenced by, 407 ff., 412, 428
Salon II, 165, 167, 348, 362, 363
Sand, George, 11, 155, 160, 305, 380
Schall, Karl, 173, 174

Schauspielerin, Die, 246
Schelling, Friedrich von, 137, 149, 152, 167
Schlegel, Friedrich, 292 ff.
Schleiermacher, Friedrich, 289, 291, 294
Schlesische Zeitung, 196
Schnitzler, J. H., 61
Schriften in bunter Reihe, 361
Schwabenspiegel, 112
Selden, Camille, 91 ff.
Seraphine, 268, 379
Sittengemälde, Heine's introduction to, 161
Société de la morale chrétienne, 63
Soireen, 317
Spaziergänge und Weltfahrten, 378, 379, 382
Spinoza, Baruch, 149, 152
Stadt Lucca, Die, 133
Staël, Madame de, 7, 174
   attack on, by Heine, 120, 166
Stanhope, Lady Hester Lucy, 33, 74, 77
Stieglitz, Charlotte, 78, 79, 82, 83
   her friendship with Theodor Mundt, 79, 331 ff.
   her death, 79, 82, 340
   her feminism, 83, 368
   Mundt's memoir of, 331, 366 ff.
   dedication of *Kritische Wälder* to, 331
   her letters to Mundt, 331, 336, 340
Stieglitz, Heinrich, 82, 331 ff., 367 ff.
Strauss, Salomon, his duel with Heine, 112
Suez Canal, 35, 36, 50, 102, 261, 263

Tagebuch von Helgoland, 428, 429
Talabot, Paulin, 20, 28, 36, 63
Telegraph für Deutschland, 268, 378
Tristran, Flora, 32
Tzschoppe, J. A. von, 184

Unterhaltungen am häuslichen Herd, Gutzkow editor of, 317
Uriel Acosta, 258, 290

Varnhagen von Ense, Karl August, 61, 69, 70, 75, 77, 90, 95, 98, 101, 108, 112, 175, 185, 382
   his connection with the Young Germans, 69, 70, 175, 342
   his sympathy with the Saint-Simonians, 76
   correspondence with Pückler-Muskau, 76

his friendship with Laube, 184
   encouragement of Mundt, 343
Varnhagen von Ense, Rahel, 60, 70 ff., 173, 382
   self-revelation in her writings, 72
   her Saint-Simonian sympathies, 73, 74
   her criticisms of Saint-Simonism, 74, 75
   letters of, to Heine, 70; to Karl Schall, 173
   her influence on Mundt, 343, 344
Veit, Moritz, 173, 179, 186, 351, 362, 392
   his friendship with Mundt, 349, 351
Vergangenheit und Gegenwart, 271, 384
Vertraute Briefe über die Lucinde, 291, 294, 295
   Gutzkow's preface to, 295 ff.
Vigny, Alfred de, 11
Voilquin, Susanne, 32
Vorrede zu Kahldorf über den Adel, 96

Wagner, Richard, 175
Wally, die Zweiflerin, 79, 244, 264, 300 ff., 421, 422
   argument of, 303 ff.
Wanderungen durch den Thierkreis, 412 ff., 420, 423, 427
Warnkönig, Dr, 65, 66
Wienbarg, Ludolf (see also under names of works), 69, 348, 351, 365, 379
   his relations with the Young Germans, 398 ff., 404, 408, 411, 417, 424
   his character and mode of life, 398, 400, 423
   patriotism, 401
   love of the sea, 401, 402
   influence of Heine on, 403 ff., 420
   Saint-Simonian ideas, 407 ff., 428
   Aesthetische Feldzüge banned, 412
   Saint-Simonian ideas developed, 412 ff.
   his feminism, 413, 414
   religious opinions, 406 ff., 415 ff.
   partnership with Gutzkow, 419 ff.
   attitude to social questions, 419 ff.
   his banishment, 422, 423
   Gutzkow's criticisms of, 422, 423 ff., 429
   mental and moral breakdown of, 423 ff.
   as a political pamphleteer, 426, 427

Wienbarg, works of
  Aesthetische Feldzüge, 239, 349,
    404 ff., 420, 423, 427
  *Holland in den Jahren 1831 und
    1832*, 420
  Rückblicke auf mein Leben, 424
  Tagebuch von Helgoland, 428
  *Wanderungen durch den Thier-
    kreis*, 412 ff., 420, 423, 427
  Zur neuesten deutschen Literatur,
    420, 423

Young German movement (see also
    under Heine, Laube, Gutzkow,
  Mundt, Wienbarg, Kühne,
    Varnhagen von Ense, etc.), 50,
    66, 67, 69, 70, 78, 80, 81
  suppression of, 84, 85

Zeitgenossen, Die, 268
Zeitung für die eiegante Welt, 173,
    182, 183, 184, 186, 234, 239,
    379, 381
  Laube, editor of, 180, 233 ff.
  Kühne, editor of, 365
Zur neuesten deutschen Literatur, 420,
    423